HANDBOOK OF YOUNG ADULT RELIGIOUS EDUCATION

HANDBOOK OF YOUNG ADULT RELIGIOUS EDUCATION

EDITED BY
Harley Atkinson

Religious Education Press
Birmingham, Alabama

Library of Congress Cataloging-in-Publication Data
Handbook of young adult religious education/edited by Harley Atkinson.
   Includes bibliographical references and indexes.
   ISBN 0-89135-098-5
   1. Christian education of adults. I. Atkinson, Harley.
BV1488.H36 1995
268'.433—dc20   94-40561
                                                                    CIP

Religious Education Press
5316 Meadow Brook Road
Birmingham, Alabama 35242
10 9 8 7 6 5 4 3 2

Religious Education Press publishes books exclusively in religious education and in areas closely related to religious education. It is committed to enhancing and professionalizing religious education through the publication of serious, significant, and scholarly works.

PUBLISHER TO THE PROFESSION

Contents

892 45

Tables and Figures

Introduction

The *Handbook of Young Adult Religious Education* is a comprehensive source covering significant issues related to the effective religious education of young adults. Following the pattern of prior handbooks in this series, the book brings together men and women who are specialists in their field. Each chapter is written in a scholarly yet readable manner, and every attempt was made to interface theory, research, and practice throughout the book.

It was our intention to include as much diversity as possible in the selection of authors. Denominationally, a wide variety of persuasions are represented—Roman Catholic, Baptist, and United Methodist, to name a few. Professionally, the writers represent several types of schools—Christian universities and colleges, seminaries, Bible colleges, and secular universities. In addition, contributors represent Canada, United States, and the Caribbean.

Summary

The book is divided into five carefully designed sections. Part one provides foundations for young adult religious education. John Elias examines the overall task of young adult religious education. He describes religious education in terms of discipleship and followership, conversion to a new way of life, community, and faith. He then includes some basic principles for religious education of young adults.

In the second chapter Fred Wilson gives an extensive summary of principles of religious education for young adults. Included are characteristics of adult learners, credos of learning, and theories of learning. In chapter three the issues of why young adults participate in religious education opportunities and why others do not are discussed.

The second part of the book is concerned with characteristics of young

1

adults. Les Steele identifies and discusses psychological characteristics, focusing primarily on identity and intimacy. M. Carolyn Clark describes the sociocultural tasks of work and establishing a career, fashioning a family, and getting an education. Donald Joy describes the spiritual journey of young adults in terms of religious, moral, and faith development.

Part three includes two chapters that focus on educational procedures. In chapter seven Trenton Ferro and Gary Dean combine their efforts in a look at the broader components of the education process including principles related to the adult learner, principles related to the facilitator or planner of young adult learning activities, and the process of planning the teaching/learning transaction. Reginald Wickett then examines methods and techniques in the areas of climate setting, learning situations, and evaluation. He describes these in relation to individual, group, and distance education.

In the fourth and most extensive section, a number of authors look at religious education of young adults in specific circumstances. In chapter nine Fred Wilson delineates ways to reach unchurched young adults through religious education. He identifies characteristics of the various age groupings of young adults, barriers to reaching them, and insights as to how they might better be reached.

Steve Fortosis looks at a group of young adults we often neglect in religious education writings—the college student. He gives a general profile of this group, further describes them in terms of social tasks, psycho-social development, moral development, religion and spirituality, and finally identifies ways of working with them in the church and on the campus. Michael Anthony explores some of the critical issues related to young single adults. He looks at the historical development of single adults in America, identifies current trends, and guidelines for implementing a religious education ministry with young single adults.

In chapter twelve Nick and Nancy Stinnett discuss family life education. They cover concepts related to family life such as family wellness, marriage success, and effective parenting, as well as methods for implementing a family life education program.

Everett Worthington deals with religious education and marital issues. In this chapter he examines marriage and spirituality within the Judeo-Christian tradition, looks at marriage in its historical context, studies social, technological, and philosophical changes that impact marriage, and describes some innovative methods related to religious education and marital issues.

The last chapter of part four is a collaboration of several authors. They examine young adult religious education of major cultural groups that exist in North America. Elizabeth Conde-Frazier looks at Hispanic-Americans, Anthony Headley focuses on African Americans, and David Wu studies Asian Americans. Key issues include the family, value systems, and identity seeking.

The final section is concerned with programming young adult religious education and includes two chapters by Trenton Ferro. In chapter fifteen he outlines the necessary components of any successful religious education program, as well as the processes by which programs are developed. In the final chapter of the book he discusses the process of evaluating the young adult religious education program.

What Is a Young Adult?

Defining young adulthood is rather difficult and assumes some ambiguity. Our society or culture has no single, definitive criterion—or rite of passage—that tells us when an individual leaves adolescence and enters adulthood. The fact of the matter is that we have several indicators—graduation from high school, acquisition of a driver's license, legal majority, or independence from parents, to name a few. However, these criteria are often in conflict. For example, an individual may be eligible to serve in the army, but not of legal drinking age. Even age of majority as prescribed by law fails to solve the problem, as legal age changes from state to state, province to province, and country to country. Furthermore legal age does not guarantee an individual is psychologically or socially mature enough to carry out the tasks adulthood may require.

In addition there is growing evidence that for many adolescence is being extended into the early twenties. More and more individuals are either remaining at home into their twenties, or moving back home after several years of college or a less than successful attempt at living on one's own. One is no longer surprised to encounter a 24 year old who has never handled his or her own bank account, or run into a 22 year old who still depends on mom to do his laundry. Some developmentalists, such as Daniel Levinson, have described this late adolescence/early adulthood as neither, seeing it rather as a transitory period—a moving from one stage of life to another.

Just as the beginning of adulthood is difficult to define, so is the termination of young adulthood. The single 40 year old who is physically fit, still engages in sports, and does not feel the constraints of family life may feel more like a 29 year old, while an out of shape 35 year old with the responsibilities of a wife and four children may feel he is already well into middle age. Developmentalists differ as to when one leaves young adulthood and enters middle adulthood. And perhaps it is best, from the perspective of religious education, to allow some ambiguity, not forcing young adults to move from one group to another because they have reached a certain age. Most theorists and religious education experts consider the ages 35 to 40 as an approximate transition to middle adulthood, and so shall it be for us. Thus for the purpose of this book young adulthood is considered to include the ages of 18 to 35 - 40.

Distinct Groups of Young Adults

It is important to recognize that young adulthood is comprised of several distinct groups, each having its own unique characteristics and needs—and each demanding special ministries and religious education programs. Many adults between the ages 18 and 40 are single—part of a growing trend in America, where one of every three households is comprised of singles. Single adults are further categorized as never-married, divorced, separated, or widowed.

Often considered as a group distinct from single adults are the college aged—a group that is most likely to be absent from church participation. They may be single, but on the other hand do not fit the typical single adult description and may prefer to think of themselves simply as not-yet-married. In some ways they are still adolescents, on the other hand they are exploring adulthood and are still making significant life decisions (including marriage). Many of these young adults may be away at college, thus the only contact with them is during the summer vacations or through the mail. However it is important to provide ministry for those who do not go to college, who have finished college, or who may attend a school in the area.

Newlyweds form another group of young adults. Young married couples retain much of the freedom and mobility that young singles do—at least until the first child comes along. This may be a group that is also noticeably absent from the church, although that often changes when they begin to raise a family. At this point most young parents want some religious foundation for their children, and this becomes a tremendous opportunity to reach the entire family.

We might consider another group of young adults as the unchurched. Research indicates that young adults are conspicuously absent from regular church worship and religious education activities. Changing culture and lifestyles, including mobility, affluence, increased education, cynicism and apathy all contribute to lack of participation. Too often we focus on the churched, while neglecting the unchurched. A critical question for religious educators is: How can we best reach the unchurched through religious education?

Finally, there are the various ethnic groups represented in young adulthood. Cultural diversity has long been a characteristic of the church, but in this country it has often been a hindrance to effective religious education. Religious education is often insensitive to the characteristics and needs brought to us by individual cultural groups. Methods, techniques, and curricula fail to take into consideration learning styles, cultural distinctives, and issues of assimilation and acculturation. The major ethnic minorities are African, Hispanic, and Asian, but we must be aware of the diversity within each of these groups, as well as the existence of other less prominent cultural groups.

Why a Book on Young Adult Religious Education?

As I scan my library shelves I see a whole row or two of books on youth ministry and religious education with youth. Likewise, it is relatively easy to find sources related to children and older adults. However, apart from edited books which might include a chapter on young adults, there is a dearth of literature on the religious education of young adults. This in itself necessitates the writing of this book, but I can think of some additional reasons.

First, according to the 1992 U.S. Census Bureau, the total population of Americans between the ages of 20 and 40 is 83,031,000. That is 33 percent of the total population! Young adults comprise a growing and influential people group.

Second, early adulthood (along with late adolescence) is a stage of life when individuals tend to drop out of church and religious education. At the same time young adulthood (late twenties) is the time when a large number of these dropouts return to the church. The church must figure out ways to retain and win back these people.

Third, understanding and ministering to young adults is not a simple task. A young adult ministry is not simply an extension of the youth group, a college and career group, or a single adults ministry. As suggested earlier, this age group is diverse and varied—including collegians, single adults (of various sorts), newlyweds, parents, and members of ethnic groups. Churches must know how to target specific needs of the various types of young adults in their congregations.

Finally, in many ways young adults are a troubled age group facing critical issues, not the least of which are the skyrocketing divorce rate and shaky marriages. To marital issues we can add the ever present pressures of achieving an education, parenting, and establishing a career. A strong religious education program can go a long way in effectively meeting the critical needs of young adults through varieties of small groups, seminars, retreats, counseling, and classes.

Acknowledgments

Finally a few words of acknowledgment to other individuals are in order, as no endeavor such as this can be carried out alone. First, let me express my appreciation to the number of writers who diligently and with excellence contributed to this edited book. I would also like to mention my colleague and good friend Donald Ratcliff who encouraged me to take on this project and advised me along the way, as well as James Michael Lee who was not only courageous in offering me this first-time opportunity, but has been extremely patient and helpful throughout the whole process.

This writing and editing project would not be possible were it not for a host of teachers and professors who taught me at various levels of my education.

Two professors, however, stand out in the sense that they provided a special measure of encouragement and assistance in the field of writing. These are Bob Radcliffe and Fred Wilson, who taught a number of my classes at Talbot School of Theology.

Finally, I am indebted to my parents, Walter and Marie Atkinson, who, though they did not come from a background of higher learning, supported and encouraged me through every level of education. To them I dedicate this, my first book.

Part One: Foundations of Young Adult Religious Education

CHAPTER ONE

Purpose and Scope of Young Adult Religious Education

JOHN ELIAS

While young adulthood has been the focus of research for psychologists and sociologists, it has not received the treatment it deserves from religious educators. Reflection on this task may offer valuable insights for understanding the purpose and scope of religious education for young adults.

Understanding Young Adulthood

A clear perspective on the scope and purpose of young adult religious education naturally begins with an understanding of young adulthood.

A Social-science Understanding of Young Adults

Most life cycle developmentalists describe young adulthood chronologically as extending from approximately age 18 to 35 or 40 (e.g., Levinson et al., 1978; Gould, 1978; Stevens-Long, 1984). They further break down young adulthood into smaller periods. For example Levinson describes a sequence of periods including Early Adult Transition (age 17 to 22), Entering the Adult World (about 22 to 28), Age 30 Transition (age 28 to 33), and Settling Down (age 33 to 40) (p. 56).

In defining young adulthood in this manner, it becomes clear that this stage of life embraces many types of young adults. Furthermore it includes men and women, the single and the married, those preparing for careers and those already established in a profession. Young adults are also found in all classes of society, and are members of various racial, religious, and ethnic groups. As is well recognized, they have assumed a multiplicity of lifestyles.

Psychosocial development. In recent years our knowledge of young adulthood has grown significantly as a result of the work of both psychologists and sociologists. Erik Erikson (1958), in his study of young Martin Luther, provided the groundbreaking work in this field, as he described the conflicts that young adults, especially those with religious outlooks, experience. Describing human development as primarily the resolution of particular psychosocial crises, Erikson identified young adulthood as a time when persons centered on the issues of arriving at their own self identity, and to subsequently forging this identity with others, in a search for real intimacy.

Erikson also described a period of moratorium that young adults pass through, in which they often make various tentative commitments in order to resolve their crises. The psychological resolution of these crises comes about with the development of the virtues of fidelity or devotion to a cause and the attainment of intimacy with others in love, work, and companionship. In his study of young Martin Luther, Erikson showed that the religious issues of dealing with parental faith, moral and religious teachings, and religious authority figures are vital concerns in human and religious development in young adulthood.

Lifespan development. Working in the psychoanalytic tradition, Daniel Levinson (1978) and colleagues describe how young male adults build a life structure that consists of occupation, love relationships, marriage and family, relations to self, use of solitude, and roles in various social contexts. An important finding is that these young adults fashion a dream and seek out a mentor in order to aid them in realizing this dream. Around the age of 30, young male adults often go through a painful transition as they begin to question certain elements of their first life structure.

Cognitive development. Another body of research that seeks to understand young adulthood is cognitive developmentalism. The works of William Perry (1970), James Fowler (1981), Robert Kegan (1982), and Sharon Parks (1986) focus on cognitive structures. Building on the work of Jean Piaget, these scholars describe young adulthood in terms of efforts to develop meaning systems and cognitive processes which stress autonomy or independence, individual choice, personal reflection, critical thinking, and decision making. This body of scholarship shows how these efforts take place in the development of personal faith systems, moral reasoning, and personality types. While cognitive development is controlled by the emergence of innate capacities, it is only fully understood in light of the social contexts of family, work, friendship, and community life in which young adults find themselves. Cognitive developmentalism has shown itself open to an under-standing of the development in religious knowledge and awareness that takes place in young adulthood.

Social psychological development. Douglas Kimmel (1980) and Robert Havighurst (1972) see development in young adulthood in terms of how young adults deal with certain developmental tasks in the social contexts of occupation, family, and community. They have explored patterns of role taking and occupational stages. In addition, this body of research has shown itself sensitive to the variables of age, religion, class, gender, and educa-tion, in understanding young adults. By taking into account the effects of belonging to a particular age cohort, these theories also describe how young adults are affected by the social events and mores of the decade in which they come to maturity. Havighurst identifies eight developmental tasks of the young adult as selecting a mate, learning to live with a marriage partner, starting a family, rearing children, managing a home, getting started in an occupation, taking on civic responsibility, and finding a congenial social group.

Affective development. While a considerable amount of effort has gone into understanding cognitive and psychosocial development, much less is written about the affective development of young adults. The affective domain con-cerns the matters of the heart—feelings, attitudes, emotions, values, and love. The *Encyclopedia of Psychology* suggests that affect is one of the least understood and most difficult problems in the field of psychology (Palmer, 1984). Yet experts argue that affective knowing is indispensable to religious education (e.g., Lee, 1985; Foltz, 1986) and faith development (Fowler, 1986).

One useful framework for understanding affective development in young adulthood identifies five growth trends that are commonly found during this period (White, 1975).

1. A Stabilization of Ego Identity: Ego identity or how one feels about oneself is influenced less by transient experiences or remarks than in ado-lescent or childhood years. The young adult begins to develop a consistent, stable, and defined sense of self.

2. Freeing of Personal Relationships: Young adults are less tied to their personal fantasies and desires than adolescents. This allows them to devel-op interpersonal relationships that are more responsive to the unique needs and characteristics of other persons.

3. Deepening of Interests: During young adulthood there is a greater involvement in specific areas of interest. While the involvements of chil-dren and adolescents are often short-lived, young adults show a greater com-mitment and deeper interest in areas such as academia, hobbies, sports, occupation, and relationships. Because of increased involvement and deepening interest, there is often greater satisfaction received from the activities.

4. Humanizing of Values: There is also an increasing awareness of human meaning in values and the way in which they function in society. Ethics and morals are not simply seen as absolute and inflexible rules, but rather are seen in a more personal light, and related more to life experiences.

5. Expansion of Caring: One's concern for the welfare of others grows in young adulthood. There is a movement toward increasing empathy with both individuals and humanity at large. The young adult tends to extend one's self more to the poor, the sick, and the oppressed.

Attitude toward religion. Sociologists have increased our knowledge of the attitudes of young adults toward religion and religious institutions. Studies show that large numbers of young adults experience alienation, dissatisfaction, and disidentification from the religious bodies in which they were raised. One study of baby boomers found that over 60 percent of these young adults dropped out of active involvement in churches and synagogues for a period of two years or more. Some left in disillusionment with a church that seemed feeble and impotent to bring about change. Many Catholics left in anger and frustration over the church's position on divorce and abortion; some in mainline denominations felt their churches were spiritually and theologically impoverished; most quit because the church did not seem relevant to them (Roof, 1993, p. 55). An interesting and surprising finding of this study is that education appears to have had little influence on this—those who did not have a college education dropped out equally with those with a college education (p. 55). A number of studies demonstrate that young adults, especially those in their early twenties, have the lowest rate of church attendance of all age groupings (e.g., Gribbon, 1981; Willits & Crider, 1989).

Religious Understanding of Young Adults

Do religious traditions have anything valuable to offer us for our understanding of young adulthood? Indeed they do. Religious movements have invariably been led by young adults who were dissatisfied with the traditional religions of which they were members. Most founders and reformers of religious institutions were young adults who were motivated by a purer ideal of religious living. Young adulthood is the stage of life where we would have to situate such leaders as Moses, Jesus, and Paul, even though we often lack precise chronological details about their lives. We know for sure that the Protestant reformers Martin Luther, John Calvin, Huldreich Zwingli, and John Knox were men in young adulthood; the founders of religious associations, congregations, and orders have been predominantly young men and women.

Given this reality of the predominance of young adults at the forefront of religious movements, it is no surprise to find that the classical religious literature contains themes, stories, and advice that have particular value for describing a religious understanding of young adulthood. Since it was to young adults like themselves that these leaders were appealing, it is understandable that what they said and wrote touched the very depths of religious faith of young adults. In these appeals of young adults to other young adults we find the religious understandings of young adulthood that should underpin educational work with adults.

A biblical concept of maturity. A religious understanding of young adulthood best includes a biblical concept of maturity as it relates to development. The classical text on Christian maturity is found in the Apostle Paul's letter to the Ephesians. Paul's desire for the church is that

> The body of Christ may be built up until we all reach unity in the faith and in the knowledge of the Son of God and become mature, attaining to the whole measure of the fullness of Christ. Then we will no longer be infants, tossed back and forth by the waves, and blown here and there by every wind of teaching and by the cunning and craftiness of men in their deceitful scheming. Instead, speaking the truth in love, we will in all things grow up into him who is the Head, that is, Christ. From him the whole body, joined and held together by every supporting ligament, grows and builds itself up in love, as each part does its work (Eph. 4:13-16, NIV).

The text emphasizes a number of characteristics of Christian maturity. Adult maturity is described as the attainment of a stability and adherence not expected of or found in children, who are tossed about and easily influenced (Schippers, 1975, p. 92). It appears that Paul uses the word "infants" to denote spiritual immaturity, "an immaturity which is culpable when sufficient time has passed for those so described to have grown out of infancy" (Bruce, 1984, p. 351).

This is not the only place New Testament writers use the terms "infants" or "children" to denote spiritual immaturity. The Apostle Paul, in speaking to the Christians in Corinth, tells them that he cannot address them as spiritual men and women, but as infants, still needing to be fed with milk rather than solid food (I Cor. 3:1-2). He later states that "When I was a child I talked like a child, I thought like a child, I reasoned like a child. When I became a man, I put childish ways behind me (I Cor. 13:11). Note that no blame is placed upon the infant for being immature or childish. In other words, maturity is relative to age, or how long one has been a convert (Bruce, 1984, p. 351). For example, a 6-year-old is mature if she acts like a normal 6-year-old. She is not immature because she is a 6-year-old and not a young adult! Thus Christian maturity, like physical growth, is a process—a process of continual growth.

This maturity is achieved, not through solitary efforts, but within the community of Christians. While each individual is called to grow in maturity the ultimate goal is that the whole "body of Christ may be built up" (Eph.4:12) and "grows and builds itself up in love, as each part does its work" (Eph.4:16).

The concept of the Christian life as a process emphasizes that together with the stability of young adulthood there also needs to be venturing out and risk taking. The powerful image of the Christian as pilgrim or wayfarer captures this insight. Growth to maturity is thus described as a journey into regions that are barely known. While there is progress in the journey, the extent of this progress is largely unknown because it is incomplete. The transcendent or other-worldly nature of maturity keeps the process open and indeterminate. In this concept of development there is a recognition that individuals may fail to develop, that they may fail God's activity in their lives.

Young adults as disciples of a religious teacher. Religiously speaking, young adults are called to be learners or disciples of the true meaning of life. All religions describe how young adults are driven to a search for true wisdom. This religious need is most often met when the adult comes into contact with a religious teacher, as well as the writings of such a person. To be a religious disciple often means to physically leave the family and the work in which one was engaged in, in order to learn from someone who is sure and offers true teaching.

While the various gospel accounts concerning the early days of Jesus' ministry describe the religious discipleship of young adults, John's gospel (chapter 1) offers the most telling details. Jesus recognizes that the young fishermen were looking for someone, a teacher. He invites them to spend some time with him in order for them to judge the quality of his companionship and teaching (Jn. 1:39). These young adults were changed by this experience, in some cases signified by the changing of names (e.g., Jn. 1:42). Once they had met this extraordinary teacher, they hastened to tell their friends about him. One by one a group of young men and women became his disciples. The scriptures speak of these disciples as leaving all to follow Jesus.

Discipleship in the New Testament refers not only to learners, but also to close followers and faithful adherents. Besides receiving the teaching that was offered to all persons, the disciples also received special instructions on how to carry out the mission which Jesus gave them. They were given opportunities to put into practice what they learned about teaching and healing (Lk. 9:1-2). Since these disciples were to be known by their unreserved loyalty to Jesus, the master, they were bidden to take their cross and follow him, since the disciples could not expect a better fate than what their master faced. It was clear that there was a high cost to this discipleship (Lk. 9:57-62).

A religious understanding of young adulthood begins with a realization that at this stage of life young adults, who are in the process of making their way in the world, have a need to learn about the spiritual and religious life. They have need for religious mentorship or sponsorship in the faith. In the midst of all of their striving for identity, intimacy, and vocation, many come to realize that the achievement of these tasks will not be possible, nor will their lives be satisfying, unless they have some way of realizing the deep desires and striving of the human person to learn the true meaning of life.

Many young adults find the religious teachings, practices, and structures of their childhood inadequate for dealing with the new life situations in which they find themselves. Many have experienced loneliness, the death of a parent, broken relationships, and failures at work. Many, if not most, are burdened with the beginnings of starting a family, raising children, and holding down a job. These life situations, added to the psychological crises that they may experience calls for creative religious education and ministerial efforts on the part of churches.

Young adults as followers of a religious leader. Closely related to discipleship is the religious concept of followership. In the New Testament, following Jesus often meant that young adults had to break with their past and leave all things to submit in faith and obedience to the salvation which Jesus offered. Following Jesus meant that young persons had to share in the conditions of his life, including his sufferings and death. In other words, followers were challenged to develop a devotion to the leader. This following also entailed the bearing of witness concerning Jesus because of the vital union with him. It even included for many who followed him a willingness to accept a martyr's death, should this be demanded. Though this following of Jesus has taken various forms in different cultural situations, it is important not to soften the radical challenge of Jesus' words (Lk. 9:23).

Jesus expressly bid the young adults around him to look to himself as a model: "I have set you an example that you should do as I have done for you" (Jn. 13:15). The Apostle Paul also urged his readers to be followers of Christ. This close following or imitation is presented as a necessary condition for union with Jesus. In fact the entire moral life of Christians has been described as a following of Jesus, as a conforming of one's activity to his. The life of the Christian is not primarily one of laws and rules, but rather a life characterized by the imitation of a person who holds out the gift of friendship and salvation. This following is not to be a mechanical one, but one in spirit and truth. The Christian community has given a special place to those men and women who have been followers of Jesus in an extraordinary way.

If an individual is to achieve religious maturity, one needs to find one's own masters and leaders. While these may still include those that one has had since early life, though now freely chosen, the religious literature bids young adults to be open and receptive to other teachers and leaders who beckon them to diverse and often deeper spiritual ideals.

While many in society rightly place great emphasis on young adults developing the qualities of leadership, religious traditions tend to state with some degree of paradox that in the spiritual life one must always remain a follower. Given the human condition, there is never a time when one can be totally responsible for the care of one's soul, when one is no longer in need of the example and exhortation of powerful leaders and mentors. It is especially in young adulthood that this is true. In the life of the spirit there is a widely recognized truth that all persons, even those who are leaders and teachers of others must remain disciples and followers.

Young adults in need of conversion to a new way of life. At the heart of the Christian message addressed to young adults is the call to conversion, the summons to turn away from one way of life in order to embrace another. Just as the young adult, John the Baptist, issued this call to conversion to potential disciples, so Jesus took up his call and made it an essential part of his ministry. The call to convert demands an internal change involving one's complete activity. The Greek *metanoiein* means to change one's mind after reflection, but includes the connotations of "going beyond the present attitude, status, or outlook; or repentance" (Gillespie, 1991, p. 26). This call, like the message of the prophets of Israel, was a call by Jesus challenging the young men and women to forsake the external observance of religion for a radically internal observance. Jesus made it clear that the full realization of this conversion would come about only in another sphere where the power of God was totally operative. This call of Jesus to conversion entailed the reappraisal of all aspects of human life and even demanded a renouncing of those things most treasured by young men and women (Mt. 16:24-26; Lk. 14:26-27).

The challenge of the concept of conversion for understanding young adults, is that it counters the secular notion that human development, including religious development, is simply a matter of natural development such as happens with plants and animals. Religious development, however, takes place only with the following of a call to radical change and conversion.

The concept of religious conversion is valuable for supplementing the social-science concept of development that is usually used to describe human growth. While development seems to imply an orderly and natural growth, conversion indicates that very often there are times of regression and times of movement forward. Furthermore, the concept of religious conversion makes clear final goals for human striving, which are left vague in social science theories on human development. Conversion brings to the fore the importance of continual striving for spiritual and religious goals and values in life, and includes the awareness that there are powers available to young adults which go beyond what persons and even communities can provide. For a more extensive treatment of conversion from theological and psychological perspectives, the reader is referred to Newton Malony and Samuel Southard's (1992) edited book titled *Handbook of Religious Conversion*, and V. Bailey Gillespie's (1991) *The Dynamics of Religious Conversion*.

Young adults as community members. While the religious call to young adults is a deeply personal one in that it summons them to convert, learn, and follow, it also includes a call to enter into a community of faith made up of like believers. Jesus called young persons to join a holy assembly and association. The scriptures speak of the Twelve, the Seventy-two, the community, and the gathering of followers. The gospels describe some sort of common life that Jesus shared with young men and women. The Acts of the Apostles emphasizes the communal life of Christians who shared things in common, prayed, and served one another. The same pattern of community faith is found in all religious bodies. In fact, the opportunity to join the life of a community of persons who intimately share life an values is one of the most appealing features of religion.

Young adults are invited to enter assemblies, churches, congregations, communities, and associations. All of these terms indicate that the group is not a static entity but one which is renewed each time new members enter. These associations are gatherings of people in concrete places and times, in the ideal open to all persons who wish to learn, convert, and follow. One enters such communities in freedom without any coercion. Within such communities there is often a fundamental equality of persons. Members of these communities are often asked to share their material and spiritual gifts. While one's giving to the community is foremost in one's mind, paradoxically the more one gives to others the more one receives in return.

One of the characteristics of young adults is their desire to belong to a larger community (Merriam & Ferro, 1986). In fact, what often attracts people to religious associations is the dramatic witness of the community's love and care for each other. Young adults, especially, are in search for associations and communities to which they may belong, now that they have begun a journey with some degree of independence from family and friends. It is within religious groups as well as within other groups that one has the opportunity to become one's true self.

Mainline denominations at times have difficulties maintaining the involvement of young adults as active members (Hoge,1981; Bagley, 1987). These traditional churches are often the exclusive preserves of Christians of middle class and middle age. Very frequently young people who find a place in a campus community of faith have difficulty reestablishing themselves within parish or local communities. Many young adults who were active in church-oriented youth groups in their teens have serious problems finding similar groups in their early young adulthood. Studies indicate, however, that young adults often return to the church in their early twenties to mid-thirties (Gribbon, 1981; Hoge, 1981).

Young adults as persons of faith. There is probably no word that appears more frequently in religious literature than faith. It is also noteworthy that some psychologists have ascribed faith or an aspect of faith as a principal virtue needed for achieving maturity in young adulthood. Fowler (1981), for example, suggests that an individuative-reflective faith is most likely to occur during young adulthood. Sharon Parks (1986) proposes that it is in young adulthood that the individual is marked by the capacity to take a self-aware responsibility for choosing the path of one's fidelity (p. 77). What religious leaders ask of the young adults they call to conversion and for whom they present themselves as teachers and leaders is faith and confidence in themselves and in the truth of their message. Jesus asked individuals to believe in his power and in his goodness, which he identified as the power and goodness of God.

Christian faith, as presented in the scriptures, is a power which brings about the forgiveness of all sins that persons have committed. It entails a firm conviction that the leader will be faithful to his or her promises and be able to fulfill them. This assent is asked for especially in cases for which there is no immediate or clear proof or evidence. Rather than reduce faith to a purely human phenomenon, religious traditions consider it a gift of God given to individuals for both their own benefit and that of others.

Religious traditions and denominations stress that the beginnings of faith in young adulthood are at times dramatic, and at other times nonperceptive. Faith can be strong and it can be weak; it can be adequate or inadequate for the task of religious living. The religious traditions know no smooth passage or development of faith, as often appears in social-science theory and research on faith development. The call of young adults to faith is a call to struggle, to fail often, and to begin the task again. The Christian scriptures detail not only the great faith of Jesus' disciples but also the periods of weak faith in the lives of the disciples Peter, Thomas, and others.

Religious faith can provide an identity of intrinsic worth and dignity, a value needed especially in the years when one is attempting to establish family, friendship, career, and community roots. Such a faith is valuable in facing many of the particular pitfalls of this period, notably a lack of confidence in oneself and in one's abilities to relate with others and to be a productive worker and colleague. The rootedness of faith can provide the sense of self needed for entering into lifelong relationships.

All educational efforts can be seen as directed at increasing religious faith as understanding, trust, and commitment. It is important to deal with the full reality of faith as a power which is at the same time intellectual, affective, imaginative, and action-oriented. All meetings of young adults should include prayer and study of scripture and on responses of faith to human problems and societal crises. At times ministers and religious educators underestimate the values of their own tradition in dealing with young adults, thinking that this age group wants more "relevant" approaches. This age group wants and expects serious grappling with all dimensions of religious faith.

Theological Principles for Religious Education of Young Adults

All religious groups are concerned with educational efforts, since they attempt to encourage people to embrace a certain religious way of life. These educational efforts are guided by certain principles, some coming from the social sciences and pedagogy, and others coming from religious traditions. While educational principles apply to all groups within religious bodies, certain principles are more applicable to one group than another, or some principles apply to one group in different ways than they do to others. With this understanding that I am presenting theological principles which apply to all faith traditions, particularly chosen for their suitability to young adults, I offer the following principles for underpinning religious education efforts among young adults.

In reflecting on education within religious groups, it is important to assume a rather broad understanding of education. While a specific definition of education describes it as an intentional activity in certain specified settings such as schools and colleges, a general definition of education also includes learnings that take place in many other settings: family, church, work, community groups, and mass media through both intentional and nonintentional efforts. In this broader view, which comes closer to the sociologist's definition of socialization, religious education takes place in family gatherings, church liturgies, work experiences, retreats and revivals, religious programming through media, personal study, and community action groups.

Religious Educators of Young Adults Should Be Present to Them

Religious education to young adults is rooted in personal presence. A campus minister I knew taught me this when he made the college cafeteria his chief setting for ministering to college students. The religious education of young adults entails that educators and ministers make the conscious effort to be present to these young people in the places where they congregate. Through the mediation of this visible presence, young adults come into contact with the religious body, its traditions and its teachings.

In Christianity, the theological root for this principle is the doctrine of the Incarnation, which for our purposes might be called the mission and ministry of presence. God was present to human beings through the person of Jesus. God became flesh and dwelt in our midst (Jn. 1:14). As one ponders the ministry of Jesus, one is struck by his going forth to fields, homes, and synagogues to meet people where they were. One thinks of, for example, his dialogues with Nicodemus (Jn. 3:1ff) and the Samaritan woman (Jn. 4:1-42), teaching in the temple during the feast of tabernacles (Jn. 7:14) or dealings with the woman taken in adultery (Jn. 8:2-7). He welcomed the people who were brought to him for healing, such as the man by the pool of Bethesda (Jn. 5:1-9).

While physical presence is necessary for this ministry of presence, it is not sufficient. We all have had experiences of being in the physical presence of persons who are not actually present to us in spirit as well as body. To physical presence must be added a presence of mind and spirit. This presence comes about when we are genuinely interested in persons in our midst. We know when people are truly interested in us as individuals, when we are more than mere clients or students to them. We know when another cares for us and is concerned with our welfare. Genuine presence means that persons are valued and loved as persons, without other considerations.

Since young adults are in a special way concerned with the quality of relationships in their lives, those who work with them must be particularly careful to be present to them in ways that foster opportunities to develop an educational or ministerial relationship. Young adults are attentive to whether or not speakers and teachers are sensitive to their presence. This ministry of presence is difficult because of the size of many churches. The larger the group the more difficult it is to establish a personal presence. Young adults, especially those who are single, are often the hidden members of these congregations. The emergence of small fellowship groups within large congregations has made it possible for more personal relationships to develop. The religious education of young adults will most often take the format of a small group of some sort.

The implication of this principle of presence is that in the religious education of young adults careful attention should be given to the quality of relationships in the educational experience. Joseph Lowman (1984) argues that one of the most important factors in student satisfaction in education is the quality of interpersonal relationships between the teacher and students. This includes a perception that the teacher cares and is concerned about them as individuals. In light of this, teachers of young adults should approach religious education opportunities not only with a didactic or heuristic mentality, but with a philetic or caring attitude as well. In other words, these encounters should include not only the giving of information or the drawing out of ideas but the creating of warm and trusting relationships between religious educators and young adults. It is only through these efforts that a presence is established that makes learning and development possible.

Religious educators of young adults should dialogue with them. In describing the principle of presence, I have already described the principle of dialogue. This is so because the two are intimately connected. Presence becomes authentic through dialogue; dialogue is only possible if there is real presence. While the truth about dialogue has been explicated by modern philosophers and educators such as Martin Buber (1970) and Paulo Freire (1968), it has its roots in religious teachings and practices.

The value of dialogue is taught in the Jewish religious tradition. The literature of the Torah presents the conventional dialogue between God and the people. Abraham and Moses are presented as dialoguing with and even arguing with God. The scriptures present the words of both parties to the conversation. The speeches of the prophets record their dialogues with God and their dialogues with the people. The wisdom literature, the most explicitly educational writings of the Jewish tradition, often uses the dialogue between teacher and students. The writings of the great rabbis are also presented in dialogue in the Talmud and Mishnah. The import of this tradition is that truth is arrived at through dialogue; people are better prepared to accept the truth if they are involved in this process.

In the gospels, Jesus is presented as a teacher within the rabbinical tradition who takes seriously the views of those whom he attempts to instruct. One account of Jesus's dialogue with his disciples is particularly instructive. In the postresurrection account of Jesus meeting the disciples traveling to Emmaus from Jerusalem, Jesus enters into dialogue with the disciples about recent events in Jerusalem his death. He listens to them, questions them, and instructs them on the Hebrew prophecies about the Messiah. Later, after he consents to stay with them and have a meal with them, the intensity of their encounter is described when they reveal how their hearts had burned while listening to his words (Lk. 24:13ff.).

Many philosophers and educators have spoken of the value of dialogue in educational processes. They point to its effectiveness in establishing relationships, setting a proper climate, and enhancing dignity and worth of the persons involved. Dialogue is especially important in educational relationships with young adults. This form of human encounter is valuable in the identity formation that is a primary psychosocial task in this period. What gives dialogue its particular power is the equality it fosters among the participants. Dialogue or communication is also the key to forging the bonds of intimacy in marriage, work and friendship, all primary focuses in the life of young adults.

Dialogue consists first of all in careful listening to the stories of young adults. There is much to be learned about these adults by having them share their experiences with us. Furthermore people learn about themselves through the process of revealing or self-disclosing themselves to others (Griffin, 1982; Tournier, 1957). Effective educators stand ready to affirm the rich and positive elements of their students' experiences. The essential attitudes of dialogue are trust, openness, love, acceptance, and respect. When these are part of the educational relationships, then elements of questioning and criticism can find a proper place.

Dialogue also entails that we be ready to tell relevant parts of our story, of our own struggles and efforts to live a spiritual life. Drawing prudently on our own successes and failures not only establishes rapport but also provides examples and motivating factors for young adults who often look to others as exemplars and mentors. it is for this reason that the religious educators with young adults should not exclusively be those of their own age group but include both middle-aged and older adults.

Religious educators of young adults should love and care for them. Implied in a prior discussion of presence and dialogue, is the important philosophical and educational principle of caring. Carol Gilligan (1982) has proposed an ethic of care which complements an ethic of justice. Educators have attempted to rethink the educational encounter in terms of caring relationships (Lowman, 1984; Lee, 1973). These writings remind us of the centuries-old Christian tradition of the care of souls, the *cura animarum* as principal task of Christian religious educators. This ethic of care sees the moral realm as not only demanding attention to rights, rules, and regulations but also as demanding a consideration of the human imperative of concern for others.

The concept of care and love are at the heart of all religious teachings. It is quite easy to find moving and beautiful prose and poetry attesting to the value placed on care for others in religious traditions. God is presented in the Jewish and Christian tradition as one who enters into a covenant of love with a people. The scriptures speak of God as simply love (I Jn. 4:8).

God's loving care for us is presented as both the motivation and the model for the care and love that we should have for others. Jesus told many stories, notably the parable of the Good Samaritan, in which the loving care of others is extolled as the preeminent religious virtue. The Apostle Paul presents loving care as the greatest virtue (I Cor.13:13), and Jesus describes it as the living witness that should be the recognizable and noteworthy characteristic for his followers (Jn. 13:35).

The word care has a number of meanings which are relevant to the educational encounter. to care means to give attention to, to be devoted to, to be anxious or concerned for. Although it is not easy to define or describe completely what we mean by care, we almost intuitively know when others care for us and are concerned for our well-being. We also know from our own experience what it is to care for others. In caring, we are so concerned with the total well-being of another that we almost feel the same emotions that they do in particular situations. Caring for others means to be sensitive to the struggles and sufferings of others. It entails being faithful to others no matter what they do, even if they cause us pain.

As a young adult, I personally experienced the attentive care of a teacher who took a special interest in my development. This man had more confidence in me that I did in myself. He knew that I could be a better student than I had demonstrated. Carefully following my progress, he gave me compliments on my successes and encouraged me to achieve even higher goals, despite my failures. Though in many ways a stern and severe taskmaster in the classroom, he warmly appealed to the best in me by pointing out to me my abilities and setting high ideals before me.

Care is manifested in many ways in religious education encounters with young adults. To care is to know the names and life situations of persons we work with. It is to become a small but significant part of their lives by willing to be with them, to listen to them, and to offer them our own insights. Care is shown in sharing joys and empathizing with sorrows. To care for others educationally is to be concerned that they learn something of value, that the experiences we offer them are worthwhile. To care means to accept respectfully the views of all students.

Since adult religious education draws predominantly middle-aged persons, church leaders need to be sensitive in a special way to the young adults (and the elderly) who at times are involved in these endeavors. Paradoxically, our care for young adults can be demonstrated more in what we allow them to do than in what we do for them. A fellowship/discussion group in which I have long been involved was regenerated when four young adults joined what had previously been a middle-aged group. Their interests now brought into the group, created a new sense of urgency and relevance which had long been lost.

Caring for young adults in religious education settings entails being responsive to both their idealism and their ambiguities. In my work at Fordham University over the years I have had many young adults in my classes. Many are preparing themselves for ministry in church settings. While these young adults enjoy spending much time in the company of their peers, they seem to seek out older adults, both students and teachers, looking for the care that is manifested through guidance and example. Teaching and mentoring these young adults is a challenging venture in that conversations are often about the direction that they might take in life. Care for such students is rewarded by greater insights into the meaning of one's own life and work.

The religious education of young adults should offer them knowledge. It is natural that there be a close connection between education and religion, since both of these are concerned with the truth and knowledge about ourselves, the world, and the spiritual realm. In fact in the early life of human groups all knowledge was viewed as religious knowledge that originated in their experiences with God. Only with the passing of time was the differentiation made between sacred and secular truth. For the religious person, however, all truth continues to have a sacred dimension to it, no matter how secular it appears.

Religions exercise their educational function by attempting to make disciples of all persons. To do this they use many methods and strategies: preaching, teaching, liturgy, guidance, and writings. All religions eventually establish schools for teaching their particular truths. The origins of schools in all societies have been closely connected with religious groups. When the formal schooling of individuals is completed, the institutional structures of religion remain for many veritable schools of learning for the remainder of their lives.

Major religious figures are primarily proclaimers and teachers of truth. Moses both gave God's law and taught about it. The prophets of Israel offered a pointed teaching relating to the moral situation in society. The wise teachers of Israel offered counsel on how every aspect of life was to be lived. Jesus is presented in the New Testament writings as the heir of these past traditions. Like Moses he was a teacher and a law giver. Like the prophets he instructed people on societal evils and their proper response to them. Like the wisdom teachers he contended that all aspects of life were to be directed so that the reign of God would be realized.

Presence, dialogue, love, and care for young adults are clearly not enough for educational experiences. To these must be added the imparting of knowledge. Young adults might simply be described as persons who are in search of knowledge. The religious knowledge they seek is not just a factual or propostitional knowledge. It is rather a knowledge of what decisions they should make and of how to go about making these decisions. What they seek are not facts but values. They seek a knowledge that will not alienate them from the world but give them an awareness of reality. The knowledge that young adults seek is one which enables them to define themselves in an authentic manner, a knowledge that may call for the transcending of what others may envision for them. This knowledge comes from face to face contact; it is deeply personal and subjective.

Young adults, in approaching religious education, need a different form of knowledge than the scholastic knowledge that they received during their formal education. The religious education that produces this knowledge might best be described as a spiritual knowledge. This knowledge comes more from spiritual disciplines than it does from book learning and study, though the latter should not be neglected. Young adults may receive this knowledge through study of sacred texts, through prayer and contemplation, and through a communal experience of religious learning. This education might better be termed a forming of the spiritual life of young adults. Such religious education takes place both in silence and in words; it attends to the meaning of things, the meaning of life. It has a place for sharing of stories and for feelings.

Teachers of young adults should offer liberation. The religious education principles which have been presented thus far have their foundation in theology, philosophy, psychology, and education. It is important to add to these a principle that relates to the social and political life of young adults. The religious education of young adults must help them to deal with the realities of their socio-political existence. It must address the reality that many young adults suffer various forms of oppression in their lives which might with profit be addressed in the context of religious education.

One of the most encouraging signs found in many religious groups in recent years is the increased attention they have given to educating people to greater socio-political awareness and participation. Churches and synagogues not only make statements on social problems but have also united to work together to address these problems. In doing this these religious groups are faithful to the historic mission of religious groups to show genuine concern not only for the city of God but also for the well-being of the city of men and women. Political theologies that place primary focus on the responsibilities of religious persons to work for the social transformation of the world, have also been formulated (Moore, 1989).

Young adults are involved in many social evils in contemporary society. Among the forms of oppression that beset this age group the following are most noteworthy. many young people are caught in patterns of addiction to drugs, alcohol, and gambling. Others suffer from lack of job opportunities, since patterns of unemployment in capitalist societies afflict young adults more than other groups. Young people who served in the armed forces must experience the pains of reentry into civilian life. The tragedy of the AIDS disease and the personal anguish over abortion often affect young adults more than others in the population. Young women and racial minorities know firsthand painful and embarrassing forms of prejudice. Young adults make up a disproportionate part of the prison population.

Religious educators to young adults can work with young adults in bringing about individual and social liberation from these ills. With many of these ills, education can help alleviate the problem and perhaps point to a solution. In other cases support can be given to young adults and their families to help them deal with their personal tragedies or issues from a religious perspective. The personal and societal tragedy of AIDS became more real to me as I visited with a dying young man and offered spiritual counseling and consolation. With many of these problems church communities must connect religious education with social and political action.

Conclusion

The religious education of young adults, like all other activities of churches and religious bodies, should be grounded in sound theological and social-science principles. Those doing religious education with young adults must be attentive to those aspects of religious traditions which pertain to the roles which young adults are able to take in religious groups and in society. They should also begin with the assumption that the religious tradition with its teachings and ritual is relevant to the life experiences and needs of young adults. Sound principles which most properly direct this activity can be found within the resources of religious groups.

Those who are responsible for religious education within religious communities must recognize that in many ways the vitality of church communities depends on the nurturing of faith in young adult members. It is these adults who are in leadership roles, or in preparation for these roles in congregations and assemblies. Special care should be paid to this group because, as the research reports, this group often distances itself from institutional forms of religion. Yet the research also reveals that for many people this period of life is the most critical for establishing firm and permanent commitments to religious bodies.

References

Bagley, R. (1987). A developmental view of young adults. In R. Bagley (Ed.), *Young adult ministry: A book of readings* (pp. 10-23). New Rochelle, NY: Don Bosco Multimedia.

Bruce, F. F. (1984). *The epistles to the Colossians, to Philemon, and to the Ephesians.* Grand Rapids, MI: Eerdmans.

Buber, M. (1970). *I and thou* (W. Kaufmann, Trans.). New York: Scribner's.

Erikson, E. (1958). *Young man Luther.* New York: Norton.

Foltz, N. (1986). Basic principles of adult religious education. In N. Foltz (Ed.), *Handbook of adult religious education* (pp. 25-58). Birmingham, AL: Religious Education Press.

Fowler, J. (1981). *Stages of faith.* San Francisco: Harper & Row.

Fowler, J. (1986). Faith and the structuring of meaning. In C. Dykstra & Sharon Parks (Eds.), *Faith development and Fowler* (pp. 15-42). Birmingham, AL: Religious

Education Press.

Freire, P. (1968). *Pedagogy of the oppressed.* New York: Seabury.

Gillespie, V. (1991). *The dynamics of religious conversion.* Birmingham, AL: Religious Education Press.

Gilligan, C. (1982). *In a different voice: Psychological theory and women's development.* Cambridge, MA: Harvard University Press.

Gould, R. (1978). *Transformations: Growth and change in adult life.* New York: Simon & Schuster.

Gribbon, R. (1981). 30 year olds and the church: *Ministry with the baby boom generation.* Washington, DC: Alban Institute.

Griffin, E. (1982). *Getting together.* Downers Grove, IL: InterVarsity Press.

Havighurst, R. (1972). *Developmental tasks and education.* New York: Mckay.

Hoge, D. (1981). *Converts, dropouts, returnees.* New York: Pilgrim Press.

Kegan, R. (1982). *The evolving self: Problem and process in human development.* Cambridge, MA: Harvard University Press.

Kimmel, D. (1980). *Adulthood and aging.* New York: Wiley.

Lee, J. (1973). *The flow of religious instruction.* Birmingham, AL: Religious Education Press.

Lee, J. (1985). *The content of religious instruction.* Birmingham, AL: Religious Education Press.

Levinson, D., Darrow, C., Klein, E., Levinson, M., & McKee, B. (1978). *The seasons of a man's life.* New York: Knopf.

Lowman, J. (1984). *Mastering the techniques of teaching.* San Francisco: Jossey-Bass.

Malony, N., & Southard, S. (Eds.) (1992). *Handbook of religious conversion.* Birmingham, AL: Religious Education Press.

Merriam, S., & Ferro T. (1986). Working with young adults. In N. Foltz (Ed.), *Handbook of adult religious education* (pp. 59-82). Birmingham, AL: Religious Education Press.

Moore, A. (Ed.). (1989). *Religious education as social transformation.* Birmingham, AL: Religious Education Press.

Palmer, E. (1984). Affective development. In R. Corsini (Ed.), *Encyclopedia of psychology*, Vol. 1 (p. 32). New York: Wiley.

Parks, S. (1986). *The critical years.* San Francisco: Harper & Row.

Perry, W. (1970). *Forms of intellectual and ethical development.* New York: Holt, Rinehart and Winston.

Roof, W. (1993). *A generation of seekers.* San Francisco: Harper San Francisco.

Schippers, R. (1975). Age, stature, maturity. In C. Brown (Ed.), *Dictionary of New Testament Theology* Vol.1 (pp. 92-93). Grand Rapids, MI: Zondervan.

Stevens-Long, J. (1984). *Adult life: Developmental processes* (2nd ed.). Palo Alto, CA: Mayfield.

Tournier, P. (1957). *The meaning of persons.* New York: Harper & Row.

White, R. (1975). *Lives in progress* (3rd ed.). New York: Holt, Rinehart & Winston.

Willits, F. & Crider, D. (1989). Church attendance and traditional religious beliefs in adolescence and young adulthood: A panel study. *Review of Religious Research*, 31 (1), 68-81.

CHAPTER TWO

Basic Principles of Religious Education for Young Adults

FRED R. WILSON

Writing in 1986 Brookfield felt that specifying generic principles for working with adults was "an activity full of intellectual pitfalls"(p. 26). Recognizing the potential pitfalls of this task, the purpose of this chapter is to present basic principles of religious education for young adults. The matrix of Table 1 will serve as the organizing structure for exploring the research and theoretical literature with special focus on young adults. Note that research and theories developed for generic learning will be surveyed before concentrating on adult learning in column two. For each of these two major foci, the top subject areas are more descriptive while the bottom areas are more analytic in their explanatory power.

Definitions: What Are We Talking About?

Most of us assume that we know what we mean when we use the terms adult and learning. An initial source for identifying basic principles is to review our understanding of them.

What Is an Adult?

Children were studied in the seventeenth century, adolescents in the early twentieth century, and the aged a few decades later. It was not until the 1940s

28

Table 1 Examining Young Adult Learning		
Explanatory Power	*Focus of Study*	
	Generic Learning	Adult Learning
↓	Definitions: Adult and Learning	Characteristics of Adult Learners
Descriptive	Learning Ability	Credos of Adult Learning
Analytical	Learning Theory	Theories of Adult Learning
		Adapted From S.B.Merriam (1987)

that gerontology was recognized as a new medical field, and only in the early 1950s that social scientists saw old age as significant for study. In the 1970s the first real interest was shown in the early adult years. Jordan (1975) points out that even in 1968 there was no article on adulthood in the *International Encyclopedia of the Social Sciences*. Graubard (1976) felt we were entering "the century of the adult, at least in America." The following table summarizes the major definitions of adult found in the literature.

Table 2 Definitions of Adult/Adulthood	
View	Definition
Social Science	Everything that happens after a certain age
Etymological Root	To grow up
Traits	Gain a status, title, achieve certain characteristics
Legal	Chronological age of majority; responsible for actions
Social-Cultural	Social perception, assuming a specific role
Developmental	Interaction of past & future, the whole person, & events

The social-science definition. Social scientists seldom raise the question, What is an adult? As Graubard (1976) comments, it "seems almost a catch-all category for everything that happens to the individual human being after a specific chronological age—whether 18, 21, or some other." It seems that adults know what adults are like, but not with any formal definition commonly accepted. Kilpatrick (1974) points out that no precise equivalent of the Anglo-American term adulthood, as a distinct stage in the life cycle, exists in any other European language. Instead, the Europeans typically speak of maturity in the sense of ripeness as applicable to any living thing such as fruit and vegetables. They have many terms as we do for meaning grown up or of legal age that carry the connotation of "responsible" or "adult." Nevertheless, neither their countries nor their languages consciously identify adulthood as a distinct stage in human development.

The root and trait definitions. The term "adult" comes from the Latin "adolescere" meaning to grow up. It suggests a process rather than the more final attainment of a specific status or title. According to Erikson (1976) "to be grown up, in any language and vision, has a particular quality of standing tall, so proudly and yet so precariously, that there is a universal need to attest and to protest that one knows where one stands, and that one has some status in the center of a new, or, at any rate, forever renewed, human type" (p. 18). Stegner (1976) suggests that qualities of adults include "sanity, normality, rationality, continuity, sobriety, responsibility, wisdom, conduct as opposed to mere behavior, (and) the good of the family or group or species as distinct from the desires of the individual" (p. 39). With such diverse opinion, it may seen difficult to determine what an adult is.

The legal definition. The law employs chronological age as a criterion for legal responsibility. Legally to become an adult is simply to reach the age of majority as defined by the law. The age of majority varies over time and from one state, province or country to another. In the United States the 1971 amendment which lowered the federal voting age from 21 to 18 is an example of such a change (Goldstein, 1976). When persons are declared adults, their parents are no longer required by law to support them. Adults are no longer legally subject to the authority of their parents. They are presumed to be able to make binding contracts, purchase and dispose of property, marry, and vote. They are supposed to be able to take care of themselves and are held responsible for their own acts.

The social-cultural definition. In another sense adulthood is a social-cultural concept in that people do not determine for themselves whether they are adult, rather they are perceived by others to be adult or not. This also refers to socially assigned roles that a person fills, roles that then determine what his or her social behavior should be. The role of grandmother, retired person, or old man are examples of socially ascribed roles for the aged. These roles also vary greatly from one era or culture to another.

A developmental definition. Psychologists most strongly favor the life-span developmental approach to adulthood. Each phase of adulthood is viewed in terms of both what has gone before, and what is yet to come. In this approach adulthood is perceived as a lifelong process with specific life stages with antecedents and consequences. The developmental approach is concerned with the interaction of psychological, biological and social-cultural influences on adulthood. This perspective takes seriously the events and experiences affecting the whole person as we seek to teach young adults.

For this chapter a person is a young adult to the degree that the individual falls into the chronological age period from 18 to 35 or 40, performs the social roles normally assigned by our culture, and perceives herself or himself to be responsible for her or his own life.

What Is Learning?

There are volumes written on learning, the nature of learning and types of learning. Most authors writing on adult learning selectively incorporate some type of definition as a jumping off place for addressing adult learning. Knowles (1984) declares learning is an "elusive phenomenon" (p. 10). While many consider change to be a central aspect of learning, there are a variety of views on how change and learning are related. Some definitions include:

Table 3	
Definitions of Learning	
View	Definition
Boyle (1981)	Learning does not necessarily change behavior, but it does change the potential for behavior (p. 5).
Adam & Aker (1983)	Learning is more or less permanent change in behavior that occurs as a result of activity or experience (p. 3).
Brunner (1984)	Learning is, most often, figuring out how to use what you already know in order to go beyond what you currently think (p. 183).
Gagne (1977)	Learning is a change in human disposition or capability which can be retained and which is not simply ascribable to the process of growth (p. 5).

Some writers have identified types of learning. The best known seems to be Gagne's typology (1977) which lists eight types of learning ranging in complexity starting with signal learning where a person responds to a stimulus, to problem solving, which is based on using concepts in thinking.

Others differentiate between learning that is primarily cognitive in nature, covering such areas as acquiring content or knowledge, to learning that is affective or emotional with a result that there is a shift in values or change of attitude. A third learning area focuses on motor skills, the use of the body in performing shills. Thus, we have the well-repeated categories used in developing objectives that are related to knowing, feeling, or doing.

Many adult educators have focused on the concept of experiential learning as a particular kind of learning (Davies, 1981; Kolb, 1984; Thompson, 1981; Walter & Marks, 1981). Thompson (1981) proposes "experication" as an overarching concept to unify education and experience. The concept also includes integration with all types and sources of conditions. Davies (1981) identifies several approaches to adult learning. This include content, needs, activities, or "lived experience" which refers to "what is required is the ability to see into oneself, to know one's experience, one's being" (p. 232).

Learning-how-to-learn is another concept more recently brought to the adult learning scene. It involves becoming aware of one's own ways of learning and then learning how to become more effective at learning in any given learning context (Smith, 1990). Interest in this concept derives from four factors according to Candy (1980): 1. a move toward helping people learn away from teaching; 2. self-development as an acceptable goal of learning; 3. continued growth in experiential approaches to learning; and 4. recognizing learning is both personal and unique to each adult.

The definitional approaches to learning normally do not distinguish between adult and children as learners. The focus is on the act or process of learning itself, not on the learner. There are just as many definitions of adult. Those working with young adults need to reflect of the numerous definitions of adult and learning. This forms an initial understanding of "who" we work with as well as "what" we are trying to do with them.

Learning Ability

Learning ability is a broad category that includes such topics as intelligence, problem solving, memory, and cognitive style. While primarily descriptive, this literature has more explanatory power than the first box because of its attention to individual differences. Some of the learning ability research focuses on age differences. Of particular interest are the findings related to physiological functioning, personality, memory, crystallized and fluid intelligence, cognitive style, and cognitive structure (Foltz, 1986).

Physiological Functioning

Biological processes vary significantly as a function of the person in whom they occur. Aging begins by mid-adolescence for the visual and respiration processes. Genetic inheritance, physiological health or disease, environmental stress, lifestyle choices, and personality patterns all seem to be components that influence individual bio-changes and their timing. The following is a compilation of research data on young adults biological processes:

1. Between the ages of 25 and 30, most of the adult systems and organs are full-grown, but some like the ears and nose continue to grow until death (Finch & Hayflick, 1977).
2. The brain slows down in reacting to stimuli by perhaps 17 percent in speed of reaction between 25 and 40 (Bromley, 1974).

3. The production of collagen, or connective tissue, ends at about age 18; wrinkling, as the result of wear and tear on brittle collagen, begins by the twenties (Kart et al., 1978).
4. Ears may start to lose sensory function in the early twenties with loss of hearing due more to exposure to loud sounds from music, work, and noise pollution in larger cities (Kart et al., 1978).
5. Balance and kinesthetic sense are at their peak of function up through ages 40 to 50 (Kart et al., 1978).
6. The heart reaches its peak function before the age of 20 for maximum rate of speed and volume of blood (deVries, 1975).
7. The amount of oxygen that the lungs supply peaks at 17 and begins to significantly decline between 20 and 40 (Bromley, 1974).
8. Maximum muscle strength peaks between 25 and 30 although they can be developed effectively until much later (deVries, 1975).
9. Bone strength is at its peak at age 30, and remains stable until middle age (Kart et al., 1978).

Based on the above observations, the young adult seems to be at his or her maximum level of physical performance. Few young adults have chronic health problems and 90 percent of them say they are in excellent or good health. This seems to be the opportune time to introduce preventive health care. Few young adults consider how their present lifestyles (nutrition, sleep, rest, and exercise) will influence the last two periods of adulthood. In a recent longitudinal study physical health at age 30 was a significant predictor of life satisfaction at age 70, more so for men than women (Mussen, Howzik, & Eichorn, 1982). Part of the reason young adults may not take these areas seriously is their ability to "bounce back" easily from physical stress, exertion, and abuse.

Another major concern coming from the above findings is related to the speed of learning. Speed of learning involves reaction time where a person perceives a stimulus, transmission time to transmit the message to the brain, and the response time to carry out the action. On the average, young adults will perceive more quickly, think more quickly, and act more quickly than older adults (Cross, 1981). However, research shows that it is the complexity of the task and individual personality differences that most affect reaction time and not age.

Several general principles for religious education for young adults are suggested by the above findings:

1. Young adults, while at the peak of their biological functioning, need to take preventive action to develop lifestyle patterns that will maintain their health.

2. Young adults are at the peak of their perception, thinking, and performance abilities.

Personality

Research on personality change and aging shows individual personality patterns maintain remarkably consistent throughout life. Differences in personality come more from the influences of changes in life than from aging (Woodruff & Birren, 1972). Thus, 50 and 20 year olds differ more because of the experiences of social and industrial changes than because one group has lived thirty more years. Researchers have found the style of "cognitive engagement" is among the most stable characteristics of learning (Haan & Day, 1974). "Cognitive engagement" includes verbal fluency, unconventional thought, wide rages of interest, aesthetic reaction, pride in objectivity and intellectual level. Thus, personality and physical activity encourages stability in learning.

Based on this research two implications can be identified:

1. Young adults will tend to increase toward a more positive self-concept as well as a grow in their level of self-esteem as they approach their 40s and 50s (Cross, 1981).
2. Young adults have a need to try out several approaches to learning before finding the one that works. Older adults operate with greater skill and deliberation (Knox, 1977). Thus, young adults with less experience and knowledge than older adults, are more ready to take risks and explore new approaches.

Memory

Most of the research findings on storage of information and cognitive processing are unclear. Neisser (1982) challenged previous research on memory by pointing out that most of the research until that time failed to identify how people use their past experiences in learning in the present and in the future.

Much of the research is based on a model of memory that includes at least two stages: 1) primary memory, which involves initial taking in of information; and 2) secondary memory, which involves storing information (Arenberg & Robertson-Tchabo, 1977). The research tends to suggest that the movement of cognitive material from short- to long-term memory is hindered due to the need for reorganization and higher-level processing. Thus, the memory difficulty appears at the point of entry into storage, not of decay of what has been stored. If adults learn material well initially and if the amount of new information is manageable and not overly complex, recall or deterioration of memory is minor until old age (Cross, 1981).

If this interpretation of the research is accepted, the following implications for young adult religious education are important:

1. New materials should be presented meaningfully in a way that assists young adults to organize and relate it to previously learned information.
2. New material should be presented at a pace that permits the young adult to master it so that the initial learning is memorable.
3. Comprehension will be greatly assisted if new ideas are presented one idea at a time without stressing intellectual competition.
4. Retention and recall of young adults will be supported by regularly summarizing new material.

Adult Intelligence

Some theorists argue intelligence is a product of learning and it should increase from infancy to old age. Others claim that intelligence grows until the early twenties and then remains stable (Dibner, 1975). Most researchers, however, would agree that both inheritance and the accumulation of experience and knowledge are what really affects the ability to learn.

One of the major contributors to understanding adult intelligence has been based on Cattell's (1963) model of fluid and crystallized intelligence. Fluid intelligence is defined as an underlying or basic ability resulting from the interaction of physiological capacity and experience. All active processing of information, whether coding during the acquisition phase or higher thought processes such as problem solving involves this type of intelligence. This type of ability declines steadily from the late teens paralleling that of various biological processes.

Crystallized intelligence is the product of the action of fluid intelligence on life processes, sometimes defined as knowledge. This kind of ability continues to increase throughout adulthood. Sex, ethnic, cohort, and educational differences all attest to the interaction of biological and social factors in adult intellectual development. If the fluid/crystallized dichotomy is true, people can do little about improving "fluid" processes except for developing better strategies of teaching and learning. However, adults can enhance the growth of crystallized intelligence by maintaining intellectual pursuits during adulthood.

However, Sternberg and Berg (1987) question the fluid versus crystallized theory of intelligence. They believe that such theories do not allow for the challenge that comes from changes in life. Other research shows that life change and stress have a major effect on IQ performance. Shifts of 13 or more points were found in adult intelligence at the time of major life events (Schwartz & Elonen, 1975). They also found that the intelligence scores of emotionally unstable people had many ups and downs. Other researchers argue that only non-normative life events such as health or other personal crises cause marked changes in intelligence tests (Baltes & Willis, 1978). Expected events are not so upsetting because they are anticipated and prepared for in advance. These expected events do not entail the kind of stress and adaptation that unexpected events do (Fellenz & Conti, 1989).

According to Sternberg's (1985) triarchic theory, intelligence has at least three parts. "Alices" are analytic wonders who are experts at taking tests and solving problems related to academics. "Barbas" are more creative thinkers capable of pulling together internal and external aspects of experience. They may not score well on tests. "Celias" work well within a specific context where they show insight into specific situations which many who do well on exams do not possess. He argues that speed and accuracy may hinder successful completion of real-world tasks. Attempts like this to bring the measurement of intelligence into real life will help us better understand if there are age differences in adult learning.

Several basic principles are suggested by the above discussion:

1. Young adult ability to learn is affected by previous experience and knowledge. This suggests that assessment of past learning may assist in identifying the levels at which content in various areas might be approached.
2. Strategies of teaching young adults should be evaluated as to their support or hindrance to long term memory.
3. Young adult exposure to and preparation for expected life events encourages stability in learning ability while crisis events may hinder the clarity of thinking.

Cognitive Style
Recent research into cognitive style has examined the idiosyncratic way each learner processes information. At least nine types of cognitive style have been identified ranging from the well researched work on field dependent versus independence dichotomy, cognitive simplicity versus complexity, to scanning versus focusing (Knox, 1977; Long, 1983). Learning style, which relates closely to cognitive style, refers to a person's preferred way of learning (Smith, 1990; Kolb, 1984; Conti & Welborn, 1986; Bonham, 1988). Over seventeen inventories and tests to identify learning style have been identified. However, none of the research shows that young adults prefer one of these styles over another as a group or to other groups.

Another area that holds some possibility for identifying basic principles revolves around extending research into the cognitive development of adults based on the work of Flavell, Piaget, Arlin, and others (Long, 1983). Labouvie-Vief (1980) criticized Piaget's four stage model by introducing an adult contextual model. She argues that formal operational thought tends to be idealistic and may insulate the individual from pragmatic orientation to the real world. Thus, as young adults go through the 18 to 22 college years period, they tend to lose the absolute nature of logic as they become aware of multiple perspectives and alternative solutions to problems. As part of this change, young adults begin to show more commitment to specialization in their thinking about their place in the complex social system. Coming to understand the constraints of reality in adult life indicates cognitive maturity and development, not regression in this view.

In 1980 Lewis argued that adult concept attainment is a different process than that found with teenagers. Lewis saw adults as having a larger verbal repertoire, more powerful and developed cognitive strategies, and more developed intellectual skills related to problem-solving skills that are the product of age, maturity, and experience.

The work in this area suggests several basic principles:

1. Young adult learning activities must not only provide variety but appeal to a broad range of cognitive and learning styles depending on personal preferences.
2. Young adult transition from the idealism of absolute logic to the pragmatic orientation of the adult world must be supported and encouraged.

In conclusion, examining the age variable as it relates to learning ability identifies limited implications for developing basic principles of religious education especially for young adults. The vast majority of the research tends to focus on the function: how the memory works, what intelligence means, rather than on differences of functioning between various adult age-group breakdowns. Perhaps it would be wise to remember Knox 's (1977) conclusion that "although there are substantial individual differences in learning ability, little of the variability is related to age" (p. 469). Researchers believe the variability among adults is more likely to be closely connected with a person's physical health, personality, social class, or educational level (Santrock, 1985).

Affective Development

Most discussions of social development tend to overlap with emotional development. However, affective development places more emphasis on the individual's feelings and emotional responses. Lieberman and Pearlin (1979) report that adults who are young, female, or of lower economic status experience the most severe life strains. After interviewing 1,100 adults they identified ten major sources of distress in their subject's roles as workers, spouses, and parents. Half of them related to occupation, and eight applied more to women than men. The young adults more often experienced problems with employment such as job searches, being laid off, and changing jobs. Among their more persistent job problems were depersonalized work environments and work pressures.

In another study of young adults by Powell and Ferraro (1960) young adults were anxious about heterosexual relationships, their emotionality, their appearance, and their social acceptability. Smoller-Weimer (1974) found they are also likely to be concerned about their vocations and about decisions they face regarding marriage and children.

It should also be noted that the emotional stability of generations also varies according to the tensions faced by young adults during the historical period of development. For example, the tensions of the Vietnam War produced some individuals who adjusted well to adulthood while others felt "adrift, suffering from anxiety, and self doubt" (Depression and Disillusionment, 1976). By contrast, emotionally healthy individuals learn to adapt their values and personalities to changing situations through the life cycle. Smithson (1974) identified some criteria of emotionally healthy behavior: being independent and being able to accept reality, adapt to change, respond sensitively to others, and handle feelings of hostility. Rogers (1977) suggests other characteristics as well: accepting the right to be human and enjoy life, expressing anger or fear without undue guilt, controlling rather than being controlled by one's emotions, experiencing inner freedom derived from ability to handle emotions properly, expressing feelings in whatever gradation is appropriate.

Some researchers argue that whatever degree of emotional stability or health a young adult has developed by the age of 30 tends to persist into the later years of life. However, the current general thinking is that life is more a series of crises that most people face that causes the reevaluation of one's personality and emotional stability—life patterns (Levinson et al., 1978; Lowenthal, Thurnher, & Chiriboga, 1972; Neugarten, 1968). While the research may be inconclusive, it does point out the importance of developing stable patterns for handling a variety of emotional responses to life's circumstances from a religious perspective.

Several general principles for religious education for young adults are suggested by the above findings:

1. Young adults, while experiencing a variety of stresses related to work, relationships, family matters, appearance, and social acceptance, need to take preventive action to develop effective patterns that will maintain their emotional health.
2. Young adults are emotionally impacted by significant historical events as a generation that may affect their emotional health. These events and their emotional impact can not be ignored in designing young adult programs.

Learning Theory

Another source for obtaining basic principles of religious education for young adults involves learning theories. Adult learning experts have tended to summarize the learning theories by organizing them into various groupings and then identifying concepts, principles, or implications that might be made to adult learners in general (Kidd, 1973; Simpson, 1980; Long, 1983; Knowles, 1984; Cross, 1981). The general learning theories have been grouped under the headings of behaviorism, humanism, and cognitivism. Additional categories have included neobehaviorism, structuralism, developmentalism, transpersonal psychology (Boucouvalas, 1983), and psychoanalysis. Learning theories tend to take into account the following three questions:

1. What is the basic moral and actional nature of human beings as it expresses itself through each individual's dealings with his or her environment?
2. What is the psychological basis of transfer of learning to new situations?
3. What are the emphases in teaching?

An excellent summary of major learning theories and their use in the classroom is provided by Bigge (1982). While helpful principles are available from each theory, none of the learning theories are uniquely focused on adults.

After a thorough review of learning theory, Dubin and Okum (1973) observed that "no single learning theory is applicable to all educational settings" (p. 3). However, they identified thirty-five implications for instruction of adults. More recently Darkenwald and Merriam (1982) presented eight generalizations from learning theory research that they believe are applicable to adult educational practice in general:

1. Readiness to learn to some extent depends upon amount of previous learning.
2. Intrinsically motivated learning produces more pervasive and permanent learning than extrinsic factors.
3. Positive reinforcement is more effective than negative.
4. Material should be arranged in an organized manner to maximize learning.
5. Repetition enhances learning, especially that related to skill development.
6. The more meaningful the material, the more easily learned and remembered it is.
7. Active participation leads to greater learning than does passive participation.
8. Factors related to the environment in which learning takes place can enhance or impede learning (pp. 110-111).

While the insights gained from learning theories are very helpful for beginning to understand basic principles for encouraging learning, they fail to distinguish between child and adult learning. Merriam (1987) comments on this limitation: "Learning is viewed as a single phenomenon irrespective of the age of the person doing it. These theories thus explain learning but do not attend to adults in particular" (p. 4).

Several general principles for young adults are suggested by the above findings:

1. While there are a number of helpful theories of learning, no learning theory is applicable to all young adult learning settings.
2. Generalizations from learning theory can be adapted to young adults in particular.

Characteristics of Adult Learners

A large amount of descriptive material is available on the adult learner falling under the heading of characteristics of adult learners. Participation and motivation studies have examined the differences between adult and pre-adult learners in such areas as maturity, life goals, instructional methodology, relation to life, attendance patterns, degree and type of motivation, and voluntary versus required participation (Houle, 1984). Another source of helpful characteristics of adult learners has come from the research on adult development and growth.

Participation and Motivation of Adult Learners

Merriam (1987) suggests that more studies have been done on adults who participate and why than any other topic of adult education. Depending on the type of learning, formal institutional programs, individual self-directed learning, or small group cooperative learning, participation ranges from 13 percent to 90 percent (Brookfield, 1986). The research findings have been relatively consistent from 1965 (Johnstone & Rivera) to the present: the typical adult learners are more than likely to be Caucasian, middle-class, well-educated, young, and have at least a moderate level of income.

To understand adult learners, researchers have also examined why adults participate or do not participate. Long (1983) notes that analytic studies attempt to examine participation at deeper psychological levels than case studies that focus on participant's resources in relation to various demographic factors such as gender, salary level, and previous education. Most survey and interview results suggest that adults participate out of practical concerns for acquiring new knowledge or skills relevant to their life situations.

In particular one major analytic approach was developed by Houle's study of learning orientations of adults in 1961. Learners were grouped into three categories: goal oriented where learning serves as a means to accomplish something else; social oriented where people wanted to be actively engaged with other adults; and learning oriented where learners want to learn for the pleasure of learning itself (Houle, 1961). Table 4 presents a summary of various reasons identified in why adults participate in learning that is both formal and nonformal in nature.

Table 4 Reasons for Participating	
Researcher	Reasons
Hoy (1933)	Desire for knowledge, Advancement, Interest, Leisure Time, Recreation, Social Reasons
Deane (1949)	Vocational help, Utilitarian Purposes, Self Development, Escape Boredom, Recreation, Curiosity
Johnstone & Rivera (1965)	Be better informed, Prepare for new job, Better learn present job, Spend time more enjoyably, Meet new people, Learn homemaker skills, Get away from daily routine, Learn everyday tasks
Burgess (1971)	Desire to know, Desire to reach personal goal, Desire to reach social goal, Desire to reach religious goal, Desire to escape, Desire to be Active, Comply
Boshier (1977)	Professional Advancement, Community Service, External Expectations, Social Contact, Social Stimulation, Cognitive Interest
Clayton & Smith	Self-improvement, Self-actualization, Vocational, Role, Family, (1987) Social, Humanitarian, Knowledge
Wilson (1992)	Ministry Preparation, Spiritual Growth, Cognitive Learning, Relationship to God, Social Contact, External Expectations, Escape, Stimulation
Atkinson (1994)	Spiritual Growth, Obedience to God, Ministry Preparation, Cognitive Interest, Community Service, Social Contact

While many additional studies have examined this since then, Cross (1981) believes that these studies have "illuminated rather than changed Houle's basic conclusions" (p. 96).

Barriers to attending have been identified by asking for reasons for non-particpation (Darkenwald & Valentine, 1985). Table 5 summaries the basic reasons given from several research studies that are both secular and religious in nature for reasons for not attending.

Table 5	
Reasons for Not Participating	
Researcher	Reasons
Carp, Peterson, & Roelfs (1974)	Financial Cost, Time Constraints, Lack of Desire, Other Responsibilities
Apt (1978)	Affective and Situational Barriers
Cross (1981)	Situational Barriers: cost, home & job responsibilities Institutional Barriers: scheduling, strict attendance requirements Dispositional Barriers: poor past performance, lack of enjoyment, per ception of self
Darkenwald (1980)	Informational Barriers: lack of awareness of opportunities
Darkenwald & Valentine (1985)	Lack of Confidence, Lack of Course Relevance, Time Constraints, Low Personal Priority, Cost, Personal Problems
Martindale & Drake (1989)	Lack of Course Relevance, Lack of Confidence, Cost, Time Constraints, Lack of Convenience, Lack of Interest, Family Problems, Lack of Encouragement
Atkinson (1993)	Time Constraints, Schedule Conflicts, Lack of Relevance, Family Constraints, Low Personal Priority, Personal Problems, Lack of Confidence

Cross (1981) developed a Chain-of-Response (COR) model for understanding participation of adults in learning activities. It assumes that adult participation is a chain of responses rather than a single decision. Each response of the chain represents where the learner evaluates his or her position in his or her environment.

Wlodkowski (1985) reviews previous findings on adult motivation and learning and then presents 68 instructional principles that can be implemented by an adult educator to encourage motivation for learning. His practices are organized under the following six factors related to different times of the learning event and the goal accomplished:

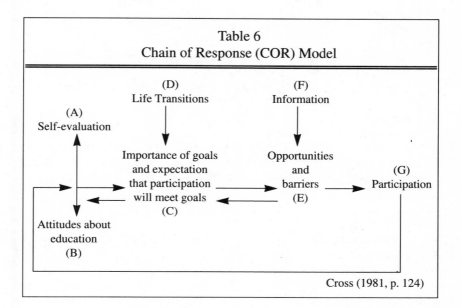

Table 6
Chain of Response (COR) Model

Cross (1981, p. 124)

Beginning	**Attitude:** positively confront the possible erroneous beliefs, expectations & assumptions (Goal: establish a positive learner attitude)	
	Needs: reduce or remove environmental components that lead to failure or fear (Goal: meet the needs of learners in learning sequence)	
During	**Situation:** make learner reaction & involvement essential parts of learning process (Goal: continuously stimulate the learners)	
	Affect: use a cooperative goal structure to maximize learner involvement and sharing (Goal: provide positive affective and emotional climate for learning)	
Ending	**Competence:** provide consistent feedback regarding mastery of learning (Goal: Increase or affirm learner feelings of competence)	
	Reinforcement: allow natural consequences to be congruently evident (Goal: Provide reinforcement of the learning sequence)	

Several general principles of religious education for young adults are suggested by the above findings:

1. Young adults tend to be involved more in self-directed learning activities than in formal learning programs.
2. Young adults choose how and what they want to learn with a focus on learning what is relevant to their life situations.
3. Young adults face barriers to participation that relate more to time and financial resources than to quality of instruction.
4. Young adults will differ on their orientations to learning: attaining goals, being with people, and learning for the sake of learning.
5. Young adult decisions to participate are influenced by multiple factors: self-evaluation, attitudes about education, life transitions, awareness of options, strength of goals and barriers to participation, past and current learning experiences.

Adult Development

A second major line of research for identifying characteristics of adult learners has focused on adult development and growth in ways similar to the major work researchers have done on the physical, psycho-social, and cognitive development of children. This approach to adults examines if and how adults change as they age. Since the 1960s many studies have attempted to chart the predictable phases or stages of adulthood. Two primary approaches can be identified: life-cycle and stage development. In contrast to the tasks and life issues that come out of a chronological look at young adulthood, there are also major personal changes taking place in the young adult's identity, intimacy, morality, and faith perspectives.

Life-cycle development. The life-cycle developmental approaches are interested in the responses people make to age and changing social phases of adulthood. Table 7 presents the periods of early adulthood based on the work of Gould (1975, 1978), Vaillant (1977), Levinson et al. (1978), and Sheehy (1976). Young adults and those who work with them should view these life-cycle tasks and events as opportunities to introduce and support spiritual transformation rather than as mere difficulties to which a young adult must adapt.

Two other authors have made their own unique contributions to chronological development with their focus on developmental tasks. Chickering (1981) identified ten developmental tasks for young adults in the 18 to 22 years old period that should guide those working with this group:

1. Becoming competent: gaining the knowledge and skills needed to carry out developmental tasks.
2. Achieving autonomy: recognition of when one is exercising independence, dependence, counterdependence, and interdependence.
3. Developing and implementing values: selecting a set of personal "chosen"

positions regarding education, sexual behavior, needs vs. wants, career, family, and personal excellence.

4. Forming an identity: a stable sense of who one is confirmed by significant others.

5. Integrating sexuality into life.

6. Making friends and developing intimacy: being able to relate to another person where sexuality is not a commodity for hire and is expressed rather than repressed.

7. Loving and making a commitment to another person: the basis of a stable marriage relationship.

8. Making an initial job or career choices based on self-knowledge.

9. Becoming active as a community member and citizen.

10. Learning how to use leisure time.

Egan and Cowan (1980) have developed an excellent workbook using these tasks to help young adults make conscious decisions in these areas.

Havighurst (1972) believes the young adult period is the fullest of "teachable moments" and the emptiest of efforts to teach. He says young adulthood is a time of special sensitivity and unusual readiness of the person to learn. He theorizes that the young adult is motivated to learn and to learn quickly if it is related to the developmental tasks of this period. Yet, little educative effort is expended by society or the church aside from formal college classes to deal with these tasks. He contends that successful achievement leads to happiness and success with later tasks, while failure leads to unhappiness in the individual, disapproval by society, and difficulty with later tasks.

When a particular stage occurs and what prompts it has been a fruitful area for researchers. Review of several approaches will give the young adult teacher insight into influences on life change in young adults.

Time perspective and cultural expectations. Neugarten (1968) describes adult activities on a continuum in which the first half of life is characterized by a future orientation and striving for the mastery of the outer world. This fosters a sense of "time lived" or one's own history as the significant factor. The second half of life is characterized by a more inward orientation, sponsorship of others, and consciousness of the finiteness of time and the need to set priorities in one's "time left to live." There are also clear differences between men and women reflecting the differences across sexes by the timing of the family and work roles.

Neugarten (1968) points out that there is a widespread cultural consensus about the proper time to leave home, go to college, marry, have children, etc. She emphasizes that the individual internalizes the culture's social norms and adapts to the external social processes. This perspective is interactive, one in which interaction between the individual and social processes regulates adult development. She claims that as a result of accumulative adaptations to both biological and social events there is a continuously changing basis within the individual for perceiving and responding to new events in the outer world. It is in this sense that orderly and predictable changes occur within the personality as well as the social environment. Changing patterns of work and childbearing are creating a much wider variation in the old timetables and revised age and cultural norms are required.

Predictable developmental crises. Another prominent theorist, Erikson (1968, 1976, 1980), argued that predictable developmental crises at each stage helped to create a vital personality. The crisis is not a catastrophe but a decisive turning point that simultaneously brings heightened potential for interpersonal integration and increased vulnerability to personality disintegration. A particular task is never mastered but rather is to be balanced with each new experience in each new period of development.

This concept offers a key for the continued development of an adult identity in young adults. They are forced to renegotiate previous resolutions of such issues as autonomy, initiative, and identity. Erikson's first stage of adulthood falls into the young adult years and is called Intimacy and Distantiation versus Self-Absorption. It represents the success or failure in one's ability to be truly open and capable of a "trusting fellowship" rather than formal separateness or pseudo-intimacy. His next stage of adult development, Generativity versus Stagnation, begins in the latter half of young adulthood. This crisis calls for the individual to create for him or herself a continuing giving of self to the world in a caretaking, creative, participatory way that is progressive and ongoing in order to avoid the pit of stagnation.

Vaillant (1977) added to Erikson's framework by using it to interpret the results of a longitudinal study of Harvard men. He describes in detail the adaptive mechanisms used as each man confronted life's challenges. He identified a new young adult task: "Career Consolidation" as a test between intimacy and generativity. Among his most interesting findings was that people cannot be expected to remember accurately the events and meanings of an earlier period of life. Instead, people reconstruct their histories as they move from one stage to another. Part of the role of a young adult teacher would be to assist them in this reconstruction process using God's Word as a basis for reflection.

In Vaillant's longitudinal study (1977), the research staff was unable to predict later psychological adjustment from personality traits observed while the men were still in college. The characteristics they thought would predict mid-life success (friendliness and humanism) were found to be unrelated to successful mid-life adaptation. Traits that were thought to predict later emotional problems (shyness, introspection, inhibition, lack of purpose, and values) also did not predict one's mid-life adjustment. Instead, the characteristics appeared to have been one manifestation of the stress of transition to adulthood. Looking back from the position of successful adaptation to mid-life, they found that those who had been seen as "well-integrated" and "practical and organized" in college were found to have been most successful in that later transition period. On the other hand, those who were "asocial" in young adulthood were the least likely to be one of those with successful adjustments to mid-life.

The 22 to 28 year phase is characterized as the time for "career consolidation of adolescent idealism" exchanged for "making the grade." Instead of questioning a choice of mate or career, he found the Harvard graduates were mainly concerned about career competition in their field. Those who were "charming" at nineteen were swallowed-up in the world of "gray flannel suits".

Expansion and contraction motives. Kuhlen (1975) proposed that the growth-expansion motives such as achievement, power, creativity, and self-actualization dominate a young adult's behavior. However, these motives may change during a person's life because they have been relatively satisfied (i.e., need for success, sex) and because the person moves to new social positions (becoming a mother, or a president of a company). He also suggests that with advancing age there is a shift away from "active direct gratifications of needs to gratifications obtained in more indirect and vicarious fashion." Thus, he sees life as a curve of expansion and contraction.

Inner development. Gould (1975, 1978) elaborates on the inner task of development through successive life stages. He emphasizes inner changes in consciousness that are the result of progressively giving up various illusions still held from childhood. Transition involves thoughtful confrontation with the reality of one's own choices and experiences—a change of viewpoint. He argues that adults seem to have an ever-increasing need to win permission from themselves to tackle these inner tasks.

In his analysis of the young adult period, the major assumption to be assimilated from 17 to 22 years old is "I'll always belong to my parents and believe in their world." Other false assumptions that must be disregarded follow from this one: "If I get any more independent, it will be a disaster"; "I can see the world only through my parents' assumptions"; "Only my parents can guarantee my safety"; "My parents must be my only family"; and "I don't own my own body." He believes marriage during this period is an expression of the need for a partner to help the person break away from the parents and gain greater independence. However, he found that such marriages have a high probability of failing since they provide more dependence, not greater independence. This was found to be especially true for women who move essentially from their paternal family to another family. The woman exchanges dependencies and fulfills a social-cultural expectation.

He describes the period from 22 to 28 as "I'm Nobody's Baby Now." To be successful, the following assumption must be disregarded: "Doing things my parent's way, with willpower and perseverance, will bring results. But if I become too frustrated, confused or tired or am simply unable to cope, they will step in and show me the right way." To do this, four misconceptions from childhood must be examined. 1) "Rewards will come automatically if we do what we're supposed to do"; 2) "There is only one right way to do things"; 3) "My loved ones can do for me what I haven't been able to do for myself"; and 4) "Rationality, commitment and effort will always prevail over all other forces." They need to learn that working hard is not enough, trying harder does not always lead to success, and that others can't provide one's own sense of satisfaction.

Another misconception is to be faced from the age of 28 to 33. "Life is simple and controllable. There are no significant coexisting contradictory forces within me." This false belief includes the assumptions such as: 1) "What I know intellectually, I know emotionally."; 2) "I am not like my parents in ways I don't want to be"; 3) " I can see the reality of those close to me quite clearly"; and 4) "Threats to my security aren't real."

This period of "Opening Up to What's Inside" involves discovering (or rediscovering) issues that were ignored or hidden during the earlier period (aspects, feelings, goals, interests, and talents). These may have been set aside because they interfered with the young adult's beliefs or goals of the earlier period. At time they may cause conflict and be suppressed. Or the issue(s) required more time than was available. There may be a fear that the time loss would hinder their effort at establishing independence and securing position for one's self in one's career and social world.

Gould believes that this transition, when adequately resolved, will result in a deeper sense of acceptance of self or perhaps the development of a personal philosophy of life. It could lead to awareness of one's strengths, weaknesses, and abilities. Young adults begin to recognize the contradictory and competing forces within with those in their social-cultural world.

Gender differences. Gender differences in how young adults handle change must not be ignored. Lowenthal (1974) reported large differences in the ways that males and females coped and developed strategies while in the same life stage. He found convergences between the sexes at the extremes (high school seniors and pre-retirees) and dramatic divergences in the middle (newlyweds and middle-aged parents). The most critical or stressful periods were different for men and women. The women consistently reported more problems and less satisfaction with their methods of coping.

Sheehy (1976) found that some women failed to really leave family: they merely left parental constraints only to enter the family constraints of a husband and children. At times women who stayed in the home were a decade or more behind in discovering their independence and developing their talents. For some women a career is a reason for returning to school. Not only do they desire a better job but have a compulsion to meet achievement needs. It also is an attempt for some women to establish and recover a distinct identity for herself apart from her family and husband.

Up to the early 1970s women were counseled to omit education during the period of child-rearing. The jobs they held prior to and after child-rearing tended to have flexible hours, require less education and were primarily in the areas of teaching, nursing, and office work. For the past twenty years there has been a stronger push for a pattern of uninterrupted devotion to education and a career to gain recognition and a sense of achievement. The period of childbearing has been moved back to the thirties for many who have gone the career route and who now desire to have children.

Lowenthal (1974) has identified four contingency schedules that women have typically taken in regards to education, marriage, career, and children during the young adult period:

1. Marriage by 22, Child-rearing from 23 - 29, Professional Training 30 - 34, then Career.
2. Marriage by 22, Professional Training 22 - 24, Initiate Career 25-27, Childbearing 28 - 35, Resume Career 36.
3. Professional Training 22 - 24, Marriage 25, Childbearing 26 - 33, Start Career 34.
4. Professional Training 22 - 24, Initiate Career 25 - 27, Marriage 28, Childbearing 29 - 36, Resume Career 37

Building life structure. One of the best known adult development studies was conducted by Levinson et al. (1978). He sees the basic task of adulthood as building and modifying ones pattern or design of life (life structure) in one area at a time. One develops by becoming more individuated in personality by resolving intrapsychic polarities such as destruction versus creation, masculine versus feminine, and attachment versus separateness. These tasks take on different character in each life period.

Levinson (1978) makes four major observations about adulthood. First, adults form and modify a "dream" that serves as an energizing vision of one's self in the world. Second, adults form mentor relationships that serve as sponsors, models, and supporters of one's place in society. Third, adult men need a "special" woman not only for affection and romance but also to help facilitate the dream. Fourth, adulthood is cyclical in terms of the rotation of a six or seven year period of relative stability and building followed by a period of four to five years of transition where one questions, experiments, and redefines one's life structure. A major weakness of this formulation is that it is based on an all-male sample.

Sheehy (1976) is a major popularizer of adult life-cycle stages. Although she relied heavily on other researchers, she makes a unique contribution on the life stage development of women and their relationship to their husbands.

The major problem of life-cycle approaches is that they falsely assume that broad predictable turning points in the lives of adults (usually men) are geared primarily to internal unfolding, a sense of natural growth. In working with individual young adults, age boundaries provide only general approximations. While they provide for individual differences, the characteristics are only rough indices. However, they provide helpful direction in programming if they are tested against the particular sub-group of young adults one may find in a particular church learning situation.

Stage development. On the other hand, the developmental stage researchers approach characteristics of adults by building on the biological metaphor which assumes continuous growth takes place from simple to more complex. Thus, rather than focusing on age and social roles defined on a horizontal level, they focus on vertical progression. These researchers focus on a primary dimension of such things as intelligence, ego development, moral development or faith development (Sell, 1985). Chapters four, five and six will focus in much greater depth on this approach to young adult characteristics.

Allman (1983) argues that adult development is the result of one's interaction with a rapidly changing social-historical time period and thus stages are not predictable. Aslanian and Brickell (1980) found, nevertheless, that 83 percent of those who were learners pointed to some past, current, or future life change as the primary reason for participating in learning. Thus, "to know an adult's life schedule is to know an adult's learning schedule" (pp. 60-61). Knox (1977, 1980, 1986), along with many other adult educators, observes that developmental issues are strongly correlational to adult involvement in learning. Thus, Fox (1981), drawing on Knox, defines learning as "the primary means by which the tension and anxiety characteristic of adult development is resolved" (p. 16).

Several general principles of religious education for young adults are suggested by the above findings:

1. Young adults will face a number of predictable developmental tasks which can help set the stage for understanding a specific individual's journey.
2. Developmental tasks of young adults provide valuable resources for program planning and formulating individual learning projects.
3. Young adults approach life from an individualistic, future perspective. Cultural timetables provide pressure that must be adequately handled and

questioned, as well as values that must be challenged from a scriptural perspective.

4. Young adults carry a number of illusions and assumptions that provide opportunity for inner growth in regards to parents, work, marriage, independence, identity, intimacy, and a philosophy of life.

5. The gender of young adults provides similar yet distinctive issues related to one's being and sexuality.

6. The socio-historical time period in which the young adult lives may provide unique issues that cannot be predicted by past research into young adults.

7. Young adult women may be in any number of combinations with regard to the interplay of timing for marriage, career training, childbearing, and career involvement.

Credos of Adult Learning

Many authors of adult learning books have identified basic assumptions or principles regarding good adult education practice. Most of these beliefs are drawn from the first four sources identified above and vary both in complexity, sophistication, and specificity to adults in general and young adults in particular. Almost no effort has been made to focus on those principles as they relate to young adults.

As early as 1926 Lindeman identified five principles of adult learning. He theorized that:

1. Adults are motivated to learn as they experience needs and interests that learning will satisfy.
2. Adults' orientation to learning is life-centered.
3. Experience is the richest resource for adult learning.
4. Adults have a deep need to be self-directing.
5. Individual differences among people increase with age (from Warnat, 1981, p. 3).

Based on speculation, Gibb, Miller, and Kidd offered some of the earliest attempts at providing principles of adult learning. Gibb (1960) offered a mixture of learning theory and procedures when he provided the following principles: learning must be problem- and experience-centered, experiences must be meaningful to the learner, the learner must be free to examine the experience, goals must be set and pursued by the learner, and the learner must have feedback on progress toward goals.

Miller (1964) attempted to identify conditions for adult learning based on cognitive development in contrast to behaviorism. However, his conditions tended to be more behavioristic as can be seen from the following restatements

Table 7			
Young Adult Stages			
Levinson	Gould	Sheehy	Vaillant

17-22 *Early Adult Transition* — *16-22 Leaving Our Parent's World* — *Pulling Up Roots* — *18-40 Intimacy & Career*

Major Tasks: Develop separate identify from parents & family; Autonomy in managing self, finances and time; Select, train for and enter career; Develop new home base; Initiate new relationships; See self as an adult

Major Events: Leave home socially or geographically; Initiate new roles & living arrangements; College/trade school, job, dating, and/or marriage

Basic Stance: Find equilibrium between "being gone" and "being in" one's family

22-28 *Entering the Adult World* — *22-28 I'm Nobody's Baby Now* — *The Trying Twenties* — *Consolidation*

Major Tasks: Explore identity & intimacy as an adult; Fashion an adult life structure; Clarify dream, Define goals; Find a mentor; Stabilize the marriage relationship or build a healthy concept of singleness; Become a parent; Career satisfaction

Major Events: 75% Select a mate who supports his/her Dream; Start the career ladder; Adjust to work world; Decide to have a child; Child starts school; Purchase a home; Community involvement

Basic Stance: Assuming responsibility for being part of society or being transient; Establishing a basis for the future

28-33 *Age 30 Transition* — *28-34 Opening Up to What's Inside* — *Passages to the Thirties*

Major Tasks: Reevaluate life commitments/values; Make commitment to changes; Explore or expand inner life as part of his/her strivings; Review sense of competence and achievement in work; Adapt dream that is more realistic; Reshaping relationships; Recognition of contradictory & competing forces in one's socio-cultural world

Major Events: Change job or career; Return for more education; Love affairs; Separation/divorce (2/3 of first divorce is by 30); Remarriage

Basic Stance: Time of questions: Why am I doing this with my life? What do I really want in life?

33-40 *Settling Down* — *Rooting & Extending*

Major Tasks: Keep own commitments; Invest self in work; Family and personal interests; Become part of one's career performers; Set goals for completing one's dream; Parenting; Develop a more satisfying marriage; Outgrow need for a mentor relationship

Major Events: Potential death of parents; Return for more education (female); Raising a teenager

Basic Stance: Make it in life; Meeting major goals; Sense of stability

Adapted from Levinson (1978), Gould (1978), Neugarten (1968), Sheehy (1976) and McCoy (1977)

of his principles: students must be properly motivated to change behavior, they must be aware of inadequacy in their current behaviors, they must have a clear vision of the required behaviors, they must have time to practice the required behaviors, they should be reinforced for correct behavior, and there must be an appropriate sequence of materials.

Kidd (1973) produced one of the major foundational works on adult learning that many adult educators highly respect. He attempted to identify central concepts rather than principles of adult learning. The source of these concepts included the changes in the adult's life span, role changes influenced by society, a collegial approach to teacher-pupil relationships, the greater variety of adult functionality and physiology, the desire of adults to be self-directing, the concept of how time changes its meaning and the attitudes related to death and aging.

More recent writers have focused on adult learning that is more widely referenced and the result of more empirically based research. Among these are Knox (1977, 1980, 1986), Brundage and Mackeracher (1980), Smith (1990), and Darkenwald and Merriam (1982). Knox's work is a monumental work weaving together adult development and learning observations. Some of these principles include:

1. Adults learn continually and much more informally in the process of adjusting to role changes as they age.
2. Adult learning achievement is modified by individual mental, social, cultural, and career considerations as well as the type of content and the learning pace.
3. Adults overemphasize past formal education experiences, underestimate their own abilities, and tend to perform below their ability.
4. Learning ability of adults is much more related to level of formal education rather than with age.
5. Effectiveness of learning was highly related to recency of formal educational experience.
6. For effective learning, there must be a search for meaning where new tasks are related to earlier learning.
7. Practice is important initially to the reinforcement of learning.
8. Prior learning may either enhance or hinder new learning.
9. Task complexity and creativity are minimally related to age but strongly related to individual differences.
10. "Almost any adult can learn anything they want to, given time, persistence, and assistance" (p. 469).

Brundage and Mackeracher (1980) identify thirty-six learning principles with specific facilitation and implication plans for each principle.

Some of their major principles include:

1. Through experience adults construct meanings and value frameworks that influence how they code and organize new data.
2. Teachers must respect past experience and assist learners to draw on this experience in handling current learning involvements.
3. The greatest amount of learning will come when the learning environment supports positive self-esteem, change, and the value of the learners status.
4. Adults are strongly motivated to learn in areas relevant to current developmental tasks, social roles, life crises, and transition periods.
5. Feedback on progress enhances learning and positive feedback serves as a reinforcement to obtaining more learning.
6. Limited arousal is necessary to initiate learning but stress blocks learning.
7. Each learner has his/her own style of learning and must be free to use it versus a prescribed mode.
8. Adults are most responsive to learning at transition points that occur at the ages of twenty, forty, and sixty.
9. A blend of individual mastery with participation in group learning provides the greatest satisfaction for learners.
10. Collaborative learning enhances self-concept and makes learning more meaningful and effective.

Smith (1990) explored how adults learn to learn. He identifies six basic assumptions about learning:

1. Learning is lifelong.
2. Learning is personal.
3. Learning involves change.
4. Learning is partially a function of adult development.
5. Learning is based on experience.
6. Learning is partly intuitive.

He also identified four key characteristics of adult learners:

1. Because adults have many roles and responsibilities, this results in a different orientation to learning when compared to children and teens. Therefore, they take responsibility for what they want to learn and they have a self-concept.
2. Since adults have accumulated many life experiences, they have distinctive preferences in learning modes and environments that comprise a learning style.

3. Since adults live through various physical, psychological, and social developmental phases, the transitions from one phase to another provides opportunity for reinterpretation and rearrangement of past experiences.

4. Adults experience anxiety and various attitudes toward learning as they attempt to be more autonomous and self-directed. Stress comes as a result of additional issues related to career, relationships and recall of prior experiences of school anxiety.

Darkenwald and Merriam (1982) identify eight principles of learning from research on the learning process. These are:

1. Readiness to learn depends on previous learning.
2. Intrinsic motivation results in more permanent and pervasive learning.
3. Positive reinforcement is effective.
4. Material to be learned should be presented in some organized way.
5. Learning is improved by repetition.
6. Meaningful material and tasks are more fully and easily learned.
7. Active participation in learning improves retention.
8. Environmental factors affect learning.

Brookfield (1986) argues convincingly that lifelong learning by adults is an empirical reality in that adults are stimulated to learn throughout the developmental stages of adulthood in response to life crises, for the innate joy of learning, and for specific task purposes. However, he believes the critical concern for formal adult learning is the nature of the teacher-learner transaction itself. He assumes six characteristics must be present in the teacher-learner transaction: willingness to learn, mutual respect, collaborativeness, praxis, critical reflection, and self-direction. These assumptions are expanded below because of their potential to stimulate further thinking in the religious education of young adults.

1. Participation in learning is ultimately voluntary, i.e., external circumstances may prompt learning, but there must be some innate desire or choice to learn. If this is true, three things are evident: there is little need to deal with learner defiance, opposition, or indifference; learners are less likely to resist participatory learning techniques; and, learners can withdraw participation when the activity does not meet their needs, make any particular sense, or is beyond their comprehension.

2. There must be respect among participants for each other's self-worth. The climate for learning is used to assist in the development of a group culture where adults can feel free to challenge ideas, otherwise it runs the risk of being nothing more than exchanges of opinion, prejudice, or lack of an

examination of beliefs, values, and behavior.

3. Teachers and learners are engaged in a cooperative activity where leadership and facilitation roles are interchangeable and assumed by different group members. Such collaboration acknowledges the accumulated experiences of adults as valuable educational resources according to Brookfield.

4. Action and reflection are closely connected in practice. Learning takes place in the context of the learner's past, present, and future. They interpret ideas, skills, knowledge, and insights in their current contexts. Thus, Brookfield argues that these are interpreted through mechanisms that learners develop, assign meaning to, codify according to categories they have evolved, and test in real life settings.

5. Critical reflection assists learners to appreciate that values, beliefs, behaviors, and ideologies are culturally transmitted and that they are potentially provisional and relative. Learning is not the uncritical assimilation of previously defined skills or knowledge. Rather, the learner develops a critical framework that is aware of underlying assumptions, norms, and uncritically accepted practices. Learners are encouraged to imagine alternative structures and paradigms. Facilitators, according to Brookfield, are to be proactive in advocating change and innovation with learners.

6. The aim of the teacher is to nurture self-directed adults. Learners are to see themselves as proactive, initiating persons engaged in a continuous re-creation of their personal relationships, work worlds, and social circumstances (Hiemstra & Sisco, 1990). They are not reactive individuals buffeted by uncontrollable forces of circumstances. Self-direction is more than skills and techniques but is, at its heart, the assumption that young adults have control over the setting of educational goals and generating personally meaningful evaluative criteria.

In spite of the variety of lists, unfortunately the research backing them is culturally specific. Often there are no control groups, most of the samples come from the United States, the samples are ethnically homogeneous, and the studies cited use a variety of methodological approaches which make baseline comparisons extremely hard to make. In most cases little effort is made to differentiate between the various adult age categories (Daloz, 1986). While it is up to the practitioner to select from the various credos of adult education researchers, several basic principles of religious education for young adults are suggested:

1. Young adults will learn throughout their life span with transitional stages serving as the immediate causes and motives for much of this learning.

2. Young adults exhibit diverse learning styles/strategies for learning and learn in different ways, at different times, for different purposes.

3. Generally, young adults like their learning to be problem-centered and related to their life situations.
4. Young adults want their learning products to have some immediate application.
5. Past experiences of young adults either enhances or hinders their current learning.
6. The young adult's self-concept influences the effectiveness of his or her learning.
7. Young adults demonstrate a tendency toward self-direction in learning.

Theories of Adult Learning

Adult theories of learning are another source of basic principles of religious education for young adults. This section contains material that is more analytic than descriptive and attempts to explain the phenomenon of adult learning. Six major adult learning theories will be surveyed. The first two are built on characteristics of adults while the next two are based on the adult's life situation in regard to roles and responsibilities. The last two theories build on the concept of transformation.

Andragogy

The best known "theory" of adult learning (Brad, 1984), Andragogy, revolves around four characteristics of adults: self-concept, experience, developmental readiness, and time perspective (Knowles, 1975, 1980). These assumptions are that, as a person matures, his or her self-concept moves from one of being a dependent personality toward one of being a self-directing human being. Second, the person accumulates a growing reservoir of experience that becomes an increasing resource for learning. Third, her readiness to learn becomes oriented increasingly to her social roles as a breadwinner, parent, and employee. Fourth, a person's time perspective changes from one of postponed application of knowledge to immediacy of application. An adult's orientation of learning changes from subject- to problem-centeredness.

From assumptions on how adults are different than children in each of these areas, Knowles develops a number of implications for the designing, implementation, and evaluation of adult learning. While often called a theory, Knowles refers to Andragogy as a "model of assumptions" (p. 43). Merriam (1987) writes that this theory "has caused more controversy, philosophical debate, and critical analysis than any other concept/theory/model proposed thus far" (p. 6). Knowles originally inferred that andragogy, with all of its focus on methodological application for teaching, represented adult learning. In contrast, pedagogy represented childhood learning. After a period of debate, Knowles modified his view so that the two approaches to learning represent a continuum from which appropriate techniques could be drawn depending on the context for the learning.

Because Knowles withdrew andragogy from being unique to adults, Cross (1981) argued that the status of the theory is "up in the air" (p. 225). Yet, the four assumptions about adult learning have continued to strongly influence most of the books written on adults.

CAL Model

Cross's Characteristics of Adults as Learners (CAL) model provides a framework by which to organize and relate the current knowledge available about adult learners (Cross, 1981). The model is designed to demonstrate the differences between adults and children in learning. Personal characteristics include physical, psychological, and socio-cultural elements. Situational elements focus on the characteristics of participants: voluntary versus compulsory, part-versus full-time study.

Table 8 CAL MODEL
Personal Characteristics
Children   Adults
------------------- Physiological/Aging --------------------
----------------- Socio-cultural/Life Phases ------------------
------------- Psychological/Developmental Stages -------------
Situational Characteristics
Children   Adults
------------ Part-Time Versus Full-Time Learning -------------
------------ Compulsory Versus Voluntary Learning ------------

The teacher of adults working on the three personal characteristics continua might create a positive learning environment to accommodate the physiological area; a cooperative, discovery learning approach on the life-phrase continuum; and the role of challenger to stimulate developmental growth on the third continuum. The CAL model provides a means for examining what and how adults learn differently from children, rather than specific implications for practice. The model provides a framework where basic insights and new data can be added and stimulate new questions in relationship to each of the variables.

Theory of Margin

McClusky's Theory of Margin (1970) builds on the assumption that adults change, adapt, integrate as they handle the discrepancy between "power," the energy needed, and "load," amount of energy available. "Load" tends to dissipate energy while "power" represents the amount of energy available to handle the load. "Margin in life" is the energy left over after subtracting "load" from "power."

When an adult is presented with a learning situation, he or she weighs how much energy is left to be expended. This interacts with the roles and responsibilities he or she carries or wants to relinquish over the course of the life cycle. The theory helps explain the energy needed to initiate learning at various times in the life cycle. It also assists the learner in identifying the need for adequate energy to handle the various adult responsibilities and adjusting roles that are part of each stage of adult life.

Proficiency Theory

Knox (1980) argued that adult learning is distinctive on two counts: adults perform several roles concurrently and adults learn so they can act outside of the educational program. Adult developmental changes provide a basis for discrepancies between current and desired proficiencies. Adults desire to perform satisfactorily when given the opportunity. To perform acceptably involves the adult in combining attitude, knowledge, and skill (p. 378). He believes society expects adults to be proficient in major social roles and as persons (p. 252). Thus, the purpose for adult learning, according to the Proficiency Theory, is "to enhance proficiency to improve performance" (p. 399).

The theory provides one perspective on explaining why adults are involved in learning. Proficiency may help explain some aspects of adult motivation and achievement in life and learning roles.

Perspective Transformation

While the first four theories focused on characteristics of adults and adult social roles, these last two theories examine the mental construction of inner meaning as it is influenced by experience. Mezirow (1985, 1991) drew on the writings of the German philosopher, Habermas. He argues that the most distinguishable characteristic of adult learning is the ability of adults to reflect critically on their lives. Humans become aware of "why meanings are attached to life, especially to roles and relationships" (Mezirow, 1991, p. 11). From this perspective, learning is not limited to adding to what a person already knows. Instead, new learning interacts with existing learning to produce a new perspective that is said to transform and emancipate the learner (Elbow, 1986).

The primary purpose of learning is to become aware of the "cultural assumptions governing the rules, roles, conventions, and social expectations which dictate the way we see, think, feel, and act" (Mezirow, 1991, p. 13). The purpose of learning is more than performing, achieving, and producing. Adult education is "to help learners make explicit, elaborate, and act upon the assumptions and premises . . . upon which their performance, achievement and productivity is based" (Mezirow, 1985, p. 148).

Theory of Conscientization

Freire's theory of conscientization (1970) is set within the framework of radical social change. Education always actively oppresses or liberates, but is never neutral. Conscientization is "the process in which men, not as recipients, but as knowing subjects, achieve a deepening awareness both of the socio-cultural reality which shapes their lives and of their capacity to transform that reality" (p. 27). The learner becomes increasingly aware of his or her situation by moving from the initial level where there is no comprehension of how forces influence one's life to the ultimate of critical consciousness. Mezirow (1985, 1991) and Freire (1970) are similar in their focus on learning as an in-depth analysis of problems, self-awareness, and self-reflection.

Several general principles of religious education for young adults are suggested by the above theories related to adult learning:

1. Young adults are different (in some way) than children in terms of their self-concept, experience, developmental readiness, and time perspective in relation to learning.
2. Young adult personal and situational characteristics require careful analysis in terms of developing learning strategies.
3. Young adults learn as they handle discrepancies in personal energy as well as proficiencies expected by society as they experience various roles and responsibilities in different stages of life.
4. Young adults learn as they reflect critically in a way that transforms their perspective on life's problems and their personal self-awareness.

Conclusion

While the author attempted to identify specific implications that are supported by research and theory, it is the practitioner who must formulate and use the basic principles of religious education for work with young adults. Our assumptions about definitions of adulthood and learning, learning ability, theories of learning, characteristics of young adults, awareness of a adult education research and theory need to be challenged if our strategies, plans, and our efforts to evaluate are to be effective.

Religious education for young adults can be examined in at least three ways: the context, the persons, and the learning itself. The overwhelming evidence of the literature is that the context for learning must be expanded beyond the four walls of the church and synagogue. Young adult learners are unique as both a group and as individuals from a number of perspectives. Learning for young adults is similar to all other adults yet different because of a number of the factors outlined above. While the above process has many "pitfalls," identifying basic principles should motivate us to continually and critically test the assumptions we bring to our task.

References

Adam, F., & Aker, G. (Eds.). (1983). *Factors in adult learning and instruction. Theory, innovation, and practice in andragogy.* No. 1. (ERIC Document Reproduction Service No. ED 228 461).

Allman, P. (1983). The nature and process of adult development. In M. Tight (Ed.), *Adult learning and education.* London: Croom Helm.

Apt, P. (1978). Adult learners and higher education: Factors influencing participation or nonparticipation decisions. *Alternative Higher Education,* 3(1), 3-11.

Arenberg, D., & Robertson-Tchabo, E. (1977). Learning and aging. In J. E. Birren & K.W. Schair (Eds.), *Handbook of the psychology of aging.* New York: Reinhold.

Aslanian, C. & Brickell. H. (1980). *Americans in transition: Life changes as reasons for adult learning.* New York: Future Directions for a Learning Society, College Entrance Examination Board.

Atkinson, H. (1993). Identifying reasons for nonparticipation in Christian education classes in Christian and Missionary Alliance Churches of the South Pacific District. *Christian Education Journal,* 13(3), 102-117.

Atkinson, H. (1994). Factors motivating participation in adult Christian education opportunities in Christian and Missionary Alliance churches of the South Pacific District. *Christian Education Journal,* 14(2), 19-35.

Baltes, B., & Willis, S. (1978). *Cognitive development and intervention in later adulthood.* The Penn State Adult Development and Enrichment Program. Unpublished symposium manuscript.

Bigge, M. (1982). *Learning theories for teachers.* San Francisco: Harper & Row.

Bonham, L. (1988). Learning style use: In need of perspective. *Lifelong Learning: An Omnibus of Practice and Research,* 11, 14-19.

Boshier, R. (1977). Motivation orientation revisited. *Adult Education,* 27(2), 89-115.

Boucouvalas, M. (1983). Social transformation, lifelong learning, and the fourth force-transpersonal psychology. *Lifelong Learning: An Omnibus of Practice and Research,* 6(7), 6-9.

Boyle, P. (1981). *Planning better programs.* New York: McGraw-Hill.

Brad, R. (1984). Foreword. In M.S. Knowles & Associates (Eds.), *Andragogy in action.* San Francisco: Jossey-Bass.

Bromley, D. (1974). *The psychology of aging.* Baltimore, MD: Penguin.

Brookfield, S. (1986). *Understanding and facilitating adult learning.* San Francisco: Jossey-Bass.

Brundage, D., & Mackeracher, D. (1980). *Adult learning principles and their application to program planning.* Toronto: Ministry of Education, Ontario.

Brunner, J. (1984). *In search of mind: Essays in autobiographies.* New York: Harper & Row.

Burgess, R. (1971). Reasons for adult participation in group educational activities. *Adult Education,* 22(1), 3-29.

Candy, P. (1980). *A personal construct approach to adult learning.* Paper available from Adelaide College, Uderdale, South Australia.

Carp, A., Peterson, R., & Roelfs, P. (1974). Adult learning interests and experiences. in K. Cross and Valley (Eds.), *Planning non-traditional programs.* San Francisco: Jossey-Bass.

Cattell, R. (1963). Theory of fluid and crystallized intelligence: A critical experiment. *Journal of Educational Psychology,* 54(1), 1-22.

Chickering, A. (1981). *Education and identity.* San Francisco: Jossey-Bass.

Clayton, D., & Smith, M. (1987). Motivational typology of reentry women. *Adult Education Quarterly,* 37(2), 90-104.

Conti, G., & Welborn, R. (1986). The interaction of teaching style and learning style on traditional and non-traditional learners. In *Proceedings of the 28th annual adult education research conference*: 49-54. University of Wyoming, Conferences and Institutes: Laramie.

Cross, K. (1981). *Adults as learners.* San Francisco: Jossey-Bass.

Daloz, L. (1986). *Effective teaching and mentoring.* San Francisco: Jossey-Bass.

Darkenwald, G. (1980). Continuing education and the hard-to-reach adult. In G. Darkenwald & Larson (Eds.), *Reaching hard-to-reach adults.* San Francisco: Jossey-Bass.

Darkenwald, G., & Merriam, S. (1982). *Adult education: Foundations for practice.* New York: Harper & Row.

Darkenwald, G., & Valentine, T. (1985). Factor structure of deterrents to public participation in adult education. *Adult Education Quarterly,* 35(4), 177-193.

Davies, L. (1981). Adult learning: A lived experience approach to understanding the process. *Adult Education Quarterly,* 31(4), 227-34.

Deane, S. (1949). *A psychological description of adults who have participated in educational activities.* Unpublished doctoral dissertation, University of Maryland, 1949.

Depression and Disillusionment (1976). *APA Monitor,* 7 (5), 13.

deVries, H. (1975). Psychology of exercise and aging. In D. Woodruff and J. Birren (Eds.), *Aging: Scientific perspectives and social issues.* New York: Van Nostrand.

Dibner, A. (1975). The psychology of normal aging. In Spencer & Dar (Eds.), *Understanding aging: A multi-disciplinary approach* . New York: Appleton-Century-Crofts.

Dubin, S., & Okum, M. (1973). Implications of learning theories for adult instruction. *Adult Education* (U.S.A.), 24(1), 3-19.

Egan, G., & Cowan, M. (1980). *Moving into adulthood.* Monterey, CA.: Brooks-Cole.

Elbow, P. (1986). *Embracing contraries: Explorations in learning and teaching.* New York: Oxford University Press.

Elder Jr., G., & Rockwell, R. (1975). Marital timing in women's life patterns. *Journal of Family History,* 1, 34-53.

Erikson, E. (1968). *Identity, youth and crisis.* New York:Norton.

Erikson, E. (1976) Reflection on Dr. Barg's life cycle. *Daedalus,* 105, 1-28.

Erikson, E. (1980). *Identity and the life cycle.* New York: Norton.

Fellenz, R., & Conti, G. (1989). *Learning and reality: Reflections on trends in adult learning.* (ERIC Document Reproduction Service No. ED 315 663).

Finch, C., & Hayflick, L. (1977). *Handbook of the biology of aging*. New York: Van Nostrand Reinhold.

Foltz, N. (Ed.). (1986). *Handbook of adult religious education*. Birmingham, AL: Religious Education Press.

Fox, R. (1981). *Current action principles and concepts from research and theory in adult learning and development*. (ERIC Document Reproduction Service, ED 203 008).

Freire, P. (1970). *Cultural action and freedom*. Harvard Educational Review, Monograph series No. 1.

Gagne, R. (1977). *The conditions of learning*. New York: Holt, Rinehart and Winston.

Gibb, J. (1960). Learning theory in adult education. In M.S. Knowles (Ed.), *Handbook of adult education in the United States*. Washington, DC: Adult Education Association of the U.S.A.

Goldstein, J. (1976) On being adult and being adult in secular law. *Daedalus*, 106, 69-87.

Gould, R. (1975, February). Adult life stages: growth towards self tolerance. *Psychology Today*, p. 78.

Gould, R. (1978). *Transformations: Growth and change in adult life*. New York: Simon & Schuster.

Graubard, S. (1976). Preface to the issue Adulthood. *Daedalus*, 105, v-viii.

Haan, N., & Day, D. (1974). A longitudinal study of change in personality development, adolescence to later adulthood. *Aging and Human Development*, 5, 11-39.

Havighurst, R. (1972). *Developmental tasks and education* . New York: McKay.

Hiemstra, R., & Sisco, B. (1990). *Individualizing instruction: Making learning personal, empowering, and successful*. San Francisco: Jossey-Bass.

Houle, C. (1961). *The inquiring mind*. Madison: University of Wisconsin Press.

Houle, C. (1984). *Patterns of learning*. San Francisco: Jossey-Bass.

Hoy, J. (1933). An enquiry as to interests and motives for study among adult evening students. *British Journal of Educational Psychology*, 3.

Johnstone, J., & Rivera, R. (1965). *Volunteers for learning*. Chicago: Aldine.

Jordan, W. (1975). Searching for adulthood in America. *Daedalus*, 105, 1-11.

Kart, C., Metress, E., & Metress, J. (1978). *Aging and health: Biologic and social perspectives*. Menlo Park, CA: Addison, Wesley.

Kidd, R. (1973). *How adults learn*, New York: Association Press.

Kilpatrick, W. (1974). Identity, youth and the dissolution of culture. *Adolescence*, 9, 407-412.

Knowles, M. (1975). *Self-directed learning: A guide for learners and teachers*. Chicago: Association Press.

Knowles, M. (1980). *The modern practice of adult education: From pedagogy to andragogy*. New York: Cambridge.

Knowles, M., & Associates, (1984). *Andragogy in action: Applying modern principles of adult learning*. San Francisco: Jossey-Bass.

Knox, A. (1977). *Adult development and learning*. San Francisco: Jossey-Bass.

Knox, A. (1980). Proficiency theory of adult learning. *Contemporary Educational Psychology*, 5, 378-404.

Knox, A. (1986). *Helping adults learn*. San Francisco: Jossey-Bass.

Kolb, D. (1984). *Experiential learning: Experience as the source of learning and development*. Englewood Cliffs, NJ: Prentice-Hall.

Kuhlen, R. (1975). Developmental changes in motivation during the adult years. In Birron (Ed.), *Relations of development and aging*. Springfield, IL: Charles C. Thomas Press.

Labouvie-Vief, G. (1980). Beyond formal operations: Uses and limits of pure logic in life-span development. *Human Development*, 23, 141-161.

Levinson, D., Darrow, C., Klein, E., Levinson, M., & McKee, B. (1978). *The seasons of a man's life*. New York: Knopf.

Lewis, J. (1980). Concept attainment among post-secondary students: Instructional design and delivery. *Educational Technology*, 20(7), 5-17.

Lieberman & Pearlin (1979). In Causes of Emotional Stress. *USA Today*, 107(2407), p. 16.

Long, H. (1983). *Adult learning: Research and practice*. New York: Cambridge.

Lowenthal, M., Thurnher, M., & Chiriboga, D. (1974). *Four stages of life*. San Francisco: Jossey-Bass.

Martindale, C., & Drake, J. (1989). Factor structure of deterrents to participation in off-duty adult education programs. *Adult Education Quarterly*, 39(2), 63-75.

McClusky, H. (1970). An approach to a differential psychology of the adult potential. In S. Grabowski (Ed.), *Adult learning and instruction*. Syracuse, NY: ERIC Clearinghouse on Adult Education.

McCoy, V. (1977). Adult life-cycle change, *Lifelong Learning: The Adult Years*, 26, 14-18.

Merriam, S. (1987). Adult learning: A review of the literature with suggestions for the direction of future research. In R.A. Fellenz & G. Conti (Eds.), *Building tomorrow's research agenda for lifelong learning: A symposium*. (ERIC Document Reproduction Service No. ED 306 455).

Mezirow, J. (1985). Concept and action in adult education. *Adult Education Quarterly*, 35(3), 142-151.

Mezirow, J., & Associates (1991). *Fostering critical reflection in adulthood: A guide to Transformative and emancipatory learning*. San Francisco: Jossey-Bass.

Miller, H. (1964). *Teaching and learning in adult education*. New York: Macmillan.

Mussen, P., Howzik, M., & Eichorn, D. (1982). Early adult antecedents of life satisfaction at age 70. *Journal of Gerontology*, 37, 316-322.

Neisser, U. (1982). *Memory observed*. San Francisco: Freeman.

Neugarten, B. (1968). *Middle age and aging*. Chicago: University of Chicago Press.

Powell, M., & Ferraro, C. (1960). Sources of tension in Married and Single Women Teachers of Different Ages. *Journal of Educational Psychology*, 51, 92-101.

Rogers , D. (1977). *Psychology of Adolescence* (3rd ed.). Englewood Cliffs, N.J.: Brooks-Cole.

Santrock, J. (1985). *Adult development and aging*. Dubuque, IA: Brown.

Schwartz, E., & Elonen, A. (1975). IQ and the myth of stability: A 16-year longitudinal study of variations in intelligence test performance. *Journal of Clinical Psychology*, 31(4), 687-694.

Sell, C. (1985). *Transition: The stages of adult life*. Chicago:Moody.

Sheehy, G. (1976). *Passages: Predictable crises of adult life*. New York: Dutton.

Simpson, E. (1980). Adult learning theory: A state of the art. In H. L. Moore & E. L. Simpson (Eds.), *Adult development and approaches to learning*. Washington, DC: National Institute of Education.

Smith, R. (1990). *Learning to learn across the life span*. San Francisco: Jossey-Bass.

Smithson, W. (1974). Emotional maturity. *Mental Hygiene*, 58(1), 9-11.

Smoller-Weimer, A. (1974). Proceedings of the 27th Annual Scientific Meeting of the Gerontological Society. *Gerontologist*, 14, 69.

Stegner, W. (1976) The writer and the concept of adulthood. *Daedalus*, 105, 39-48.

Sternberg, R. (1985). *Beyond I.Q.: A triarchic theory of human intelligence*. New York: Cambridge.

Sternberg, R., & Berg, C. (1987). What are theories of adult intellectual development theories of? In C. Schooler and K.W. Schaie (Eds.), *Cognitive functioning and social structure over the life course*. Norwood, NJ: Ablex Publishing.

Thompson, R. (1981). *Experience as a mode of learning in adulthood*. (Doctoral Dissertation, University of Washington, 1981). Dissertation Abstracts International, 42(4) 1442A.

Vaillant, G. (1977). *Adaptation to life*. Boston: Little, Brown.

Walter, G., & Marks, S. (1981). *Experiential learning and change*. New York: Wiley.

Warnat, W. (1981). *Adult learning potential: A matter of the mind*. (ERIC Document Reproduction Service No. ED 202 994).

Wilson, F. (1992). Why church volunteers attend religious training programs. *Christian Education Journal*, 12(3), 69-85.

Wlodkowski, R. (1985). *Enhancing adult motivation to learn*. San Francisco: Jossey-Bass.

Woodruff, D., & Birren, J. (1972). Age changes and cohort differences in personality. *Developmental Psychology*, 6, 252-59.

CHAPTER THREE

Participation of Young Adults in Religious Education Activities

HARLEY ATKINSON

Those who are involved in the religious education of adults are often frustrated by the lack of interest and participation in educational activities. According to one study, while an excess of twenty million adults participate in planned educational activities each year, the church accounts for among the smallest percentage of participants. Furthermore most churches have difficulty in reaching more that 50 percent of their adult members with religious education (Harton, 1986a).

Other studies reflect even less optimism. McKenzie (1982) discovered the proportion of adult education participants in the parishes he studied ranged from a disappointing 4 to 10 percent. The 1991 Barna report indicates that only 28 percent of adults surveyed regularly attend Sunday School and 29 percent participate in a small group. Roehlkepartain (1993) says "In most congregations, Christian education includes only a faithful remnant. Christian education involvement plummets after childhood, when 60 percent of children attend Christian education. By adulthood, only an average of 28 percent of churchgoing adults actively participate in Christian education" (p. 26).

The status of adult education in the church is described by Lucien Coleman (1986) as marginal at best. He says that "for even the most committed, it often amounts to no more than a forty-five-minute Sunday School session each week. And the majority of adult church members are not that involved in learning endeavors" (pp. 282-283).

Young Adults and Religious Education Participation

There is no reason to believe that young adults are any more committed to religious education than the larger adult population. For example, in 1983 in the Southern Baptist Convention the number of young adults enrolled in Bible study was 28 percent of the total adults reported, while the same group accounted for more than 51 percent of the adults baptized (Stubblefield, 1986). A study by Hines (1975) indicates that older adults tend to have a more positive attitude toward Sunday School than do younger adults.

Another report indicates that 24 percent of those in the 18 to 25 age bracket, and 28 percent of those in the 26 to 44 bracket regularly attend a Sunday School class. The numbers are very similar in regard to participating in small groups, with the likelihood of participation in small groups increasing significantly as a person gets older (Barna, 1991).

The Task of Engaging Young Adults in Religious Education

John Elias (1982) argues that the needful task of today's religious educator is to engage a greater number of adults in valuable religious learning experiences. The critical question is, "How do we involve more young adults in the important process of religious education?" Typically the adult education program of a church is developed and controlled by a pastor or Religious Education Director, and built around subject matter or available curriculum. Recent developments in adult education, however, suggest that leaders begin by focusing first on the needs, interests, and motivations of adults rather than subject matter. In other words, a clear understanding of what motivates an adult to participate in a learning activity, or conversely what deters attendance, is key to developing a well-atttended program.

The field of study related to adult education motivation might be divided into two categories. One body of work tends to be more theoretical in nature. It includes several models that attempt to identify and characterize the psychological and sociological forces that motivate adults to take part in educational activities. Another body of work is more research oriented and is largely contrived from the motivational models. This research seeks to identify the specific factors or reasons adults give for either participating or not participating in educational opportunities. It is hoped that an understanding of (a) the reasons young adults give for taking part in religious education, and (b) the reasons other young adults give for not participating in religious education, will give religious educators a picture of what must be done to increase attendance.

This chapter will first summarize some of the key theories of motivation, as will as implications for the study of adult participation. Second, the chapter will focus on what impels young adults to participate in religious education, and finally the barriers or deterrents to participation will be explored.

Theories of Motivation

A number of motivational theories or models of adult participation in education have been formulated. Collectively, the models suggest that an understanding of adult participation is complex and involves much more than simply identifying reasons for participation or nonparticipation. They indicate a need for exploring the psychological and sociological influences that surround the individual and suggest the reasons adults give for participating or not participating differ according to variables such as age, sex, past education, socioeconomic status, and ability to earn. Several of the key theories are summarized below.

Force-field Analysis

The force-field analysis of Miller (1967) attempts to relate socio-economic status directly to participation in adult education. He applied Maslow's (1954) needs hierarchy and Lewin's (1947) force-field analysis to education. Maslow says that people cannot be concerned about higher human needs—such as self-acualization and self-esteem—until the more basic needs of survival, safety, and belonging are met. Taking Maslow's idea that people cannot be concerned about higher needs until lower needs are met, Miller suggests that people from lower classes of society will be interested in education opportunities which help meet survival needs (e.g., job training). Members of upper classes, on the other hand, will participate in learning activities that lead to self-realization and personal achievement.

From Kurt Lewin (1947) he derives the idea of positive and negative forces. According to Lewin, the learner experiences positive psychological forces moving him toward the learning goal, and negative ones taking on the form of resistances. When negative forces (e.g., limited access, hostility to education) are stronger than positive forces (e.g., survival needs, changing technology), there is relatively little motivation for participation. Thus for Miller, the strong negative forces lower class people encounter—such as lack of job opportunities and weak family structures—result in little motivation. On the other hand stronger positive forces of the middle classes—such as satisfied survival need and changing technology— result in high motivation.

This approach is helpful in identifying the need for recognizing the possible influence of socio-economic factors in understanding why young adults participate or do not participate in religious education. Is it possible that young adults from lower classes will be less involved in religious education because they are consumed with survival needs? Unfortunately little if any research related to young adult religious education is available to refute or support this theory. However it is still helpful in that it suggests possibilities for further research and does imply some possible strategies. For example, churches might take an active role in helping young adults from lower socio-economic stratas in the struggles of parenting, aiding them in food and housing, and providing job placement services.

In addition, his theory brings attention to the fact that the learner or potential learner is faced with positive and negative forces, pointing to the need for exploring both motivating (positive forces) and deterring (negative forces) factors. Miller (1964) suggests that rather than try to increase the strength of the positive force, we would do better to remove the resistances.

Expectancy-valence Paradigm

Rubenson (1977), in his expectancy-valence model, also focuses on competing forces. However he is more concerned with the psychological, rather than the external barriers to participation. The "expectancy" aspect of Rubenson's theory refers to (a) the expectations of personal success in the learning activity and (b) the expectations that success in the activity will in turn lead to positive consequences. If an individual does not perceive oneself as able to participate successfully, or that there will no reward for doing so, there will be a lack of motivation to participate.

The "valence" part of the formula is concerned with the sum values the individual places on the anticipated outcomes of education—either positive, negative, or indifferent. For example, attending a class might bring a promotion and salary increase, but it may also mean less time spent with the family.

Once again, Rubenson's theory places significantly less emphasis on external barriers such as cost or transportation and draws attention to the psychological forces. In other words, the strength of the theory is that it brings to the understanding of participation and nonparticipation the idea that the removal of external barriers (such as cost, transportation problems) does not guarantee participation. Conversely, it includes the idea that a potential barrier such as cost will cease to be a barrier if the individual values the opportunity enough. Maximum motivation occurs when the potential learner expects to be successful in the experience and the learner places value on the experience and its consequences.

Religious educators of young adults can gain at least three important lessons from this model:

1. Removing external barriers such as transportation, cost, and child constraints does not guarantee participation in bible studies, seminars, or classes.
2. Possibility of participation is increased if young adults perceive the religious education as being of value—that is, if they are relevant, are related to real life experiences, and meet specific needs.

3. Possibility of participation is increased if young adults perceive that they can be successful in the endeavor. One's perception of success can be enhanced if the religious education experience takes place in a supportive, person-centered, psychologically and emotionally warm learning climate. Furthermore the religious education of young adults should occur in a noncompetitive environment, with less focus on debate and argument, and encouraging honest efforts in answering questions even when responses are incorrect.

Congruence Model

Boshier (1973, 1977) suggests that participation and nonparticipation are related to the congruence or agreement between the learner and his environment. His theory suggests that the greater the incongruencies between an individual and other students, the teacher, the institution, or even between self and one's ideal self, the greater the possibility of nonparticipation or dropout. The greater the sum of the incongruencies, the greater the likelihood of nonparticipation.

His model further defines people as either being "growth" (life-space) motivated or "deficiency" (life-chance) motivated. Growth oriented people are intrinsically motivated and participate in adult education primarily for expression. Deficiency oriented people participate in education because of the need to survive and satisfy the lower-order needs on Maslow's hierarchy (belonging, safety, and survival needs). The model suggests that enrolling for deficiency reasons leads to incongruence and dropout, while growth motivation is associated with congruence and satisfaction.

Obviously, the way to increase the likelihood of participation in religious education of young adults is to reduce the incongruencies or disagreeing factors between learners and the environment—teachers, other adult learners, facilities, or content. How can this be done? The best advice for leaders is to sustain a sensitivity to situations and variables, always open to possible incongruencies. For example, an individual is not comfortable with the other people in the class or group. Efforts might be made to help the individual find a small group or class with people he or she has more in common with or feels more comfortable with.

Chain-of-Response (COR) Model

The chain-of-response model of Cross (1981) assumes that participation in a learning activity is not a single act but the result of a chain of responses. Cross identifies six variables that contribute to the participation in adult education:

1. *Self-evaluation*. This is the beginning point. The model suggests that confidence in one's abilities plays an important role in motivating one to par-

ticipation. Individuals who lack confidence in their own abilities will avoid putting themselves in a position where they are in some way challenged intellectually, or put to the test.

2. *Attitudes Toward Education.* One's present attitude will reflect past educational experience and attitudes of significant others. Young adults who had a disdain for school as children may be hesitant to return to the scene of their former embarrassment or emotional pain.

3. *Goals and Expectations That Goals Will Be Met.* If a goal is important to an individual, the motivation to participate will be increased.

4. *Life Transitions.* Here Cross is referring to periods of change, whether they be gradual or sudden. She suggests that these changes often trigger a desire for education into action. Examples of life transitions are divorce, loss of a job, additions to the family, and geographical moves.

5. *Barriers or Opportunities.* Individuals who are highly motivated will get over modest barriers. On the other hand, modest barriers may preclude participation by the weakly motivated.

6. *Information.* Available information that joins the learner to the opportunity is the final step to encourage participation.

Cross has the benefit of drawing from a number of existing theories and demonstrates this in a broad, encompassing approach. Her model is helpful to the understanding of young adult participation in several ways:

1. Before committing to a religious education activity, many young adults must be convinced that the setting will be safe, non-threatening, and emotionally comfortable—a learning situation free from possible embarrassment, hurtful conflict, competition, or failure.

2. Religious education must provide young adults with worthy, reachable goals. If the goal is not particularly important, or likelihood of success is in doubt, motivation will decrease accordingly. Some religious education programs or small groups place high demands, goals, and accountablity on members. While this presents an exciting challenge to some, others will drop out or refrain from participating because they feel they may not be able to reach the goals.

3. Leaders must work hard to find out what barriers to participation exist and what can be done to overcome these barriers. Is the time of the learning activity not appropriate for most? Is child care a problem? Transportation? Cost? Removal of these barriers may lead to increased attendance.

4. Life transitions of young adults may trigger a desire or provide an incentive for religious education. Life transitions of young adults may include marriage, divorce, loss of a job, and birth and raising of children. Thus the best

or right time to teach a couple about child development is when they are expecting or raising children.

5. Religious education opportunities for young adults should be well promoted. Posters, church bulletin announcements, mail-outs or personal invitations are good ways to relay the information and create interest.

Social Participation Theory

Cookson (1986) developed a theoretical framework directed at "understanding aspects of the human condition which influence an individual's involvement in purposeful activities" (1986, p. 131). His assumption is that human behavior—in this case participation in learning activities—is determined, to some extent, by aspects of both the person and the environment. He identifies the following variables:

1. *External Contextual Factors* such as climate, geography, transportation, and government policies that affect education.
2. *Social Background and Social Role Factors* such as physical features, social positions, and experience.
3. *Personality and Intellectual Capacity Factors.*
4. *Attitudinal Dispositions* such as values, expectations, and intentions.
5. *Retained Information* such as images, beliefs, knowledge, and plans.
6. *Situational Barriers* such as cost or family constraints.

Like other models, Cookson focuses on the coinfluence of internal and external variables. He reminds us that to best understand the practice of young adults in religious education we must be aware of both environmental and psychological factors.

Implications for Research in Adult Education Participation

Motivation theory is of value to research in adult education participation because it aids in developing a framework for ordering research in who participates and does not participate, and why (Cross, 1981). Collectively, the theories contribute in several ways:

1. The theories demonstrate the need for understanding participation as interaction between the individual and his environment. For example, Miller (1967) suggests that those from a lower socioeconomic stratum (demographics: environment) value education for different reasons (psychographics: value system) than those from an upper-class stratum. Thus, reasons or barriers to participation are more than just a demographical issue (e.g., class); there is an interaction between environment (class) and the individual (values).

2. They demonstrate a need for exploring both the motivating and deterring factors in understanding participation patterns. In other words, simply to know why adults do participate in learning activities does not explain why others do not.

3. They help identify possible motivating or deterring factors to participation. For example Cross's life transitions (divorce, job loss, geographical moves) identify possible motives, while Cookson's (1986) external contextual factors (climate, transportation, geography) reveal possible barriers.

4. The theories give evidence to the complexity of the issue, and suggest that reasons will vary from group to group. For example, Miller's (1967) theory suggests that members of lower classes will participate in education opportunities for different reasons than those of upper classes. Cookson (1986) says social roles (e.g., gender) are influential factors. This is partially explained by the fact that different groups are faced with different external or internal influences. Men may give different reasons than women because of different characteristics or social roles. Young adults may give different reasons than older adults because of contrasting needs, desires, and characteristics.

Factors Motivating Participation

A growing body of research seeks to identify factors motivating participation in adult educational opportunities. Paul Burgess (1971) identifies four approaches to determining the reason adults are active in educational opportunities. They are: a) inferring reasons by analyzing the kinds of activities the adults participate in, b) asking adult learners to put in their own words why they participate, c) asking learners to check from a list of possible reasons for participation, and d) concentrating of adult's orientations toward learning.

The results of these studies have been helpful in understanding why adults take part in learning activities, and consequently in aiding programmers and teachers. This section will examine reasons for participation in adult education (including young adults) and adult religious education, before focusing specifically on young adults.

Reasons For Participation in Adult Education

Studies concerned with participation in educational activities date back to 1933 when Hoy identified reasons given by workers in a large British industrial city for taking evening classes. He classified the reasons into six categories: desire for knowledge, advancement, interest, leisure time, recreation, and social reasons.

Three years later Williams and Heath (1936) reported reasons given by working class adults in England, Scotland, and Wales as to why they attended classes. They grouped the reasons into four categories: the escape motive, restoring the balance, the respite from economic ends, and the discovery of fellowship.

A 1949 study by Deane identified four groups of reasons given by American adults as to why they took a particular course. The classified groups were: practical vocational help, practical utilitarian purposes, general self development, and escape from boredom, recreation, or curiosity.

Much of the current work in the field of adult education participation, however, can be traced to the efforts of Houle (1961), who emphasized a learning orientation approach. Houle reported the results of interviews with twenty-two continuing learners and identified three sub-groups of adult learners. "The first, or, as they will be called, the goal-oriented, are those who use education as a means of accomplishing fairly clear-cut objectives. The second, the activity-oriented, are those who take part because they find in the circumstances of learning a meaning which has no necessary connection, and often no connection at all, with the content or the announced purposes of the activity. The third, the learning-oriented, seek knowledge for its own sake" (pp. 15-16).

Houle's typology has been highly influential in succeeding research. For example Sheffield (1962), based on the concepts presented in Houle's book, developed a list of fifty-eight reasons why adults participate in educational activities and identified five components: learning orientation, desire-activity orientation, personal-goal orientation, societal-goal orientation, and need-activity orientation.

A national survey by Johnstone and Rivera (1965) compiled eight possible reasons for enrolling in adult studies and asked participants to indicate whether any of these had a bearing on their most recent enrollment. The results were:

1. Become a better informed person	37%
2. Prepare for a new job or occupation	36%
3. To better learn present job	32%
4. Spend time more enjoyably	20%
5. Meet new and interesting people	15%
6. Learn homemaker skills	13%
7. Get away from the daily routine	10%
8. Learn every day tasks	10%.

In an interview style similar to Houle's (1961), Tough (1968) endeavored to understand what motivates people to participate in self-directed learning. He identified three learning patterns as: (a) those with an awareness that they wanted or needed to do something that required new or more learning, (b) those who were curious about an issue or issues relevant to the learner and (c) those who had a desire to spend more time learning, followed by a decision as to what to learn.

In 1971 a pair of instruments based on the Houle typology were developed. Burgess (1971) developed the *Reasons for Educational Participation* (REP) instrument, which included seventy reasons. He administered it to over a thousand respondents in the St. Louis area and identified seven factors as: the desire to know, the desire to reach a personal goal, the desire to reach a social goal, the desire to reach a religious goal, the desire to escape, the desire to take part in an activity, and the desire to comply with formal requirements.

Boshier (1971) compiled a 48-item *Education Participation Scale* (EPS), that was administered to randomly selected adults involved in continuing learning. He identified fourteen first-order factors, which were further clustered into seven second-order factors.

Boshier (1977) and others (Morstain and Smart, 1974; 1977) refined the EPS and it is now published commercially (Boshier, 1982). The present scale is a 40-item questionnaire with a six-factor scoring key. The following factors are identified:

1. *Professional Advancement*. This is an educational preparedness factor. High scorers tend to be vocationally oriented.
2. *Community Service*. High scorers tend to be concerned with community affairs and service to mankind.
3. *External Expectations*. High scorers tend to pursue study in order to comply with the suggestions or requirements from agencies or institutions with which they are affiliated.
4. *Social Contact*. High scorers reflect a desire to fulfill a need for associations and friendships.
5. *Social Stimulation*. High scorers reflect a need for stimulation and relief from boredom.
6. *Cognitive Interest*. High scorers reflect a basic intellectual inquiry motivation. There exists a desire to acquire content for content's sake.

A survey of research on adult education participation done within the last twenty years reveals a strong interest in the subject matter. While Boshier's (1982) instrument has proven to be the most popular tool, it is not the only source of data.

Grabowski (1972) used Burgess's (1971) REP instrument to study factors motivating adult learners enrolled in an independent study program at Syracuse University. He found the first five factors to be identical to those of Burgess but discovered two others to be different. Grabowski's sixth factor was desire to study alone, and the seventh was desire for intellectual security.

A national survey of part-time students between the ages of 18 and 60 asked respondents why they engaged in their studies (Carp, Peterson, & Roelfs, 1974). They found that out of a possible twenty answers, the most important reasons centered around knowledge for its own sake. Personal fulfillment reasons and job-related reasons were next in importance.

One of the purposes of a study by Morstain and Smart (1974) was to replicate Boshier's (1971) EPS study of adult learners in New Zealand, by using a sample of adults participating in continuing education courses in the United States. Their study showed significant similarity in between the two samples.

Further study by Morstain and Smart (1977) endeavored to develop a typological framework for assessing adult learner's reasons or motivating factors that had influenced them to pursue further educational activity. Using EPS scores and selected demographic characteristics, the researchers identified five learner types as: (a) nondirected learner, (b) social, (c) stimulation seeking, (d) career oriented, and (e) life change.

Apt (1978) examined both the negative and positive factors that might influence or determine adult education participation in rural western Iowa. She identified four factors, two of which were barrier factors and two of which were motivational in nature. The two motivational factors were self-development and career. The self-development factor included items related to self/image, citizenship, curiosity, relationships and awareness. The career factor included statements related to career or job improvement.

O'Connor (1979) sought to identify reasons for the participation of nurses in continuing education. Using Boshier's (1971) EPS instrument, he identified seven motivational factors. The study indicated that nurses participated primarily for reasons related to maintaining professional currency and improving their ability to serve the public.

Boshier and Collins (1985) did a secondary analysis of EPS studies done up to that point (54 files and over 13,000 cases). The analysis identified the broad outline of Houle's (1961) three-factor typology, but more important it confirmed the six-factor scale developed earlier by Boshier (1982).

The purpose of a study by Clayton and Smith (1987) was to determine whether motives for returning to college among reentry undergraduate women could be grouped into patterns and by motive types. They identified eight general motives: self-improvement, self-actualization, vocational, role, family, social, humanitarian, and knowledge.

An investigation into the research related to participation of adults in education demonstrated significant diversity in identifiable motives. Boshier and Collins' (1985) EPS and Burgess's (1971) REP instruments identified only three comparable factors: knowledge, social contact, and requirements. Even when the same instruments were used, there were contrasting results.

For example, Grabowski (1972) found only five of seven factors to match those of Burgess. O'Connor (1979), using Boshier's (1977) EPS, identified seven factors as compared to six by Boshier.

Explanations for such discrepancies are twofold. First, dissimilarities can be anticipated when surveys are conducted among diverse populations. It can be expected, for example, that nurses will give significantly different reasons for continuing their education than randomly selected residents of rural Iowa.

Second, surveys and statistical analysis are limited by the nature of items included by the researcher. For example, Burgess (1971) included items related to religious activities and consequently identified a religious factor. Boshier (1971, 1977), on the other hand, did not include items related to religious participation thus his research did not identify a religious factor. Such diversity reinforces the theoretical assumptions that reasons differ greatly according to the group studied and that conclusions cannot readily be transmitted to other populations.

Reasons for Participation in Adult Religious Education

The first to identify a religious factor was Burgess (1971), who suggested that a strong force in adult education was a "desire to reach a religious goal." Boshier (1976) countered that because a factor was identified, it did not necessarily follow that people enrolled or attended for the reasons described. He rightly suggested that a factor could emerge because everyone "indicated they *were not* enrolled for the reasons described" (p. 30), and that an examination of item means or factor scoring was necessary to understand the quality of the factors. In other words, Boshier was not convinced that Burgess had identified a significantly influential motivation based on factor identification alone.

However, researchers have begun to explore motives for participation in church related learning activities, recognizing that while there may be similarities to the larger adult population, there may also be significant differences (Phillips, 1992). Phillips (1983) investigated the motives for participation in adult Sunday School programs of the local church in the Portuguese Baptist Convention. He developed a Portuguese edition of the REP instrument, and identified seven motivational factors. In order of significance, they were:

1. The desire to reach a religious goal
2. The desire to reach a social goal
3. The desire to know
4. The desire to take part in a social activity
5. The desire to comply with formal requirements
6. The desire to reach a personal goal
7. The desire to escape

Utendorf's (1985) study of lay Catholic workers identified religious factors and through the inclusion of item mean scores showed them to be highly influential. He adapted the 40 item EPS to include 5 "religious" items and performed a factor analysis on the 45 items. Two religious factors emerged, Personal Religious Development and Church and Community Service having the highest and second highest mean scores respectively.

Following the example of Utendorf, several studies adapted the EPS in order to study adult participation in church related education. Atkinson (1994) investigated attenders of Christian and Missionary Alliance (C&MA) churches of the South Pacific District and identified six significant factors. In order of importance they were:

1. The *Personal Spiritual Growth* factor indicates a desire to improve one's relationship with God and to deepen one's faith.
2. The *Obedience To God* factor is concerned with one's response to God and reflects a desire to please God through obedience to him.
3. *Ministry Preparation* is concerned with the individual's desire to minister to others and a need to improve one's ability to carry out that ministry.
4. The *Cognitive Interest* factor indicates a desire to seek learning and knowledge for its own sake.
5. *Community Service* reflects an interest in being equipped to serve in the community and do community work.
6. The *Social Contact* factor identifies a desire to enhance social and personal relationships.

In this study Spiritual Growth and Obedience to God factors provided much influence in motivating participation. Ministry preparation and cognitive interest provided moderate influence, while community service and social contact provided minimal influence on their attending.

Fortosis (1991) studied young single adult (aged 22-33) attenders of Evangelical Free Church Sunday Schools in Southern California. In order from strongest to weakest, the factors were spiritual growth, relationship with God, social contact, social stimulation, emotional support, external expectations, and escape.

Wilson (1992) explored the reasons church volunteers attended the Greater Los Angeles Sunday School Convention (GLASS), a convention designed to provide training, spiritual refreshment, and motivation for adults involved in Christian education. He identified eight motives as ministry preparation, spiritual growth, cognitive learning, relationship to God, social contact, external expectations, escape, and stimulation. Ministry preparation, spiritual growth, and cognitive learning were found to be the primary reasons for attending, with the other factors having little to no influence.

Reasons for Participation in Young Adult Education

While most studies are interested in the relationship between age or life stages and reasons for participation in educational opportunities, consistent and specific findings related to young adults are elusive. One of the problems is that there is little consistency in the definition of young adulthood. For example, one study considers young adulthood as 20 to 30 years old, while another might define a young adult as one between 18 and 35. Nonetheless writers agree that age functions as a significant determinant of motives to participation. Boshier (1977), for example, argues that "individuals have to respond to critical psycho-social stages in their life which may be resolved through participation in adult education" (p. 97).

According to the national survey of Carp, Peterson, and Roelfs (1974), learning for a degree, certification or new job, declined after age 34, although learning for reasons of knowledge did not decline. Escape, feeling a sense of belonging, and personal fulfillment reasons were more important to younger adults. Serving the church as a motivator varied little with age.

Morstain and Smart (1974) administered the EPS to students enrolled in adult education courses in a U.S. college. They found that while more importance was placed on professional advancement and cognitive interest for all age groups, mean scores on the social relationships scale tended to decline with increasing age. In other words, compared with other groups, the desire for meeting new people and engaging in group activities seemed more important to men and women in the youngest age group (ages 21-40).

Another Morstain and Smart (1977) study identified five learner types as nondirected, social, stimulation seeking, career oriented, and life change. They found that 81 percent of the social and 70 percent of the life change learners were 30 years of age or younger. The social learners were characterized by an interest in creating or improving one's social interactions and personal associations. The life change learners demonstrated a need to improve several aspects of one's life, including career and occupation, intellect, and social relationships.

Reasons for Participation in Young Adult Religious Education

Several studies focused on young adulthood as a variable in religious studies. Fortosis (1989) tested fifty single young adult (ages 20-30) Sunday School attenders in a Southern California church and identified six motivating factors. In order of priority they were spiritual growth, cognitive interest, social welfare, social relationships, escape and stimulation, and external expectations.

For the young adults (ages 20 to 40) in Atkinson's (1994) study, spiritual growth and obedience to God provided much influence in motivating participation. Ministry preparation and cognitive interest provided moderate influence, while social contact and community service contributed little influence. The mean scores for young adults were not significantly different from those of middle (40 to 60) and older adults (60 and over). The lone exception was social contact, where young adults had significantly higher mean scores than older adults.

In Fortosis' (1991) second study of young single adults, spiritual growth and relationship with God had highest mean scores. He concluded that young single adults are not satisfied to be simply entertained with contemporary issues but desire to mature spiritually and nurture their relationship with God. A second grouping included factors related to human relationships—social contact, social relationships, and emotional support.

Wilson (1992) divided his GLASS respondents into five age groupings (18-22, 23-29, 30-39, 40-49, and 50 and over). By comparing mean scores he concluded that 18 to 22 year olds attended more than other age-groups because of the influence of another person and less than other groups for reasons related to spiritual growth and ministry preparation. Those from 30 to 39 came more for stimulation (relief from boredom, getting away from responsibilities, a break in routine) than the next two older groups.

Suggestions for young adult religious education. The studies indicate that young adults participate in religious education for a multiplicity of reasons. These include a desire for spiritual development or growth, an interest in gaining knowledge and understanding of Bible content and life related issues, a need to be equipped for ministry or service, and a desire for social activity and interpersonal relationships. In light of this, it is recommended that churches develop a systematic strategy whereby a healthy balance of classes and courses concerned with spiritual growth (Eph. 4:13; Col. 1:28), ministry and service training (Eph. 4:12; II Tim. 3:16), content and knowledge (Prov. 1:2-3; Col. 1:9), and interpersonal relationships (I Thess. 5:11) are offered.

Churches can be more effective in this regard by doing long-term planning, perhaps one or five years in advance. Large churches might offer several kinds of classes each quarter, while smaller churches could offer one class each quarter, providing a different focus or emphasis each quarter. Another option would be to offer classes which consider a combination of motivational factors. For example a single class or study might be designed to accommodate personal spiritual development, social interaction, and equipping for ministry. Churches and young adult ministries are advised to involve their adults in the choosing of course content and curriculum development. This might be done through assesment surveys which ask adult participants to identify the types of classes or course content they would like to see offered.

Research (Fortosis,1989, 1991; Wilson, 1992; Atkinson, 1994) also indicates that spiritual growth or development serves as a strong impetus for young adults to participate in religious education. A strong young adult ministry then, will be sure to offer a variety of classes and studies which focus on personal spiritual growth. This means including classes related to spiritual disciplines such as prayer, spiritual gifts, personal Bible study, worship, stewardship, servanthood, and obedience to God.

Several studies identify social contact and interpersonal relationships as contributing factors. The nonreligious studies of Carp, Peterson, and Roelfs (1974), and Morstain and Smart (1974, 1977) indicate that social relationships seem to be more important for younger adults than for older age groups. Fortosis (1989, 1991) also found social relationships to be a strong motivator, while Atkinson (1994) found social contact to provide minimal influence. Nonetheless young adults in this study had significantly higher mean scores than older adults on this factor.

These findings stress the need to provide education opportunities that place a strong emphasis on meaningful relationships and social interaction. Roehlkepartain (1993) argues that the strongest areas of adult education involve classes that are warm and inviting, while Anderson (1990) suggests successful churches have addressed the need for building relationships by establishing networks of fellowship and support groups.

It is clear that churches desiring to attract and interest young adults will do so primarily through the implementation of small groups, which can take the form of growth groups, home Bible studies or support groups. Other types of religious education classes can be made more appealing to socially oriented learners through the provision of refreshments, allowing some time for informal talking, and encouraging discussion and sharing during class time.

Careful attention should be given to the selection of leaders for classes and small groups. Teachers and study leaders should be extraverted and friendly, capable of encouraging and nurturing the development of relationships through modeling, creating a warm climate for learning, and the facilitating of interaction.

One of the most neglected areas of adult education is the equipping or preparing of lay people for ministry and service. Yet studies indicate young adults desire such training (Fortosis, 1989; Atkinson, 1989; and Wilson, 1992). Classes designed to equip for service or ministry might include how to lead small groups, principles of teaching, leadership skills, personal evangelism, public speaking and lay counseling.

Some (Morstain & Smart, 1977; Aslanian & Brickell, 1980; Cross, 1981) identify life change as a significant incentive to educational involvement. Life change issues for young adults include leaving home, selecting a mate, marriage, having children, divorce, getting established in an occupation or career, losing a job, and entering university or college. Churches should offer classes and provide small group ministries to help young adults deal with these timely issues. They might consider classes for newly marrieds or those preparing for marriage. They could offer classes on parenting children or adolescents, or how to manage your money. They could provide support groups, for example, for those who are divorced, those who have lost their job, or those dealing with grief and loss.

Barriers To Participation

While considerable research has focused on what impels participation, little research comparable in nature has examined the deterrents. Furthermore, Darkenwald and Valentine (1985) suggest that most inquiries have either been descriptive surveys or untested theoretical assumptions. Yet Scanlan and Darkenwald (1984) have argued that the concept of deterrents to participation is crucial to understanding and predicting involvement in adult education. It is as important to know why adults do not participate as to why they do (Cross, 1981). This section will seek to identify a) reasons the general adult population gives for nonparticipation, b) reasons for nonparticipation in adult religious education, and c) reasons young adults give for nonparticipation.

Reasons for Nonparticipation in Adult Education

In the national survey by Carp, Peterson, and Roelfs (1974), respondents were asked to indicate all the reasons, from a list of 24, they felt were important in keeping them from learning what they wanted to learn. They cited financial cost, time constraints, lack of desire, and other responsibilities as the most significant barriers.

The items were further grouped by Cross (1981) into three broad categories of situational barriers, institutional barriers, and dispositional barriers. Situational barriers were those arising from situations in life such as cost, and home and job responsibilities. Institutional barriers included those that arise out of the institutions themselves, and included items such as scheduling and strict attendance requirements. Dispositional barriers were those related to attitudes and perceptions about oneself as a learner. This category included items such as poor past performance or simply a lack of enjoyment in learning. A fourth category called informational barriers—those related to awareness or lack of awareness of existing opportunities in adult education—was added by Darkenwald (1980).

In Apt's (1978) effort to identify both the motivating and deterring factors to adult participation in higher education, two barrier factors were identified. The affective barrier included six items reflecting negative feelings or attitudes toward schooling. The situation barrier included situational restraints such as time, cost or transportation and was rated potentially of greatest importance in participation and nonparticipation decisions. The affective barrier appeared to be least significant.

As a result of concern for lack of quality research in nonparticipation, Scanlan and Darkenwald (1984) developed a *Deterrents to Participation Scale* (DPS) and administered it to a random sample of health professionals. A factor analysis yielded six factors they labeled as disengagement, lack of quality, family constraints, cost, lack of benefits, and work constraints.

Scanlan and Darkenwald (1984) and Darkenwald and Valentine (1985) agreed that while this scale (DPS) was a significant step in the study of barriers to participation, it nevertheless had limitations. The major concern was its constricted validity, or the fact that the results could not be generalized to the general public. Taking this into consideration, Darkenwald and Valentine (1985) revised the DPS for the general population. The new generic scale (DPS-G) was a 34-item scale and identified the following six factors:

1. *Lack of Confidence*. Nonparticipation exists because of self-doubt and low self-esteem.
2. *Lack of Course Relevance*. Nonparticipation exists because the course does not meet perceived needs and interests.
3. *Time Constraints*. Nonparticipation exists due to lack of time or time inconvenience.
4. *Low Personal Priority*. Nonparticipation exists because of a lack of interest or low priority when compared with other interests.
5. *Cost*. Nonparticipation exists because of an inability to meet expenses.
6. *Personal Problems*. Nonparticipation exists due to situational difficulties such as child care or health problems.

Like participation studies, the explanations given for nonparticipation in adult education are varied. The diversity of responses can be explained by the dissimilarities of the populations themselves, as well as differences in the instruments used.

Reasons for Nonparticipation in Religious Education

Several dissertations examined the reasons for nonparticipation of adults in church based education. A study by Ruffner (1983) of the Indiana Church of Christ identified the following six factors: a) resistance to education (does not value education or the education offered in the church), b) confusion (respondent experienced some sort of confusion in past learning experiences), c) social nonaffiliation, (feelings of being unwanted and unwelcome), d) nonrelevance (programs are not in harmony with the needs and interests of the adult), e) marginality (indicates the individual is a nominal member), and f) activity (other responsibilities keep him from attending).

Brown (1985) explored reasons given for nonparticipation in church education programs in the Indiana Baptist Convention. He identified eight reasons as: a) fulfillment gap (church education is not fulfilling their needs), b) religious nonaffiliation (lack of felt need), c) social nonaffiliation, (not interested in church social activities), d) alienation (a feeling of unacceptance), e) inability (inability to attend), f) self-direction deficiency (lack of self direction), g) education bias (some sort of dislike of education), and h) inconvenience (opportunities are not convenient).

Another study sought to discover the reasons Southern Baptist adults give for not participating in church related education (Harton, 1985). Six factors were found: a) secular orientation (church is no longer a viable alternative for investment of time), b) resistance to education (not orientated toward education), c) estrangement (feeling of exclusion from the rest of the congregation), d) aversion to church-based education (do not believe church education programs have anything to offer them), e) marginality (generally not active in church activities), and f) activity (other activities take too much time).

Finally, Atkinson (1993) modified the Darkenwald and Valentine (1985) DPS-G scale and identified seven nonparticipation factors in a study of Christian and Missionary Alliance church attenders. In order of importance they were a) time constraints, b) schedule conflicts, c) lack of relevance, d) family constraints, e) low personal priority, f) personal problems, and g) lack of confidence.

From general observations of factor mean scores, it appears that most nonparticipation in this study stemmed from the fact that adults were excessively busy. This was demonstrated by the nature of three of the first four factors: time constraints, schedule conflicts, and family constraints. Simply put, these factor scores indicated that adults found other activities and responsibilities to be restrictive in allowing them to attend Bible studies or other types of classes.

Reasons for Nonparticipation in Young Adult Education

As one might expect, young adults often identify reasons for nonparticipation that are different from those of other adults. Carp, Peterson, and Roelfs (1974), and Darkenwald and Valentine (1985) found cost to be a deterrent primarily for young adults. Darkenwald and Valentine also found their personal problems factor (including items such as child care and family problems) to be a greater deterrent to younger women.

Certain situational barriers makes education participation difficult for young adults. "Lack of time due to job and home responsibilities, for example, deters large numbers of potential learners in the 25-to-45 year-old age group. Lack of money is a problem for young people and others of low income. Lack of child care is a problem for young parents" (Cross, 1981, p. 98).

Harton's (1985) church-based study found young adults (18-35) to identify with four of six factors. He found them to be a) more resistant to education, b) more resistant to church-based education specifically, c) more estranged from the rest of the congregation, and d) busier in other activities, with less time for church education.

In Atkinson's (1993) study young adults had highest mean scores on time constraints, schedule conflicts, and family constraints. This seems to indicate that many young adults in this study were simply too busy for participating in religious education. When compared to other adults on these factors, young adults had significantly higher mean scores than older adults on time constraints and schedule conflicts. They also had significantly higher mean scores than both middle and older adults on the family constraints factor.

Suggestions for young adult religious education. In most studies, lack of time or being too busy is mentioned by young adults as the most significant deterrent to taking part in education opportunities. Apparently this is also recognized by most coordinators of Christian education as a significant problem. In Roehlkepartain's (1993) study, 72 percent saw busy schedules of adults as a major or somewhat major problem of their religious education program.

It is important for churches and leaders to be sensitive to this matter—to recognize that young adults have busy schedules and lead complex lives. They must also seek to discover ways to reach them in spite of their satiated lifestyles. Efforts should be made to make classes more available to these potential attenders. This may mean abandoning traditional hours and finding out what times are best suited for a particular group. For example if many church attenders commute for two hours after work, it may be difficult to attract adults to a evening Bible study at 7:00 P.M. It means, as much as is possible, offering a variety of opportunities at varied times, so that choices are available. Some possibilities, in addition to the traditional Sunday School hour classes are Sunday evening classes, lunch hour classes, early morning studies, Saturday morning classes, evening sessions, home Bible studies and small groups, and weekend seminars or workshops.

It also means that it may be unrealistic to expect an adult or couple to attend more than one learning opportunity a week. Young adults should be encouraged to choose one meaningful class or small group study and be faithful and committed to it. In addition, the teaching and preaching the church should be such that it encourages adults to recognize the need for religious education and to make every effort to set aside a time for the same.

Family constraints such as home responsibilities and lack of child care also deters many young parents (Darkenwald & Valentine, 1985; Cross, 1981; Atkinson, 1993). This problem can be easily solved by providing adequate child care and children's ministries so that young parents can be freed to participate in their activities. Some churches are reaching mothers of preschoolers (MOP's) by providing child care for the whole morning. While the children are being taken care of the mothers take part in a variety of activities such as a Bible study, aerobics, lunch, and even a trip to the shopping mall.

A third deterrent that young adults identify with is cost. Generally this is not an issue in religious education because classes and studies normally do not require tuition or books. Occasionally, however, retreats and seminars are included in the programming of young adult ministries. Remember that many young adults may not be able to attend because of financial constraints. This problem can be alleviated somewhat by adhering to the following two simple suggestions. First, keep expenses to a minimum by avoiding expensive and extravagant facilities. Second, efforts should be made to make money available for those who could not otherwise afford to attend.

While not necessarily identified as being more predominant among young adults than others, studies indicate that there is often a resistance to education that is reflected in different ways. Some feel that they will not profit from educational experiences, or that classes and studies lack relevance to their needs and interests. Harton (1986b) says that "All other details properly attended to, they are more likely to participate if they perceive that the educational activity will meet an educational need or interest they have identified" (p. 144).

He goes on to suggest that literature on adult development and life tasks are rich with insights into the needs of adults. In addition adults themselves provide the best source of information in regards to their needs and interest. Barna (1993) argues that the church has failed miserably in this task of being relevant—at least to the Baby Boom generation. He says, "Churches expected the same programs and style of instruction that they had been using for years and years to satisfy the needs of these young adults. That expectation proved to be unrealistic. . . . When churches offered only pat answers to increasingly complex issues, Boomers took their quest for spiritual enlightenment elsewhere. Sunday School, worship services, prayer chains, potluck dinners, and committee meetings simply did not address the needs of this maturing generation" (p. 189).

A second way resistance to education is demonstrated is through the belief that religious education is for children (Ruffner, 1983). Roehlkepartain (1993) identifies this as one of the key, and most damaging, myths of religious education. What is needed, he says, "is a view of Christian education as a lifelong process" (p. 29).

Summary

Church leaders and coordinators of religious education are often frustrated by lack of participation of adults in religious education opportunities.

The purpose of this chapter has been to better understand what motivates young adults to participate, or deters young adults from taking part in religious education experiences, with the further intent of providing suggestions which might lead to increased participation. The following insights are summarized:

1. Participation and nonparticipation in learning activities is understood best through an analysis of the interaction between an individual and his or her environment.
2. The potential learner is faced with positive and negative forces. Possibility of participation can be increased, though not guaranteed, with the removal of the negative forces or barriers.
3. If an individual does not perceive oneself as able to participate successfully, or if there is no reward for doing so, there will be a lack of motivation to participate.
4. The greater the incongruencies between an individual and his environment, the greater the possibility of nonparticipation.
5. One's past educational experiences will affect the attitude an adult currently has toward taking part in a learning activity.
6. Life transitions such as divorce or having a child may trigger a desire for education into action.
7. If an individual is highly motivated he or she will get over most barriers; modest barriers may preclude participation to the weakly motivated.
8. Available information that joins the learner to the opportunity is the final step in encouraging participation.
9. Young adult participate in religious education for a variety of reasons. These include a desire for spiritual development or growth, an interest in gaining knowledge and content of the Bible and life-related issues, to be equipped for ministry or service, and a need for social activity and interpersonal relationships.
10. For young adults, lack of time or being too busy is the most significant deterrent to taking part in learning activities.
11. Family constraints such as home responsibilities and lack of child care deters many young parents.
12. Adults often resist learning activities in the church because the classes often lack relevance to their needs and interests, or because of the notion that religious education is primarily for children.

REFERENCES

Anderson, L. (1990). *Dying for change*. Minneapolis: Bethany House.
Apt, P. (1978). Adult learners and higher education: factors influencing participation or

nonparticipation decisions. *Alternative Higher Education*, 3(1), 3-11.

Aslanian, C., & Brickell, H. (1980). *Americans in transition*. New York: College Entrance Examination Board.

Atkinson, H. (1993). Identifying reasons for nonparticipation in Christian education classes in Christian and Missionary Alliance Churches of the South Pacific District. *Christian Education Journal*, 13(3), 102-117.

Atkinson, H. (1994). Factors motivating participation in adult Christian education opportunities in Christian and Missionary Alliance churches of the South Pacific District. *Christian Education Journal*,14(2), 19-35.

Barna, G. (1991). *What Americans believe*. Ventura, CA: Regal.

Barna, G. (1993). *The future of the American family*. Chicago: Moody.

Boshier, R. (1971). Motivational orientations of adult education participants: A factor analytic exploration of Houle's typology. *Adult Education Journal*, 21(2), 3-26.

Boshier, R. (1973). Education participation and dropout: A theoretical model. *Adult Education*, 23 (4), 255-282.

Boshier, R. (1976). Factor analysis at large: A critical review of the motivational orientation literature. *Adult Education*, 27(1), 24-47.

Boshier, R. (1977). Motivational orientation revisited. *Adult Education*, 27 (2), 89-115.

Boshier, R. (1982). *Education participation scale*. Vancouver, Canada: Learningpress.

Boshier, R., & Collins, J. (1985). The Houle typology after twenty-two years: a large-scale empirical test. *Adult Education Quarterly*, 35(3), 113-130.

Brown, W. (1985). Factors contributing to the non-participation of adults in the educational programs offered by churches of the Indiana Baptist Convention (Doctoral Dissertation, Indiana University, 1984). *Dissertation Abstracts International*, 45, 9276A.

Burgess, P. (1971). Reasons for adult participation in group educational activities. *Adult Education*, 22(1), 3-29.

Carp, A., Peterson, R. & Roelfs, P. (1974). Adult learning interests and experiences. In K. Cross & Valley (Eds.), *Planning non-traditional programs* (pp. 11-52). San Francisco: Jossey-Bass.

Clayton, D., & Smith, M. (1987). Motivational typology of reentry women. *Adult Education Quarterly*, 37(2), 90-104.

Coleman, L. (1986). Adults are the church now. In J. Stubblefield (Ed.), *A church ministering to adults* (pp. 278-283). Nashville: Broadman.

Cookson, P. (1986). A framework for theory and research on adult education participation. *Adult Education Quarterly*, 36 (3), 130-141.

Cross, P. (1981). *Adults as learners*. San Francisco: Jossey Bass.

Darkenwald, G. (1980). Continuing education and the hard-to-reach adult. In G. Darkenwald & Larson (Eds.), *Reaching hard-to-reach adults* (pp. 1-10). San Francisco: Jossey-Bass.

Darkenwald, G., & Valentine, T. (1985). Factor structure of deterrents to public participation in adult education. *Adult Education Quarterly*, 35(4), 177-193.

Deane, S. (1949). *A psychological description of adults who have participated in educational activities*. Unpublished doctoral dissertation, University of Maryland, College Park, MD.

Elias, J. (1982). *The foundations and practice of adult religious education*. Malabar, FL: Krieger.

Fortosis, S. (1989). Perspectives on community: Young singles in the congregation. *Christian Education Journal*, 10(1), 39-50.

Fortosis, S. (1991). *Reasons for single young adult participation in Sunday school pro-

grams within Evangelical Free Churches in Southern California. Unpublished doctoral dissertation, Biola University, La Mirada, CA.

Grabowski, S. (1972). *Motivational factors of adult learners in a directed self-study bachelor's degree program.* Unpublished doctoral dissertation, Syracuse University, Syracuse, NY.

Harton, R. (1985). A factor analytic study of reasons for non-participation church-based education among Southern Baptis adults (Doctoral Dissertation, Indiana University, 1984). *Dissertation Abstracts International, 45,* 3050A.

Harton, R. M. (1986a). Importance of adult education. In J. Stubblefield (Ed.), *A church ministering to adults* (pp. 13-31). Nashville: Broadman.

Harton, R. M. (1986b). Program planning models for adult education. In J. Stubblefield (Ed.), *A church ministering to adults* (pp. 144-161). Nashville, TN: Broadman.

Hines, B. (1975). *An investigation of the effect of multiple curriculum and/or social grouping choices upon attitudes which adult learners have toward Sunday School in selected Southern Baptist churches.* Unpublished doctoral dissertation, Southwestern Baptist Seminary, Fort Worth.

Houle, C. (1961). *The inquiring mind.* Madison: University of Wisconsin Press.

Johnstone, J, & Rivera, R. (1965). *Volunteers for learning.* Chicago: Aldine.

Lewin, K. (1947). Frontiers in group dynamics: Concept, method, and reality in social science. *Human Relations,* June (1), 5-41.

Maslow, A. (1954). *Motivation and personality.* New York: Harper & Row.

McKenzie, L. (1982). *The religious education of adults.* Birmingham, AL: Religious Education Press.

Miller, H. (1964). *Teaching and learning in adult education.* New York: Macmillan.

Miller, H. (1967). *Participation of adults in education: A force-field analysis.* Boston: Center for the Study of Liberal Education for Adults, Boston University.

Morstain, B., & Smart, J. (1974). Reasons for participation in adult education courses: A multivariate analysis of group differences. *Adult Education,* 24(2), 83-98.

Morstain, B., & Smart, J. (1977). A motivational typology of adult learners. *Journal of Higher Education,* 48(6), 665-679.

O'Connor, A. (1979). Reasons nurses participate in continuing education. *Nursing Research,* 28(6), 354-359.

Phillips, W. (1983). Motives for participation in the adult Sunday School program of local churches in the Portuguese Baptist Convention (Doctoral Dissertation, University of Georgia, 1982). *Dissertation Abstracts International,* 43, 3486A.

Phillips, W. (1992). Reasons for participation in learning activities: Implications for the adult Sunday School program. *Christian Education Journal,* 10(3), 36-45.

Roehlkepartain, E. (1993). *The Teaching Church.* Nashville, TN: Abingdon.

Rubenson, K. (1977). *Participation in recurrent education: A research review.* Paper presented at the meeting of National Delegates on Developments in Recurrent Education, Paris, France.

Ruffner, K. (1983). Demographics associated with non-participation in church-based adult education: A factor analytic study (Doctoral dissertation, Indiana University, 1982). *Dissertation Abstracts International,* 44, 959A.

Scanlan, C. & Darkenwald, G. (1984). Identifying deterrents to participation in continuing education. *Adult Education Quarterly,* 34(3), 155-166.

Sheffield, S. (1962). *The orientations of adult continuing learners.* Unpublished doctoral dissertation, University of Chicago, Chicago.

Stubblefield, J. (1986). Young adult years: Spread your wings and fly. In J. Stubblefield (Ed.), *A church ministering to adults* (pp. 52-64). Nashville, TN: Broadman.

Tough, A. (1968). *Why adults learn: A study of the major reasons for beginning and continuing a learning project.* (Monograph in Adult Education No. 3). Toronto: Ontario Institute for Studies in Education.

Utendorf, J. (1985). Reasons for participation in Roman Catholic lay ministry training programs. *Review of Religious Research*, 26(3), 281-292.

Williams, W., & Heath, A. (1963). *Live and learn.* London: Methuen.

Wilson, F. (1992). Why church volunteers attend religious training programs. *Christian Education Journal*, 12(3), 69-85.

Part Two: Characteristics of Young Adults

CHAPTER FOUR

Psychological Characteristics of Young Adults

LES STEELE

The purpose of this chapter is to identify general psychological characteristics of young adults and reflect on strategies which religious education can utilize in facilitating growth and development in young adults.

The psychology of adulthood is itself a developmental phenomenon. When the history of developmental psychology is traced it begins as child psychology, moving to adolescents, and finally to adulthood. For instance, notice the trajectory of Erik Erikson's work: *Childhood and Society*, 1951; *Youth: Identity and Crisis*, 1968; *Adulthood*, 1978; *Life Cycle Completed*, 1982; and *Vital Involvement in Old Age*, 1986. The point is that we have only begun in the past twenty years or so to take seriously the developmental characteristics of adulthood.

Approach

The approach taken here to describe the psychological characteristics of young adulthood is developmental, systemic, and teleological. It is developmental in that it views young adulthood as a period of the life cycle with inherent potentials and limitations. Young adulthood is understood as a period of the life span that brings to it both positive and negative resolutions of developmental tasks from previous age periods. These resolutions have direct impact on the way the tasks of young adulthood are negotiated. The psychological characteristics described here are drawn predominantly from both the psychosocial and cognitive-structural developmental theories.

The approach is also systemic. Essentially, this means that behavior, thought, and affect of an individual must be interpreted in light of the "system" of interaction which serves as the individuals primary basis of relationship. Those involved in the system include parents, siblings, extended family, and friends. The approach is not behavioristic in that the young adult is simply the product or victim of a system. The young adult is active in the system, and it is the very dynamic of the interactions that influence psychological characteristics. The central issues of identity and intimacy and the specific tasks of young adults are not independent variables but operate systemically in the development of the young adult.

Finally, the psychological description of young adults presented here is teleological. Teleological implies that a specific direction and trajectory underlines the notion of healthy development. The trajectory for human development and specifically young adults described here is drawn from practical theological insights. Christian theology and psychology provide insights on optimal human development and in particular the direction of growth desired for young adults.

The chapter will describe the factors which function systemically to influence the development of young adults then discuss two central issues of young adulthood; identity and intimacy formation. Following this the age periods of young adulthood will be described. Finally, a comparison of generational cohorts will be made and the direction of growth in young adults summarized.

Factors

Before beginning an attempt to describe the psychological characteristics of young adulthood it is important to speak to the factors which interact systemically to influence growth and development. It is important to remember the systemic nature of these factors. Obviously, at various periods of the life cycle certain factors predominate over others. It does appear, however, that young adulthood is one of the first age periods in which each of the factors mentioned here converge as the individual attempts to construct an initial adult life structure. The factors which converge are biological issues, family, social, and historical/cultural issues.

With the rise of psychological images of adulthood it seems as if we have diminished the influence of biological factors in our potential growth and development. At stake here is the age-old question of nature or nurture. We must refuse the either/or construction of the question and recognize that it is both/and. As young adults attempt to find their place in the adult world, they find some doors open and others closed primarily on the basis of innate endowments which influence choices in career and lifestyle. My spirit may wish to be a professional athlete but my flesh may be inadequate to the goal. It is also a harsh reality that given a culture which is preoccupied with physical attractiveness, the resolution of the intimacy issues at young adulthood are directly affected by innate endowments.

Family issues also carry impact for the developing young adult. Today, perhaps more than at any other time, we are aware of how our family of origin affects our adult lives. The negotiation of a young adult life structure is affected by the way in which the young adult has been parented and indeed how their parents were parented. Erik Erikson speaks of the "cogwheeling" of generations and how family issues come to bear on an individual's development. By cogwheeling, Erikson means the interaction of multiple family generations. This has both a positive and a negative effect on all members of the family. Connected with this is the individual's own ideas and dreams about family life. Clearly, if a traditional family structure is my ideal for family life this will have direct influence on my dealing with intimacy issues.

The social context of young adults also has significant impact on their development. Included with social context are issues of economic class, level of education, occupational role, religion, and one's circle of friends and acquaintances. Each of these variables present both positive and negative aspects to the developing young adult. The economic class from which a young adult comes and to which they aspire has direct impact on occupational and lifestyle choice. Religious factors play a significant role for some young adults as they are concerned that their choices fall within the will of God. Also important here is the realization that aspects of this age period are defined by society (Chickering & Havighurst, 1981, p. 19). Bernice Neugarten speaks of the "social clock" (Neugarten and Hagestad, 1976). By this she implies that societal norms play a significant role in the negotiation of adult life tasks. For the young adult this may manifest itself in the intimacy question. Society seems to place time parameters around when one "ought" to be married. There are also gender issues which come to play at this point. For the young woman, if she is not married by the "appropriate" age then she and others worry about her possibilities to marry. It still appears however, that a sex bias exists here in that the same concerns are less obvious for males. "On time" also implies not being too early. Again if a young woman marries she may do so earlier than the social grouping deems "on time." Either way, the notion of the social clock affects the growth and development of young adults in all of their adult developmental tasks.

Finally, the broader culture and historical moment affects the negotiations of young adulthood. Culture implies the mores and expectations of the social arena broader than an individuals primary social group. This includes social forces that affect young adults' choices. Robert White (1966) suggests four aspects of American culture that affect young adulthood (pp. 107-112). He recognized the "competitive" nature of American culture. If young adults do not exhibit the appropriate amount of competitiveness they will get nowhere. He also spoke of our "faith in material progress," our reliance on practicality and common sense, and our basic tendency toward conformity. We may wish to discuss if these are true today, yet it is still important to recognize the cultural myths which shape the young adult's vision of adulthood. The historical moment also impinges upon the young adult's development. In fact, each of the factors here mentioned are historically conditioned. The "acceptable" images of beauty, family, occupation, social context, and culture all flow with the currents of history.

We will now consider the primary developmental issues to be negotiated by young adults. The above factors all interact as young adults attempt to form an initial adult life structure by negotiating the psychological tasks of identity and intimacy.

Identity Formation in Young Adults

A central psychosocial crisis of young adulthood is the continuation of the formation of an identity. Erikson (1980) locates the point of ascendancy for the identity formation process in adolescence. However, he also is clear that the process is ongoing. Current research also substantiates the ongoing nature of identity formation through young adulthood (Orlofsky et al., 1973). Distinctions between adolescence and young adults in the identity formation process will be discussed later, for now let us define what is meant by identity.

Erikson suggests that the psychosocial task to be negotiated is Identity versus Identity Confusion (1980, p. 94). Identity is a very confusing notion which at times may correspond with what some refer to as the "self." For Erikson, identity includes two primary components; 1) a "perception of one's self sameness and continuity in time" and 2) "the simultaneous perception of the fact that others recognize one's sameness and continuity" (1980, p. 22). The perception of self sameness grows primarily out of the individual's creating an ideology, clarifying occupational goals and gaining confidence in human relationships. The danger, however, is the inability to make any progress in these areas. The individual becomes confused and unable to make decisions. If identity is achieved, the primary strength to be developed in the personality is fidelity— the ability to make and keep commitments.

Young adults (18-22) are at the end of this psychosocial crisis. By this age they will have developed tentative resolutions to the identity question. Much work, however, remains for the young adult. Whereas adolescents are gathering the raw material for framing the identity, young adults are putting on the finishing touches.

If young adults are at this point in identity formation they will manifest group confidence, self-awareness, and stepping out into the world. "Identity achievement is accompanied by a psychological state of inner assurance, self-direction, and self-certainty (Adams, Markstrom, & Abraham, 1987, p. 292). There is a sense of "coming of age" characterized by confidence and engagement with the public arena. Young adults turn their attention from the private work of identity formation to the public work of identity formation (Merriam & Ferro, 1986). Sharon Parks (1986) states, "I propose, then, that the threshold of young adulthood is marked by the capacity to take self-aware responsibility for choosing the path of one's own fidelity" (p. 77). For young adults the formation of an ideology is the task of making meaning. In essence the young adult is weaving a unified philosophy of life, a coherent system of beliefs and values to center the identity.

Young adult identity formation is also associated with the tasks of negotiating greater autonomy both physically and psychologically. Gould (1978) asserts that adults at different periods must challenge false assumptions in their lives. For young adults from 17-28 he suggests they must challenge the assumption that "If I get any more independent, it will be a disaster" (Kimmel, 1974, p. 98). Parks (1986) finds the movement here to be from counter dependence to interdependence to interdependence (p. 54). By counter dependence Parks implies an opposition to authority. This form of dependence is found primarily in the early phases of identity formation. Young adults are negotiating the latter two forms. They are realizing that they are included in the realm of authority. They have a voice. The move to interdependence may best be characterized as the realization of being one voice among many. Young adults begin by using their voices for solos and hopefully will blend them with the choir.

Emotionally, the movements toward autonomy carry the exhilaration of freedom with the fear of vulnerability. The path toward autonomy is wrought with danger and requires courage to move on. An essential element in the movement toward autonomy and interdependence is the family system.

There is a great deal of interest today in family systems particularly in describing dysfunctional families and how these affect an individual's emotional well-being. It is clear "that individuation from one's family of origin is important to the establishment of a mature ego identity during late adolescence" (Anderson & Fleming, 1986, p. 785). Research further indicates that in family situations characterized by fusion and/or triangulation young adults attempting to form a mature identity will not have adequate strength to do so (p. 786). On the contrary in situations where young adults perceive parental emotional support and encouragement toward independence there is increased growth toward mature identity (p. 788).

A part of the process of developing autonomy from parents is developing a mentor/sponsor relationship. Levinson (1978) found that a mentor plays a significant role in the young adult's identity formation and autonomy efforts. For young adults seeking to find verification for their identity a sponsor becomes significant. Parks (1986) states that a sponsor can "anchor the vision of the potential self" (p. 86). Sponsors can be college faculty, older friends or older co-workers. In some ways they function as transitional objects as the young adult continues to move toward interdependence.

Issues of gender have impact on identity resolution. For example, Carol Gilligan (1982) has convincingly argued a male bias in Erikson's attention of identity. The bias becomes more evident in Levinson's (1978) understanding of the trajectory of adult development. In both Erikson and Levinson great value is placed on autonomy, independence, and achievement. The emphasis on the independent, autonomous adult is at the expense of committed relationships. This understanding needs to be corrected to incorporate the voice of women. Gilligan (1982) states, "The elusive mystery of women's development lies in its recognition of the continuing importance of attachment in the human life cycle" (p.445). We must understand identity formation not in terms of independence but interdependence.

Identity formation in young adulthood is a continuation of the process initiated in early adolescence. It is, however, much more sophisticated and the stakes are much higher. The young adult is keenly aware of the freedom and vulnerability they now possess. They must take seriously the task of forming a coherent view of life which serves to direct the building of an adult life structure. Relationships also take on a formative role in the life of the young adult.

Religious Education Tasks and Identity Formation

Religious education can provide support and encouragement as young adults establish their identities. Obviously, religious education must continue to educate young adults in scripture and doctrine, but what programs can religious education offer to foster identity formation? First, religious education can assist young adults in forming a philosophy of life. It can offer courses, workshops, and retreats that focus on the need for young adults to make meaning in life. Programs should focus on helping young adults affirm a relevant faith that centers their identity. Walter Brueggemann (1979) states that when we seek to understand ourselves in relationship to God the question shifts from who I am to whose I am. We must assist young adults in affirming an internally motivated faith that gives substance to identity. Associated with this is the need to help them utilize a relevant faith in developing an ethical system. Courses which focus on clarifying values and discussing Christian ethics can be helpful.

Second, we can assist young adults in dreaming. Quite often as young adults attempt to form dreams of adult life their field of vision is limited. They need to be made aware of the enormous possibilities and needs that exist in the world so that their dream can be magnified. By involving young adults in service projects, sponsoring speakers from all walks of life, and by having them hear the stories of older adults we can assist them in forming a dream consistent with their faith and gifts.

Third, we must help them understand the possibilities and pitfalls of their attempts at autonomy. For some, this will mean providing support systems which encourage them to risk being more independent. For others, it will mean exhorting them to beware of an overextended independence. It may be useful to offer courses which help young adults explore their families of origin. By doing this they may gain insight into their fear of autonomy or their desperate need of autonomy.

Intimacy

It is clear that a major developmental task to be addressed in young adults is that of developing an intimate relationship with one or more persons. Intimacy here refers secondarily to intimate relationships with others which are also deep and abiding. A problem here is how many truly intimate relationships can an individual maintain. Most argue that it is very difficult to have more than three or four truly intimate relationships at any one time. The primary issue for our consideration is the task young adults address as they attempt to understand what an intimate relationship is and can they or do they want to be a part of an intimate relationship.

Erikson (1982) defines intimacy as the "capacity to commit oneself to concrete affiliations which may call for significant sacrifices and compromises" (p. 70). This affiliation includes shared work, sexuality, and friendship. The relationship needs to be complementary-reciprocal. Intimate people share work. They have something like a "life project" that brings them together. For many this project is children but can be any project that brings two people together around a common cause. Shared sexuality is crucial to truly intimate relationships. One of our current dilemmas is how we have attempted to trivialize sexuality into nothing more than a human need driven by instinct. Sexuality provides two people with the opportunity "to know as they are known." To be vulnerable and "naked" before another is one of the most fearful acts humans can encounter. It can also be one of the most profound acts of concrete commitment to another.

Friendship is central to intimacy. Friendship means to have another who is willing to be with me, to hear me, to be happy with me, to mourn with me, and then to turn this around—for me to hear, to laugh with, to cry with, to care for their welfare. These are central issues of intimacy. Beneath these issues is the crucial component of intimacy—commitment. Intimacy is the capacity to commit. The capacity to commit implies an awareness of the need to sacrifice for the other and a willingness to do so. Chickering and Havighurst (1981) state that loyalty is the only critical norm to intimate relationships.

As mentioned previously, commitment and intimacy are related to identity. Erikson (1980) states, "The condition of a true twoness is that one must first become oneself" (p. 101). There is a need for individuals to have a "reasonable" sense of identity before true intimacy is possible. Research on intimacy status in college males illustrates the point. Orlofsky (1973) identified five intimacy statuses. The "intimate" individual forms deep and open relationships with friends and is involved in a committed love relationship. The "preintimate" has peer relationships that are deep and open but is not involved in a committed love relationship. "Stereotyped Relationships" individuals maintain superficial friendships. "Pseudo intimates" have entered permanent relationships, but the relationships lack depth and transparency. The "isolate" withdraws from social settings and has only a few acquaintances. Research by Orlofsky (1978) also indicates that college males described as "preintimate" can also be described in an "identity moratorium" status. That is, they are highly involved in coming to a sense of identity. The identity work takes precedence over developing a love relationship but is greatly assisted by deep and open friendships. Research by Adams, Markstrom, and Abraham (1987) indicates that being "identity-achieved" is associated with a greater willingness to reveal one's self and a greater willingness to be less self-conscious. Both of these characteristics are crucial to true intimate relationships.

Clearly, there is a relationship between identity and intimacy. The basic relationship seems to be identity followed by intimacy. This must be clarified to see identity formation as developmentally prior to but further facilitated by intimacy formation. Gilligan (1982) states, "Intimacy precedes, or rather goes along with, identity as the female comes to know herself as she is known, through her relationships with others" (p. 437). What she observes regarding women seems to be an important ideal for men as well.

The relationship is further clarified by considering unhealthy relationships. Kegan (1982), in discussing artificially intimate relationships, states, "What might appear to be intimacy here is the self's *source* rather than its aim. There is no self to share with another; instead the other is required to bring the self into being" (p. 97). The relationship Kegan describes is currently named codependency. Many individuals seeking to find themselves prematurely commit to permanent relationships which draws them away from the necessary identity work. The relationship often appears wonderful, but after a few years, if the individual has an opportunity to resume identity work, the relationship is revealed as counterfeit. Vaillant (1977) observes, "In other words, to marry too young, before a capacity for intimacy was developed, boded as poorly for successful marriage as to exhibit a delayed capacity for intimacy" (p. 216).

Isolation is the negative resolution of the intimacy crisis. Erikson (1980) defines isolation or distantiation as "the readiness to repudiate, to isolate, and, if necessary, to destroy those forces and people whose essence seems dangerous to one's own" (p. 101). This definition seems to connote an assertiveness by the self which is not the case. Isolation is most characterized by fear. It is the fear of disappearing as a self. It is also the fear of remaining separate and unrecognized. Young adults are in the midst of a difficult psychosocial crisis. It is indeed fearful and frightening to become vulnerable to others with the possibility of rejection or worse disappearing into the other.

Positively, however, one is reminded of the words in the first Epistle of John "perfect love casts out fear." Erikson (1982) suggests that the strength of the personality which is a result of a positive resolution of the identity crisis is love. He defines love as, "mutuality of mature devotion that promises to resolve the antagonisms inherent in divided function" (p. 71). There is no sentimentality here. Love is seen as a cognitive and affective strength of the individual which allows the person to be open and giving. When we allow another into our lives we allow for the possibility of personal transformation. Kegan (1982) states, "Who comes into a person's life may be the single greatest factor of influence to what the life becomes" (p. 19).

Religious Education and Intimacy

As with identity, religious education can assist young adults in negotiating the issues of intimacy. First, religious education can educate young adults in a mutual understanding of friendship. Religious education can offer courses on listening, empathy, and general social skills such as how to meet new people. Religious education can also offer opportunities for young adults to socialize. Care must be taken to avoid the tendency to create uncomfortable settings due to tacit or explicit expectations to form couples. We must provide contexts for developing committed, mutual friendships.

Second, religious education can educate for a realistic understanding of love. Our culture continues to perpetuate an overly romantic notion of love and the "white knight" myth. Religious education must help young adults recognize the socialization which has created unreal expectations for intimate relationships. The "white knight" story where the "one" will come and rescue me from my loneliness is sexist and untrue yet continues to operate in the minds of many young adults—male and female. Courses and seminars which educate to expose these untruths and help young adults establish honest and realistic expectations for marriage are necessary.

Third, religious education can assist young adults in developing an ethical understanding of sexuality. Clearly, issues of gender are important here as in the totality of our self-understanding. In regard to sexuality, religious education can address the problems of sexual dominance and violence. The most often hidden issues of sexual coercion must be addressed openly. A theological understanding of relationships must be taught to assist young adults in seeing relationships and sexuality as related to their being created in the Image of God. A theology of love can be developed for young adults by exploring biblical images of love and care. Hopefully by openly addressing these issues young adults can create sexual values which translate into appropriate sexual behavior.

Young Adult Developmental Tasks

The story is told that Freud was once asked about what constitutes healthy adulthood. His response: *"arbeiten und lieben."* To work and to love. To work—to find ways to be both productive and creative as we attempt to make a living. Erikson identified occupational commitment as central to identity formation. To love—to try and understand how to be a friend and have friends; to explore whether or not we will commit ourselves to a long-term relationship.

Having discussed the major psychological characteristics of young adulthood we turn now to consider how these characteristics manifest themselves in more concrete developmental tasks of work and love. Within the entire young adult age period (18-35) most theorists identify three specific periods. These are ages 18-24; 25-30; 31-35. We will discuss the characteristics of these periods and their contribution to the development of a young adult life structure. Specific attention will be given to the tasks of work and love.

Eighteen to Twenty-Four

Within the North American context, the age period 18 to 24 is the traditional period to attend college. College offers many an opportunity to work on the issues of identity and intimacy, work and love. It is a time and place traditionally understood as allowing for personal exploration and growth in order to be better prepared for engaging the adult world. We may wish to discuss if this is now the case or ever was the case, but that discussion must be deferred. It must also be pointed out, although obvious, that not all 18-24 year olds attend college. The percent of 18-24 year olds attending college is 60 percent as of 1990. This means that 40 percent of 18-24 year olds are negotiating the developmental tasks outside the college environment. Research is lacking on the differences between how college attendees and non-college attendees deal with their age tasks. The majority of research on this age group is done with college attendees for two obvious reasons. First, they are a convenient sample, whereas non-college attendees are more difficult to gather data on. Second, the research is being done to help colleges determine curricular and service decisions. In general, both paths have their own strengths and weaknesses as 18-24 year olds deal with their developmental tasks. These young adults are "novice" adults.

No matter which path is chosen the direction of the early young adult is up and out. Gail Sheehy (1976) refers to it as a period of "pulling up roots," Roger Gould (1978) speaks of "breaking out." Obviously, the primary task is leaving the home of one's parents. Many parents and adolescents look forward to this time. However, as in any transition in life, it is a period of both gain and loss. The emotionally charged language of both Sheehy and Gould carry the reality of painful separation. As young adults leave their family of origin there is pain and a sense of vulnerability. There is also a sense of expectation and hope as young adults launch out in order to create a tentative adult life structure.

This experience of leaving home affords the opportunity of not only physical separation and space but also the possibility of emotional space. If young adults are to continue identity formation and the development of intimate relationships they must have the emotional space to grow.

This period is also a period of dreaming. Young adults reflect on their futures—persons, places, things. They create visions of what an ideal life might be for them. This dream typically has two central themes; love and work. Values and attitudes about relationships are further clarified as young adults prepare themselves for marriage and family life. This preparation includes the primary question of whether or not they see themselves in a long-term commitment and if children appear in their dream. For some, their observations of bad marriages make them very hesitant to move in that direction. For others, it serves as a challenge to create a good marriage. If this question is settled, there is the further question of family. "Do I desire children?" If so, "When?" These questions of marriage and family tend to make 18-24 year olds keen observers of marriages and families.

A related task is the managing of a home. Finding a place to live, eating, paying bills are all essential tasks of this age. Despite the apparent mundaneness of these issues, they can prove to be the greatest threat to the adult life structure. As folk wisdom states it, "It is not the mountain ahead that wears you down, it's the grain of sand in your shoe." Individuals without the practical survival skills may find themselves paralyzed and unable to take initiative in other areas of adult life. Their sense of competency is challenged thus eliciting feelings of inferiority which impact the entire sense of self.

In order to pay the bills, young adults must find work. Eighteen to twenty-four year olds tend to experiment with and explore options. Career choice is a frightening task. Young adults must evaluate their skills and abilities, their likes and dislikes and their values. They must consider the options available and make choices, and they must consider the economic realities which impinge upon their choices.

For college attenders, career choice is typically associated with choice of degree major. The assumption is that they will work in a career directly associated with the major chosen. There is ample evidence that shows this to be an untrue assumption, yet it still operates as a tangible expression of career exploration. Research also supports the observation that college students' career plans are superficial and quickly abandoned (Chickering & Havighurst, 1981). Simply consider the number of times students change majors and you can see the tentativeness and exploratory nature of early choices.

It is also clear that career choices are highly influenced by family expectations. Pragmatically, parents are concerned that young adults will be able to pay for their education and become financially self-sufficient. In terms of ideals, families may hope young adults will perpetuate a particular career path of the family or may hope that they will be the generation of the family that advances socially and economically.

The path of non-college attenders tends to be one of job experimentation. This entails taking jobs that have some level of interest and making some contribution to paying the bills. Exploration comes in their attempts to move from job to job. In a weak economy exploration is difficult and quite often young adults end up in careers by coincidence.

Career choice cannot be seen as an isolated decision but must be seen in relation to identity formation. Research in this area illustrates the systemic interplay of career choice and identity. Some research indicates that young adults with a clear sense of identity continue to engage in career exploration (Blustein, Devenis, & Kidney 1989). One could conclude from this that identity formation allows for career exploration. Research, however, also suggests that, "career exploration may provide a means for individuals to learn about themselves in ways that may be relevant to other important aspects of personality development" (Blustein et al., 1989, p. 200). Therefore, career exploration facilitates identity formation. The systemic reality is that career and identity are mutually facilitative. As I consider identity issues, I must consider career choices. As I consider career choices I must see how these fit into my sense of identity. Chickering and Havighurst (1981) state that a "key vocational developmental task is reconciling self-perceptions with perceptions of work and workers" (p. 217). Can I see myself in this career? Do I want to be like those I see in this career? For both college attenders and non-college attenders the tasks of the 18-24 year old period are similar:

achieving independence, exploring relational options and considering career choices. It is an initial attempt to establish an adult identity.

Religious education tasks for 18 to 24 year olds. Religious education tasks related to the psychosocial crises of identity and intimacy were previously discussed. Most of these issues appear throughout young adulthood. However, there are some which are more specific to particular age periods in young adulthood. For 18 to 24 year olds religious education can assist in tangible ways related to autonomy, intimacy and career.

As "novice" young adults sense the need for autonomy, religious education can provide both emotional support, as previously discussed, as well as practical support. Two particulars come to mind. First, young adults need physical help to move out. At a church in Illinois the young adult group created a service simply entitled, "Cheap Movers." Many in this group were moving out of their parents' homes for the first time while others were moving from apartments to newly purchased homes. The service was simple. Anyone moving would make their need known and the "Cheap Movers" sprang into action. They would coordinate transportation and human power to handle the move. They would also coordinate a potluck meal to be shared by all involved. This service not only contributed practical assistance to achieving autonomy but provided the contexts to develop friendships and care in commitment.

Religious education can also offer courses for specific home management skills. Quite often young adults have never been made aware of many of the mundane yet essential tasks related to establishing their own home. Seminars and courses could be offered in a variety of areas. Searching for an apartment or house, understanding lease/rent agreements, engaging utility services and many others could be of great service. Courses on money management can help young adults establish patterns of financial responsibility.

In regard to intimacy, 18 to 24 year olds may be considering the options of singleness or marriage. Some may be sensing that singleness is their only option and in need of assistance in maintaining a healthy sense of self. Others may be experiencing an inordinate need for marriage and need assistance in clarifying their feelings. Religious education can help young adults explore the question of singleness and marriage so that they are making more careful and informed choices.

Religious education can also assist these novice young adults in career exploration. Vocational interest inventories can be made available and direction given. Career interest groups can be coordinated utilizing older adults representative of various careers. Young adults could meet in groups with these persons and ask questions to gain insight into particular careers. Related to this could be the creation of a mentor/sponsor program to pair up older adults with young adults. These sponsors would act as advisors, clarifiers, information sources and cheerleaders as the young adult explores possibilities.

Twenty-Five to Thirty

Young adults now move from a "novice" phase to "middler" phase. During the novice phase young adults lack confidence as they negotiate the early adulthood tasks. Middlers, however, have possibly gained a degree of confidence and now press on more boldly in further refinement of the tasks before them. Along with increased confidence comes the realization that stakes are getting higher. Changing occupations becomes more difficult and relationships become more complex. In essence, the increased awareness of responsibility for decisions qualifies the manner in which young adults continue to develop.

Turning again to the issues of love and work, we find in relationships evidence for increasing complexity. During this period the marriage rate for women is about 45 percent and about 42 percent for men. The average age of marriage in 1987 was 23.6 for women and 25.3 for men. Whereas the novice phase could be characterized as learning how to have serious relationships, the middler phase can be characterized as having relationships. The task now becomes learning how to live in relationship. Young adults must decide why they do or do not desire a permanent loving relationship. In past generations marriage seemed to be the means to fulfilling one's role in society and to care for another. Today it appears that self-fulfillment predominates as the reason for marriage (Yankelovich, 1981; Bellah, 1985).

Work also takes on a more refined nature. In novice young adults the balance between career commitment and career exploration leans to the exploratory pole. In middler young adults the balance begins to shift toward commitment. In essence, choices are refined.

George Vaillant (1977) suggests that this is a period of "career consolidation." He found that between Erikson's intimacy crisis and the generativity crisis young adults work hard to establish their careers. Vaillant states, "from age twenty-five to thirty-five they tended to work hard, to consolidate their careers" (p. 216). Energy is diverted from romance, play, and avocations to establish occupational credibility. Once idealistic and possibly critical of materialism, these young adults buckle down. At times it appears a major personality change occurred. Vaillant goes on to say, "Men who at nineteen had radiated charm now seemed colorless, hardworking, bland young men in 'gray Flannel suits'" (p. 217). The middler period of young adulthood (25-30) is a period of increased competency and confidence as young adults address the tasks of work and love. Obviously, there are those who do not do well in negotiating these tasks. In place of competency and confidence, insecurity and a lack of self-confidence keeps these young adults from successfully developing a functional adult life structure.

Religious education tasks for 24 to 30 year olds. Religious education could be helpful as "middler" young adults continue to negotiate work and love. In regard to work, religious education could continue offering support in exploration through seminars and sponsors. For this group, however, it is more important to help them develop a theology of work. This is the age group which quite often invests much of their energy in career consolidation, often to the neglect of other areas in their lives. Courses and seminars which educate young adults in vocational balance could do much to further positive growth. Studies which help young adults reflect on materialism could help maintain perspective as many careers lure them toward the love of money.

In regard to love, it is appropriate with this group to explore more specifically issues of marriage. Seminars for engaged couples are useful. Here education to assist in adjusting to the early years of marriage can help young adults prepare for the sometimes difficult first years. Courses and seminars for those already married can also be important. These could include topics such as communication, household management, dual career marriages, and dealing with the in-laws. Religious education's key role in marriage is to assist couples in developing a spiritual basis for their marriage. Many young adults marry without considering the subtle strength of their religious and spiritual history. This often means they marry someone who does not share that history which may become an obstacle to forming a spiritual basis in their marriage. These issues could be explored as well as helping them develop spiritual practices as a couple and individuals.

For single young adults this may be a difficult time period. The "social alarm clock" still tends to go off in young women, in particular, if they are not in a serious relationship by their late twenties or early thirties. Religious education can assist these young adults in understanding their singleness. This can include affirming the gift of singleness and supporting them in living out that gift or adjusting to singleness as an unchosen gift.

Thirty-One to Thirty-Five

If we characterize the novice phase of young adulthood (18-24) as developing an initial adult self and the middler phase (25-30) as developing an outer adult self, then we can characterize the "senior" phase of young adulthood as developing the inner adult self. In the middler preoccupation with occupation young adults can become more outer directed than inner directed. There is the tendency to listen to mentors, significant others and the myths of particular occupational cultures as one attempts to clarify values. The same tends to be true with relationships. Middler young adults often look to their friends' relationships for comparison—why isn't our relationship like theirs?

"Senior" young adults begin to develop an inner adult self. Gould (1978) characterized this as a period of "opening up to what's inside." He sees it as a time of discovery or rediscovering feelings, goals, and interests that were hidden or ignored. Clearly, when one is preoccupied with ordering one's outer world, these concerns get lost.

Levinson (1978) finds here a period he names the Age Thirty Transition. He describes this as a bridge period in which individuals terminate, alter, or refine parts of the earlier adult life structure. This is done in order to prepare for a more satisfying next stage of adulthood. The initial young adult life structure is re-worked based upon more intrinsic motivators and self-reflection. There is a sense that the more exploratory and tentative nature of earlier young adulthood is disappearing. Life is becoming more serious or real and the stakes are higher. Young adults may think that if they do not change dissatisfying aspects of their adult life structure now, they may not have another opportunity to do so. The changes may be minor fine tunings which require little effort. They may, however, be major choices which require enormous time and energy.

The issues continue to be work and love. In regards to work the change may require further education. Today's increased population of "adult learners" at colleges and universities as well as theological seminaries bears testimony to this. Young adults may have come to a point where further progress requires a college degree or graduate education. They must make hard choices to press on, remain in their current situation or change direction completely.

Relationally, the transition to inner directedness can lead to a willingness to be more honest in primary relationships and to be more secure. There may be minor mid-course negotiations to make a marital relationship more mutually satisfying to both partners. For the current cohort of "senior young adults" it may also mean having children. The trend is toward delaying parenthood from the earlier phases of young adulthood until "senior" young adulthood when some of the other aspects of the life structure are more settled.

The transition may also result in more radical alterations such as divorce. Marriages may be perceived as obstacles to ongoing individual development, or the relationship may be simply inappropriate. Quite often early marriages, those entered prior to an adequate sense of identity for one or both partners, are most vulnerable to divorce.

A final aspect of developing the "inner adult self" during this last period of young adulthood is avocational interest. Hobbies and leisure activities may have taken second place to love and work. If they did, this is a period where those interests may be rediscovered. Time use is readjusted to make room for hobbies, sports, classes, or other activities which round out the adult life structure.

Religious education tasks for 31 to 35 year olds. Religious education with "senior" young adults becomes a task of assisting them in reflecting upon their adult life structures. Continued marriage and parenting courses are helpful. These may become more crucial as marriages are reevaluated and children demand more attention. In regard to parenting, young adults are concerned with basic child care education.

Senior young adults may be reflecting on changes in career. Religious education could once again provide opportunity for exploration as well as encouragement for continued growth in careers. There is also the need to continue developing a theology of work. This should include helping young adults gain or regain balance assuming they over-invested in their career.

Senior young adults were characterized as nurturing their inner adult lives, but this must be qualified by recognizing their growing call to responsible citizenship. It may be helpful to offer religious education programs to these senior young adults which makes connections between their lives and Jesus'. This is the point where Jesus entered public ministry. Exploring Jesus' life may provide a context for these young adults to both reflect on their life structures and to move out in public ministry through a variety of roles.

Generational Comparisons

Let's think about these theoretical generalizations in light of how the current young adult cohort is negotiating their developmental tasks. Previously, three age groups were identified in young adulthood; novice young adults (18-24), middler (25-30), and senior young adults (31-35). To consider generational trends we will combine the novice and middler phases into one generational cohort and the senior young adults the other. The younger group has gained much attention in recent years and is variously described as the "Twentysomethings," "Thirteeners," "Busters," and "X'ers." "Twentysomething" obviously signifies age. "Thirteeners" signifies this cohort as being the thirteenth generation in America. "Busters" refers to the group born after the "Baby Boom." "X'ers" refers to a generation which is "x-ed out," forgotten and ignored. Here they will be referred to as "X'ers." This is the cohort of young adults born between 1964 and 1973. Both of these generational cohorts attract attention as being either spoiled or ignored. It could be that the attention given to any cohort of young adults is a manifestation of "generational narcissism." That is, each generation of young adults believes that their story is truly unique and must be heard. With this disclaimer in mind let us now consider these two cohorts.

The senior young adults are those born between 1958 and 1963. Although considered a part of the "Baby Boom" they are considerably different than older boomers. For the sake of discussion they will be referred to as "Back

Door Boomers." They missed much of the flair of the "Front Door" of the Baby Boom yet find themselves considered a part of this cohort. Consider the world into which these Back Door Boomers were born, when they came of age, and who they are now.

The Back Door Boomers were born into an American culture of hope and attainable affluence. Dwight Eisenhower or John Kennedy was president at the time of this group's birth. As a part of the larger Baby Boom, they are considered privileged children. The majority were raised in intact families with a mother at home. The nations and individual family resources were directed toward their education and well-being. They were raised to expect much and were expected to produce much. It is generally assumed that Boomers grew up in the mythologized 1960s when everyone was demonstrating for peace and love. The problem is, however, Back Door Boomers were too young to come out and play.

When they came of age (1972-1977) and could come out to play, the nation had changed. The economy was in recession, there was no gasoline for their cars, and they watched the corruption of government exposed. It also became clear at their adolescence that the job market was dismal. Not only had economic troubles contributed to unemployment so had the size of their generational cohort. There were so many of them that jobs were scarce. If they were attending college or graduating from college it became clear that they would be underemployed. In 1982 forty-four percent of college graduates 24 years or younger were in non-college jobs (Littwin, 1986, p. 29).

Home life had changed considerably for this group as well. The idealized intact, mom-stay-at-home family was an endangered species. The divorce rate doubled from 1955 to 1975. Mothers were going to work in order to try to get ahead or keep up financially. Clearly, not all in this generational cohort had shared this home life, but it was still the operative cultural myth. The myth was being exposed.

As Back Door Boomers approached the novice phase of young adulthood and considered the tasks of work and love, the possibilities and ideals for both of these tasks were gone. They delayed marriage and settled into underemployment.

While Back Door Boomers were school age children and adolescents, the X'ers were being born. The "X Generation" is made up of those born between 1964 and 1973. In essence, when Back Door Boomers were coming of age, X'ers were just arriving. The political and social events of these years had the most direct effect on the Back Door Boomers but clearly had indirect effect on the X'ers.

The X'ers were born in a period when their parents and Boomers observed some of the darkest moments in American politics. Still reeling from John F. Kennedy's assassination, they experienced the assassinations of Martin

Luther King Jr. and Bobby Kennedy. They watched as we finally put an end to our involvement in Vietnam. X'ers' parents were numbed as the Watergate hearings culminated in Nixon's resignation.

Possibly as a response to the despair over national events and in reaction to their parents' extreme self-denial, X'er parents indulged themselves. Yankelovich (1981) observes how basic ethical stances shifted from self-denial to self-fulfillment. In homes where both parents were present, both parents were absent. That is, even if the marriage was intact both parents were working. More X'er children grew up with working mothers than any previous generation (Gollub, 1991). Even if the parents were physically present, they were emotionally absent. Parents were preoccupied with their own lives resulting in emotionally undernourished children. These X'er children became "adultified." They were expected to take on inordinate degrees of responsibility, to take care of themselves both physically and emotionally, and to decide upon their own values. They had TV and other material goods to occupy themselves but as Littwin (1986) states, "To be a child back then was to have everything, except maybe an on-duty mother, a protected childhood, and a stable family" (p. 23).

X'ers came of age in an era of denial. This cohort turned 17 between 1981 and 1990. Ronald Reagan was the only president in this period. They too, as with Back Door Boomers, began considering their occupational and economic futures in a period of high unemployment and economic uncertainty. But we denied the facts. The message of the 1980s was "buy now, buy now, buy now." It seems we forgot the companion to this statement—pay later. Along with economic and work confusion came continued political dismay. The scandal for these adolescents was the Iran-Contra Affair. In regard to adolescents attempting to understand their sexuality a new acronym was introduced to their vocabulary: AIDS.

Who are these Generation X'ers as young adults? What generalizations can we carefully make and how are they approaching the developmental tasks of work and love? Douglas Coupland (1991) asserts that the "X Generation" is a generation "purposefully hiding themselves" (p. 56). They have been described as cultural orphans, a generation forgotten. This has led to detachment and disengagement. They are in no hurry to grow up any further. Having been forced to grow up too soon, they find a world unfriendly and not ready for them. X'ers can be characterized as pragmatic in comparison to the idealism of the Front Door Boomers. They seem to feel that preoccupation with ideals has left necessary tasks unattended. Now X'ers must serve as the clean-up crew to get basic issues addressed.

The X'er pragmatism manifested itself in 1984 as political conservatism. Fifty-nine percent of 18-24 year olds voted for Ronald Reagan. In light of the 1992 elections however, their conservatism needs to be reinterpreted as an outcome of their pragmatism. In pre-election polls a substantial amount of Ross Perot's support came from the Twentysomething cohort. His message of "We have a mess— Let's fix it," was appealing to their nonpartisan pragmatism. It appears that a significant number in this cohort finally voted for President Clinton. This may be the result of the denial embedded in the Reagan and Bush administrations combined with a sense of hope that Clinton may get something done. It was not a partisan vote, for X'ers are clearly suspicious and guarded about business as usual.

How do they see the future? Levine (1980) suggests that they seem to be hopeful about their personal future yet doubtful about the future of the world. This is a curious mix, yet it may illustrate the resiliency which accompanies their pragmatism. Economically, they are realistic and angry. Sixty-five percent of X'ers agree that "it will be much harder for people in my generation to live as comfortably as previous generations (Coupland, 1991, p. 183). As Coupland puts it, "You can either have a house or a life" (p. 142). The economic realities have created a situation which in turn yields yet another name for this cohort—"boomerangs." Twentysomethings who have attended and graduated from college return home. Non-college attenders either do not leave or return due to financial difficulty. According to the U.S. Census Bureau, in 1992 fifty-five percent of 20-24 year olds lived with their parents. This is more than any other generation since the Great Depression (Howe and Strauss, 1992, p. 78). They, therefore, are realistically attempting to re-create some dream for themselves.

Their realism is not without emotion. They are angry at what they perceive as a greedy and selfish generation that immediately precedes them. They see the Boomer generation as a "Pacman" generation which devoured all that was in their path. They are particularly angry at the subgroup of Boomers labeled "Yuppies." These Young Upcoming Professionals, which actually only describes about one in twenty Boomers, are seen as the most flagrant in their greed. X'ers perceive them as grossly greedy in their consumption of goods and occupying all the good jobs. This is not to say X'ers would not do the same if they could. Coupland (1991) defines Yuppie Wannabes: "An x generation subgroup that believes the myth of a yuppie lifestyle being both satisfying and viable" (p. 91). One way some X'ers attempt to fulfill their yuppie desire is to live at their parents home and use their personal income to purchase clothes, toys, and experience.

How are the X'ers in negotiating the tasks of work and love in young adulthood? Before addressing work and love separately, it must be said that X'ers tend to delay addressing both. Having been forced to be adultified children, Gollub (1991) states, "Now they have become childlike adults, who cannot weigh options and decide" (p. 234). Where previous cohorts experience mid-life crises in their forties, X'ers face a paralyzing "mid-twenties crises." They have a very difficult time making choices and clarifying values.

However, when they do consider work, what is the result? Clearly the result of their delay combined with a poor economic and employment situation is what Coupland calls "McJobs." These young adults settle for and/or are forced to settle for jobs which they are overqualified for and underpaid for. They receive low wages with little or no benefits for health care or retirement. These jobs can serve a useful role as buffers to provide time for young adults to explore other more satisfying options, but this is often not the case. More often they serve to provide money and absorb time which does not allow exploration. In essence, they are often occupationally stuck.

When X'ers have the opportunity to select careers, they have admirable ideals. Fifty-eight percent of 18-29 year olds agreed that, "there is no point in staying at a job unless you are completely satisfied" (Coupland, 1991, p. 183). Coupland illustrates this in the following comments of the employer of one of his novel's characters. "I just don't understand you young people. No workplace is ever okay enough. And you mope and complain about how uncreative your jobs are and how you're getting nowhere" (p. 20). Healthy work environments; stimulating, interesting, and creative work; a possibility for promotion: these are qualities which X'ers hope for in a good career. Past generations also hoped for these but were more willing to settle for less, hoping for improvement.

Whereas in work there is an idealistic desire for immediate work satisfaction, in love there is a willingness to delay relationships. One X'er defined this response to love relationships as "commitophobia"—a fear of making commitments. The reality is that this cohort of young adults is delaying long-term love relationships. The age of first marriages has been increasing for years; for females it has moved from 20.2 in 1955 to 24.1 in 1991 and for males from 22.6 in 1955 to 26.3 in 1991. Marriage may not be the only indicator of young adults' willingness to commit to long-term relationships, but it does help us verify what we observe. Why are X'ers delaying long term relationships? There is no doubt that this is a complex question with many variations, but it could have something to do with their past experiences.

During their childhood the divorce rate doubled. What X'ers observed was the failure of long-term relationships. This undoubtedly makes them very wary of such commitments. It is fair to generalize that many X'ers heard their parents say something like, "Our relationship is stifling each of our own personal growth. We need to separate so we can take care of ourselves." They may have also heard more than their fair share of, "Tell me what you're feeling." The result could be that their observations and self-confusion have caused them to be emotionally hardened and hesitant to share their innermost feelings. Again, they watched as "care of self" and "sharing of feelings" resulted in their neglect. Because of this experience, they are very cautious of long-term relationships.

They are not, however, giving up on long-term loving relationships. There are three general trends in the X'ers approach to love. First, dating is redefined. Whereas the Boomers, including Back Door Boomers, had unchaperoned individual dates, probably dinner and a movie, X'ers are group dating. Groups of five or more will hang out together, see a movie, do dinner, or whatever. The date will be in the safety of a group where platonic relationships can first develop. In one sense this may serve as a new form of the "chaperoned" date. Not only is this emotionally safer but also physically safer as we have become more aware of date rape and other forms of violence.

When two persons are attracted to one another they will probably have a preliminary date such as "doing coffee" during the day. There seems to be an attitude that dinner and a movie represent a higher degree of commitment than is appropriate early on. Economically, this may be very true. Who initiates the preliminary date is open to either sex, though some express a desire for the "old days" where the guidelines were a bit clearer.

A second difference for X'ers is sexual intimacy. While supposedly sex became free in the 1960s and 1970s, it has now become very costly. Casual sex is becoming, fortunately, a thing of the past among young adults. (Unfortunately, this does not appear to be true for adolescents). Obviously this difference is brought about by the AIDS epidemic but may also be associated with the general skepticism which X'ers have toward relational patterns of the immediate past. There seems to be a realization that sex does not make a relationship.

This may be connected with the ideals which X'ers express about marriage. Gollub (1991) observes that there seems to be a desire for a life of the 1950s, yet it must be shaped by the gains of the 1960s and 1970s. Others observe, "Attitudes that are a curious hybrid of fifties conservatism and the sixties' liberalism: a pragmatic blend uniquely of the Nineties" (de Leon, 1993). From the 1950s, X'ers desire the ideal of building a life together. When they consider family life, they place high priority on caring for children and spending time together as a couple and family. They believe they have learned from their experience of neglect. From the 1960s and 1970s, they want to appropriate the gains of the feminist movement. They do not desire hierarchical relationships where genetics determines authority. They want truly shared leadership relationships where the tasks of building a life together are distributed not according to gender but according to interest, ability, and availability. We may see more marriages with males at home or where both take part time jobs in order to share the home building tasks.

Back Door Boomers and Generation X'ers are two cohort groups that make up the current young adult age group. In many ways the two cohorts are quite similar. Both experience the prospect of unemployment and/or under-employment. Both entered young adulthood during times of economic insecurity which makes them less than hopeful for their future standard of living. In terms of love, both cohorts have delayed long-term commitments. The Back Door Boomers experienced some of the effects of out-of-control divorce rates. The X'ers, however, are the first to deal with the deadly threat of AIDS. Much of what is said about both groups, but particularly X'ers, appears negative. I do not believe such a view is completely accurate. Their pragmatic approach to economic problems combined with their ideals of both work and love may yield rich changes. I believe this cohort of young adults has the possibility to creatively and concretely address our problems.

Conclusion

This chapter began with a discussion of the factors which influence the psychological growth of young adults. Given these factors it was also suggested that a useful approach to understanding the psychological characters of young adults includes developmental, systemic, and teleological components. The primary issues of identity and intimacy were discussed. Age periods of young adulthood were discussed focusing particularly on the themes of work and love. Finally, generational comparisons were reflected upon in order to illustrate the historical and cultural effects on the psychological characteristics of young adults. Throughout, suggestions for religious education were offered.

In conclusion, I would like to bring into focus the direction of growth in young adulthood. That is, if we are attempting to foster healthy psychological adjustment in young adults, then what are the primary areas of growth? What is a compelling vision for young adults?

Robert White (1966) suggests five growth trends in young adulthood. First, there is a hope for stabilizing of ego identity. The identity of young adults becomes more consistent and competent. With this consistency comes increased self-confidence. Single events, which in adolescents destabilize the identity, lose their power. What is hoped for in young adults is this increasing capacity for self-awareness which stabilizes and centers the identity. As the identity becomes more stable, young adults need to consolidate their system of values. White suggests that young adults realize that values have human origin and are related to social stability. From the perspective of Kohlberg's stages of moral reasoning young adults are appreciating social contracts and their importance in human relationships. As young adults become more independent they must humanize and consolidate their value systems (White, 1966).

Third, White recognizes a deepening of interests. Young adults need the deepening of interests. Young adults need the opportunity to gain satisfaction from both job and hobby simply for the joy of the task. Jobs need to become more than paychecks. Hopefully, young adults can begin to express their creativity and imagination in their work. Also, it is anticipated that they will find satisfaction in hobbies, family and, civic responsibilities. These directions can occur if young adults are in secure situations with someone encouraging their growth (White, 1966).

Fourth, White speaks of the freeing of relationships. As young adults become more experienced in intimacy they learn the value of free and honest relationships. The film "Everyone Rides the Carousel" is a depiction of Erikson's eight cycles of life. At stage six, Intimacy versus Isolation, two young adults exemplify the freeing of relationship. They begin a conversation on their future and are depicted wearing masks. While each mask speaks what it assumes the other wishes to hear the individuals behind the masks are expressing his and her doubts and concerns. Eventually, one of them gives voice to the real issues and the masks disappear. The direction of growth in relationships is hopefully toward unmasked, honest, and careful expression and away from masked, anxious, and defensive expression.

Finally, White suggests an expansion of caring in young adults. In Erikson's language this is a beginning of generativity . The focus of care moves beyond self, beyond work and the primary relationship to include children, community, church, and the global situation. The self and spouse are not neglected but nurtured by giving the self in caring ways.

There are many opportunities for religious education to nurture the psychological growth of young adults. Our theological traditions affirm and support the directions of growth and our faith may give encouragement as young adults strive to grow.

References

Adams, R., Markstrom, C., & Abraham, K.G. (1987). The relations among Identity development, self-consciousness, and self-focusing during middle and late development. *Developmental Psychology*, 23, 292-297.

Anderson, S., & Fleming W. (1986). Late adolescents' identity formation: individuation from the family of origin. *Adolescence*, 21, 785-796.

Bellah, R. et al. (1985). *Habits of the heart*. Berkeley: University of California Press.

Blustein, D., Devenis, L., & Kidney, B. (1989). Relationship between the identity formation process and career development. *Journal of Counseling Psychology, 36*, 196-202.

Bruegemann, W. (1979). Covenanting as human vocation. *Interpretation*, 33, 115-129.

Chickering, A. & Havighurst, R. (1981). The life cycle. In A. Chickering (Ed.), *The modern American college* (pp. 16-50) San Francisco: Jossey-Bass.

Coupland, D. (1991). *Generation X*. New York: St. Martin's Press.

de Leon, F. (1993, Jan. 10). *Singles*. The Seattle Times. pp. K1-2.

Erikson, E. (1950). *Childhood and Society*. New York: Norton.

Erikson, E. (1968). *Identity: Youth and crisis*. New York: Norton.

Erikson, E. (1978). *Adulthood*. New York: Norton.

Erikson, E. (1980). *Identity and the life cycle* (A Reissue). New York: Norton.

Erikson, E. (1982). *The life cycle completed*. New York: Norton.

Erikson, E. (1986). *Vital involvement in old age*. New York: Norton.

Gilligan, C. (1982). *In a different voice*. Cambridge, MA: Harvard University Press.

Gollub, J. (1991). *The decade matrix*. Reading, MA: Addison-Wesley.

Gould, R. (1978). *Transformations*. New York: Simon & Schuster.

Howe, N., & Strauss, W. (1992). The new generation gap. *The Atlantic*, 270, 67-89.

Kegan, R. (1982). *The evolving self*. Cambridge, MA: Harvard University Press.

Kimmel, D. (1974). *Adulthood and aging* (2d ed.). New York: Wiley.

Levine, A. (1980). *When dreams and heroes died: A portrait of today's college student*. San Francisco: Jossey-Bass.

Levinson, D., Darrow, C., Klein, E., Levinson, M., & McKee, B. (1978). *The seasons of a man's life*. New York: Knopf.

Littwin, S. (1986). *The postponed generation*. New York: Morrow.

Merriam, S., & Ferro, T. (1986). Working with young adults. In N. Foltz (Ed.), *Handbook of adult religious education*. (pp. 59-82). Birmingham, AL: Religious Education Press.

Neugarten, B., & Hagestad, G. (1976). Age and the life course. In R. Binstock & E. Shanas (Eds.), *Handbook of aging and the social sciences*. New York: Van Nostrand Reinhold.

Orlofsky, J., Marcia, J., & Lesser, I.M. (1973). Ego identity status and the intimacy versus isolation crisis of young adulthood. *Journal of Personality and Social Psychology*, 27, 211-219.

Orlofsky, J. (1978). The relationship between intimacy status and antecedent personality components. *Adolescence*, 51, 419-441.

Parks, S. (1986). *The critical years*. San Francisco: Harper & Row.

Parham, T. (1989). Cycles of psychological nigrescence. *The Counseling Psychologist*, 17, 187-226.

Sheehy, G. (1976). *Passages*. New York: Bantam Books.

Vaillant, G. (1977). *Adaptation to life*. Boston: Little, Brown.

White, R. (1966). *Lives in progress* (2nd ed.). New York: Holt, Rinehart and Winston.

Yankelovich, D. (1981). *New rules*. New York: Random House.

CHAPTER FIVE

Sociocultural Characteristics and Tasks of Young Adults

M. CAROLYN CLARK

If young adulthood is characterized by anything, it is the assumption, in a relatively short period of time, of multiple adult roles and responsibilities. When young adults move out of their families of origin to establish their own lives separate from their parents, they must construct more than one new reality. At a minimum they must establish a home and support themselves with a job. They must develop a social network in these new settings and consider the options of marriage and family. And they must find their place within the larger social community. As a result, the beginning of adult life is experienced as a constellation of emerging identities: worker, spouse, parent, citizen. Merriam (1984) argues that the clustering of these tasks makes young adulthood unique. It is tempting, then, to address the sociocultural dimension of adult development strictly in terms of the assumption of those various adult roles and responsibilities.

However, I believe that simply doing that would miss the deeper significance of this period in the life cycle. In addition to exploring possibilities in marriage, family, work, career, and citizenship, central tasks of young adults are to begin to make sense of these events and experiences and to fashion meaning, attitudes, and values from them. From within the multiple new contexts in which they find themselves, they must bring coherence to all these discordant new experiences. Their task is to make adulthood meaningful.

The church can play a critical role in this process of meaning-making for young adults, helping them understand the complexities and the implications of their new experiences. But it is essential first that those in religious education have an informed understanding of the multiple forces that are at work in the lives of young adults. In the previous chapter Steele examined the inner world of young adults—their psychological characteristics and tasks. But human beings are embedded in a social context, and that world exerts a great influence on our lives. In this chapter I will focus on that outer world, examining the sociocultural tasks and expectations that young adults face. As we will see, more is involved than simply assuming particular social roles and responsibilities.

Conceptualizing Sociocultural Tasks

How do we think about our relationship to the social world? Most often we think in terms of social roles. Sociologists conceive of the social world as a system of interlocking positions, such as parent and child or teacher and student; a role addresses the content of any of these positions (Bee, 1987). However, roles must be understood not only as behaviors expected of an individual but also as behaviors that serve a particular function for society. There are several levels to any analysis of these roles. The first involves a simple description of what is expected of a person in that position, almost in behaviorist terms. The best example we have of this is the work of Robert Havighurst (1952).

In *Developmental Tasks and Education*, Havighurst identified a series of developmental tasks that confront a person across the life span. He defines these as "the physiological, psychological, and social demands a person must satisfy in order to be judged by others and to judge himself or herself to be a reasonably happy and successful person" (Chickering & Havighurst, 1981, p.25). In young adulthood these tasks derive primarily from the assumption of new social roles, as well as from personal aspirations. Havighurst notes that this is a time of particular stress as the person makes a transition from the age-graded world of childhood to the social status-graded world of adult society. Havighurst (1952) originally listed eight tasks for this stage in the life cycle:

> selecting a mate
> learning to live with a marriage partner
> starting a family
> rearing children
> managing a home
> getting started in an occupation
> taking on civic responsibility
> finding a congenial social group.

He believed these tasks together captured the central roles and responsibilities of young adults in American society.

That first level of analysis is straightforward; we see what it is that young adults are expected to do. The second level is implicit, namely the function of these various roles for society. The development of families contributes to the stability of society and serves as the primary means of socialization of children. Likewise, entry into the workforce supports the economy, and active engagement with the wider community advances the project of a democratic society. But there is a further level of analysis. What hidden forces are at work here that shape these social roles in particular ways that lead to very different experiences for different people? I refer particularly to the forces of gender, race, and class. While Havighurst (1952) refers in a limited way to the role of class in the discussion of his model, he does not adequately address issues of gender or race. Yet these are powerful dimensions of our life and they must be considered in any analysis of the life course. They provide the essential caveat to any generalizations we might make about the social roles and responsibilities of young adults, since the interpenetrating factors of gender, race, and class significantly alter those roles.

Bee (1987) notes that gender, race, and class set a trajectory for an adult's life that exerts a powerful force on the life course. All three social constructions serve to limit opportunity for the development of certain people; women, racial minorities, and those with few or no financial resources do not have access to the life experiences available to middle class or affluent white men. There is no level playing field in our society, and both the structure of that field and the rules of the game are designed to maintain the power of the privileged few. Consider some common statistics. In 1990, women earned $.72 for every dollar earned by men (*Working Women*, 1991). The life expectancy of nonwhites in 1990 was 72.4 years, while whites could expect to live 76 years (*Statistical Abstract*, 1992). And overall life satisfaction is lowest for those of lower social status (Bee, 1987). The diversity of life experience pointed to here must be taken into account in any discussion of adult social roles. We cannot, for example, speak of parenting in young adulthood as an abstract concept. It exists only in particular social contexts, and these contexts shape the experience. Consider the differences between the parenting experiences of an upwardly mobile white couple and that of an African-American woman on welfare who is a single parent. These differences are significant and must be accounted for.

Young adulthood is not simply a life stage with identifiable roles and responsibilities; it is a situated condition within a diverse social fabric. In this discussion I will try to address something of the complexity of these realities. Building on Havighurst but expanding the analysis to include the effect of gender, race, and class, I turn now to the specific sociocultural tasks that confront young adults. My primary focus will be on two, entry into the workforce and establishment of a family, because they are the social expectations that are viewed as the essential dimensions of adulthood. These tasks are addressed for the first time in young adulthood, as is the formidable challenge of balancing the two domains, which I will also address. Finally I will briefly address the role that education plays as young adults learn to be part of a larger world.

Get a Job!

The first imperative of the young adult is to become self-supporting, and that means entering the job market. Work is a fundamental aspect of adult life, and it serves several functions. There is, of course, the bottom line—we work to provide food and shelter and other necessities for ourselves and others. But it is also part of our personal identity, one shaped even in childhood. The question, "What are you going to be when you grow up?" usually elicits an answer that identifies a particular occupation, like teacher or astronaut. This is a statement of *doing* rather than being; the doing of something is essential to our status as adults. This connection between work and identity is particularly clear for those who have ever experienced a period of unemployment, an event which in many triggers an identity crisis and loss of self-esteem.

The greater majority of adults are in the labor force. According to the 1990 census, 76.1 percent of men and 57.5 percent of women are employed or seeking employment (*Working Women*, 1991). Significantly, this reports only those in paid employment, leaving uncounted the 21 percent of women 25-54 years old who are full-time homemakers (*Working Women*, 1991), and rendering their contribution to the economy invisible. There is a further distinction between those who have jobs and those who have careers. Perlmutter and Hall (1985, p.382) define jobs as "occupations in which upward advancement is limited and movement is primarily horizontal," whereas careers "are characterized by interrelated training and work experiences, in which a person moves upward through a series of positions that require greater mastery and responsibility and that provide increasing financial return." Career positions are typically more stable since they are less subject to economic fluctuations.

Getting Started

Choosing an occupation is a highly personal process. Schaie and Willis (1986) argue that the process begins in childhood where families exert influence through socialization and by providing or failing to provide important opportunities like education. Class differences are operative in this regard, with circumstances directing lower-class children to jobs and higher-class children to careers. One way this happens is through formal education. Anyon (1989), in her study of elementary schools in different social class communities, shows evidence of a "hidden curriculum" which serves to prepare students for the type of work appropriate to their class. For example, in the working class school, teachers stress the importance of following a predetermined procedure and give students few opportunities to make decisions, whereas in the affluent professional school the teachers emphasize creative expression and application of ideas and concepts. This aptly presages the different characteristics of work done by working class and professional adults. Education is a further means of stratification in that children of middle-class families are far more likely to attend college and therefore be eligible for the better paying professional occupations than the children of working-class families who have fewer resources and more limited expectations.

There are other influences as well. Gender certainly is a factor. Through sex-role socialization, women are directed toward occupations that continue their role as caretaker and nurturer—teacher, nurse, secretary, waitress. These traditional women's jobs have lower pay and lower status than the jobs that are considered traditionally male, namely, the professions. Other influences on occupational selection are geographic proximity and luck. A young adult in the Midwest will be more likely to consider farming than someone growing up in Detroit. And then there is the role of chance: the person with the skills happens to meet the person who needs the skills, and employment results. Finally there is personality. Several psychological instruments, such as Holland's vocational interest typology and the Strong-Campbell interest inventory, are built on the assumption that different personality types are suited to different jobs (Schaie and Willis, 1986). While this clearly plays a role in job satisfaction, it is only one of many factors that influence selection.

Developing Experience

Having selected an occupation, the young adult begins a course of work that will unfold in some patterned way. Unfortunately, most of the studies on work in adulthood have been done on middle-class men; we know considerably less about the work experience of working-class men and of women of all classes. We have data on the continuous work patterns that characterize professional careers of men, not the discontinuous patterns of working-class people subject to fluctuations in the economy, nor the discontinuous patterns of most women who are the primary caregivers of families. However, some of this research provides interesting models for comparison.

Perhaps the most noteworthy is Levinson's (1978) study of male development, one of the rare studies that does include discontinuous work. He took care to include diverse occupations in his sample—executives, biologists, factory workers, and novelists—and while it was not his object to outline career patterns, his data suggested a certain progression these men experienced. In early adulthood he noted two stages. The first is the trial or establishment stage, which Levinson believes can last till the man is 30. This is a time of experimentation, as the man looks for a challenging job that fits his interests and abilities. Bee (1987) notes that men frequently change jobs during this period, more so than at any other time. Once an occupation is decided on, the man must then learn how to do it, and Levinson found that for many that meant finding a mentor, a more experienced person who through example and influence helps them advance their career. He also found that the men had a Dream, an image of their eventual success, and that they actively worked toward its achievement. This is particularly true in the second stage, that of stabilization, which he placed between 31 and 45. Most promotions happen during this period. The process of forming an occupation is thus a protracted one, in Levinson's model.

How is the pattern different for women? The most obvious difference is continuity. Bee (1987), summarizing multiple studies, estimates that "something like one quarter of all women in recent cohorts have worked continuously through their adult lives. The modal pattern, however, describing the work histories of perhaps half of adult women, is to stop work for at least several years while children are young, with a later return to the work force" (p.228). There is a direct correlation between career achievement, and its corollary, high salary, and a continuous work pattern (Van Velsor & O'Rand, 1984), suggesting that following the male career pattern is the way to succeed.

The number of working women has grown steadily. Bee (1987) notes that in 1953, one in three women worked outside the home; in 1985, women became the largest group in the work force, outnumbering white men. Today women constitute 45.6 percent of all workers (*Statistical Abstract*, 1992). However, there are major inequities in the type of work these women do. More women are in clerical, sales, and service jobs positions with low status and pay; current figures place 59 percent of women in the work force in these jobs (*Statistical Abstract*, 1992). In all other occupations they are disproportionately found in the lower ranks. This explains the longstanding inequity between women's salaries and those of men; whereas women earned $.63 for every dollar men earned in 1955, they now earn marginally more, at $.72 to the male dollar (*Working Women*, 1991). Furthermore, the benefits necessary for working women who have children to succeed are absent: affordable child care, flextime, and paid maternity leave. Women are systematically disadvantaged in a work world controlled by men.

A number of work trends hold true for both women and men. Work satisfaction increases with age, as does commitment to a specific job (Rhodes,

1983). For those in professional careers, a college education is a critical factor in career success (Bray & Howard, 1983). Those who are promoted early in their careers advance further (Rosenbaum, 1984). Finally, the achievements in young adulthood are the most important, since most career advancement occurs at this stage (Bee, 1987).

It is also important to see work experience as a sociological reality that changes across time. Spenner (1988) notes four major changes in the American workforce over the course of this century: the increased number of working women, the lengthening of the average work life, the increased overall complexity of work, and the ever greater connection between work and personal identity. It is reasonable to expect further changes in the future, providing more challenges to this generation than those foreseen now.

Consequences for Religious Education

Given the importance of work in young adult development, how can religious educators make a contribution? Certainly they can play a major role as counselors and guides for young adults facing important career decisions. Considering those questions within a religious context enables young adults to assess their options from a moral perspective and to better understand the impact of their decisions on others. Further, religious educators can focus on the process of decision making itself and introduce young adults to the prayerful process of understanding God's will in their lives. While this process is not limited to career decisions, the saliency of career issues in young adulthood offers a significant opportunity for this kind of faithful exploration.

Young adulthood, then, is an important time of career development. The role of worker which is assumed for the first time in young adulthood shapes adult identity in major ways and defines to a large extent the degree of social attainment possible in later adulthood. But work constitutes only part of a healthy adult's life; let's turn now to consider how a young adult addresses the issue of relationships.

Fashioning a Family

One of the psychological issues of young adulthood is development of the capacity for intimacy, the establishment of meaningful relationships with others that are so necessary for a satisfying life. We are, after all, social beings; our development as humans is linked to our connection with others. But these relationships present both opportunities and challenges.

Intimacy is expressed most commonly in the social institution of marriage. The vast majority of American adults are married, and about 90 percent do so before they are 35 (Schaie & Willis, 1986). While there are other forms of intimate relationships, as we will see, there is a strong social expectation that marriage will occur during the young adult years. Young adults are also biologically primed to select a mate and start a family. This is hardly a minor decision; many would agree that it presents probably the largest change in adulthood. It is important, therefore, to understand some of the complexities that are involved here.

Choosing a Partner

There has been much speculation about how partners choose each other. Despite our romantic notions of marriage in this country, many social factors influence this choice. Similarity and proximity are major factors; we marry someone we already know and who is most like us. Murstein (1982) proposes three stages to the process of mate selection: the stimulus stage, in which there is mutual attraction; the values stage, in which the couple checks for congruence of beliefs and values; and the roles stage, in which both test out the viability of the lived experience of the relationship. Bee (1987) summarizes the research on the relationships of couples who eventually marry and notes a pattern: "Feelings of belongingness and attachment increase over time as do 'maintenance behaviors' (disclosing feelings, trying to solve problems, being willing to change in order to please the partner). Both ambivalence and conflict also increase early in relationships, with the peak just before a commitment to marriage is made, after which they decline" (p.185). There are differences by gender in this process: men form attachments earlier, while women engage in more maintenance behaviors, no doubt due to sex-role socialization pressures.

Once both adults commit to the relationship, cohabitation or marriage occurs. The choice to live together before marriage is made by a small but growing percentage of couples, most often those with dual careers. Interestingly, research appears to indicate that what is often perceived as a training period for marriage does not work that way; couples who cohabited first have the same divorce rates as traditional couples (Bee, 1987).

The age at which adults first marry in this country has been rising steadily. Now the median age for men is 26, while for women it is 24 (Cavanaugh, 1990). This varies by class, however. The longest delays occur among women who postpone marriage to pursue a career. In her study of both working class and professional families, Rubin (1976) noticed that working-class couples married younger and had a higher incidence of pregnancy before marriage. She attributes the difference to the absence of other routes to independent adult status, particularly for women, within working-class families.

Marriage is correlated with increased happiness for both women and men, as well as with better physical and mental health (Bee, 1987). This makes sense if we see happiness as a function of social support, since social supports increase when people marry. However, there is a gender difference here. Bee (1987) notes that while both women and men benefit from marriage, that benefit is greater for men. This is largely because sex-role socialization places greater burdens on women to provide nurture and support in the relationship. Additionally, women's roles are given lower status and involve more routine or unpleasant tasks than do men's roles.

Having Children

Satisfaction with marriage appears to be highest in the first few years, then drops off with the birth of the first child. Schaie and Willis (1986, p.53) call the first birth a "profound disruption" in the couple's life, if for no other reason because they are assuming new roles as their dyad becomes a triad. The timing of this change seems to vary by class. Rubin (1976) noted that the working class couples she studied had their first child seven to nine months after the wedding, whereas the professional couples had theirs three years later. The additional time as a dyad allowed the professional couples to deepen their marital relationship; it also enabled them to advance their careers and save more money. Delayed parenting, therefore, offers both social and economic benefits.

A major reason for decline in marriage satisfaction with the onset of parenting is role conflict and role strain. Conflict comes because the child demands time and attention, from the mother particularly, and that means that less time and attention can be directed toward the spouse. Bee (1987, p.163) argues that "it is precisely this sense of not enough time, particularly affectionate or nurturant time with one's spouse, that marks this transition." Role strain comes with the assumption of new roles which are as yet unfamiliar. Bee goes on to suggest that role conflict and role strain can be mitigated by clarifying and sharing the child care tasks, and by redefining the priorities of other housekeeping roles. Despite the decline in both happiness and marital satisfaction at the birth of the first child, it is important to note that having a child does benefit the couple, especially in producing a sense of purpose and the feeling thatthey are now "grown up" (Harriman, 1983).

Once again there are differences here by class. Rubin (1976) found more stress among working-class couples, mostly because they have fewer economic resources to cope with the demands of child care and are therefore less free to address their needs as a couple. There is also more conflict with in-laws in working-class families, because there is more contact between them (professional couples tend to live apart from their families of origin, usually due to relocations for school or work purposes) and more dependence on them for child care and sometimes for economic support.

More salient still are the gender differences in parenting. Perlmutter and Hall (1985) point to social role expectations as the major source of these differences. The mother is expected to be the primary caregiver, whereas the father's interaction with the child is less frequent and focuses on social interaction. When she picks up the baby, it is usually to tend to its needs; when he picks up the infant, it is usually to play. Additionally, household tasks tend to be assigned disproportionally to the woman after the birth of the first child, even if they were shared more equitably before. Finally, the management of the more complex family system created by children falls to the woman; she is expected to make things run smoothly and is given little support or thanks for this role. Maccoby (1980) links this to the reduced self-esteem and depression often found among young mothers.

Divorce

If the overwhelming majority of adults marry, it cannot be assumed that those original marriages will last. Unfortunately, divorce is a frequent occurrence in young adulthood because marriages tend to fail rather quickly. Cavanaugh (1990) reports that in the United States half of the divorces happen before the seventh wedding anniversary. Divorce rates have been rising by about 10 percent per year, though this trend may be slowing. Overall, couples who married recently have only a 50-50 chance of staying married for life. He also notes racial and age differences here; the divorce rates are higher for African-Americans than whites, and higher for those who marry before they are 20 than those who marry later. Economic factors are mixed. A husband's higher income leads to a more stable marriage, but a wife's high income increases the chances for divorce. Relative economic independence means that women are free to leave unsatisfactory relationships (Chase-Lansdale and Hetherington, 1990).

Clearly there has been a cultural change in our attitudes toward divorce. Divorced adults are not stigmatized today as they once were; instead, divorce has become a more acceptable choice. Cavanaugh (1990) argues that this shift is related to changed expectations of marriage: "More people now expect marriage to be a positive experience and to be personally fulfilling. When a marriage fails to produce bliss, divorce is often considered as the way to a new and better partner" (p.377). This shift is reflected in legal changes toward no-fault divorce, rather than the earlier requirement that proof of cause, such as infidelity or nonsupport, be presented.

The effects of divorce are significant, however, and are felt differently by women and men. While men experience more psychological distress in the short run, women are both socially and economically disadvantaged in the long run. Men are three times more likely to remarry than are women, and this is especially true for women with children (Schaie & Willis, 1986). If there are children, custody is awarded to the mother over 90 percent of the time, yet while her parental responsibilities increase, her disposable income drops to 73 percent of what it was before the divorce. The father, on the other hand, experiences a 42 percent rise in income (Cavanaugh, 1990).

Divorce and remarriage create a variety of family constellations and the assumption of what can be a confusing assortment of new roles—there are relations to establish with stepchildren, the former spouse and the new spouse's former spouse, former and new in-laws, and more. This in turn can create further role conflict and role strain. Bee (1987) speculates that these increased demands for adaptation may foster personal growth. While plausible, this possibility has yet to be studied.

Variations on the Family

While marriage is clearly the dominant social expression of intimacy, it does not always follow the traditional pattern of two parents with children. The so-called traditional family is no longer the norm; Bee (1987) estimates that only 40 percent of families today could be categorized this way. There is great diversity in family type. Some possibilities include: couples with children, childless couples, single-parent households, and adult children caring for parents. Each of these configurations provides different life experiences, and those experiences again vary by gender, race, and class.

Single-parent households face particular challenges. While the numbers of single parents are steadily rising, their experience is one of stress and isolation. Most single parents are divorced mothers, but others are fathers with custody, never- married mothers, widows or widowers with children, or single adults who have adopted children. Currently there are approximately 11.3 million women and 2.9 million men who are heads of households (*Working Women*, 1991). A primary source of stress is role overload, as one parent assumes the responsibilities of two for child care, household management, and income production. One result is that the children assume more responsibilities than is true in dual-parent families, making them mature more quickly (Perlmutter & Hall, 1985).

Single parents face significant social problems, however, particularly in a social world oriented to married couples, and must be creative to address those personal needs that children cannot meet. Dating is often difficult, both because of the shortage of other single adults, and because the children may resist a new relationship. It is important for the single parent to construct a support system for themselves. Social groups like Parents Without Partners can help address these social and emotional needs.

If there are multiple variations on the theme of the traditional family, there are even more possibilities that are to varying degrees nontraditional. One that is parallel to marriage but largely remains socially unaccepted is that of the homosexual couple. The percentage of the U.S. population that is homosexual can only be estimated; Bee (1987) suggests that 2 to 5 percent of American adults are exclusively homosexual, and 3 to 5 percent are typically but not exclusively homosexual.

Another alternative is group living. In many cases this is entered into for convictional reasons, for example, religious communities or political communes. Rather than committing to one other person, a commitment is made to a group sharing the same core beliefs. Other groups choose to live together to establish a type of extended family spanning several generations. Schaie and Willis (1986), in fact, suggest that all group living is a form of extended family. It could be that participation in such groups allows adults to work through some issues related to their family of origin.

The final alternative is the one from which young adults begin and to which many of them return, at least temporarily, several times over the adult years, namely singlehood. Cavanaugh (1990) estimates that about 75 percent of men and 57 percent of women between 20 and 25 are single. Overall approximately 5 percent of adults never marry, though this number may be on the increase (Perlmutter and Hall, 1985). In the early stages of young adulthood, being single is viewed as a time of exploration and development preliminary to marriage. Cavanaugh (1990) reports that the decision to remain single usually occurs between 25 and 30; those most likely to make that choice are adults with less than a fifth grade education and women with graduate degrees. Single adults are not isolated but instead build extensive social networks with family and friends. Perlmutter and Hall (1985) note that single adults have a range of options about intimate relationships, from multiple sexual partners to celibacy. While public attitudes toward the single adult may be improving, it is still not a fully acceptable choice in a culture as couple-and family-centered as ours. Young adults who choose to remain single are, to some extent at least, viewed with some suspicion and disapproval. Here there are clear gender differences; it is less socially acceptable to be a single woman than it is to be a single man. Class and racial differences are less clear.

Singlehood is most often experienced as a temporary state, given the high incidence of divorce in this country. But there are gender and age differences here as well. About 80 percent of those who divorce remarry within three years (Cavanaugh, 1990). The incidence of remarriage is far greater among young adults, because more partners are available, and among men of all ages, because men tend to marry younger women. Divorced women are increasingly less likely to marry as they age, and women with advanced degrees are the most likely to remain single. Women are also more likely to survive their husbands, making singlehood in the final years of life a predictable experience for women. Despite the likelihood that an adult will spend a number of years single at different points in the life span, being single is more likely to be understood in terms of what it is not (not being married) than what it is. Our understanding of this state is therefore limited.

Consequences for Religious Education

The overwhelming variety of options for establishing intimate relationships that are available today create many opportunities for religious education. Young adults who have a religious affiliation already express their desire to relate to others in a meaningful way, and in all probability they would be open to involvement in specific groups to address particular relationship issues. The more obvious ones would be classes or counseling for couples preparing for marriage, as well as courses for new parents. These would provide opportunities to understand these traditional roles within a religious perspective and help young adults develop the necessary skills and attitudes to function effectively and happily in these roles. Also necessary are religious supports for nontraditional situations—the divorced, those who choose to remain single, single parents—in the form of support groups or counseling. Religious educators can play a role in each of these contexts to enable young adults to meet the challenges they face more effectively and faithfully.

We have seen something of the complexity of the web of close relationships that are possible choices for young adults. It is important to remember, however, that adults deal with these issues at the same time as they are managing their jobs and careers. How it is possible to deal with both domains simultaneously is our next concern.

Balancing Work and Family

Young adults not only must establish themselves in careers and fashion a family in some form, they must also learn how to balance both of these domains. Clearly the roles of spouse/parent and worker are each demanding; one also has an effect on the other over time. Learning how to deal with conflicts between the two and how to achieve satisfaction in both is a primary task that is carried across the adult years, but it begins in young adulthood.

Particular notice is given to the added role strain on women who combine career and family, and doing so guided by the ideal of the superwoman. Rapoport and Rapoport (1980) identify four sources of strain in dual-career families, most of which fall disproportionately on women: work overload; society's negative reaction to working mothers; role conflict; and social network dilemmas created by too many responsibilities and too little time. But they are careful to note some benefits as well. Families have more money and women are more self-actualized and satisfied with their lives. Bee (1987) summarizes the tensions and dangers implicit in the superwoman goal. "The research tells us this is an extremely difficult combination to carry off. A successful career virtually requires continuous employment and a strong work commitment. But a strong work commitment by a wife, especially if there are children, is likely to decrease marital satisfaction, increase the risk of divorce, and certainly increase overall role conflict and role strain. This does not imply that there is a conspiracy of some kind to prevent women from achieving both work success and family satisfaction. It does mean that our society has not yet evolved good methods to deal with such combinations of roles" (pp.236-237).

These difficulties, great as they are for middle-class families, are even more pressing for working-class women and men who have the additional burdens of less satisfying work and lower wages which provide them fewer resources to cope with the strains. Perlmutter and Hall (1985) note that working-class women with children are less satisfied with their lives when they work outside the home.

When the marriage relationship is seen in terms of power, work by both spouses has an interesting effect. Working wives have power in the relationship commensurate with the amount of income they bring to the family (Bee, 1987). This power is manifested in greater shared decision making. There is a fine line here, however; some men are threatened if their wives earn as much or more money than they do. Too much power for the woman could threaten the stability of the marriage.

There is a clear effect on the division of family labor in dual-career families and it does not benefit women. While this picture is slowly changing as more egalitarian ideas about sex roles take hold in our culture, it nonetheless remains true that "women have the major responsibility for both rearing children and keeping house, whether they work or not" and there has been "only a small or moderate increase in the number of hours per day or per week that husbands of working wives spend in household tasks" (Bee, 1987, pp.234-235). This produces for working married women what is often referred to as the second shift; they work eight hours or more a day for pay, and then work another shift at home without pay, tending to household maintenance and child-care tasks. The resultant overload creates strain for women in both domains.

It is important for adults to develop skills and strategies to address these sources of conflict and strain in dual-career families. Bee (1987) suggests several strategies. First, learn how to manage time more effectively. It is possible to do many tasks more efficiently. Second, restructure family roles so responsibilities are shared more equitably among husband, wife, and older children. This also involves deciding what tasks can be left undone or be done less often. And third, adjust sex-role definitions. This exercise in cognitive restructuring enables people to get beyond the constraints of those roles to which they were socialized and to find a more meaningful way to construct an understanding of themselves in relation to one another. These and similar adjustments would significantly reduce the strain induced by balancing work and family.

Merriam and Clark (1991) found a different way to examine the relationship between career and family. They conceptualized those domains more broadly as work and love. Work was defined as those activities engaged in for pay or done voluntarily, and included being a student; love encompassed interpersonal relationships, family events, social life, and leisure. They asked men and women to rate their experiences in each domain over a twenty-year period as good, OK, or bad. They found three patterns of relationship between the domains. In the first, love and work move together; when one improves or declines, the other does as well. For this group stability comes from the balanced and sustained rhythm of the domains. In the second pattern, one domain remains unchanged, almost always rated as good, while the other fluctuates freely. In this group, stability is achieved by locating personal identity in the steady domain, whether it is love or work. In the third pattern, both love and work fluctuate independently of one another. Here stability comes from the emphasis placed on work and the personal control it brings. There were no differences by gender among these three patterns; women and men were equally likely to have any one of them. This study suggest that, while balance or stability between work and love is achieved in different ways, all three patterns contribute to a sense of organization and control in adult life. This and other studies link the balance between the domains to overall psychological well-being in life, indicating the importance of both realms in adulthood.

For many women, the price of working away from home is too much. They sense the tension of holding a job, sustaining a marriage and family, and handling household duties. George Barna says, "The 'second shift' that women work at home after spending time at a job is wearing down millions of women. Reports of illnesses, acute fatigue, emotional exhaustion, depression, and unfulfilled expectations suggest that many women are not satisfied with their existence. Even the forms of assistance designed to make the 'super mom' possible, such as child-care centers, have failed to provide the kind of help that women need" (1993, p. 182).

Whereas in the seventies most adults supported women's entry into the work force, the pendulum seems to be swinging in favor of the stay-at-home wife and mother. One survey found that Americans favor a model where the mother stays at home by a margin of four to one (Barna, 1993, p. 184).

Consequences for Religious Education

The challenges presented by work and family to individuals also present opportunities for religious educators. Here too the church can help young adults learn how to deal effectively with both life domains by providing education and support. Particularly useful would be classes on understanding changing social roles for women and men. Bringing a faith perspective to these issues would enable young adults to put such changes in a larger framework and be more accepting of them. Tensions between work and family in young adult life also present opportunities for religious educators to counsel adults and help them develop more effective coping skills. For those women who choose to remain at home, rather than work, the task is to affirm them in this choice and provide opportunities to equip them to be most effective in this role.

Learning to be Part of a Larger World

Along with the assumption of these new roles of spouse/parent and worker, young adulthood also is the site of some changes in an old role. Those young adults who go back to college or on to professional schools become students again, but there is a big difference between being a student as an adult and filling that role as a child. And while not everyone goes back to college, all adults experience the role of learner in other settings, either on the job or in the community. In this section I will explore the new dimensions of learning that open up before young adults and look at the implications of that learning.

Adult learners differ from children in a number of ways. Merriam and Caffarella (1991) sum these differences up in three areas. First, the learning contexts are not the same. Children's learning occurs primarily in the home and at school, and it is directed toward a distant goal—preparation for adulthood. Learning is central in their lives, and compulsory. Adults, on the other hand, add learning to their other responsibilities, and it is more often directed to an immediate and practical goal. Learning is something they choose to do in order to improve their situation in some way. Second, the two groups have different characteristics as learners. Adults have a range of experiences which serve as a resource for learning, unlike children. They also have different developmental tasks and different transitions to negotiate. Third, there are some differences in the learning process itself, but the most significant is probably the issue of meaningfulness. Children learn because they have to; learning for adults, on the other hand, is linked more closely to their life situation so it must be meaningful to them.

Taken together, these factors describe a distinct shift in the learning role as men and women enter adulthood. Learning becomes a way to cope with the demands of life, a way of functioning more effectively as adults. In that sense it becomes a practical tool. Young adults, therefore, come into a new relationship to learning, a much more pragmatic one.

While learning is a more conscious choice now, there are more outcomes of the learning experience than the practical benefit to be gained. Learning changes the learner. This is probably best illustrated by the work of Perry (1981), who studied the effects of a liberal arts education on intellectual and ethical development. While his original study was with Harvard undergraduates, subsequent research (see, for example, Lavallee, Gourde, & Rodier, 1990) suggests that life experience produces results equivalent to those produced by higher education. Perry outlines nine positions or stages that describe how the world is viewed. King (1978) clusters these into four categories. In the first, Dualism, knowledge is absolute and is the province of Authority. There is neither ambiguity nor uncertainty, and alternative points of view have no legitimacy. The second, Multiplicity, moves to the opposite pole. Here there are multiple perspectives and they are all equal; evaluation of the merit of an argument is not possible. With the third category, Relativism, the various points of view are subject to evaluation and knowledge is seen as contextual. Reaching Commitment in Relativism, the fourth and final category, enables the person to make "an active affirmation of themselves and their responsibilities in a pluralistic world, establishing their identities in the process" (King, 1978, p.39). This movement away from absolutes and toward a committed stand within relativism describes a process that may not begin or end in young adulthood but which makes significant strides during those early years.

In an even broader sense, learning in adulthood can be understood as a widening of perspective. Mezirow (1991) outlines a comprehensive theory of adult learning which is conceptualized as the ongoing restructuring of meaning as a person engages life experience. Mezirow argues that all human beings interpret experience through a personal meaning structure. These structures are complex constructs which are the product of socialization and enculturalization, as well as being shaped by personal history. In that sense they are learned rather than inherited. These meaning structures function as a lens or filter through which personal experience is mediated and by which it is interpreted, thereby bringing coherence to those experiences. As an experience passes through the meaning structure, it becomes assimilated into it, either reinforcing the original form if it was completely congruent with past experiences, or gradually reshaping the structure if less congruent. Thus, over time, a person's perspective can change. Often these changes are gradual, the normal developmental process adults experience as they change social roles, but the changes can also be more dramatic, such as those occurring from unexpected traumatic or otherwise significant events. Learning then "may be best understood as the process of construing and appropriating a new or revised interpretation of the meaning of one's experience as a guide to decision and action" (Mezirow, 1988, p.223).

If we think of learning in Mezirow's terms, then it is easy to see how important this new role of the learner is in the lives of young adults. It offers a way of understanding how they are able to negotiate the major life changes facing them. But even if we think of learning in narrower terms, as participation in formal education, it also plays a significant role.

Learning in formal environments is a common feature of young adult life. For many that means either returning to college, if they did not continue on or complete their degree right after high school, or working on a graduate or professional degree. Patterns here have changed somewhat. While once the traditional practice was to go to college right after high school and complete the program without interruption (except, perhaps, for military service), now it is common for college students to interrupt or delay their course of study. The number of returning young adults enrolled in college increases steadily; in 1992 68 percent of college administrators polled reported an increase in adult enrollment over the 1991 levels (*Chronicle of Higher Education Almanac*, 1992).

There is also the possibility of education in other contexts. There are multiple opportunities for adults to learn through educational programs at work and in the community. There have been many studies of participation in adult education programs across the country, and the number of adults engaging in formal learning activities ranges from 14 percent to nearly 80 percent, depending on how education is defined. Interestingly, adult learning is far more prevalent among young adults than any other age group; those 25 to 34 years old account for 34 percent of the participation (Merriam & Caffarella, 1991). Men and women participate in adult education about equally, but the distribution by race is overwhelmingly white. It is also significant that the best predictor for participation is prior education. Those most in need of adult education are not getting it, for a variety of reasons.

Education plays a significant role in adult life, not the least because it influences social attainment. Bee (1987) notes that this functions primarily through job patterns: "How far you can travel on the 'job ladder' over your lifetime is strongly influenced by the rung at which you enter it. And the rung-of- entry is itself strongly influenced by the years of education you have completed" (p.53). For women handicapped by a discontinuous work pattern, an education credential can make a major difference in getting a job. Bee argues that education, through its impact on work history, has a powerful impact on social class.

Learning, then, plays a very important role in the lives of young adults. It is not too much to assert that it is a major force in shaping adult lives. After all, adults learn how to be workers, how to establish relationships, how to balance work and family, and even how to be adults.

Conclusion

Whenever we are presented with information of any kind, it is important not only to assess its truth value but also to ask about its usefulness. Now that we know something about the sociocultural tasks facing young adults, what difference does it make? How can this knowledge inform practice? This closing discussion addresses exactly that question.

If we pull back and look at the totality of the sociocultural terrain through which young adults are moving, several features stand out. The first is the amount and degree of change present in this life stage. The assumption of adult roles cause sea changes in their lives, and those changes come quickly and often simultaneously in different arenas. It is obvious that young adults must be thoughtful, knowledgeable, and perhaps above all adaptive if they are to succeed.

If we pull back even further and look at the nature of the times in which we and they are living, we see still more change. The historian Barbara Tuckman compared our own time to the fourteenth century, which she termed "an Age of Disruption" in that it was "so distinctly an age where everything was disappearing, everything people believed in" (Kidder, 1989, p.47). Hers is a compelling image as we watch our country's infrastructure decay, our position in the world economy erode, and social fabric tear at its worn seams. And this mirrors the situation across the globe. Barber (1992) identifies two central principles that tear us at cross purposes. The first he calls "Jihad . . . the retribalization of large swaths of humankind . . . in the name of a hundred narrowly conceived faiths against every kind of interdependence, every kind of artificial social cooperation and civic mutuality"; and the second he dubs "McWorld . . . [created by] economic and ecological forces that demand integration and uniformity . . . pressing nations into one commercially homogenous global network" (p.53). An Age of Disruption indeed.

What does it mean to be a faith community in such a context? Fowler (1981) links faith to the process of forging meaning in our lives. He defines faith broadly, including but going beyond religious realities to encompass "those various interrelated dimensions of human knowing, valuing, committing and acting" (p.92) that are involved in meaning formation. Parks (1986), agreeing with Fowler, examines the religious challenges of young adulthood. She calls this life stage "the critical years," in no small measure because of the "experience of the dissolution and recomposition of the meaning of self and world and its challenges to faith" (p.xii) which characterizes those years. She too places meaning-making at the center of the human enterprise, and she understands faith as fundamentally a meaning-making activity. "The meaning-making that constitutes what we are calling adulthood is a self-aware composing and maintaining of pattern, order, and significance in the most comprehensive dimensions of our awareness. In other words, whenever we organize our sense of a particular object, series of activities, or institution, we are also compelled to compose our sense of its place in the whole of existence. We speak of this activity as composing a 'world.'

But even 'world' becomes a provincial concept as our awareness of 'cosmos' increases. This is to say that all human beings must compose and dwell in some conviction of what is ultimately true. Human beings self-consciously or unself-consciously compose a sense of the ultimate character of reality" (Parks, 1986, p.16).

At the beginning of this chapter I said that, in my view, the central task facing young adults is to make adulthood meaningful. I believe it is the task of any religious community doing religious education with young adults to offer them a place where they can do that. If Fowler (1981, p.92) is right, and I believe he is, when he describes faith as "a way of leaning into and finding or giving meaning to the conditions of our lives," then the community of faith is where we all do that together. Guided by our religious traditions, by our belief in God's presence with us, we daily go about the business of making our lives meaningful. Sharing that dynamic character of faith does not provide answers to the many questions challenging young adults, but it does provide a context in which they can deal with those questions and which will enable them to construct meaningful answers for themselves.

References

Almanac (1992). Vol. 39. (August 26, 1992). Washington, DC: *The Chronicle of Higher Education*.

Anyon, J. (1989). Social class and the hidden curriculum of work. In J. H. Ballantine (Ed.), *Schools and society: A unified reader* (pp. 257-279). Mountain View, CA: Mayfield.

Barber, B. (1992). Jihad vs. McWorld. *The Atlantic Monthly, 269 (3)*, 53-65.

Barna, G. (1993). *The future of the American family*. Chicago: Moody.

Bee, H. L. (1987). *The journey of adulthood*. New York: Macmillan.

Bray, D. W., & Howard, A. (1983). The ATandT longitudinal studies of managers. In K. W. Schaie (Ed.), *Longitudinal studies of adult psychological development* (pp. 266-312). New York: Guilford.

Cavanaugh, J. C. (1990). *Adult development and aging*. Belmont, CA: Wadsworth.

Chase-Lansdale, P. L., & Hetherington, E. M. (1990). The impact of divorce on life-span development: Short and long term effects. In P. B. Baltes, D. L. Featherman, & R. M. Lerner (Eds.), *Life-span development and behavior, vol. 10* (pp. 107-150). Hillsdale, NJ: Erlbaum.

Chickering, A. W., & Havighurst, R. J. (1981). The life cycle. In A. W. Chickering (Ed.), *The modern American college* (pp. 16-50). San Francisco: Jossey-Bass.

Fowler, J. W. (1981). *Stages of faith: The psychology of human development and the quest for meaning*. San Francisco: Harper & Row.

Harriman, L. C. (1983). Personal and marital changes accompanying parenthood. *Family Relations*, 32, 387-394.

Havighurst, R. J. (1952). *Developmental tasks and education*. New York: Longmans, Green.

Kidder, R. M. (1989). *An agenda for the 21st century*. Cambridge, MA: The MIT Press.

King, P. M. (1978). William Perry's theory of intellectual and ethical development. In L.

Knefelkamp, C. Widick, & C. A. Parker (Eds.), *Applying new development findings.* New Directions for Student Services, No. 4 (pp. 35-51). San Francisco: Jossey-Bass.

Lavallee, M., Gourde, A., & Rodier, C. (1990). The impact of lived experience on cognitive ethical development of today's women. *International Journal of Behavioral Development, 13,* 407-430.

Levinson, D., Darrow, C., Klein, E., Levinson, M., & McKee, B. (1978). *The seasons of a man's life.* New York: Knopf.

Maccoby, E. E. (1980). Commentary and reply. In G. R. Patterson, Mothers: The unacknowledged victims, *Monographs of the Society for Research in Child Development, 45 (5),* 56-63.

Merriam, S. B. (1984). Developmental issues and tasks of young adulthood. In G. Darkenwald & A. Knox (Eds.), *Meeting educational needs of young adults : Vol. 21. New directions in continuing education* (pp. 3-14). San Francisco: Jossey-Bass.

Merriam, S. B., & Caffarella, R. S. (1991). *Learning in adulthood.* San Francisco: Jossey-Bass.

Merriam, S. B., & Clark, M. C. (1991). *Lifelines: Patterns of work, love, and learning in adulthood.* San Francisco: Jossey-Bass.

Mezirow, J. (1988). Transformation theory. *Proceedings of the Annual Adult Education Research Conference, 10,* 223-227.

Mezirow, J. (1991). *Transformative dimensions of adult learning.* San Francisco: Jossey-Bass.

Murstein, B. I. (1982). Marital choice. In B. B. Wolman (Ed.), *Handbook of developmental psychology* (pp. 652-666). Englewood Cliffs, NJ: Prentice-Hall.

Parks, S. (1986). *The critical years: The young adult search for a faith to live by.* San Francisco: Harper & Row.

Perlmutter, M., & Hall, E. (1985). *Adult development and aging.* New York: Wiley.

Perry, W. G., Jr. (1981). Cognitive and ethical growth: The making of meaning. In A. W. Chickering (Ed.), *The modern American college* (pp. 76-116). San Francisco: Jossey-Bass.

Rapoport, R., & Rapoport, R. N. (1980). Three generations of dual-career family research. In F. Pepitone-Rockwell (Ed.), *Dual career couples* (pp. 23-48). Beverly Hills, CA: Sage.

Rhodes, S. R. (1983). Age-related differences in work attitudes and behavior: A review and conceptual analysis. *Psychological Bulletin, 93,* 329-367.

Rosenbaum, J. E. (1984). *Career mobility in a corporate hierarchy.* New York: Academic Press.

Rubin, L. B. (1976). *Worlds of pain: Life in the working-class family.* New York: Basic Books.

Schaie, K. W., & Willis, S. L. (1986). *Adult development and aging.* Boston: Little, Brown.

Spenner, K. I. (1988). Occupations, work settings and the course of adult development: Tracing the implications of select historical changes. In P. B. Baltes, D. L. Featherman, & R. M. Lerner (Eds.), *Life-span development and behavior,* vol.9 (pp. 244-285). Hillsdale, NJ: Erlbaum.

Statistical abstract of the United States, (1992). U. S. Department of Commerce. Washington, DC: U.S. Government Printing Office.

Van Velsor, E., & O'Rand, A. M. (1984). Family life cycle, work career patterns, and women's wages at midlife. *Journal of Marriage and the Family,* 46, 365-373.

Working women: A chartbook. (August 1991). Washington, DC: U.S. Department of Labor.

CHAPTER SIX

Religious, Moral, and Faith Development of Young Adults

DONALD JOY

We have one real-life exchange in which Jesus may have focused every issue we need to examine in the religious, moral, and faith development domain for young adults. We call the encounter, perhaps unfortunately, the story of "the rich young ruler." We keep bumping into it, once in Matthew 19:16-30, again in Mark 10:17-31, and finally in Luke 18:18-34. A caution that the encounter was not even understood by the first hearers and Jesus' own disciples who watched it unfold play-by-play has not prevented us from oversimplifying the story by naming in a way that focuses on wealth and royal class. Both they and we seem to miss the fact that this is a news report on a young man who suffers from a nagging feeling of uncertainty—echoing the young adult gut vacuum: "Is that all there is?" Or is he the modern yuppie, out to cut a deal to get the very best? Max Lucado, in *The Applause of Heaven* (1990, p. 28 ff.) describes the guy as rich. "Italian shoes. Tailored suit. His money is invested. His plastic golden. He lives like he flies—first class." Having mastered the three "Ps" of yuppiedom, "Prosperity. Posterity. Power," he asks "what good thing must I do to get eternal life?"

Lucado analyzes him: "The wording of his question betrays his misunderstanding. He thinks he can get eternal life as he gets everything else—by his own strength."

So in unraveling the research and demographics on young adults and their journeys of religious, moral, and faith development, take a straight reading of this surprisingly contemporary slice of young adult issues:

"A certain ruler asked him, [Jesus] 'Good teacher, what must I do to inherit eternal life?' 'Why do you call me good?' Jesus answered. 'No one is good—except God alone. You know the commandments: "Do not commit adultery, do not murder, do not steal, do not give false testimony, honor your father and mother."' 'All these I have kept since I was a boy,' he said. When Jesus heard this, He said to him, 'You still lack one thing. Sell everything you have and give to the poor, and you will have treasure in heaven. Then come, follow me.' When he heard this, he became very sad, because he was a man of great wealth. Jesus looked at him and said, 'How hard it is for the rich to enter the kingdom of God! Indeed, it is easier for a camel to go through the eye of a needle than for a rich man to enter the kingdom of God.'

"Those who heard this asked, 'Who then can be saved?' Jesus replied, 'What is impossible with men is possible with God.'

"Peter said to him, 'We have left all we had to follow you!' 'I tell you the truth,' Jesus said to them, 'no one who has left home or wife or brothers or parents or children for the sake of the kingdom of God will fail to receive many times as much in this age and, in the age to come, eternal life.'

"Jesus took the Twelve aside and told them, 'We are going up to Jerusalem, and everything that is written by the prophets about the Son of Man will be fulfilled. He will be handed over to the Gentiles. They will mock him, insult him, spit on him, flog him and kill him. On the third day he will rise again.' The disciples did not understand any of this. Its meaning was hidden from them, and they did not know what he was talking about" (Lk. 18:18-34, NIV).

"Hey," Lucado replays the naive first response, "'a piece of cake. I've done all of these. In fact, I've done them since I was a kid.' He swaggers a bit and hooks a thumb in his belt. 'Got any other commandments you want to run past me?'"

Jesus' final probe turns out to be "impossible" with humans—something calculated to bring one yuppie's arrogance down a notch. But such integrity is possible only by connecting to the heart and character of God—with whom "all things are possible."

Forever Contemporary

Consider some current young adult values, conflicts, and paralysis points compared to this encounter with Jesus.

Inner Yearnings

"Blessed are those who hunger and thirst for righteousness, for they will be filled." Jesus focused the fourth beatitude on the young man's emptiness. Eventually, in this chapter, the beatitudes come for a "curriculum inspection" because of their significant attention to deep and real human needs.

The yearning for significance and meaning in life likely reaches a third and final peak in the early young adult years. While the years from birth to age 6 are the "primary" or even "exclusive" years of attitude and value development, the teen years with their cognitive development acceleration and emergence of the unique "self" emerge as the first time for choosing one's own attitudes and values. But the early young adult years open the doors of the real world in which attitudes and values matter. "Early adulthood constitutes the third and probably final life period during which an individual's attitudes can or do undergo marked change" (Lee, 1973, p. 110). These deep hungers for embracing life and career, and/or marriage, and one's own family continue to fuel the furnace of young adults. And a key issue is that of inner wholeness, spiritual wellness, a sense of being reconciled with the moral center of the universe—a hunger and a thirst for righteousness, integrity—in short, for God. So the question the young, moral, affluent, well parented adult asked resonates with that of virtually every young adult today.

Needing a Formula to Follow

The belief that the emptiness comes from a feeling of neither "doing things right" nor "doing the right things" may also be universal. Males, it is assumed, are more likely to think that they can "fix it" by themselves. Women, we hear, are more likely to jump in to "fix relationships" for themselves and everyone else in sight. If we read the story with both agendas in mind, the star of the street interview does ask a "doing" question. Most of our religious traditions caution against a "works-based salvation" and stress "salvation by faith alone" and "grace, not performance-based" religion. Yet, in this rather detailed exchange, Jesus did not seem to draw a distinction between "believing" and "doing," between "status" and "performance." He seems to assume that the two sides of the coin are connected right down the middle and that an appeal to action reveals an X-ray of a person's belief system. Cognitive-behavioral therapy makes much the same conclusion when it urges changes in behavior in order to alter pathological beliefs traumatized by past experiences. We may find that we serve young adults best by nurturing their deep hungers instead of by feeling sorry for them and setting up programs to "fix the world" for them. The deepest hunger among young adults is for honesty. Religious education that invites candor, blesses tough questions, accepts agendas for which there are no slick and quick solutions will be magnetic to young adults. Traditional religious education curricula have advertised their genius in sticking with material on which the majority of Christians agree. But tough questions from real life must be brought into collision with traditional, simplistic theological ideals and biblical pat answers. The depth of scripture and theology offers an open invitation to bring doubt, even skepticism and tough questions to church.

Lifestyle Check

Watch the Teacher-Physician work at "diagnosis" when the young adult discloses his symptom of restlessness: keep the commandments. And Jesus lists them, beginning with the one about sexual integrity and working in a sort of spiral through the relational section of the Decalogue (commandments 7-6-8-9-4, Deut. 5) ending with concern for honoring parents. Since we know the plot line in the story and that it eventually focuses on material possessions, we may miss the importance of Jesus' first point of diagnostic assessment, the lifestyle check: sexual integrity, respect for life, respect for property of others, honesty, and respect for parents.

Young adult lifestyle issues today have not escaped the painful inventory with which Jesus started. The young adult in this gospel story claimed to have passed the entry level test—integrity of life and relationships—every way. So the religious, moral, and faith journeys of young adults today may need to pause and get the "behavior therapy" under way on the "big five" commandments Jesus cited. If he answered too quickly, without acknowledging that a perfect moral track record is impossible, Jesus may have countered with the ultimate sacrifice demand to get his attention. Indeed, Jesus' response is, "What is impossible for mortals is possible for God." It may be that what Jesus is trying to show the young man is the impossibility that he has kept the basic moral law. So Jesus may be trying to show him his own EKG. To claim such perfection is to be a conspicuous fraud. Yet note, the acid test of the man's moral and spiritual maturity is a "behavioral test."

Demands That Break Us

The diagnosis is completed without any further questions. Jesus finishes with a prescription: "You still lack one thing. Sell all that you have and distribute it to the poor, and you will have treasure in heaven; and come, follow me." Matthew 19:19 adds the last half of the "new commandment" to the old ones, "You shall love your neighbor as yourself." The prescription Jesus gives is in the spirit of this uniquely Jesus way of defining one's love for God—by the acid test of loving one's neighbor. Evidently Jesus was suspicious that the young man answered too quickly, was too slick in his high moral claims. So the moral task—of total material bankruptcy—may have been the deeper test of character.

Young adults who volunteer to do medical or construction or teaching missions in other cultures simply have to grind down to a moral and spiritual core that is deeper than moralistic philanthropy. "Getting right down there with the people" is never going to happen to moralistic, materialistic folks. So, "What must I do to inherit eternal life?" may always have an answer with pain and self surrender in it. Only when we have been wounded, seen our vul-nerabilities, faced our own failures, will we have credentials God can use with other hurting people. It is the mark of young adult culture in North America that their vulnerabilities are carefully hidden, and they might even line up to lie shamelessly that "all of these good things I've been doing since I was a kid." But if we are enveloped in secret shame and damaged self-value we will be dangerous in reaching out to honestly vulnerable folks. And the "counter-dependent" (Weinhold & Weinhold, 1992) aristocratic, short-term vacation "missioning" we prefer to do turns out to be more often an exercise in cross-cultural shaming than in offering grace and forgiveness and help to the wounded. Shame wrapped as we are in our pride and arrogance, we would do our neighbors a favor to warn them if we ever decided to enter on a cru-sade to "love our neighbors" in the same way we despise ourselves.

Affluence Test

The command to "sell all," to "come" and to "follow" Jesus is frightening to all of us who are enveloped in comfortable affluence. If we object to charges that we are affluent, usually because of our bills outstanding, and our bank loans on everything we live and move in, H. Stephen Glenn and Jane Nelson offer a check list which measure affluence:

1. Do you have more than one pair of shoes?
2. Do you have more than one choice about what you will eat for each meal?
3. Do you have access to your own means of transportation?
4. Do you have more than one set of underwear?

"If you answered 'yes' to three or more of these questions, then by the overall standards of the world, you are affluent. Fewer than 10 percent of all people who have ever lived have been able to answer 'yes' to three or more of these questions at any one time in their lives" (Glenn & Nelson, 1989, pp. 44-45).

And it is in this "material test" that young adults in the Western world are most vulnerable, after passing the basic moral integrity test of the selected five commandments. The years between 18 and 40 are the years of acquisition, of establishing identity through achievement, and of displaying that status through symbols of success. Add to that the fact that our success symbols are also luxury accessories of convenience and soft-indulgent comfort, and we may see why suffering and deprivation correlate so strongly with the highest reaches of religious, moral, and faith development. So what is Jesus prescribing for young adults today?

Carolyn Koons, of Azusa Pacific University in California, recruits hundreds of college and older young adults to spring break work trips. It is the Mexicali Project, a week or two of gut-wrenching construction, evangelism, and rescue work in Mexico. Religious education projects which put muscle alongside money are sorely needed for young adult volunteers who will give a sabbatical year to teaching English in Hungary or China. Mountain Top, in Tennessee, or the Christian Appalachian Project are only two agencies which offer volunteers specific United States-based service missions.

Most of our religious traditions become zealous over words and doctrines. Yet in this gospel story and challenge, and in other teachings of Jesus, the behavior is proof of and precedes "belief" and theology. We are often uncomfortable with Jesus' retort to the challenge of his authenticity: "My doctrine is not mine, but his that sent me. If a man will do *his will* [italics mine] he shall know of the doctrine, whether it be of God, or whether I speak of myself" (Jn. 7:16-17, KJV).

With this amazingly accurate diagnostic story of young adult agendas straight from the pages of three gospels, it will be appropriate for us to look now at research and speculative models which examine the religious, moral, and faith development of young adults.

A Hunger for Righteousness?

We will always be in debt to Jean Piaget (1961) for opening the research windows which have given us a theory about how humans everywhere cognitively "make meaning" of life experience. His field research among children in Zurich and Neuchatel, Switzerland, has now been replicated almost worldwide. Sometimes referred to as "cognitive developmental theory" or "moral development theory," the ripening field of research and inquiry tends to be defined as the field of "structural development." By "structural" researchers agree that humans in any social environment inevitably are "constructing" meaning from experience. What is more, the meaning is being "made" within a uniquely human moral capacity—a "structure"—which in any culture moves in predictable developmental patterns. These patterns of structural development are commonly called stages, and Lawrence Kohlberg (1958, 1981, 1982) observed that they unfold in an invariant sequence.

Many of us have been intrigued by human growth and development in the religious and faith dimensions of their experiences and have applied structural development research to issues of children's developing conscience (Joy, 1969). Others have explored university student's moral development in secular and religious environments (Dirks, 1988). Still others have measured the development of moral and spiritual sensitivity in comparative parochial day-school environments (Stewart, 1974). We have chosen structural development paradigms both because of their plausibility in explaining complicated human responses to life experience, and also because of their validity potential in measuring subjects' ways of "making meaning." And we have also turned to Piaget and Kohlberg kinds of research because we observe complex religious and faith patterns within traditions we know well. Without exception, those of us who have designed structural research in religious and faith community settings have been rewarded by impressive findings.

In an obscure chapter on "Development and the Idea of Justice," Piaget (1961) documented children's advancing ability to make moral judgments on the basis of increasingly complex understandings of justice. Abraham Heschel (1962) examines Old Testament uses of the concept of justice to note that justice is not simply an attribute of God but is essential to the core character of God—is in all God's ways. So, what Piaget discovered in his street experiments may be larger than some evolutionary humanistic phenomenon. He may have actually been the first social science researcher to identify and describe a core "image of God" in humans.

The unfolding pattern of justice across childhood, Piaget observed—and many of us have verified—moved from a naive and egocentric sense of fairness with punitive and expiatory consequences for violating that self-protecting-projecting sense of moral right across two more grand transitions. Given wide life experience, humans advance to a new organizing center for justice: heteronomous equality. This center of justice is kept in place by judgments which demand an exact match between a violation and its consequence, called reciprocity. And among everyone guilty, the demand is for equality. Kohlberg organized his research at the University of Chicago (1958) around three levels, the first two of which were grounded in Piaget's developmental justice findings—preconventional and conventional. Finally, Piaget, and later Kohlberg, saw the peak of justice understandings organized around equity, which Piaget described as "an advanced form of equality" in which the ability of the person to perform was taken into account and the judgment was tempered to reflect those circumstances. Piaget described children's objection to strict enforcement of the rules when children were too little or otherwise able to perform as "commutive justice." So postconventional moral reasoning in Kohlberg's Stages 5, 6, and 7 is loosely grounded in this advanced form of moral reasoning Piaget documented by listening to children while they solved moral problems on the streets of two Swiss cities.

Here is a quick summary of structural stage progression across the tapestry of justice:

Level A: Preconventional Moral Thinking. Orientation to Prudence.

Right and wrong are determined by physical consequences.

Stage 1: If I get hurt or penalized, I did wrong.

Stage 2: If I get what I want with no pain, I did right.

For both Level A stages, justice is seen as immediately evident: people who get caught have done a bad thing. If they do not get caught they did right and should be boastful and swagger a bit.

Level B: Conventional Moral Thinking. Orientation to Authority. Right and wrong are determined by other people.

Stage 3: What significant other people expect from you.

Stage 4: What the public law or rules require of you as a member of the ordered society.

Justice is reciprocal and applies to everybody the same. Wrongs should be "put right." The idea that justice reconciles all irregularities, settles all debts, and exacts penalties and fines to guarantee a community "balance sheet" becomes very important.

Level C: Postconventional Moral Thinking. Orientation to Principles. Right and wrong are determined by unchanging values.

Stage 5: Communities simplify their rules by organizing everyone to achieve higher concepts of respect, equity, and understanding. These principles are codified by voluntarily contracting and fully participating members who arrive at a community consensus. Policing is necessary to protect the common good from invasion and terrorism by bandits and grossly immoral and out of control folks.

Stage 6: Individuals, even though they participate in Stage 5 "common good" consensus and craft the highest principles for the protection of the rights, dignity, and worth of individuals, may find themselves isolated by a higher call which is reported to the community. Although rejected at that time for community ratification, they resolve to encircle the community for a yet higher good. They do so in patience, peacefully optimistic that the walls will one day come down and a higher principle can be embraced by the community.

In examining the religious, moral, and faith development of the young adults, we will be helped by noting some general findings from structural research:

1. Progression through the stages of moral reasoning is orderly. No stages are missed.

2. Each stage is transformed and carried forward, incorporated, into the subsequent stage. This illustrates the principle of hierarchical integration: new structures are simply the ripening of previous ways of organizing meaning. Nothing is ever lost out of experience or memory, but everything is in the pro-

cess of being transformed "from one degree of splendor to another" (2 Cor. 3:18).

3. Progression through the stages is not guaranteed by biological ripening, but is the effect of the individual's full participation as a "meaning maker" in a rich and moderately conflictual social environment.

4. People tend to understand justice solutions only one stage beyond their present, preferred stage structure, and to hold in contempt previous—that is, lower—stage structures of justice.

5. People tend to settle down or center in on a stage structure of justice when a) that structure is adequate to solve the typical justice problems which occur in the person's environment, or b) when social or political norms codify and enforce justice issues in ways which hold a person hostage to a compromised journey of justice growth.

Religious education of young adults most often betrays them by supporting the fallacy that "they have it made," that they "are too busy at this time," or that all religious, moral, and faith growth potential is now behind them. "Arrest" and "comfort with the status quo" are major enemies of the higher ground of moral, faith, and religious experiences which await young adults unless they 1) persistently bring their negative life experiences to the religious education arena as a primary curriculum, 2) chronicle their own pilgrimages through remembered story sharing, through journals, reviews of family and personal photo and video records, and 3) track on deeper faith studies which deal with issues of justice, theodicy (the problem of God's goodness balanced against God's interventions), reconciliation, and forgiveness. Parenting issues, singleness concerns, marriage and divorce questions— these are always changing, never fully resolved domains which must constantly be reworked with the deeper and wiser perspectives of young adults in the process of moral, religious, and faith exploration.

Fast Lane Gusto Grabbers

The young adult years are profoundly vulnerable to needs for social approval. We often speak of peer pressure on teens, but at worst their need for peer approval is only a warm-up scrimmage compared to the needs for success-oriented adults for keeping their approval ratings high.

Opportunities

In an era when the moral majority was thought to be the major political force, anyone wanting to win an election might compromise conscience for the sake of pleasing the announced criteria of the moral majority. But ten years later when the doctrine of pluralism had replaced the moral majority as a force to be reckoned with, it might be important to shift positions on abortion or the homosexual lifestyle. And in such a pressure cooker to take the right opportunistic stance, young adults of United States were shocked that evangelist Billy Graham would accept an invitation to spend the night in the Lincoln Room as a guest of George and Barbara Bush on their final night in the White House and then would be the singular clergy to participate—both invocation and benediction—the next day for the swearing in of Bill Clinton on the Capitol steps. Graham answered the "culture of opportunism" questions on inauguration night on Larry King Live by saying that his commitment was to deeper and unchanging values of the Christian gospel and grace. Furthermore he was committed to keeping open his lines of communication with everyone. But a baby boomer generation tends to be significantly in the grasp of a Stage 3 relativism which finds "going with the flow" more urgent than moving ahead with a moral, religious, ethical, and faith journey.

Crowds were fickle in Jesus' day and are in ours. The Stage 3 orientation on justice issues reads like this: "What I think should be done is beside the point. What is the crowd saying?" More specifically, the question is, "What are the people I want to impress clamoring for?" And at a Stage 2 delayed developmental stage, as always, the question is, "Who can give me the best and biggest deal? What is in it for me?" The Stage 2 con artist and the Stage 3 pragmatist are half-siblings, and since the Watergate scandal of the 1970s, American morality has shifted significantly toward opportunism—getting whatever you want if you can do it without getting caught. The persistent question in our culture today is precisely that of Luke 18:18, "How can I be saved and still hang on to my symbols of status, popularity, and power?"

Going with the Flow

Young adults, like all of the rest of us, tend to be engulfed by the values and appetites of our culture. If extravagant consumption is the American way, then adopting a simple lifestyle and cutting to the bone on fossil fuel consumption, the use of plastics and other non-biodegradable materials takes a lot of intentionality and a significant amount of work. So we slide quickly back into the popular ways of buying and disposing. "I would rather be dead than out of step with my generation" cut to the heart of a pastor whose son was finishing his first semester at the university and was abandoning family beliefs and values. "Free to choose" is often as coercive as a police state—because our friends are the "police."

Young adults in an extravagant consumption culture are ready for religious education explorations of issues related to conservation, recycling of nonrenewable resources, and saving the planet for future generations of larger populations. But young adults are also prime authorities on recovery issues, themselves having come back, in many cases, from losses, disorders, and addictions. Consider the urgency of arranging training seminars focused on turning life experience into much needed skills such as convenors, facilitators, even parish counselors working with recovery groups under the umbrella of religious education services.

Angry Rebels and Agnostics

Check the rosters of "missing" young adults whose faces were standard features at your church during their childhood and youth program years. Some are missing because they were caught up in the fast lane values of opportunism and going with the flow. But among the most difficult to reach and to retrieve for the faith journey and for congregational life are the cynics and agnostics. Stage 4 orientation to righteousness and justice tends to hold that there is an absolute and ordered universe of truth. This often includes the idea that bad things do not happen to good people and that God will take care of those who are faithful to him. The craving for specificity which characterizes Stage 4 reasoning expects perfection from leaders, and expects to deliver perfection of performance as a junior participant. So congregations in which rules proliferate and in which failures are well hidden behind facades of denial and even deception can expect a crop of Stage 4 cynics to walk away, often for a lifetime. And when emerging young adults bite the bullet of feeling betrayed by their religious systems, their fall tends to be spectacular. Some rebel and criticize the religious institution in which they were conceived and cradled. But most act out their rebellion by wildly violating the values and beliefs they once embraced. They are more likely to dip into Stage 2 appearing behaviors which are the ultimate put-down for a conserving family and congregational system: alcohol abuse, drug abuse, and sexual promiscuity are powerful theological statements in the arsenal of weapons in use by young adult rebels.

Stage 4 1/2 was defined by Kohlberg during the 1960s to describe the "almost principled" alienated young adult population which confronted American institutions with moral accusations of fraud and deception. Most of the unrest occurred on university campuses. President's offices were frequent targets of sit-ins or other disorder. When Kohlberg and his Harvard team of moral development researchers went to Berkeley to "stage" these rebels, they found 80 percent of those scoring Stage 6 were protesting, 50 percent of those scoring Stage 5. Stages 4 and 3 were not significantly involved. Then a surprise: 50 percent of Stage 2 scoring students were protesting— going along for the thrill of it—going with the flow of excitement (Kohlberg, 1981, p. 45).

Phantom of Intimacy

Erik Erikson's (1950, 1980) speculative model of eight stages of human development was evidently put in motion by his own journey into young adulthood under surveillance of Adolf Hitler's Jewish genocide machine. His own Scandinavian father had abandoned his German mother before his birth. She had quickly married her pediatrician, a Jew. So at mid-teens, wise enough to know his Jewish moniker would do him no good, he spread a cover of anonymity over his Jewish name and dubbed himself, in a gesture toward Scandinavia, Erik, Son-of-Erik. He then took off to travel.

That was before World War II, but by the 1960s Erikson's Childhood and Society (1950) with its center chapter on the "eight stages of man" was being clutched in the hands of protesters taken to jail, arrested on American university campuses. The book understood them. They were having an identity crisis, they said, and one had to read Erik Erikson to frame a meaning for the phenomenon. The transition to adulthood, Erikson had found, necessarily goes through a search for meaning, uniqueness, and significance. He had called that the adolescence life task—tugging between identity and identity diffusion, or confusion and meaninglessness.

The scheme of eight stages of human development consists of eight pairs of competing magnets. Erikson insisted that both magnets are at work, but that one will tend to prevail in the struggle with life's agenda stage by stage. He further observed that people who make a negative resolution at one stage, tend to follow with a negative resolution at the next. A religious education concern would be to support the growing person with resources and agendas which predict effectively that the candidate would make choices which would lead to positive resolution, stage after stage. here are those eight pairs of magnetic and competing poles:

8. Mature years	Integrity	vs.	Disgust and Despair
7. Adulthood	Generativity	vs.	Self-absorption
6. Young Adulthood	Intimacy	vs.	Isolation
5. Adolescence	Identity	vs.	Identity Diffusion
4. School Age	Industry	vs.	Inferiority
3. Play Age	Initiative	vs.	Guilt
2. Early Childhood	Autonomy	vs.	Shame and Doubt
1. Infancy	Trust	vs.	Mistrust

One can see that if a child of 2 to 4 years of age is unable to master the autonomy tasks of early childhood such as bowel control, the resulting orientation of shame predicts that the initiative and industry worker-bee characteristics of the healthy pre-pubertal child are likely to be resolved instead into feelings of guilt and inferiority. If so, then pray God for a miracle that gathers up the young teen in a community of grace and moves retroactively into healing the roots of mistrust, shame, doubt, guilt, and inferiority before sexual ripening blows open the doors of the identity vs. role diffusion or ambiguity battle.

Applied to the young adult agendas, if the identity conquest fails and one is swallowed up in a sea of role diffusion and uncertainty about a sense of origin, destiny, and immediate role, the next task, intimacy, may founder and slide into a negative resolution of isolation.

Erikson defines the intimacy achievement expressly in confidential and exclusive sexual intimacy. With this vulnerability exposed, a necessary trust with one's secrets is bound in a lifelong mutual respect, and isolation is defeated, or at least held at bay with the sense that in all the universe, there is one exclusive other who fully knows me and values me all the more.

Studies in observing exclusive, monogamous human "pair bonding" note the same phenomenon of vulnerability as a prerequisite to moving forward to intimate sexual contact. For example, at Desmond Morris's Step 6 which he describes as "arm to waist" there is the disclosure of secrets as a final clearing of possible fatal personal flaws by full disclosure, Past relationships, previous temporary sexual relationships, the shame enveloped abortion—all of these come to the surface as if to say, "here goes my darkest secret. I could not bear to lose you if we move further toward marriage and intimacy. So you need to know that there is an old secret that haunts me, and I need to tell you what it is."

The summary of demographics on singles versus married in the population of United States was prepared by Carolyn Koons and Michael Anthony in their Single Adult Passages (1991, p. 51). They offer possible factors which may have enhanced the option of singleness or otherwise have influenced its rise or decline.

Any measure of intimacy in the young adult sector today suggests a rising trend toward isolation. The rising number of single housing units, of divorce, of single parent households documents a creeping alienation across these decades of early adult life experience. And the majority of recovery participants in 12-step and other programs are from these young adult decades as well.

Sexually transmitted diseases (Joy & Hager, 1993), children given up for adoption, abortion, family stress (Joy, 1988, 1990), broken relationships, and divorce (Joy, 1986, 1989) constitute the greatest wound stripe among young adults today. Religious educators have no alternative but to have a needs driven program-curriculum design which flexes to meet widening needs in these highly sensitive areas.

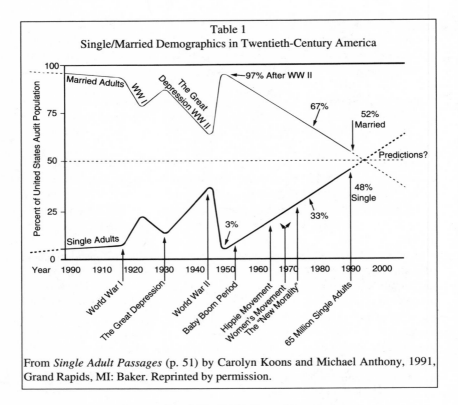

Table 1
Single/Married Demographics in Twentieth-Century America

From *Single Adult Passages* (p. 51) by Carolyn Koons and Michael Anthony, 1991, Grand Rapids, MI: Baker. Reprinted by permission.

James Fowler's Faith Development

James Fowler (1986), first at Harvard Divinity School, and now at Emory University and Candler School of Theology devised a faith development research model. It was Doug Sholl, then a Vietnam era divinity student at Harvard, who stumbled onto early Lawrence Kohlberg research and determined to write a thesis based on "The Contribution of Lawrence Kohlberg to Religious and Moral Education" (Sholl, 1971). Fowler, who accepted the mentor's role in the thesis project, began his serious look at Kohlberg in response to Sholl's need for guidance and defense. Fowler first tested his faith development model in Harvard classes where theological pluralism was profound. So his design of "faith" was necessarily empty, to accommodate any faith or nonfaith tradition whatever. Only after establishing his theory through *Stages of Faith* (1981) did he turn to offering faith development in specific Christian terms (1984, 1987, 1991).

Fowler's faith development theory is an amalgam of structural research, Erik Erikson's psycho-dynamic theory, and strands of Paul Tillich and Carlyle

Marney concepts informing the faith development stage grid. The justice key of Piaget and Kohlberg—mirroring the image of God dimensions of righteousness is not played out in the faith development theory. The young adult life agendas are illuminated by examining Fowler's faith stages focused on pastoral care (1987), in which he crafts them to combine Robert Kegan's (1982) ego developmental language. The typical young adult structural windows on faith likely span Fowler's Stage 3 through 5 as represented in the outline below:

7. Universalizing Faith and the God-grounded Self
6. Conjunctive Faith and the Interindividual Self
5. Individuative-Reflective Faith and Institutional Self
4. Synthetic-Conventional Faith and the Interpersonal Self
3. Mythic-Literal Faith and the Imperial Self
2. Intuitive-Projective Faith and the Impulsive Self
1. Primal Faith the Incorporative Self

Fowler suggests that Stage 5 Individuative-Reflective Faith is unlikely to occur before young adulthood. Many adults likely remain in a Synthetic-Conventional state of faith, perhaps lifelong. But the so-called Baby Boomer generation has tended to remain in a privatistic impulsively self-centered Intuitive-Projective sort of idea about having a religion that does what you want when you want it. Others have appeared to arrest within the imperial Mythic-Literal perception of a corporate faith which matches visions of success and grandeur, and rewards religiosity by showering raises, Cadillacs, and Mercedes benefits according to "the Lord gave me" whims. Religious education designed to invite these self-serving adults to begin to enlarge their "window" of faith to include the unanswered prayers of suffering people and their own unresolved problems will need to hook them in immediate needs. Still the dress for success, look good in public syndrome may make it difficult for many of them to sign on for an "Unfinished Business" (see Joy, 1989) class, like the one David Thompson hosts. There his own "family of origin" issues have been the gangplank many of us have walked to revisit our own painful pasts as we tell the truth and thus enter into new and deeper levels of Individuative-Reflective faith in the corporate life of shared community. In that setting, we recently spent four weeks opening the agenda of early childhood sexual trauma around our own cases, linking "image of God" first awareness with our present sense of God's witness through our sexual identity and experience (Joy, 1993; Joy & Hager, 1993)

Maturing in Discipleship

Neil Hamilton has critiqued Fowler's movement toward a universilizing faith with its widening tolerance for pluralism. In his *Maturing in the Christian*

Life: Biblical and Theological Resources for Faith Development (1984), Hamilton draws a model from the gospels which does not move toward universalistic indifference, but to a focused Christian commitment:

> 5. Maturing in the Church: Body and Mission
> 　4. Intimacy, "Friend," and Sanctification
> 　　3. Disillusionment, Despair, Betrayal
> 　2. Triumphalist, Illusion, Ethnocentric
> 1. Following: Pupils Attaching to Jesus

While Hamilton offers no specific "stages," he substitutes the story details from the gospel accounts for "empirical data" and traces the original apostles in their naive and bumpy road to empowerment for the Pentecost explosion of witness and mission in the worlds

Trajectory of Suffering

Robert Sears offers a theory of spiritual and faith development traced over a journey of suffering:

> 5. Suffering as Glory—Mission Faith, Pentecost
> (We) View: God suffers with us and for us.
> 　4. Vicarious Suffering—Communitarian Faith,
> Jesus: Servant (I-Thou)
> 　　3. Suffering as Witness—Individualizing Faith:
> Jeremiah and Job (I).
> 　2. Suffering as Discipline—Familial Faith: Mosaic law.
> 1. Suffering as Penalty—Initial Faith: Abrahamic basic trust view; there ought to be no suffering

Sears (1983, 1988) sees growth in grace as progressive into trinitarian life. The ground of faith is the inner life of the Trinity: I-Thou-We. Stages 1 and 2 are seen as innocent suffering, but that view gives way to Stages 3 and 4 as voluntary suffering. Finally, with Stage 5, suffering is redemptive.

The unreflected "upward journey" into positive and philosophical tranquillity, which seems to characterize the moral and faith development theories of Piaget and Fowler, spins toward suffering and pain by Hamilton and Sears. Add to these pain theorists the fictional masterpiece of Walter Wangerin, and the negative trajectory toward mature faith continues.

Classical Myth as Model

America's gospel storyteller laureate may have done his best and most classic work in *The Orphean Passages: The Drama of Faith* (Wangerin, 1986).

In an intricate and layered novel, Wangerin unfolds the classic Greek Myth of Orpheus, his love of Euridice, his loss of her, his mourning, his pursuit of that lost love which leads to his own death, and thereby, to an eternal reunion and ultimate bliss, The myth is spread evenly through six chapters of the six stages of young minister-to-be Orpheus. He is a little boy, Orphay. He grows up to be a minister—eloquent, compassionate, vulnerable, exploited, humiliated, and professionally dead before he breaks through to a real world of integrity without costume. Wangerin, entirely untutored by Piaget, Fowler, or Kegan managed to weave a plot and revive a classic myth, crafting them into his own pastoral version of a "theory" of faith development. Here are the chapter titles which constitute a trajectory:

The Sixth Passage: "I Have Called You by
Name"Resurrection
The Fifth Passage: Guilt and The Final Refinement,
Dying
The Fourth Passage: Faith, Conviction, and Not Seeing
The Third Passage: Mortification, Supplication
The Second Passage: Death and Mourning
The First Passage: Experience and Language

Like Fowler, Wangerin urges us to regard "faithing" as a verb, not a frozen noun.

Beatitudes as Curriculum

Elsewhere I have offered a life curriculum model in the eight beatitudes of Jesus (Modgil & Modgil, 1985; Dieter & Berg, 1984). After hearing the pastor's sermon suggesting a developmental structure to the beatitudes, I turned to John Wesley's sermons on the beatitudes to discover that he had noted the life pilgrimage trajectory there: "Some have supposed that [Jesus] designed [the beatitudes] to point out the several stages of the Christian course; the steps which a Christian successively takes in his journey to the promised land. . . . It is undoubtedly true, that both poverty of spirit and every other temper which is here mentioned are at all times found, in a greater or less degree, in every real Christian. And it is equally true, that real Christianity always begins in poverty of spirit, and goes on in the order here set down, till the 'man of God is made perfect'" (Wesley, 1872, p. 252).

Here is the "ladder" of unfolding life agendas from infancy to moral, spiritual, and political maturity, as seen through the beatitudes:

8. Advocates of victims
7. Peace makers
6. Pure hearted
5. Merciful
4. Hungerers for righteousness
3. Victims of forced constraint: Meek
2. Victims of grief: Mourners
1. Victims of poverty

Young adults will be able to trace the helplessness of childhood extending into adolescence. They can also calculate their losses and do their grief work. The can document their "forced labor," the disciplines of rigorous parents and teachers, or the alternate bondage of no supervision and the lessons from the street. At any rate, the young adult years will be rich if there is an unrelenting hunger and thirst for righteousness, for nailing down issues of value and justice for oneself and for others. The upper reachers are likely a lifelong quest. And the rewards always lead to intimacy with God—the kingdom, the attributes of righteousness, mercy, holiness, and compassion for all who suffer.

Gender Differences in the Developmental Journey

There are two support systems to young adult journeys in moral, faith, and religious development which seem to vary by gender. Carol Gilligan (1982), first a student of Kohlberg, then a colleague at Harvard's Center for the Study of Moral Development, has convincingly demonstrated that women follow a unique path in valuing and making moral choices. Similarly Mary Belenky (1986) with her colleagues makes a case for *Women's Ways of Knowing*.

Ways of Reasoning
Gilligan first observe that while males reason around issues of justice in making moral choices, females from childhood tend to make choices based on relational or "attachment" grounds—how people are affected by the choice. She demonstrated that Piaget and Kohlberg, who had worked almost exclusively with male samples, had developed tests and problems that discriminated against girls and women—almost always reducing them to a Stage 3 as a maximum developmental destination. Gilligan found that development in women is across a series of observable stages in which they describe themselves in the context of relationships:

Perspective III: Aware of inner voice. Self plus others.

Perspective II: Aware of self. Absorbed in social responsibility.
Perspective I: Unaware of self. Absorbed in social matrix.

Most enlightening to men and women, however, are Gilligan's (1990) findings in *Making Connections: The Relational Worlds of Adolescent Girls at Emma Willard School.* She chronicles the "abandonment of self" as girls hit sixth grade. Their way of making meaning out of their world requires that they curb their questioning and their spontaneous approach to learning and social development Women teachers coach them, often subtly, to prepare them for a woman's passive role in life. Sixth grade boys are encouraged by the same teachers to argue, ask questions, and move ahead with their social and intellectual development.

Ways of Knowing

Mary Belenky and her colleagues (1986) report and document that women in educational environments which include men, tend to go *silent*— matching the sixth grade coaching Carol Gilligan observed at the Emma Willard School. Such girls and women tend to rely too much on "authorities," and subsequently become dependent. Belenky describes other ways women learn. *Received knowing* tends to take the silently absorbed knowledge and may even pass it on, without owning and transforming it. *Subjective knowing* is a woman's way of internally affirming what is true. This way of knowing, should it surface, may be subject to harsh judgment from the authorities around her. *Connected knowing* refers to the process women tend to use more than men do—a way of weaving new knowledge into old connections William Perry's (1968) findings, again mostly with men, described a pattern of analytical, separated, objective ways of knowing. These variations between *separate and connected knowing* are not gender specific, and anyone working in a schooling environment will likely become competent at *separate knowing*, but most women and many men learn best using Belenky's sort of *connected knowing* strategies.

Catherine Stonehouse (1980), herself a research seasoned moral development specialist, and my colleague both in national religious education careers and now in graduate school mentoring, offers extensive treatment of Gilligan and Belenky in a chapter titled "Learning From Gender Differences" (1993).

Transformation Across the Young Adult Years

Religious education with young adults consists of the widest possible array of potential energy, gifts, and capacity to respond to service and mis-

sion. What we less often notice is that the need spectrum is equally complicated and complex. Here, in a final section, is an invitation to consider both
needs and energies among them and generic program-curriculum planning
appropriate to these decades of recruits and disciples.

Full Service Communities of Faith

Lyle Schaller has dubbed the effective congregations in United States
"full service churches." These are congregations which, facing the enormously complex needs of their communities and accumulating members,
create special programs to meet special needs of its people. Such a congregation is a "full service" or "seven-day-a-week church" in Schaller's (1992)
description.

David Michael Henderson (1980) shook down the phenomenon of the
Wesley revival in England to sort out its "adult education" dimensions.
Looked at through the lens of contemporary religious education he exposed
a "full service" sort of comprehensivess in the five levels of the early
Methodist community.

1. The society. Preaching/teaching dominated these meetings. Admission
was by ticket, renewable every three months. Since the meetings were illegal under English "established church" law, admission was restricted and
an absolute prohibition prevented reporting out what was said at the meetings.
Confidentiality was spread across the remaining four levels, as well.
Henderson notes that this "no talk back" sort of meeting was principally
cognitive education.

2. The class. Established regionally in households of not more than a
dozen, a "class leader" circulated to collect one penny per week to help
retire debts incurred in restoring or building facilities for the society to use.
Henderson reports evidence that the house calls gave opportunity to inspect
the lifestyle patterns of the member—in the crucible of lived daily life.
Irregularities of behavior, even domestic stresses, were confronted by the
leader and a member would be brought to accountability and correction of the
destructive behavior pattern. Henderson identifies the unique education concern of the classes as lifestyle accountability. All society members were
required to be members of a class.

3. Bands. Bands were volunteer groups organized by gender and by marital status within convenient geographic regions. Normally bands met on
Monday nights and one other evening convenient to the group. A strict agenda included a punctual time to close the meeting and suggested ways of
doing it. The agenda of the band was reporting in on your daily pilgrimage
of life Both positive and negative experience were to be reported, and the
"band" was your unconditional, confidential support system. Henderson
observes the affective curriculum in the bands.

4. Penitent bands. For people struggling with alcoholism or past life as a prostitute—both groups were evidently plentiful in Wesley's societies—long-term recovery was arranged through specialized groups. Here, again, the agenda was your own story of growth and of failure. You would find yourself entering a penitent band on "referral" from the society, the class leader, or from your first volunteer band. Once referred, you were expected to continue so long as your recovery was still marked by irregular lifestyle patterns. This further affective program extended to recovery agendas and anticipated the 12-step program by two hundred years. Penitent bands met on Monday nights and normally chose Saturday night—the weekly time of their greatest vulnerability rooted in past lifestyle—for the second meeting. Wesley was criticized for permitting the penitent bands running much later in the night on Saturdays than was published in the agendas, but he observed that they needed to invest their energy in singing and praising God on a night they had once used for other purposes.

5. Leader bands. Another "referral group" was the potential class leader pool. It was voluntary, of course, but the educational purposes were obvious. By sharing their own life journeys and engaging in Bible study, they were being formed to walk among society members and to nurture the entire complex system of Wesley's "full service" program.

Recovery and Survivors

Today's full service young adult religious education ministries accumulate survivor and recovery programs much like Wesley's "bands," customized to respect the unique adult stories which unfold in the presence of a community of healing grace.

Recovery. 12-step programs abound for the recovering alcoholics, for those with eating disorders, for those dealing with sexual addictions, gambling addiction, or drug problems.

Survivors. Divorce recovery runs parallel in many ways to dealing with bankruptcy, cancer, adultery, incest, rape, abortion, death of a spouse, death of a child, or with incorrigible children. Virtually all of these are organized around therapy recommended for those who suffer from post-traumatic stress disorder in which anniversary reactions and survivor guilt and depression are hallmarks. Children's curricula is available for child care programs that occur during adult participation in a recovery or survivor group (Kondracki).

Relationship training. Family life seminars (Joy, 1990; Smalley, 1991), developing positive couple patterns that lead to sexual intimacy in marriage (Joy, 1986), "getting the love you want" within marriage, represent a beginning list of kinds of short-term and repeatable seminars needed where young adults gather. Publishers continue to feed new resources in this arena of

love, sex, marriage, and family dynamics to meet the ever intensifying needs
of singles, marrieds, singles again, and remarried young adults.

Equipping and Empowering

Nothing promotes growth in Christian discipleship and moral maturity better than investing in meeting more desperate needs of others. Full service programs are showing an increasing opportunity for short-term, "stop out" year,
and career shift mission work in North America and overseas. These range
from immediate application of expert skills in another culture to soloing as
a teacher of English as an employee of a foreign government or school system. Physicians, dentists, and surgeons, for example, are volunteering their
services for two to six weeks in medically deprived places in the world.
Young adults who want to combine a holiday trip with putting in a hard
day's work on building homes or a church may volunteer for service abroad
through their church, denomination, or other agency prepared to broker such
experiences.

Conclusion: Young Adult Religious Education as Midwife to Lifelong Growth

Young adults contain the energy that shapes the world and opens the
doors to whatever future we will leave for the next generation. Pastors,
Directors of Religious Education, and other professionals who work with
them will celebrate their journeys. Until the mid-twentieth century, it was commonly thought that moral and spiritual growth was completed by about 12
years of age. So, Sunday Schools were seen as for "children." A mark of
adulthood was to drop out and settle in for a long rocking-chair existence at
that high plane of maturity known as adulthood.

Today, we celebrate the journey of adults, knowing that potential for
growth in perception, wisdom, and service is a never-ending trajectory of high
reward and celebration. The theoretical models developed since mid-cen-
tury all hold out "stages" toward which we point, but which we rarely grasp
consistently or fully. We press toward the mark of the high calling of God in
Christ Jesus, and continue well beyond age 40, where the focus of this chapter ends.

References

Belenky, M. F., Clinchy, B. M., Goldberger, N. R., & Tarule, J. M. (1986). *Women's ways
of knowing: The development of self, voice, and mind.* New York: Basic Books.
Dieter, M., & Berg, D. (1984). *Wesleyan perspectives on the church.* Anderson, IN:
Church of God Publishing House.
Dirks, D. H. (1988). Moral development in Christian higher education. *Journal of*

Psychology and Theology, 16, 324-331.

Erikson, E. (1950). *Childhood and society.* New York: Norton.

Erikson, E. (1980). *Identity and the life cycle.* New York: Norton.

Fowler, J. (1981). *Stages of faith: The psychology of human development and the quest for meaning.* San Francisco: Harper & Row.

Fowler, J. (1984). *Becoming adult, becoming Christian: Adult development and Christian faith.* San Francisco: Harper & Row.

Fowler, J. (1987). *Faith development and pastoral care.* Philadelphia: Fortress.

Fowler, J. (1991). *Weaving the new creation: Stages of faith and the public church.* New York: Harper Collins.

Gilligan, C. (1982). *In a different voice: Psychological theory and women's development.* Cambridge, MA: Harvard University Press.

Gilligan, C., Lyons, N. P., & Hanmer, T. J., (Eds.) (1990). *Making connections: The relational worlds of adolescent girls at Emma Willard School.* Cambridge, MA: Harvard University Press.

Glenn, H. & Nelsen, J. (1989). *Raising self-reliant children in self-indulgent world.* New York: St. Martin's Press.

Hamilton, N. (1984). *Maturing in the Christian life.* Philadelphia: Geneva Press.

Henderson, D. (1980). *John Wesley's instructional groups.* Bloomington, IN: Indiana University Press.

Heschel, A. (1962). *The prophets (Vol. I).* New York: Harper & Row.

Joy, D. (1969). *Values oriented instruction in the church and in the home.* Bloomington, IN: Indiana University Press.

Joy, D. (1985). *Bonding: Relationships in the image of God* [Video]. Wilmore, KY: Center For The Family.

Joy, D. (1986). *Rebonding: Preventing and restoring damaged relationships.* Dallas: Word.

Joy, D. (1988). *Parents, kids, and sexual integrity.* Dallas: Word.

Joy, D. (1989). *Unfinished business: How a man can make peace with his past.* Wheaton: Victor.

Joy, D. (1990). *For parents only: Risk-proofing your family!* [Video Assisted Curriculum]. Lexington, KY: Bristol House.

Joy, D. (1993). *Celebrating the new woman in the family.* Lexington, KY: Bristol House.

Joy, D., & Hager, D. (1993). *Women at risk: The real truth about sexually transmitted disease.* Lexington, KY: Bristol House.

Kegan, R. (1982). *The evolving self: Problem and process in human development.* Cambridge, MA: Harvard University Press.

Kohlberg, L. (1958). *The development of modes of moral thinking and choice in the years 10-16.* Chicago: University of Chicago Press.

Kohlberg, L. (1981). *The philosophy of moral development.* New York: Harper & Row.

Kohlberg, L. (1982). *The psychology of moral development.* New York: Harper & Row.

Kondracki, L. *Confident kids!* Whittier, CA: Recovery Partnership, Box 11095.

Koons, C., & Anthony, M. (1991). *Single adult passages: Uncharted territories.* Grand Rapids, MI: Baker.

Lee, J. (1973). *The flow of religious instruction.* Birmingham, AL: Religious Education Press.

Lucado, M. (1990). *The applause of heaven.* Dallas: Word.

Modgil, S., & Modgil, C. (1985). *Lawrence Kohlberg: Consensus and controversy.* Sussex, UK: Falmer Press.

Perry, W. G. (1968). *Forms of intellectual and ethical development in the college years.*

New York: Holt, Rinehart and Winston.

Piaget, J. (1932, 1961). *The moral judgment of the child* (Trans.). New York: Free Press.

Schaller, L. (1992). *The seven-day-a-week church.* Nashville, TN: Abingdon.

Sears, R. (1983). Healing and family spiritual/emotional systems. *Journal of Christian Healing, 8,* 10-23.

Sears, R. (1988) A Catholic view of exorcism and deliverance. In W. Swartley (Ed.), *Essays on spiritual bondage and deliverance* (pp. 100-117). Elkhart: Institute for Mennonite Studies.

Sholl, D. (1971). The contribution of Lawrence Kohlberg to religious and moral education. *Religious Education, 66,* (5) 364-372.

Smalley, G. (1991). *Hidden keys to loving relationships.* Paoli, PA: Relationships Today.

Stewart, J. S. (1974). *Toward a theory of values development education.* Unpublished doctoral dissertation, Michigan State University, Lansing, MI.

Stonehouse, C. (1980). *Patterns in moral development: A guidebook for parents and teachers on facilitating the Christian moral development of children, youth, and adults.* Dallas: Word.

Stonehouse, C. (1993). Learning from gender differences. In K. Gangel & J. Wilhoit (Eds.), *The Christian educators handbook on adult education* (pp. 104-120). Wheaton, IL: Victor.

Wangerin, W. (1986). *The orphean passages: The drama of faith.* San Francisco: Harper & Row.

Weinhold, J. B., & Weinhold, B. K. (1992). *Counter-dependency: The flight from intimacy.* Colorado Springs, CO: Circle Press.

Wesley J. (1771/1872). *The works of John Wesley (Vol. 5).* Grand Rapids, MI: Zondervan.

Part Three: Educational Procedures

CHAPTER SEVEN

General Principles and Procedures

TRENTON R. FERRO AND GARY J. DEAN

Good teaching does not just happen! It results when religious educators understand their learners, when they demonstrate appropriate attitudes and behaviors, when they prepare and plan carefully and thoroughly, and when they bring all these elements together skillfully in the actual teaching/learning transaction. Consequently, any person who has a genuine interest in working with young adults, who truly wants to facilitate their development and growth, and who possesses the appropriate content knowledge and skills to be taught and learned can develop the requisite capabilities for working with groups of young adults in learning and change situations.

The purpose of this chapter is to help both prospective and experienced religious educators of young adults gain and develop an understanding of, and appreciation for, the characteristics of young adults as learners; the role and function of those who plan and conduct learning for young adults; and processes which can help them plan learning situations with greater awareness, conscientiousness, and thoroughness. Specific principles and procedures involved in actually facilitating the learning interaction are discussed in the following chapter.

Educational Principles Related to the Adult Learner

A certain number of young adults might participate in the programs offered by a religious organization to which they belong out of loyalty to that organization or because they have developed and maintained from their youth the habit of regularly participating in that agency's programs. However, most will participate because they see some gain for themselves—and, likewise, those who stay away perceive little benefit in the activity or have decided that some alternate pursuit has greater merit. Therefore, the religious educator of these young adults must understand what prompts them to participate, what motivates them to learn, and what deters them—in short, what are the characteristics of young adults as learners.

As background to this discussion, it is important to recall the developmental characteristics of young adults presented in the previous three chapters. In summary, psychological issues which young adults face are independence, identity, and intimacy; the sociocultural tasks with which they struggle include becoming financially independent through work, setting up their own family units, and making commitments to their community (Merriam, 1984; Merriam & Ferro, 1986). In fact, it would be fair to say that young adults are consumed with these concerns. The religious educator who includes these issues as important and regular features of program offerings will experience greater success and satisfaction than one who does not.

Characteristics of Adult Learners

From 1960 onward various national studies have been conducted to determine who participates in adult education and why (see, for example, Aslanian & Brickell, 1980; Cross, Valley, & Associates, 1974; Johnstone & Rivera, 1965). These studies were based on different definitions of who is an adult, what is adult education, and what comprises an adult education setting. In addition, different methodologies were used to collect data. As a result, the findings vary from one study to the next. For instance, the reported percentage of the adult population involved in learning activities varies from 14 percent to 49 percent (Merriam & Caffarella, 1991). Other studies which incorporate or concentrate on independent and self-directed learning report participation rates as high as 90 percent (Penland, 1979; Tough, 1979).

In spite of these variations, a number of helpful interpretations of the findings have been published (Brookfield, 1986; Cross, 1981; Darkenwald & Merriam, 1982; Merriam & Caffarella, 1991). In Brookfield's (1986) words, "Of perhaps greatest statistical significance is the general finding that it is previous educational attainment and participation that is the most statistically significant variable in determining future participation in formal education" (p. 5). Related to this finding are other demographic variables: participants tend to be younger, earn higher incomes, are employed full time, and are more likely to be white (Merriam & Cafarella, 1991). However, there is little difference in participation between white and black adults when the level of educational attainment is comparable (Darkenwald & Merriam, 1982).

What does all this say? There is a broad spectrum of young adults in terms of their involvement in various types of learning opportunities and settings. In many cases, their participation depends on personal perception of the benefits to be gained from involvement in the proposed activity and on the nature of their relationship to the host organization. Even the definition of what constitutes learning can have a bearing on potential participation. Brookfield (1986) says "We should conceive adult learning to be a phenomenon and process that can take place in any setting. Indeed, it will often be the case that the most significant kinds of adult learning that are identified as such by adult learners themselves occur in settings not formally designated as adult educational ones. Such settings include families, community action groups, voluntary societies, support networks, work groups, and interpersonal relationships" (p. 4).

The research findings reported above may not be applicable to every individual setting or group of potential participants because they cut across the entire adult population and often describe participation in more formal settings. Yet the astute religious educator, by paying attention to the profile given above of typical participants, can take compensatory action to make the religious organization's programs more attractive and accessible to those who are less likely to participate in other settings.

Why Adults Participate—And Why Not

Many of the studies referenced above have also attempted to ascertain the reasons why adults do or do not participate in learning activities (Cross, 1981; Merriam & Caffarella, 1991). Reasons for participating are considered "motivators" in that they attempt to explain the internal urges or drives which propel people to become involved in growth and developmental opportunities. These studies also endeavor to describe those forces that keep adults from participating. Such forces are called "detractors" or "barriers."

Motivators. A seminal study on this topic, conducted by Houle, was reported in *The Inquiring Mind* (1961). Houle developed a three-way typology for classifying groups of people in order to explain why they are active learners. First, there are the *goal-oriented learners* who use learning primarily to attain some purpose or objective. People in this group see learning as a series of episodes, each of which is initiated by identifying some need or interest. The episode ends when the need or interest is satisfied.

Second, *activity-oriented* learners participate primarily for the sake of the activity itself rather than to achieve the purpose or objective of the activity. Such learners, for example, may join a group for the social contact and opportunity to interact with other participants.

Third are the *learning-oriented*. They pursue learning for its own sake, and their pursuit is lifelong. Their drive or fundamental desire is to know more and to grow through the very activity of learning. While some adults may fit into only one of these groups, others may fit into more than one. In addition, peoples' orientation can change over time and depending on the situation. The groups are not mutually exclusive.

Beginning with Houle's (1961) theoretical framework, Boshier (1971, 1973, 1977) has developed and refined the *Educational Participation Scale* (EPS). Morstain and Smart (1974), in turn, have run factor analyses on data collected when using the EPS and have found six factors which explain why adults participate in learning: Social Relationships, External Expectations, Social Welfare, Professional Advancement, Escape/Stimulation, and Cognitive Interest. The Social Relationship and Professional Advancement factors relate closely to Houle's goal-oriented learner; Social Relationships and Escape/Stimulation, to the activity-oriented learner; and Cognitive Interest, to the learning-oriented adult. The Social Welfare factor appears to relate to both the activity-oriented and learning-oriented adult.

Other researchers have observed the relationship between changes in people's lives and their involvement in learning. Havighurst (1972) developed the concept of the "teachable moment" to link together age-appropriate tasks and behaviors (those which arise from and relate to specific developmental phases and periods in a person's life) and the motivation or urge to participate in learning activities. There are moments in people's lives when they are particularly sensitive or open to participating in growth opportunities, so that they might better meet and deal with such age-related tasks and behaviors capably and confidently. For young adults, these tasks might include selecting a partner, marriage preparation and enrichment, beginning and raising a family, and selecting and preparing for a job or career. Similarly, based on the findings of their national study, Aslanian and Brickell (1980) reached the conclusion that life changes or transitions serve as "trigger events" for motivating adults to become involved in learning. Most of the transitions triggering learning related to career and family. To a much lesser extent were concerns related to health, civic responsibilities, religion, and the arts.

Detractors and barriers. Just as researchers have attempted to understand why adults participate in various educational settings and situations, they have tried to determine why adults do not take advantage of learning opportunities (Cross, 1981; Darkenwald & Merriam, 1982; Merriam & Caffarella, 1991). Accomplishing this is a more difficult task than identifying motivational factors; finding nonparticipants to include in a research project is a much more difficult undertaking than locating participants. Brookfield (1986) also warns against an inappropriate attitude which can develop about nonparticipants:

Viewing nonparticipants in education and training courses as disadvantaged is, of course, pernicious. It is easy to accept, almost without being aware of it, a stereotype of the nonparticipant in formal education as inadequate, deficient, and somehow unfulfilled. This view is fundamentally flawed, [sic] for two important reasons. First, to be disadvantaged is not an individual phenomenon, but a social product. . . .

Second, viewing nonparticipants in formal education as somehow disadvantaged may be premised upon the highly arrogant assumption that only participants in formal education are engaged in purposeful learning (pp. 6-7).

Nevertheless, detractors or barriers to participation in learning have been identified. Programmers, facilitators, and institutions can improve participation by taking appropriate action to remove those barriers over which they have control.

Johnstone and Rivera (1965) were the first to categorize barriers into clusters in order to better understand this phenomenon. They identified two types of barriers, external or situational and internal or dispositional. Cross (1981) expanded the number of categories to three. Using data from a national study, she grouped twenty-four nonparticipation items under three headings.

Situational barriers, those which relate to a person's situation in life at a given point in time, include lack of time due to work or familial responsibilities; insufficient funds to pay for the expenses—tuition, books, child care, for example—connected with taking classes; no child care; lack of transportation; and either lack of support from, or outright opposition by, friends and family.

Institutional barriers "consist of all those practices and procedures that exclude or discourage working adults from participating in educational activities" (Cross, 1981, p. 98), including lack of information, inconvenient schedules or locations, full-time fees for part-time study, lack of information about offerings, attendance requirements which are too strict, and lack of access to administrative offices and student services.

Dispositional barriers, arising from a person's attitudes about oneself and perceptions of oneself as a learner, include concerns about one's age, lack of confidence, concerns caused by previous poor educational experiences and performance, and lack of interest.

In addition to situational and institutional barriers, Darkenwald and Merriam (1981) refer to *informational barriers*. These include not only the failure of institutions to communicate adequately with their intended audiences but also to the inability or failure of adults to pay attention to, or seek out information about educational activities. They also include psychosocial barriers—beliefs, values, attitudes, and perceptions about oneself or the educational setting which inhibit involvement. This latter category is similar to what Cross (1981) and others call attitudinal or dispositional barriers.

A few studies also have looked at barriers to participation in adult religious education. McKenzie, for example, (1978, 1980) found seven dimensions of nonparticipation: 1) programmatic nonrelevance, 2) involvement in other activities, 3) physical incapacity or confusion, 4) alienation from church activities, 5) negative attitude toward education and resistance to change, 6) estrangement or a feeling of not belonging, and 7) marginality or a non-joining lifestyle. Dimensions two and four are particularly true of young adults, while one, six, and seven are descriptive of young adults as well as adults in other age categories.

Being alert to these various factors which describe and explain why adults do and do not participate will help the religious educator plan and conduct learning and growth opportunities which will attract and retain young adults. Reasons are complex and multifaceted; they vary; they change. An individual may be more inclined at one time and less at another to participate because of changing life circumstances. Knowing these elements will also improve the processes of conducting needs assessments and planning programs, topics which are discussed in Chapter Fifteen.

The Concept of Andragogy

A term which has been used for some time in Europe and which was first introduced to adult educators in America in the 1920s has been adopted and given popular currency by Malcolm Knowles. In a series of widely read books, Knowles (1975, 1980, 1984; Knowles & Associates, 1984) has developed the concept of andragogy as a set of assumptions which have important consequences for the religious education of young adults.

The need to know. Participants in schooling (K-12 as well as most colleges and universities) carry out their assignments for grades, credits, and degrees. Sometimes the usefulness and applicability of what they are doing is explained; oftentimes it is not. On the other hand, most young adults want to know why they are learning what they are studying. Beginning any learning episode with such an explanation will greatly enhance the active involvement of participants.

The learners' self-concept. This is a cornerstone of Knowles' approach to working with adult learners. Just as young adults possess a concept of being responsible for their own lives and decision, so they want to be responsible for their own educational decisions and activities. Yet their previous educational experience inhibits both facilitators of, and participants in, young adult learning settings from acknowledging and using this natural "instinct." According to Knowles (1980, 1984), the adult educator's major responsibility is to help participants become independent and self-directed learners.

The role of the learners' experience. A theme which runs throughout adult education literature is that adults enter the learning situation with a wealth and variety of life experience. This treasury of expertise becomes a valuable resource for the facilitator of young adult learning; each group of young adults includes a number of experts on a variety of topics and skills. Consequently, all members of a group, facilitator and participants alike, become both teachers and learners. Tapping this well of life experience also affirms the personal worth and self-esteem of the members of the group.

Readiness to learn. This assumption underlies adult educators' intense interest in the phases of adult development and the studies which explain why adults participate in growth activities, both of which have been discussed above. Young adults become ready to learn when they are faced with real-life situations for which they feel they lack the requisite knowledge and set of skills. As stated previously, paying close attention to the life situations of participants which create these "needs to know" provides educators with ample ideas for workshops and courses and encourages educators to constantly relate content to these life situations.

Orientation to learning. This is a natural extension and corollary of the previous point: young adults are life-, task-, and problem-centered in their orientation to learning. They "are motivated to devote energy to learn something to the extent that they perceive that it will help them perform tasks or deal with problems that they confront in their life situations. Furthermore, they learn new knowledge, understandings, skills, values, and attitudes most effectively when they are presented in the context of application to real-life situations" (Knowles, 1984, p. 59).

Motivation. Most young adults are prompted by internal pressures to become involved in learning activities. The most potent motivators are related to felt needs to improve oneself, to develop job-related skills and improve career possibilities, to enhance self-esteem, and the like—in general, to respond to the kind of life transitions and trigger events which have been described above and in earlier chapters. According to Tough (1979), it is natural for adults to want to continue learning and growing throughout their lifetimes unless that natural motivation is deterred by the barriers discussed earlier.

These assumptions, developed fully in Knowles' *The Adult Learner: A Neglected Species* (1984) and *The Modern Practice of Adult Education: From Pedagogy to Andragogy* (1980), are discussed in the context of adult religious education by McKenzie (1982).

Religious educators can enhance participation in their offerings by gearing offerings to the concerns, life situations, and interests of young adults; by enhancing motivators and removing barriers; and by observing sound adult education principles. Furthermore, relating scriptural and theological concepts and insights to daily life establishes the religious institution's interest in the participating young adults and enhances the likelihood of their continued involvement in the sponsoring organization.

Education Principles Related to the
Religious Educator of Young Adults

Religious educators of young adults should be aware of and possess certain characteristics regardless of the topic or the circumstances in which they are teaching. These characteristics can be divided into four categories: 1) values, beliefs, and assumptions regarding the purpose of the religious education activity; 2) personal attributes which contribute to successful teaching; 3) interpersonal skills which enhance the learning transaction; and 4) knowledge and skills needed to implement specific teaching and learning techniques and methods appropriate for young adult learners. The first three areas are the subject of this section; the fourth is addressed in Chapter Eight.

Values, Beliefs, and Assumptions of Religious Educators of Young Adults

The values, beliefs, and assumptions referred to here are those related to understanding, nurturing, and directing the learning process of young adults and are independent of religious or theological beliefs. While religious and theological beliefs, as well as the interpretation given to those beliefs, will often be implicit or explicit in the subject matter chosen, research-based beliefs about how young adults learn and the role of the young adult religious educator in that process are the major concern of this section.

Philosophical assumptions affect the way religious educators treat learners and how they plan and conduct learning activities. The most compelling reason for getting in touch with philosophical orientations is that behavior is affected by them whether religious educators are aware of their influence or not. The purpose of the learning activity will often be defined by the context in which it occurs, whether it be, for example, a retreat, a self-help group, or an intensive study of the scriptures. The specific goals of young adult religious educators, however, are a result of their beliefs, values, and assumptions regarding the learning process. These personal goals of young adult religious educators can be identified at the societal, institutional, instructional, and individual levels.

The first question one might want to ask, then, is, "What do I believe to be the nature of the learning process?" This question can be refined into several more discrete parts: "What is the purpose of the learning experience for the learner, for the young adult religious educator, for the sponsoring institution, and for society as a whole?" A review of philosophical principles and beliefs about young adult learning and the role of the young adult religious educator will help to answer these questions. Religious educators of young adults should try to identify the ideas that most closely describe their beliefs regarding why it is important for young adults to participate in religious education.

Several schemas have been used to conceptualize philosophical orientations in adult education. Brookfield (1989) suggests three primary paradigms from which adult educators operate: the behaviorist, the humanist, and the critical. Elias and Merriam (1980) identify six basic philosophical orientations which appear to guide most adult educators. These include liberal, progressive, behaviorist, humanist, radical, and analytical adult education. Elias (1982) has also discussed these philosophical orientations within the context of adult religious education. Darkenwald and Merriam (1982) enumerate five philosophical orientations for adult educators, including cultivation of the intellect, individual self-actualization, personal and social improvement, social transformation, and organizational effectiveness. Each orientation to adult education is based on different assumptions about learners, learning, and the purpose of education.

The organizational scheme of Darkenwald and Merriam (1982) is used here to further explore the relationship of the young adult educator to the young adult in religious education activities.

Humanistic. The humanistic approach states that the acquisition of knowledge, skills, and attitudes is primarily for the benefit of the individual learner. For the humanist adult educator, the purpose of education is to help learners grow and develop as human beings, become more whole, and eventually become self-actualized. For example, McKenzie (1982) contends that "religious educators must be concerned with the development of the total adult, and with the manifold educational needs and interest experienced by adults" (p. 22). Girzaitis (1977) states that adult religious education concerns itself with helping the adult to "free self from a narrow and closed vision of life in order to see everyday experiences as a call to growth" (p. 20). Religious educators operating from a humanistic perspective may focus on self-development, interpersonal relations, self-understanding, and personal growth. Self-actualization is often identified as the ultimate outcome of the humanistic learning process.

Progressive. This approach implies that the personal growth which results from the acquisition of knowledge, skills, and attitudes should be used for the betterment of society. Society is improved because there are better people in it, and the next generation of people are better off because the society in which they live has been improved. This notion is based on the writings of

John Dewey (see, for example, Dewey, 1963) and has been termed by Bergevin (1967) "the civilizing process." Examples of young adult religious education goals illustrating the progressive philosophy are related to social responsibility, the church and society, peace and justice, and helping of others.

Liberal. The liberal approach (where liberal is used as in the term "liberal arts") emphasizes the acquisition of knowledge, skills, and attitudes to transmit our cultural heritage. Elias (1982) highlights the major dimensions of liberal religious education as follows: "The wisdom presented in theological classics is the primary focus of education; intellectual understanding of ideas and values found in these classics is promoted; moral education takes place through exposure to and dependence on values in religious classics; and religious and spiritual growth is through initiation into a way of living and a way of thinking celebrated in a religious community" (p. 159). Examples of liberal goals for young adult religious education might include studies of the theology of the religious group or denomination and its development, church history and influential figures in the past, the arts and religion, and religious interpretations of historical events. Most catechetical programs, for both youth and young adults, are informed by the liberal perspective.

Social transformative. The social transformative, or radical, approach emphasizes the transformation of society through young adult religious education. This approach can be compared to the progressive approach. In the progressive approach, society is changed because people are changed. The changes in society are evolutionary and the direct result of adult learners possessing better knowledge, skills, or attitudes. The radical approach also encourages the improvement of society through religious education. However, the changes in society are often more sweeping. Learners are encouraged to implement their new knowledge, skills, and attitudes to make profound changes in society. An underlying assumption of this approach is that religious education is a political activity and curricular decisions are political decisions (Freire, 1970, 1973; Groome, 1980). Missionary work is often transformative in that missionaries are expected to encourage those they are helping to bring about major social and cultural, as well as personal, changes. Also, peace, justice, racial, gender, and environmental issues are often framed within the social transformative orientation. Liberation theology, especially as it has been developed in Latin America, and much feminist theology are representative examples of this perspective.

Organizational. The organizational, or behavioral, approach emphasizes the acquisition of knowledge, skills, and attitudes for the improvement of the institution sponsoring the adult learning activity. Examples of this approach include learning how to conduct meetings, increasing knowledge about church governance, and learning how to serve as an emissary of the religious organization. Most proponents within the ranks of religious educators of what Elias (1982) calls socialization-behavioristic theories have concentrated their efforts and concerns on the processes to be used in enculturating children into the various religious traditions.

The foregoing discussion underscores the fact that there are many different reasons for undertaking religious education with young adults. Harmony and cooperation will often result when there is unanimity of purpose among the Director of Religious Education, the young adult educator, and the young adult learners. When there is disparity of purpose, however, confusion and lack of cooperation can result (Ferro, 1993). In order to ensure that the outcome is cooperation rather than confusion, adult religious educators need to reflect on what they believe the purpose of the learning activity to be and to determine if others (the DRE and young adult learners) are in congruence with them.

Personal Attributes of Young Adult Religious Educators

Young adult religious educators must combine their personal philosophical orientations with the personal attributes they possess. This combination, when understood and harnessed, provides the basis for effective young adult religious education. As discussed earlier, effective teaching of young adults is based on several assumptions: adult learners are valued as individuals, their contributions to the learning process are valued, and the young adult teacher is not threatened by the learners or what they have to say. It should be noted that the religious educator of young adults is often in a position different from that of a teacher of youth. Teachers of youth are typically respected because they are seen as the content expert, they are in a position of authority, and they are older than the learners. None of these conditions may apply to the religious educator of young adults. The young adult religious educator may be working with young adults who are as equally well informed on the topic as the instructor, the learners may be peers of the instructor in other aspects of life, and they may be as old or older than the young adult educator. Some personal self-reflection will help identify the attributes the adult educators possess and which they can apply to the teaching and learning process.

Many lists have been developed to describe effective adult educators. It is helpful to view the various lists as goals to which effective and growing young adult religious educators aspire. Draves (1984) suggests that adult educators should love their subject, desire to share it, and be competent in it. Seaman and Fellenz (1989) identify needs manifested by teachers of adults which may impact their teaching as popularity, pride of accomplishment, self-confidence, desire to be helpful, expression of personality, self-improvement, and financial gain. In addition, teachers of young adults must learn how to communicate those needs to others, especially administrators and young adult learners. Dean and Ferro (1991) provide the following list of characteristics of good adult educators: a belief that adults can change and learn, enthusiasm about both the learners and the topic, patience and willingness to listen to others carefully, knowledge of the topic, ability to clearly articulate material, flexibility, openness, and a sense of humor. Though critical for the success of a young adult learner, the intangible qualities identified above are often difficult to measure. How can young adult religious educators tell if they possess enough of the right qualities? One way to address these issues is to ask the learners and other young adult religious educators for an assessment. Identifying a personal list of qualities may be a difficult, even painful, process, but it is a highly beneficial one for both the young adult religious educator and the learners.

Interpersonal Skills of Young Adult Religious Educators

Successful religious educators of young adults build upon their personal qualities and philosophical assumptions by developing their ability to understand and relate to others. These abilities, known collectively as interpersonal skills, are the underlying skills of good young adult religious educators and contribute to successful learning experiences. A little reflection on the past may help illustrate the importance of effective interpersonal skills. By recalling the best teachers they ever have had, young adult religious educators can identify what made them outstanding teachers. Chances are it is not what they taught, but how they taught that stands out. In short, it was how they treated learners that made the lasting impression. It might also be noted that the worst teachers can often be identified for the same reason but for, hopefully, an entirely different set of characteristics.

Knox (1986) notes that "teaching tends to be quite intuitive and implicit, largely reflecting the instructor's personal qualities and habits" (p. 43). Effective teachers build upon an intuitive sense that allows them to understand and respond to the needs of their young adult learners; they display interpersonal skills that encourage and support learners. These interpersonal skills can be roughly divided into three categories: attending skills, questioning skills, and presentation skills.

Attending skills. The skills used to encourage and support young adult learners can be referred to as attending skills. These skills find their basis in the belief that the teacher and learners are equal partners in the learning process and that both will benefit from it. Knox (1986) identifies the essence of attending skills when he states that effective adult educators (1) "are supportive and encourage participants to be resources for the learning of others as well as active agents of their own learning"; (2) "accommodate participant needs and expectations that fit program purposes"; (3) "let participants know early where their reasons and program purposes match and help them seek resources and assistance to meet needs that some learners may want to pursue beyond [the] program"; (4) "help participants understand their characteristics related to learning and will provide options for individuals as well as the group"; and (5) use information "about adults' current proficiencies . . . in selecting examples, concepts, and procedures likely to be helpful to the participants at their current stage of development" (pp. 44-45).

The most fundamental of attending skills is active listening. Good teaching starts with good listening. Before religious educators can help young adult learners acquire the desired knowledge, skills, and attitudes, it is vital that they understand their learners. Understanding learners depends to a very great extent upon listening to them. The first step in effective listening is to stop talking and focus on the learner. Several guidelines may help in the development of effective listening skills: concentrating on the learner, not on oneself; making eye contact with the learners; listening for both the "information" and the "feelings" in the learner's message; repeating or rephrasing the learners' questions or comments to ensure that the facilitator and the other learners understand; and allowing the learners to finish what they have to say without cutting them off or putting words in their mouth. These guidelines are based on the assumption that the young adult learner deserves to be treated with the same respect as the teacher or, for that matter, as any adult.

Questioning skills. Sanders (1990) notes that questioning "is probably the most fundamental instructional methodology available" (p. 119). He further notes that questions serve several different purposes: to gain the learners' participation in a class, to demonstrate what learners' know about a subject, to focus the attention of a learner, to lead discussions, to review subject matter, to stimulate thinking, and to test the learners' knowledge. In addition, questions may be used to enhance the relationship between the teacher and the learners or among the learners themselves. Questions of this sort often deal with the process of learning, such as, "Are you with me?" and "How can I better help you to understand this material?"

One approach to understanding the use of questions is to contrast the role of closed versus open-ended questions. Closed questions seek a specific bit of knowledge, usually a fact, and typically have one right answer. Open-ended questions are used to elicit ideas, opinions, alternatives, or solutions to problems possessing multiple right answers. Also, questions can be asked of a particular student or addressed to the group as a whole.

Closed questions addressed to a particular learner usually serve the purpose of assessing that person's retention of previously acquired knowledge, skills, or attitudes; establishing the learner's current understanding of the subject matter; or determining if the learner is with the teacher and the group. An example might be: "John, do you recall the names of the twelve disciples?" Open-ended questions addressed to an individual elicit that person's opinions and give the participant a nonthreatening opportunity to participate in the group: "Mary, what do you think is meant by the passage we are discussing?" Closed questions for the whole group can focus the attention of group members on a topic or an important fact: "Does anyone know the names of the major religions of the world?" Open-ended questions addressed to the whole group serve to invite participation by all members of the group, to elicit a variety of opinions or ideas, and to develop a list of options or alternatives. An example of this type of question might be: "In how many different ways might we respond to this situation?"

One of the most serious problems exhibited by teachers regarding questions is the failure to allow sufficient time for a reply. Waiting three to five seconds before talking again gives the learners time to process the question and form a response. Providing learners insufficient time to respond sends the message that the young adult religious educator really does not value their response. If this practice is repeated, the learners will soon learn not to respond at all.

Presentation skills. Margolis and Bell (1984) identify the fundamentals of making effective presentations. Their advice includes the implementing of the following principles: using effective body language; being natural and not trying to put on an act; avoiding inappropriate behaviors such as making noises (for example, clicking one's pen and jingling change) and distracting movements (staring, swaying, and pacing are examples); maintaining physical contact with the learners by arranging the furniture so that everyone can see and hear the teacher and each other; maintaining psychological contact by mixing with the learners before, during, and after the learning activity, maintaining eye contact with the learners, and treating the learners with respect; establishing an appropriate pace and tone for the presentation by talking naturally; maintaining a balance between being too formal and too informal; being responsive to the needs of the learners; using humor appropriately; and summarizing the main points frequently.

In addition, Margolis and Bell (1984) provide a list of "do nots." Their list includes the avoiding of clichés, jargon words, and buzzwords; avoiding body language, vocal sounds, and other behavior which might prove distracting to the learners; not taking oneself too seriously, rolling with the punches, and acknowledging one's humanity; not making excuses or apologizing unnecessarily (such behavior only calls attention to the problem); not talking to the chalkboard, flip chart, or wall; and avoiding language and stories that might offend or alienate the learners.

The Role of the Young Adult Religious Educator

Young adult religious educators must be able to identify the roles they are called upon to play and to be flexible enough to switch roles as necessary. The many roles include content expert, learning facilitator, organizer, encourager, guide, and role model. Sometimes several roles are being played simultaneously as the young adult religious educator responds to different situations and the needs of different learners. Flexibility is only successful, however, when it is based on a solid foundation of self-understanding and clear purpose. This foundation is achieved by developing a clear sense of values, beliefs, and assumptions about the purpose of learning; awareness of one's personal attributes as a young adult religious educator; and a commitment to constantly enhancing interpersonal skills to help other adults learn.

Planning the Teaching/Learning Transaction

To this point the chapter has discussed characteristics of young adults as learners and the attributes of effective religious educators of young adults. The process of planning the learning experience brings together these elements. This planning process is presented in two parts: determining what is to be learned (the developing of goals and objectives) and deciding how that learning will take place (the identifying of appropriate learning activities).

Developing Goals and Objectives

To ensure the success of a learning activity, the teacher must have a clear picture or conception of where that activity is going, that is, it must have goals. "A goal is a general statement of a desired outcome of the learning process. A goal can usually be divided into several objectives and need not be stated in behavioral terms, but should fit into one or more of the learning domains" (Dean, 1994).

The concept of instructional domain was developed by Bloom, Engelhart, Furst, Hill, and Krathwohl (1956) who identified three: cognitive, affective, and psychomotor. The *cognitive domain* consists of a hierarchical series of learning outcomes beginning with the simple recall of facts and developing through comprehension and application into the ability to analyze, synthesize, and evaluate information. The *affective domain* deals similarly with beliefs, attitudes, and values. Likewise, the *psychomotor domain* refers to the acquisition of physical and motor skills.

The concept of instructional domain is useful in two ways. First, it helps identify the potential range of learning outcomes so that activities can be designed to achieve them. Second, it makes specific the desired outcomes so that both facilitator and participants have a clear and consistent understanding of the direction of the learning activity.

Goal statements can be divided into several, more discrete outcomes called objectives. Mager (1984) identifies three components which constitute an effective objective: 1) the terminal behavior, 2) the conditions under which the behavior will be demonstrated, and 3) the criteria of acceptable performance. Terminal behavior refers to what the learner should be able to do upon completion of the learning activity. Some examples include reciting the books of scripture (cognitive domain), making life decisions based on theological principles (affective domain), or singing the weekly anthem on pitch (psychomotor domain).

Conditions refer to how the learners will demonstrate what they have learned. For example, learners can demonstrate their knowledge by participating in a discussion, taking a test, or performing a skill which they have acquired. Criteria for acceptable performance refer to how well learners need to demonstrate what they have learned. For example, a passing score on a test may be 70 percent. This last component may not be applicable in many religious education activities designed for young adults, but it is important when a specific level of competence is required.

Mager's (1984) prescription for writing objectives is intended for highly structured learning situations. Since most young adult religious education takes place in less formal settings, the following guidelines may be more useful. According to Dean and Ferro (1991), each goal or objective statement should consist of three elements. First, the goal or objective begins with reference to the learner, making the learner the subject of the statement. This can be referred to as LWBAT, "the learner will be able to" (Dean, 1994). Second, the domain is identified by using an active verb which states the desired action to be accomplished by the learner. Examples of active verbs in the three domains are listed in Table 1. Third, the object of the statement identifies what is to be learned.

Examples of goal and objective statements can be presented in the context of a series of workshops designed to prepare young couples for marriage. A goal statement in the cognitive domain might be:

A. Learners will be able to understand the interpersonal dynamics of a marriage relationship.

Some learning objectives designed to achieve this goal might be:
A1. Learners will be able to identify factors contributing to a positive, functional relationship.
A2. Learners will be able to identify factors contributing to a dysfunctional relationship.
A3. Learners will be able to compare and contrast factors contributing to functional and dysfunctional relationships.

A goal statement in the affective domain might be:
B. Learners will be able to apply theological principles in making positive relational decisions.

Table 1
Verbs for Use in Goals and Objective

Domain	Verbs for Goals	Verbs for Objectives
Cognitive (Information, Knowledge, and Problem Solving)	Know Understand Comprehend Apply Analyze Synthesize Evaluate	Recall Define Identify List Solve
Affective (Feelings, Beliefs, and Values)	Value Believe Appreciate	Choose/Reject Approve Dispute Select Show Interest In Advocate Adopt Argue For
Psychomotor (Skills)	Exhibit Imitate	Demonstrate Act Build Design

From AKC Judges Institute Instructional Design and Teaching Manual by G. J. Dean and T. R. Ferro, (New York: American Kennel Club, 1991), p.53. Used by permission.

Some learning objectives designed to achieve this goal might be:

B1. Given the opportunity to participate in an extramarital affair, learners will be able to choose behavior consistent with the theological principles of the religious group.

B2. When presented with options related to birth control, learners will be able to advocate a position in keeping with the theological principles of the religious group.

A goal statement in the psychomotor domain might be:

C. Learners will be able to exhibit effective interpersonal skills.

Some learning objectives designed to achieve this goal might be:

C1. Learners will be able to demonstrate active listening skills by paraphrasing their partners' statements of feelings.

C2. Learners will be able to use body language which demonstrates an attentive attitude.

Identifying Appropriate Learning Activities

Learning activities are the means by which goals and objectives are achieved; they are the "stuff" of the learning process. Since goals and objectives are used to identify learning outcomes in the three domains, appropriate learning activities need to be selected which lead to the desired learning outcomes specified for each domain. Appropriate learning activities in the cognitive domain include lecture, exhibits, demonstration, panels, interviews, field trips, case studies, simulations, and role plays. Appropriate learning activities in the affective domain—those which encourage the acquisition and demonstration of attitudes, values, and beliefs—include case studies, discussion, simulations, and role plays. Appropriate learning activities in the psychomotor domain—that which fosters the development of physical and motor skills—include modeling, demonstration, and practice.

Questions which religious educators of young adults might ask to help them select appropriate activities include:

1. Will the young adults respond to the learning activity? Do the activities encourage active or passive participation? Is that level of participation desirable?

Figure 1
PLANNING GUIDE

WORKSHOP TITLE _____ PAGE _____

INSTRUCTOR _____ DATE _____ TIME _____

GOALS	OBJECTIVES	ACTIVITIES	TIME	MATERIALS & MEDIA	FACILITIES	OTHER FACTORS

From Gary J. Dean & Trenton R. Ferro, *AKC Judges Institute Instructional Design and Teaching Manual* (New York, NY: American Kennel Club, 1991), p. 71. Used by permission.

2. Is the religious educator comfortable using the particular learning activity?

3. Are the facilities and equipment necessary for using the particular learning activity available?

4. Will there be adequate time to conduct the learning activity?

5. Do the learning activities fit the expectations of the sponsoring organization?

A well-planned and organized class, workshop, or seminar depends on sequencing goals, objectives, and learning activities to accommodate both the learners and the content. The content must flow in such a way that the learners can perceive the logic of the sequence and achieve the desired outcomes. In addition, learners must be comfortable with both the activities and the order of activities. Using a Planning Guide such as the one in Figure 1 can help the adult religious educator identify all the factors necessary to conduct a successful learning experience. After the goals, objectives, and activities have been placed in proper sequence, the educator can determine how much time each activity will require for satisfactory completion, the materials and media needed to conduct each activity, the facilities required (the configuration of space and furniture), and any other factors which must be taken into account. In addition, a column can be added to describe assessment procedures when such are appropriate.

Conclusion

Three major topics were addressed in this chapter: the characteristics of young adults as learners, the characteristics of adult educators, and the process of planning learning experiences for adult learners. Any successful learning experience begins with an understanding and consideration of the learner. In addition to understanding the learners, religious educators of young adults must be in touch with their philosophical understandings of learning, their personal attributes, and the interpersonal skills they possess. Building upon their understanding and knowledge of the learners, and employing their self-understanding, young adult religious educators can then engage in the planning and facilitating of young adult learning with the confidence that a quality experience will result for the learner, the teacher, and the sponsoring institution.

References

Aslanian, C. B., & Brickell, H. M. (1980). *Americans in transition: Life changes as reasons for adult learning.* New York: College Entrance Examination Board.

Bergevin, P. (1967). *A philosophy of adult education*. New York: Seabury.

Bloom, B. S., Engelhart, M. D., Furst, E. J., Hill, W. H., & Krathwohl, D. R. (1956). *Taxonomy of educational objectives: The classification of educational goals. Handbook I: Cognitive domain*. New York: David McKay.

Boshier, R. (1971). Motivational orientations of adult education participants: A factor analytic exploration of Houle's typology. *Adult Education, 21*(2), 3-26.

Boshier, R. (1973). Educational participation and dropout: A theoretical model. *Adult Education, 23*(4), 255-282.

Boshier, R. (1977). Motivational orientation re-visited: Life-space motives and the Education Participation Scale. *Adult Education, 27*(2), 89-115.

Brookfield, S. D. (1986). *Understanding and facilitating adult learning*. San Francisco: Jossey-Bass.

Brookfield, S. D. (1989). Facilitating adult learning. In S. B. Merriam & P. M. Cunningham (Eds.), *Handbook of adult and continuing education* (pp. 201-210). San Francisco: Jossey-Bass.

Cross, K. P. (1981). *Adults as learners: Increasing participation and facilitating learning*. San Francisco: Jossey-Bass.

Cross, K. P., Valley, J. R., & Associates. (1974). *Planning nontraditional programs: An analysis of the issues for post secondary education*. San Francisco: Jossey-Bass.

Darkenwald, G. G., & Merriam, S. B. (1982). *Adult education: Foundations of practice*. New York: Harper & Row.

Dean, G. J. (1994). *Designing instruction for adult learners*. Malabar, FL: Krieger.

Dean, G. J., & Ferro, T. R. (1991). *AKC Judges Institute instructional design and teaching manual*. New York: American Kennel Club.

Dewey, J. (1963). *Experience and education*. New York: Collier.

Draves, W. A. (1984). *How to teach adults*. Manhattan, KS: Learning Resources Network.

Elias, J. L. (1982). *The foundations and practice of adult religious education*. Malabar, FL: Krieger.

Elias, J. L., & Merriam, S. B. (1980). *Philosophical foundations of adult education*. Malabar, FL: Krieger.

Ferro, T. R. (1993). The authority of the word. In P. Jarvis & N. Walters (Eds.), *Adult education and theological interpretations* (pp. 35-52). Malabar, FL: Krieger.

Freire, P. (1970). *Pedagogy of the oppressed*. New York: Seabury.

Freire, P. (1973). *Education for critical consciousness*. New York: Seabury.

Girzaitis, L. (1977). *The church as reflecting community: Models of adult religious learning*. West Mystic, CN: Twenty-Third Publications.

Groome, T. H. (1980). *Christian religious education: Sharing our story and vision*. San Francisco: Harper & Row.

Havighurst, R. J. (1972). *Developmental tasks and education* (3rd ed.). New York: McKay.

Houle, C. O. (1961). *The inquiring mind*. Madison, WI: University of Wisconsin Press. [Reprinted, 1988, with additional Foreword by H. B. Long and Afterword by C. O. Houle. Norman, OK: Oklahoma Research Center for Continuing Professional and Higher Education.]

Johnstone, J. W. C., & Rivera, R. J. (1965). *Volunteers for learning: A study of educational pursuits of adults*. Hawthorne, NY: Aldine.

Knowles, M. S. (1975). *Self-directed learning: A guide for learners and teachers*. New York: Association Press.

Knowles, M. S. (1980). *The modern practice of adult education: From pedagogy to andragogy* (rev. and updated). New York: Cambridge.

Knowles, M. S. (1984). *The adult learner: A neglected species* (3rd ed.). Houston: Gulf.

Knowles, M. S., and Associates. (1984). *Andragogy in action: Applying modern principles of adult learning.* San Francisco: Jossey-Bass.

Knox, A. B. (1986). *Helping adults learn.* San Francisco: Jossey-Bass.

Mager, R. F. (1984). *Preparing instructional objectives* (2nd ed.). Belmont, CA: Pitman Learning.

Margolis, F. H., & Bell, C. R. (1984). *Managing the learning process.* Minneapolis: Lakewood Publications.

McKenzie, L. (1978). Non-participation in parish adult education: An empirical study. *Living Light, 14*, 3.

McKenzie, L. (1980, October 24). The case for adult religious education. *National Catholic Reporter*, pp. 9, 11.

McKenzie, L. (1982). *The religious education of adults.* Birmingham, AL: Religious Education Press.

Merriam, S. B. (1984). Developmental issues and tasks of young adulthood. In G. G. Darkenwald & A. B. Knox (Eds.), *Meeting educational needs of young adults* (pp. 3-13). (New Directions for Continuing Education, No. 21). San Francisco: Jossey-Bass.

Merriam, S. B., & Caffarella, R. S. (1991). *Learning in adulthood: A comprehensive guide.* San Francisco: Jossey-Bass.

Merriam, S. B., & Ferro, T. R. (1986). Working with young adults. In N. T. Foltz (Ed.), *Handbook of adult religious education* (pp. 59-82). Birmingham, AL: Religious Education Press.

Morstain, B. R., & Smart, J. C. (1974). Reasons for participation in adult education courses: A multivariate analysis of group differences. *Adult Education, 24*(2), 83-98.

Penland, P. R. (1979). Self-initiated learning. *Adult Education, 29*, 170-179.

Sanders, R. E. (1990). The art of questioning. In M. W. Galbraith (Ed.), *Adult learning methods: A guide for effective instruction* (pp. 119-129). Malabar, FL: Krieger.

Seaman, D. F., & Fellenz, R. A. (1989). *Effective strategies for teaching adults.* Columbus, OH: Merrill.

Tough, A. (1979). *The adult's learning projects: A fresh approach to theory and practice in adult learning* (2nd ed.). Austin, TX: Learning Concepts.

CHAPTER EIGHT

Specific Educational Procedures: Methods and Techniques

R.E.Y. WICKETT

A close examination of the special nature of young adulthood persuades us of the need to teach in ways that are consistent with the unique characteristics and general nature of this age group. Yet we must also recognize the diversity that is based upon individuality of learners. The key for young adult religious educators is to consider all the relevant individual factors while incorporating the special features of young adulthood into the planning and implementation of religious education processes.

Methods and Techniques

This chapter contains sections which refer to instructional procedures—that is methods and techniques—in the areas of climate setting and facilitation of learning. James Michael Lee defines methods and techniques as follows: "*Method* is the internally ordered set of pedagogical procedures which are arranged in discrete generalized bodies or classes. Method serves to furnish the larger tactical unit of the teaching-learning act. Examples of method are problem solving, teacher-pupil planning, socialized teaching, individualized teaching, and affective teaching. *Technique* is the concrete, tangible, specific way in which a pedagogical event is structured in a given teaching-learning situation. Technique functions as a specific procedure which is actualized in a definite instructional circumstance. Lecturing and telling,

role playing, project, discussion, and panel are all examples of technique"
(1973, p. 34).

Types of Religious Education Learning

Further reference will be made to individual, group, and distance religious education.

Individual learning. Individual learning occurs when a young adult works
through a course of study alone, or under the supervision or personal help from
the religious educator or tutor. The situation in many small congregations,
especially rural areas where there are small numbers of people to begin with,
will find this approach most conducive in meeting religious education needs
which would otherwise remain unmet. Others "will need the individual activity and freedom and flexibility which comes from that situation in order to
learn what they require" (Wickett, 1991, p. 83).

Malcolm Knowles (1975), who refers to this type of education as *self-
directed learning*, suggests individualized learning is valuable for several
reasons. First, there is evidence that people who take the initiative in learning learn more and learn better than do those who sit passively at the feet of
teachers. Second, as we grow and mature we develop an increasingly deep
psychological need to be independent of parental control, teachers, and other
adults. A third reason is that with the explosion of knowledge and information it is no longer realistic to define the purpose of education simply as
transmitting what is known. The main purpose of education must be to develop inquiry skills (pp. 14-15). He concludes by saying "the ability to learn on
one's own . . . has suddenly become a prerequisite for living in this new
world" (p. 17). Jeanne Tighe and Karen Szentkeresti (1986) include appren-
ticeship and tutorial as types of individual learning opportunities.

Group learning. This type of religious education needs little explanation.
It refers to the standard religious education setting where two or more young
adults meet with a teacher or leader for the purpose of pursuing a particular
course of study. Small groups, Sunday School classes, seminars, and workshops are examples of group learning opportunities.

Distance religious education. Distance religious education "is characterized by some degree of separation from the teacher and the other learners"
(Wickett, 1991, p. 152). Correspondence study is a good example of this
type of religious education. Distance religious education is helpful for whom
"the normal schedule of life precludes participation in either full-time or
part-time studies through the standard course or classroom format" (Wickett,
1991, p. 153). Distance education models are frequently popular with young
adults because they enable further religious education on a flexible, somewhat
individualized basis. Much learning in distance religious education requires
the individual to work independently. Furthermore the specific location and

timing of the learning are determined by the learner in light of his or her convenience and availability. For more extensive descriptions of distance education the reader is referred to R.E.Y. Wickett (1991) and Desmond Keegan (1990).

It is clear that religious educators must use different methods and techniques in alternate settings and situations. The requirements for working with individuals or groups in a face-to-face situation are different from those used in distance education or independent studies.

Instructional Procedures and Critical Issues
in Young Adult Development

Good religious education methods and techniques for young adults should foster the developmental processes which enable maturation and continuous growth. The methods and techniques the religious educator uses should support the developmental processes which are occurring in the young adult learner. The struggles for independence, identity, and intimacy, as described by Sharan Merriam and Trenton Ferro (1986) lead us to important guiding principles for the facilitation of the learning process.

Merriam and Ferro also discuss the importance of vocational and religious development of the young adult. The opportunities to pursue careers and jobs have a direct influence on young adults, particularly because of society's emphasis upon the job in relation to personal identity. They also cite James Fowler's (1981) work as an indicator of the possibilities for faith development in the lives of young adults.

Fowler builds on the psycho-social framework of Erik Erikson (1968, 1980) in conjunction with the work of other social-scientific theorists, to develop a concept of faith development which incorporates issues of intimacy and identity. Identity and intimacy have important consequences for the religious educator of young adults. If we agree with Fowler and Erikson in this respect, identity will be an issue for the earliest part of young adulthood, while intimacy will be an issue for the latter part of young adulthood.

There are theorists who would argue that identity or identity related issues will also occur at other times in life after early young adulthood. Such prominent theorists such as Roger Gould (1978) and Daniel Levinson (1978) see identity issues in other phases of young adulthood, as well as middle adulthood. Although one must agree that identity issues do emerge at times in life other than early young adulthood, it might be argued that they have a particular importance to those emerging from parental guidance and school, into the world of independent living and careers.

The issue of intimacy is relevant to young adult religious educators as it must emerge from a central position of good interpersonal relationships.

Effective interpersonal relationships are relevant to work which involves the educator and learner in various circumstances and contexts. Close personal relationships which are consistent with the Eriksonian concept of intimacy, will emerge more readily for individuals who learn how to relate effectively with others.

Independence is an issue for adult religious educators because we need to recognize the adult status of the learner. This recognition implies our ability to accept the learner's rights as a fully functioning, autonomous person in society and within the context of the learning situation. Independence rather than dependence should be our goal for the learner.

Methods and techniques which are consistent with these principles enable the individual to establish a sense of self, as well as nurturing relationships with the religious educator and other group members. Methods which foster identity and intimacy include those which enable an individual to experience a positive, relational climate.

Procedures for Climate Setting in Young Adult Religious Education

Classroom climate involves physical surroundings, as well as interpersonal arrangements and rapport (Westmeyer, 1988). Physical arrangements—the nature of the furniture and the way in which it is arranged—will influence both comfort and other factors such as communication patterns.

Reasonably comfortable chairs (though not too comfortable) with a writing surface for activities and note taking are preferred. A circular approach allows each person to have a direct sight line and individual communication with each group member. When set up in this manner, no one is isolated or denied his or her identity. This enables the religious educator to become part of the group, as opposed to being up front and separated from the others.

In regard to the relational climate, an effective model of young adult religious education calls for a setting that fosters interpersonal relationships and positive feelings. Joseph Lowman (1984) identifies the following teacher characteristics that contribute to a warm relational climate: 1) demonstrates a strong interest in students, 2) acknowledges student's feelings and encourages students to express their feelings, 3) encourages students to ask questions and express personal viewpoints, 4) communicates openly and subtly that each student's understanding of the material is important, and 5) encourages students to be creative and independent in dealing with the material and to formulate their own views (p. 17). Westmeyer (1988) suggests that such a model calls for a setting of mutual respect and collaboration.

Climate Setting in Individual Learning

The relational climate in the individualized learning situation should be as open and friendly as possible. One-on-one situations are ideal for getting to know each other in a personal way. Relaxed and friendly settings such as the kitchen table or coffee shop are ideal.

The religious educator's deployment of effective interpersonal skills and questioning techniques is helpful in establishing both contact with the learner and a deeper understanding of the individual. It is important that the religious educator begins with personal but nonthreatening issues first, and then moves to the content related issues.

After introductions have been completed, some attempt should be made to review the purpose which brought the learner and the religious educator together. The desired content for the learning may require clarification first, followed by the process itself.

Learners often need assurance that the learning process will be successful for them. Young adults will value a recognition of their interests and their concerns at this early stage.

Climate Setting in Group Learning

A climate setting exercise which allows people to have their identity established within the group context is the best approach to take. Young adult learners can be identified to each other on a one-to-one basis, or within the group verbally and visually, and with respect to relevant aspects of their personalities.

There are three options which need to be considered in the introduction process of the climate setting exercise. The first option involves the decision to have the person introduce themselves verbally or through another medium involving symbolic representation in print or picture. Verbal introductions are the easiest to accomplish, but are more effective when combined with some form of print or symbols.

Most young adults have experienced the opportunity to introduce themselves briefly to other members of a small group or religious education class. The length and quality of the introductions vary. Some participants feel uncomfortable about the process while others love the stage. The decision to have individual introductions in a group setting should depend upon the size of the group and the comfort level which individual learners will require to help make it a positive experience. Time will also be a factor.

Another option is to have members meet first in pairs, and then follow up with the introductions of their respective partners. This can be very effective, particularly if the partner makes short written notes on a card. This avoids the tendency to include too many thoughts. We also feel less self conscious about the introduction of another person when we simply relay information.

Print is also an effective form of making introductions. It is quick and simple, and the focus of thought is on the content of the information to be shared. Once information is in print on a card or small piece of paper, it can be shared quickly and easily with other participants. The leader of the young adult group can retain the information for future reference. It is important to remember, however, that print literacy is an issue in a society where there are numerous illiterates. The religious educator who works in a context where there are young adults with low levels of literacy should avoid the use of procedures which rely on print or written communications.

Symbolic representation may be used with virtually everyone, if it is stressed that *simple* symbols are to be used. The religious educator might remind the young adult participants that one does not have to draw well, then introduce him or herself with simple symbols. Participants might use stick figures for people and the easiest symbols they can think of for other items. Objects for leisure activities such as a baseball bat, tennis racket, or basketball are all quick to draw in simple form. These symbols are placed on any reasonable sized piece of paper or a 5" by 7" index card for easy sharing and storage. See Figure 1 as an illustration of this symbolic form.

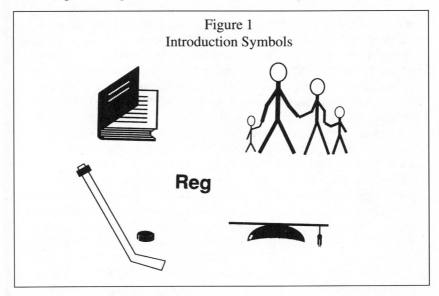

Figure 1
Introduction Symbols

An important fact to remember about symbolic representation is that it will require some form of explanation so that group members will understand the full meaning of the symbols. For example, a tennis racket needs to be interpreted as to the nature and level of participation. It will be important to provide the participant with an opportunity to comment upon the symbols they have drawn.

The level of comfort at the interpersonal level needs to be translated into comfort with the content and process of the chosen procedure. Young adult learners need to be assured that the learning they have come to expect will emerge from the process. Discussions of the content of the course will allow the religious educator to understand any special needs of the young adult learners, and they will provide clues for any special illustrations which may be needed to clarify the theories or principles. The learners will feel that their interests are being considered when the religious educator indicates the point in the process where certain items the learners have mentioned will be included in the religious education process.

If there are to be new experiences in the learning process, this might be a good time to assist the learners in preparation for these experiences. Sharing the positive features of a proposed activity and indicating how it fits into their learning may be a major benefit to the learners.

Following is an outline of proposed procedures for interpersonal climate setting in a group:

1. Before learners arrive, insure that the physical setting is such that it will be supportive of interpersonal rapport. This includes the physical surroundings and structure of chairs and possibly tables. Some prefer a circle of movable, comfortable chairs where all participants can see each other as well as the teacher, and whereby chairs may be moved easily into diads or triads (groups of two or three). A preference of others is to meet around a conference table, so that legs and feet are not exposed to other group members (Westmeyer, 1988).

2. Greet participants as they enter the room to insure that no discomfort arises during the opening minutes. Refreshments are helpful in creating a warm and friendly relational climate. As people enter, they may be met and introduced to others by a designated greeter.

3. Give participants a friendly invitation to take their seats. Local expectations and circumstances should dictate whether the leader or teacher starts exactly on time or waits for a few moments.

4. A personal introduction by the religious educator may assist the group in thinking of what they might say in their introductions. Humor is often used to help the young adult learners relax and see the leader in a positive light, but the important factor in the use of humor is its appropriateness.

5. After the religious educator's introductory remarks, give the young adult group members the opportunity to consider what they will share about their personal identity with other members of the group. Distribute 5" by 7" cards to all members of the group and then provide some time for reflection and

writing or drawing, to allow them to communicate appropriate items about themselves.

6. Ask members to write their names at the top of the card. Have them underline the name by which they are normally addressed by friends.

7. Participants should then write five things about themselves which will help identify them to others. They might indicate that they save stamps or enjoy watching a particular television program (see figure 2).

8. Ask the group members to identify another person in the group whom they do not know or, in the case of the group which has some prior contact, with whom they are the least familiar.

9. Ask members to approach the person identified (see number 8) and exchange cards. They should spend approximately two and one half minutes talking with the other person about the card contents. Allow up to three minutes if they are to introduce each other to the group, because clarification of certain items may be necessary. It is important that the introductions be appropriate and the introducers feel comfortable.

Figure 2
Introduction Card

Reg Wickett
University professor
Husband and father
I live in a three generation household
I enjoy reading mystery novels
I am active in "old timer" sports

The next step is to insure proper climate setting concerning the content and process of the course. Young adult learners wish to know that the content of the religious education class will be appropriate for their needs and interests. Give both the young adult religious educator and the learners time to share their views on the proposed content. The leader or teacher can share an overview of the proposed content from his or her perspective, as well as from the institutional perspective. The latter perspective is important because pre-course advertising by the institution may have led learners to choose the class for particular reasons.

The learner's perspective is shared because the young adult religious educator will need to confirm individual interests. The leader will need to be able to show the connections between the proposed content and the learner's interests, and to use the information in preparation for the sessions. This latter point is important. Special references to learners' interests, when made at the appropriate moment during sessions, will enable the learners to develop a deeper level of understanding of the content.

It would be helpful to have learners share comments on their reasons for participating in this class, as well as lists of objectives or what they hope to gain from the sessions. They could share these either verbally or in written form. One way of doing this is to have learners record their objectives on newsprint sheets in large print, and then tape these sheets about the room. Learners can review the sheets together and make comments or ask questions. The religious educator may comment on these items, perhaps indicating when certain items will be covered.

The following procedures may assist this process and should take place before any further discussion of content:

1. Provide each learner with a sheet of newsprint, a large felt-tipped pen, and pieces of adhesive material to attach the newsprint to the wall.
2. Ask each learner to work independently, indicating on the newsprint in large letters the specific items they wish to learn.
3. Give learners sufficient time to perform this task. Suggest that they take a few moments to consider what they would like to write, then proceed.
4. When finished, have each participant to attach the newsprint at eye level on the walls of the meeting room.
5. Indicate that they are to examine the other sheets of newsprint as people finish the process. Allow sufficient time for all to review the sheets.
6. Lead a discussion which highlights the similarities, when materials will be covered, as well as special interests. Allude to resource materials at this time as well.
7. Tape the sheets to the walls and leave them there throughout the duration of the class, as a reminder of the needs of the group members.

The religious educator cannot give too much emphasis to the importance of conducting both aspects (content and process) of climate setting. The group will function well or poorly based upon much that occurs at this time in the religious education process.

Climate Setting in Distance Religious Education

Climate setting for distance religious education with young adults is equally important. Although there will be young adults who will not feel the need to be in contact with the religious educator, there will be those who will require interaction. An early personal contact will encourage future contacts which normally do not occur in this type of religious education unless stimulated. Contact may occur with an individual situated at the central location, or with a local contact person.

Distance religious education situations may include a group meeting prior to the beginning of the actual learning activities. Stress must be placed upon openness to future contacts and accessibility through an easy system of contact. Telephone numbers where the learner can reach the religious educator with some regularity, as well as a good system for taking messages will enhance the distance religious education process.

Should the religious educator find it necessary to contact participants by telephone prior to the course, he or she should make the initial conversation as positive and friendly as possible. One creates an impression with only the sound of the voice and the content which it conveys.

The following suggestions will assist the religious educator in the initial telephone contact:

1. Make certain the time of the conversation is convenient for the young adult learner and will occur without undue distractions.
2. Make personal introductions in a friendly manner, but also make clear the institutional relationship to the learner.
3. Indicate a desire to learn about the learner's course involvement with respect to convenient periods for course work as possible future telephone contacts.
4. Answer any preliminary questions about the course content, materials, and process.
5. Indicate clearly the process whereby the learner will be able to make contact and the telephone number or numbers which can be used to do so. Make it clear that appropriate contact is welcome, and suggest the best times for such activity.

Procedures For Teaching Young Adults

This section of the chapter discusses individual, group, and distance religious education methods and techniques. Each method or technique is selected for its consistency with the developmental tasks of identity seeking, intimacy, and independence.

We can enhance the exploration of identity in young adulthood through an educational process which respects and incorporates the young adult's life experiences into the learning situation. Methods and techniques which incorporate the young adult learner's prior experiences will help validate that experience in the mind of the learner.

Cooperative methods and techniques will promote interpersonal relationships and skills among group participants (Meyers & Jones, 1993). The ability to relate effectively with others will enhance the learner's normal attempts to establish forms of intimacy in other life situations.

Activities which promote autonomy and respect the learner's right to make decisions in the learning process are of value in promoting a sense of independence. Although relationships are important, they should not promote inappropriate dependence on others.

Methods and Techniques for Individual Learning

Individual learning has already been defined as that which occurs when a young adult works through a course of study alone, or under the supervision from the religious educator. This section will make a distinction between independent learning and one-to-one learning. In addition, the learning contract, a technique that is helpful for both types of individual learning, will be discussed.

Independent learning. The independent learner has the lowest level of involvement with the religious educator. Most independent learners interact primarily with resources which are nonhuman in nature—printed materials, videos, films, workbooks, and so forth. Others may relate to the religious educator at certain times during the process. This interaction would enhance their learning but not reduce their feeling of independence. The religious educator should be accessible and available to the young adult independent learner, but assistance must be nondirective and unobtrusive (Wickett, 1991).

The religious educator plays a threefold role in assisting the independent learner. The first is to make available necessary resources to the learner. The second is to insure the learner can utilize the resource base. The third is to be available to the learner in the case that the young adult desires interaction or contact (Wickett, 1991).

One-to-one learning. One-to-one learning differs from independent learning primarily in the level of involvement of the religious educator. Whereas the independent learner prefers to work alone, this method assumes a relationship between the learner and the religious educator. However the responsibilty and control for learning are still placed in the hands of the young adult learner. This method, therefore, should not be used in situations where the learner demands a considerable amount of attention or direction (Wickett, 1991).

The following steps summarize the procedures involved in one-to-one learning:

1. Build a relationship which includes an indication of acceptance and support.
2. Use good questioning techniques and listen to the answers.
3. Organize meetings at appropriate and mutually agreeable times.
4. Have resource materials available at meetings based on the answers to your questions.
5. Be prepared to get more involved, if the learner so desires.

6. Help the learner to bring the relationship to an appropriate closure.
7. Indicate future resources and information to assist continued learning as requested by the learner (Wickett, 1991, p. 96).

For more information on this approach, read Wickett's (1991) chapter "The Learner-Centered Model" in *Models of Adult Religious Education Practice*, and Knowles (1975) book *Self-directed Learning*.

Learning contracts. A very effective procedure to use in an independent learning situation is the learning contract or covenant. A contract, Knowles (1975) reminds us, is a binding agreement between two or more parties or persons. It is increasingly popular for teachers to make such covenants with students for course work and grades. In self-directed learning, however, one might contract with herself or with a religious educator. The contract will specify how the young adult learner will go about accomplishing the task and how she will know when she has arrived.

A simple, yet effective way of writing up a learning contract is adapted from Knowles (1975). The learner, in consultation with the religious educator, draws three columns on a sheet of paper. The three columns should include in order: 1) the learners learning objectives, 2) learning resources and strategies, and 3) criteria and means of validating evidence. Figure 3, taken from Wickett (1991, pp. 104-105) provides of an example of a possible draft.

The following outline provides procedures for the religious educator in developing the learning contract:

1. Ask the learner to review material related to the learning contract. Three recommended sources are Wickett's (1991) *Models of Adult Religious Education Practice* (chapter 13), Knowles' (1975) *Self-direct Learning* (pp. 26-28), and Knowles' (1986) *Using Learning Contracts: Practical Approaches to Individualizing and Structuring Learning*.
2. Have the learner consider his or her specific area of interest.
3. Provide a short explanation and clarification of the learner contract technique.
4. Ask the young adult learner to identify his or her particular interest, and discuss this for deeper understanding by both the young adult religious educator and learner.
5. Have the learner begin work on a draft of a written contract.
6. Review the draft with the learner, paying close attention to issues such as clarity, feasibility, and accessibility of resources. The covenant should include resources and process.
7. Make sure the learner leaves the second session with clear insight into what should be done to prepare a final written contract.
8. Review and approve the document in the third session. Make arrange-

Figure 3
Learning Contract

Learning Project: Developing Skills for Lay Ministry   Duration: 4 months

Learning Objectives	Learning Resources and Strategies	Criteria and means of Validating Evidence
1. To develop skills in conducting church-related visits to elderly and infirm people.	Organize a biweekly roster of people to be visited who are hospitalized, bed-ridden, or in nursing homes.	Invite a supervisor to attend at least three visits and to rate me on my ability to a)communicate b) show concerns.
2. To enhance my understanding of types of care offered by the church	a) Participate twice a month at centers which distribute free food and and clothing b) Organize a social event each month to welcome newcomers. c) Attend self-help groups sponsored by the church at least once a week.	Write a comprehensive description of services offered by the church. Discuss these services in light of the needs of those in the church community.
3. To develop skills as a facilitator at educational events	Conduct and observe education activities such as Bible studies, Sunday school, teacher training classes.	At the end of at least three teaching sessions have participants rate the effectiveness of my teaching methods and behavior.
4. To increase my ability to conduct worship events.	a) Read information on the music and traditions of worship. b) Participate in contemporary forms of worship.	Plan and conduct worship services bimonthly employing a variety of worship styles.
5. To gain skill in conducting the administrative function of the church.	a) Be present at and assist in a goal-setting workshop. b) Assist in preparing the financial budget for the next fiscal year.	Request a supervisor to observe and comment on work done in the administration of church duties.

ments at this time for the monitoring of the contract.

9. Continue to provide support for the learner until the final session, when the learner brings closure to the experience through self evaluation and response from you, the religious educator.

Methods and Techniques for Group Learning

There are a number of instructional procedures which promote a sense of group involvement while allowing the young adult learner to express his or her individual concerns for learning.

The tip of the iceberg. The "Tip of the Iceberg" refers to the amount of learning which occurs in young adult religious education classes in comparison to the larger base of the iceberg, which symbolizes learning that takes place outside of the context of the classroom. The procedure, developed and practiced by Allen Tough in the Department of Adult Education at the Ontario Institute for Studies in Education (see Herman, 1980), is described more extensively by Wickett (1991) in *Models of Religious Education Practice* (Chapter 14).

The procedure "is based upon a group situation where there is some flexibility in the overall content to be learned. It is possible to have a common element of content for all students in the group situation while also encouraging each student to pursue those individual interests which are related to the general content area outside of the classroom" (Wickett, 1991, p. 112). The time spent outside the group will be much more significant in terms of overall learning for most of the young adult learners. The learning in the class or group is seen by the religious educator, but is only "the tip of the iceberg." The greater part of the learning takes place outside the class in informal discussion, while reflecting or reading, and so forth, is below the waterline and generally unseen (Wickett, 1991).

The specific procedures for working with young adults in this method are as follows:

1. Encourage learners to examine and work in areas of personal interest.
2. Suggest readings and activities based upon feedback concerning areas of interest identified by group learners.
3. Encourage individual learners to continue their efforts in particular areas of study outside of class.
4. Provide an opportunity at each session for group members to identify resources and findings which may be of interest to other participants. Increasing awareness through continuous interaction in group sessions will promote understanding of the needs and interests of other learners. Positive reinforcement of any attempts to assist other learners will result in more openness to such possibilities.

Learning contracts for group learning. Learning contracts can be used in group learning settings as well as in individualized situations. The emphasis here is on personal learning with any benefits of group cooperation almost coincidental. "Learners should not be forced to adapt to the group's interest in any way. Rather, the group should provide the atmosphere within which the individual will continue to pursue a covenant based upon individual needs and interests" (Wickett, 1991, p. 108).

The religious educator might employ the following steps along with the procedures previously described in relation to individual contracts.

1. Organize all young adult learners into learning partnerships during the initial group meeting. Have group members identify their specific or shared areas of interest.
2. Involve all learners in a deeper discussion of their particular areas of interest through learning partnerships.
3. Encourage all learners to share information questions, and concerns with their partners, between group sessions.
4. Request learners to share their draft learning covenants with their partners during the second session. This discussion should involve constructive feedback and support.
5. Encourage participants to contact their partners in regards to any concerns they might have as they prepare the final contract document.
6. Involve the learning partners in the process of examining and responding to the final draft of the covenant.
7. Arrange for the learning partners to attend sessions together where the religious educator and the learners can maintain contact for the purpose of solving any problems which may occur, as well as continuing interaction.
8. Arrange for learning partners to present the results of their covenant learning in a predetermined sequence during the final sessions.

The study circle. The study circle method will be most appropriate for young adult religious education situations where a sense of group cohesion is important (Wickett, 1991). Still both the learner's individuality and rights must be affirmed in this procedure to be consistent with the guiding principle of identity formation. The rights of the individual to comment and to participate in the decision-making process of the group are paramount to the success and effectiveness of the method.

Study circles have no teachers, students, nor externally determined curriculum. They are composed of young adult members and a religious educator whose task is related more to the process than to the content or resources of learning. The physical arrangement for this method is, as suggested in the name, a circle—a seating formation in which no individual, including the facilitator, has prominence over any other. Study circles work best when comprised of five to twenty members with a trained facilitator or leader (Wickett, 1991).

The following points taken from Wickett (1991) outline the basic process of this method:

1. Advance information is shared with all potential participants. All members of the community must receive it.

2. The formation of the study circle occurs in the initial meeting as people become aware of its purpose and methods.

3. Participants share ideas and interest within the general context of the circle's purpose.

4. Discussions occur to enable clarification of ideas and interests and the role which the study circle can play for the group and its members.

5. The group determines its plan of action by democratic decision making. The facilitator is an equal member.

6. The resources and data are gathered and shared within the group.

7. Plans can be changed and developed through mutual agreement in a democratic fashion.

8. The group evaluates its own process of learning (pp. 130-131).

Methods and Techniques for Distance Education

When preparing for distance religious education courses, the religious educator should be flexible and adaptable with the scheduling of resources (such as print materials, video and audio based media) and activities (written or other assignments). Too much external control will take away from the learner's sense of personal independence.

Personal contact between the learner and religious educator should foster a sense of independence on behalf of the learner, as well as participation in any decision making. Telephone contact may be the only vehicle for this form of communication, although some systems for distance education, such as the British Open University, do use occasional interpersonal contact (Perry, 1976). Personal contact should be utilized as much as is necessary.

It is important that assignments not simply require redescription of textual or other material. Rather, the religious educator should emphasize integration with the learner's existing knowledge. Questions should provide the opportunity to reflect upon personal experience, and to assimilate or integrate new information.

An example of integration might involve a question such as the following, which would be part of a written assignment in a correspondence section of a distance religious education course.

Assignment:
Consider the implications of the biblical story of the Good Samaritan for your personal life. Describe a personal experience in which you have been involved directly or an event which you observed directly or indirectly through the media, and then describe the appropriate ways in which people should have acted under the circumstances.

This form of question enables the young adult learner to relate to the relevant portions of the bible story through a life experience of more recent origins. The choice of event an its retelling will contribute to an understanding of the meaning.

In implementing distance religious education, the religious educator should employ the following procedures:

1. All facilitators and teachers should be well-trained in order to maximize the effectiveness of the implementation phase.
2. Learners should be provided with an orientation to this approach to learning.
3. Learners should be provided with an accessible and approachable contact person who will guide and support them while in the system.
4. In-person sessions should occur at early stages to give people the confidence and support needed to proceed.
5. Materials on content and for support activities should be provided on a regular basis with the intention of keeping the student active but not overloaded.
6. The learner should be assisted to withdraw from the process at the end of the learning or at any other time, if necessary (Wickett, 1991, p. 157).

Conclusion

Specific methods and techniques for young adult religious education should respect the elements of identity, independence, and intimacy in the learning experience, and in the working relationship which evolves between the religious educator and the young adult learner. These methods and techniques must enhance the sense of emerging self identity in the earliest stages of young adulthood. The sense of independence, which is a clear mark of the achievement of adulthood in our society should not be diminished during the learning process. Indeed it should be enhanced by the learning experience. A respect for the lives of learners beyond their interaction with religious educators, including their close relationships with others, will make the task of religious education more effective.

References

Erikson, E. (1968). *Identity, youth and crisis*. New York: Norton.

Erikson, E. (1980). *Identity and the life cycle*. New York: Norton.

Fowler, J.W. (1981). *Stages of faith: The psychology of human development and the quest for meaning*. New York: Harper & Row.

Gould, R.L. (1978). *Transformations: Growth and change in adult life*. New York: Simon & Schuster.

Herman, R. (Producer & director). (1980). *The tip of the iceberg*. [videotape] Toronto: Department of Adult Education, the Ontario Institute for Studies in Education, and Ryerson Polytechnic Institute.

Keegan, D. (1990). *Foundations of distance education* (2nd ed.). London: Routledge.

Knowles, M .S. (1975). *Self-directed learning: A guide for teachers and learners*. Chicago: Follett.

Knowles, M.S. (1986). *Using learning contracts: Practical approaches to individualizing and structuring learning*. San Francisco: Jossey-Bass.

Lee, J.M. (1973). *The flow of religious education*. Birmingham, AL: Religious Education Press.

Levinson, D.J., Darrow, C.M., Klein, E.B., Levinson, M.H., & McKee, B. (1978). *The seasons of a man's life*. New York: Knopf.

Lowman, J. (1984). *Mastering the techniques of teaching*. San Francisco: Jossey-Bass.

Merriam, S.B., & Ferro, T.R. (1986). Working with young adults. In N.T. Foltz (Ed). *Handbook of adult religious education* (pp. 59-82). Birmingham, AL: Religious Education Press.

Meyers, C., & Jones, T.B. (1993). *Promoting active learning*. San Francisco: Jossey-Bass.

Perry, W. (1976). *The open university: A personal account by the first vice-chancellor*. Milton Keynes, UK: Open University Press.

Tighe, J., & Szenthkeresti, K. (1986). *Rethinking adult religious education*. New York: Paulist.

Westmeyer, P. (1988). *Effective teaching in adult and higher education*. Springfield, IL: Charles Thomas.

Wickett, R.E.Y. (1991). *Models of adult religious education practice*. Birmingham, AL: Religious Education Press.

Part Four: Focused Religious Education For Young Adults

CHAPTER 9

Reaching Unchurched Young Adults Through Religious Education

FRED R. WILSON

Bill is in his first year of college. He's not sure what career direction he's going so he's taking courses in business, political science, and art to see if he likes one over the other. Bill has had several different part-time jobs and is debating whether he wants to live in the dorms or rent an apartment with several other fellows while finishing university. Bill used to attend Sunday School until his parents allowed him to stop going at around 12 years old.

Bill's older friend Toni has held a number of jobs including shoe salesman, delivering newspaper bundles, and waiting tables. He recently signed up for a hitch in the U.S. Army to get some job training. He has dated around but has no plans for marriage. He's not interested in "religion" right now.

John and Mary are another set of Bill's friends. John graduated from high school two years before Bill. John and Mary met at college. Dating led to marriage. They both dropped out of college to set up home and earn some money to continue their college studies. John is merely attending church to please Mary who is helping teach a toddler Sunday School class. She hopes to teach in an elementary school when she completes her education sometime in the future.

Sam and Lonie are another couple that Bill enjoys spending time with. They have been married almost seven years and have a son, Jimmy, who is 4 years old. Grandmother watches Jimmy while both parents work. Lonie is a manager in a computer services business and spends a lot of miles on the road while Sam works as a high school P.E. teacher. He and Bill thrive on playing a lot of basketball and tennis together. Sam invited Bill to attend a small Bible study group at Christmas break but Bill was not open to it.

Linda is also a friend of Bill. She helps out with the church youth group and is the mother of an 8 year old girl. Her first husband divorced her after nine years of marriage for another woman. She entered the church through a course offered for recent divorcees at the church. Linda is currently looking for a job in a store while attending college two evenings a week. She hopes to eventually buy her own ladies wear store to help put her daughter through her education. Mom and dad have invited her to live with them while she gets things together after the divorce.

Young Adults

While each of these individuals is unique, they are going through similar but diverse experiences related to autonomy, career, education, personal goals, marriage, and adjustment to new experiences. They have one common characteristic: each is called a "young adult" in our society because they fall into the 18 to 35 year age range.

These and other young adults are facing a number of developmental issues and events based on their age and past life experiences. However, young adults have also lived through similar and different events and trends as a group and in subgroups. This has produced several common generational trends in how they perceive the world and act in it. To reach unchurched young adults, it is wise to recognize these distinctive generational views toward life in general and the church in particular. We can no longer assume that young adults have the same experiences and values as older adults.

After examining the distinctive generational patterns of young adults, this chapter explores the relation of young adults to the church in terms of their prior religious experience. Since there are strong indications that young adults are beginning to return to the church, we will also review significant research findings on why young adults have returned to the church. This chapter will conclude with specific suggestions on how religious education may assist in reaching unchurched young adults.

Living before, during, or after a major historical event has a significant impact on how one tends to think and act as a person. There is a major difference in reading or watching a TV program about the Vietnam War and living through or fighting in it. Because young adults born in the same years and decades share many similar events and express many common values, they tend to fall into one of several generational groups that can be clearly differentiated from other generations. Currently, at least four generational group identities have been identified: the Youth Market (born after 1977), Baby Busters (born between 1965 and 1976), Baby Boomers (born between 1946 and 1964), and the 50-Plus Market. Table 1 summarizes some of the basic characteristics of Baby Boomers and Baby Busters.

Table 1	
Characteristics of Baby Boomers and Baby Busters	
Baby Boomers	Baby Busters
Low loyalty	Sense of entitlement
High expectations	Lack of deferred gratification
Seek meaning	Prefer individualism
Weak relationships	Enjoy isolation
Tolerance for diversity	Postpone education, marriage,
Comfortable with change	children and working
Anti-establishment	Fast paced
Favor hands-on leadership	Unfocused
Media conscious	Undecided
Entrepreneurial	Indecisive
Focus on experiencing life more	Blurred sex roles
than possessions	Comfortable with contradictions
Favor fun over duty	New approach to humor
Favor candor over tact	
Favor professionalism/excellence	
Adapted from Anderson (1990), Miller (1992). Light (1988).	

The Baby Boomers and Baby Busters will be examined more closely as the two generation groups overlapping in the young adult age frame.

Baby Boomers

Baby Boomers are anywhere between 45 and 27 years old. They grew up as the first standardized generation, drawn together by the history around them, the images of television, and the crowding of their sheer numbers as children and adults (Light, 1988). They experienced the great financial expectations of the 1950s, the fears of Sputnik, the dawn of nuclear power, the hopes of the New Frontier of John F. Kennedy and Lyndon B. Johnson's Great Society. They experienced the disillusionment of three major assassinations, the Vietnam War, Watergate, resignation of a vice president and later of a president (Miller, 1992).

Baby Boomers grew up in homes with kitchens meeting standard building codes that came into being in the 1940s. They experienced the standardized curriculums and universal access to education of the 1950s. They share the standardized fear of bomb drills, and the war deaths of the 1960s in Vietnam. They share common ideas about tolerance and rejection of social and political traditions.

Boomers are different from their parents in values and basic orientation to life. Fifty percent of Boomers versus 32 percent of Boomer parents believe drug testing is an invasion of a person's privacy. Boomers are two times more likely than their parents to approve of living together without marriage (61 to 30 percent), are 25 percent more likely to approve of a woman calling a man for a date (84 to 59 percent), and are much more willing to take positions than parents on issues whether they know something or not (Washington Post/ABC News Poll reported in the Washington Post, May 27, 1986). Some believe this is due to Boomers having more education and self-confidence than their parents. Boomers also have less political party loyalty, have less use for terms such as liberal and conservative, and are more tolerant of social diversity. The above suggests that unchurched Boomers will have a variety of different opinions and values than the older generation making up many of the church's educational programs.

Current management literature characterizes the generation differences between Boomers and the 50-Plus Market as follows (Carson, 1986): Baby Boomer managers are seen to have no code of loyalty, no desire to demand loyalty from workers, have unusual optimism for the future, have an unquestioning faith in capitalism, are eager to take risks and willingly change companies, are more comfortable with numbers and are searching for autonomy and instant gratification. The 50-Plus Market are described as preoccupied with security, demanding of a pledge of loyalty from everyone, are perceived of as more cautious, resistant to change, comfortable in bureaucracies, more people oriented, and harder workers. The above suggests that religious education leaders should be prepared to work with a variety of expectations in the leadership styles of those who help to develop programs for unchurched young adults. Also, they will have a history of criticizing the "establishment." They will be much more participative and democratic in their management style. They will oppose unilateral decisions and are more process oriented. They are attuned to the ongoing need of change and are more entrepreneurial in their approach to decision making.

Light (1988) argues that there were three major distinctive crises that imprinted Boomer values. First, Boomers reacted more intently to the major political events of the 1950s and 60s because they were younger and more impressionable than their parents. In a ten-year span they experienced the assassination of three major political figures, the implementation of the 1964 Civil Rights Act with over thirty-eight major marches with five to twenty million Boomers involved, the Cuban Missile Crisis, Vietnam, Watergate, OPEC

Oil embargoes. Light (p. 39) argues that these events tore away the remaining myths of innocence the generation possessed about war, warriors, and politics. Older Boomers lost interest in politics due to disillusionment based on the failure of the dream that they grew up with during the 1950s as the U.S. having the best form of government. Younger Baby Boomers started life with no illusions at all.

Second, a social revolution has occurred in the family of Baby Boomers with the result that there is a new definition of the family. For some it has become the collapse of the family through divorce and mothers entering the work force. Up to 1950 children were raised to obey strict social rules regarding family and work. Such rules as women don't work and husbands provide for the family were taught to ensure the system that husband and wife stayed together. However, these strong normative controls have been modified so that women made up 15 percent of the work force in 1950, 30 percent by 1960, and 50 percent in 1980. Divorce laws have been greatly modified so that up to 50 percent of Boomer marriages are now expected to end in divorce. This suggests that unchurched Baby Boomers will have a need for strong relational type activities that revolve around establishing small groups that promote positive family values, fellowship, and support.

Third, there has been a major economic crisis directly affecting Baby Boomers. The economy of the 1970s and 80s experienced three recessions, double digit inflation and unemployment, an increase of 20 percent in mortgage rates, price and wage freezes, two oil embargoes, and a 600 percent increase in the price of education. Between 1972 and 1987 inflation figures show the price of homes up 294 percent, average mortgage payments up 282 percent, Federal taxes up 175 percent, Social Security up 331 percent and state and local taxes up 520 percent with an increase of income of only 153 percent (Light, 1988, p. 44).

What are Baby Boomers' general attitudes toward life? In light of these three crisis? When asked to tell if they had accomplished what they had expected at their high school graduations, 1/3 said it was less, 1/3 better, and 1/3 about the same. When asked about finances, the same breakdown existed (Ehrenreich, 1986). In a Harris Poll, 75 percent felt they face more competition from others their same age for jobs, promotions, and a chance to get ahead. Thirty-six percent find themselves blocked by the older generation, 67 percent had to wait much longer than their parents to be able to buy a new house and 40 percent felt people who hold the power have kept Baby Boomers from the more important roles in politics and governing (Ehrenreich, 1986). A Roper Poll (American Demographics, 1987) found 50 percent of Boomers believing the American Dream was slipping away from them.

The above findings suggest that unchurched Baby Boomers will have high expectations for religious education programs if they attend. They will also tend to respond well to high expectations being placed on them. At the same time, their low loyalty suggests that they will be very open to exploring alternative programs until they find a religious education program that meets their needs and expectations. They will also tend to be highly suspicious of institutions, their labels and their programs, but more likely to trust a creditable and trustworthy person.

Differences Between Baby Boomers

With almost two decades between the first and last Baby Boomers, they have been arbitrarily divided into Front End and Back End Baby Boomers to distinguish unique aspects of this generational group. The Front Enders, or Old Wave, were born between 1946 and 1954. They are at different points in the life cycle and have different social and political history than the Back End or New Wave Boomers who were born between 1955 and 1964 (Light, 1988).

Front Enders remember atomic bomb drills, freedom marches during the Vietnam War, John F. Kennedy's assassination, are more likely to have children and high mortgages, and are likely in their second or third marriages. They have received the lion's share of economic and social benefits and have considerably more experience with politics and society.

New Wavers, on the other hand, are starting and testing their first careers, are early in their marriages, and remember MIA bracelets, Earth Day, Robert Kennedy's assassination, and some still live at home. They are 12 percent less likely to watch network news every day, 10 percent less likely to be interested in the elections, less likely to know congressional candidates, and less confident about their ability to influence the political system. Over 65 percent say they don't vote if they do not care about the election outcome. They disapproved more of Ronald Reagan and George Bush's handling of the job as president and are less likely to support their foreign policy and economics.

Front Enders still support Lyndon B. Johnson's concept of a Great Society. Forty-seven percent believe his programs improved society while only 14 percent of Back Enders believe it made things better and 41 percent say it made no difference. Front Enders have higher incomes, lower mortgage rates, lower personal debt, are further along the career ladder and have higher earnings (CBS News/New York Times Poll, January 1986).

Perhaps the most telling differences relate to how each was parented and the resulting effects it had on their perspectives toward life (Wares & Crandall, 1964). Front End Boomers tended to experience the stress of being first born in the birth order. They received more prolific babying and were offered more help as children whether needed or not by their mothers. They tended to be sheltered from potential psychological and physical frustrations and dangers. Mothers gave them more open affection, used approval more than punishment, and gave children more freedom than mothers in the 1940s. This sense of nurturing and freedom provided a sense of protected individualism so that Front End Boomers explored the limits of life without fear (Wares & Crandall, 1964). In addition, 80 percent made it through childhood without experiencing their parents' divorce or at least not until they were older adolescents (Hofferth, 1985). They entered college to explore a philosophy of life.

On the other hand, Back End Boomers experienced dwindling attention from their parents, schools, and economy. Parents adopted a different child rearing philosophy in light of the spreading fear of delinquency. Benjamin Spock revised his baby book in 1957 from a stricter philosophy of discipline and less spoiling of the child. Mothers showed less direct affection and approval, imposed even fewer restrictions on their children, and were more ambivalent in placing limits on behavior because more of them returned to the work force (Wares & Crandall, 1964). Fifty percent of Back End Boomers experienced divorce, and by age three 10 percent had experienced divorce (Hofferth, 1985). Back End Boomers are more interested in getting through the day, have fewer illusions about divorce, lack of care, the unsheltered, and the world as an uncertain place. They are more afraid of nuclear war and have experienced less material success than Front End Boomers.

Back End Boomers, according to the comparison of high school seniors polls in 1960 versus 1980, are more interested in making money than Front Enders who wanted to develop a philosophy of life. Making money took top priority and increased by 30 percent for Back Enders (Light, 1986). Developing a philosophy or meaning for life had decreased down to 4 percent. Back Enders were also more liberal on gender and equality issues than Front Enders (Klein, 1985).

Reaching Back End Baby Boomers through religious education will mean making efforts to build relationships and being sensitive to needs and hurts, due to the great numbers who have experienced divorce in their past. They will not necessarily be drawn to religious education programs focusing on the meaning of life but on living life. As they establish their first adult life structures they will be the young adults most likely to seek new congregational involvement. They will provide the fertile ground for religious education to serve since they are so open to experiencing something worthwhile in the spiritual realm.

Baby Busters

Baby Busters were born after 1964 and make up the second major generational grouping that fits under the rubric of young adults at the end of the twentieth century. These young adults have been raised in smaller families, attended smaller schools and studied in smaller classes, and have often experienced closure or consolidation of schools or classes due to the decrease in students. They had older teachers, experienced less competition, and found it easier to make sports teams, win scholarships, get accepted to college, and get a job. While it may be too early to characterize a generation that is in its mid-twenties, Baby Busters have broken the Baby Boomer mold. Howe and Strauss (1992) write: "Today's teens and twentysomethings present to Boomer eyes a splintered image of brassy looks and smooth manner, of kids growing up too tough to be cute, of kids more comfortable shopping or playing than working or studying. Ads target them as beasts of pleasure and pain who have trouble understanding words longer than one syllable, sentences longer than three words. Pop music on their Top 40 stations—heavy metal, alternative rock, rap—strikes many a Boomer ear as a rock-and-roll end game of harsh sounds, goin'-nowhere melodies, and clumsy poetry. News clips document a young-adult wasteland of academic nonperformance, political apathy, suicide pacts, date-rape trials, wilding, and hate crimes" (p. 75).

Baby Busters have had different experiences than Boomers. Busters have not had to fight as hard for women's rights. They do not have the fears associated with the Cold War, nuclear attacks, or Vietnam. They have a strong sense of entitlement that grows out of their experience of two wage earners in the home who desired to give their children the best of everything. They are not prepared for the shock of real life because of their general protection from hostility. The competitiveness of Baby Boomers is a surprise to them.

In addition, the have experienced a general sense of instant gratification. They have had so many needs met so quickly that they live for now without worry for tomorrow. They have missed the hand-me-downs of larger Boomer families and have learned to live on plastic money. Their dreams have tended to be met on demand (Littwin, 1986).

Baby Busters have experienced life primarily as individuals in isolation from others. Whether it be CD player, cassette player or radio, they have enjoyed the private world made possible by headphones. Many of them have been children of divorce and experienced unstable family relationships, single and blended parents. Because of mobility, they have lacked family to turn to for help in crisis experiences. This suggests that unchurched Baby Busters will have a need for strong relational type activities that revolve around establishing small groups that promote positive values, fellowship, and support.

In addition, they have lived through a period when the general culture has emphasized the devaluation of children (Littwin, 1986). Children are now seen as financial and social liabilities. Cases of child abuse, whether sexual, physical, or psychological are only now coming to light in unprecedented numbers. Parents are anxious for them to leave home and often expect them to fend for themselves. The Baby Busters have little concern for others and seem totally self-absorbed to onlookers. They are the embodiment of the narcissism of the age with a self-understanding that they are important, value high self-esteem, and are the fulfillment of their parent's dreams.

Baby Busters are often called the "postponed generation" because they graduate from college later, decide to marry later and have children later than Boomers (Littwin, 1986). Perhaps a part of the reason is that they have had too many choices and feel immobilized by the options before them. Perhaps the experiences of a parents failed marriage has encouraged them to delay until they are willing to take the risks involved. To eventually possess their material desires the have learned to depend on birth control and abortion. They have a much bleaker view of the future than Boomers. They believe the future will be much harder for them to get ahead than it was for their parents. They are very pessimistic about the fate of the United States and their generation. Howe and Strauss (1992) write: "They sense they're the clean-up crew, that their role in history will be sacrificial—that whatever comeuppance America has to face, they'll bear more than their share of the burden. It's a new twist, and not a happy one, on the American Dream" (p. 75).

More than ever, the transition between leaving home and entering the adult world is being delayed for Busters. This may be the result of the fast-pace and unfocused view they have of the world through television. They have few burning causes and have instant reporting of every major event around the globe. The sheer speed and amount of information has exposed them vicariously to more of life than past generations experienced in a lifetime. No wonder they seem so undecided and indecisive. They tend to float from one school, one job, one relationship, one set of convictions to another. Perhaps they feel they need to try everything before they decide. To them nothing is permanent. Their options must be left open for whatever may come next. At least home is a "safe" place to stay until they decide to leave (Lasch, 1979).

The Baby Busters have blurred sex roles to the extent that some call them the first unisex generation (Anderson, 1990). Having been taught the equality of the sexes since birth, male and female have every career option open to then that was limited to one gender over an other in the past. Clothing has focused on jeans and sweatshirts. Dresses are the exception for females. Coed dorms at colleges is a norm. Some argue that the sexes have grown up so close together that they are more like friends than the mystery of the past. There is no such thing as date. They just do things together and take turns paying the bill. They understand sexual relationships but tend to lack a perspective on gender roles in marriage and the family.

In contrast to Baby Boomers, Baby Busters are more comfortable with contradictions in terms of dress, hair styles, and ear rings. They have a highly eclectic style of dress. What they have in common is that they are so unique from each other. They find no problem with holding contradictory beliefs, things, and feelings. They lack integration of the various aspects of their lives. Some would call it flexibility while others call it a lack of consistency. With so many Baby Boomers ahead of them, this may be their way to give themselves meaning as the generation in the shadows.

Howe and Strauss (1992) characterize Baby Busters as a group ready to emerge when they write, "Notice a counter-mood popping up in college towns, in big cities, on Fox and cable TV, and in various ethnic side currents. It is a tone of physical frenzy and spiritual numbness, a revelry of pop, a pursuit of high-tech, guiltless fun. It's a carnival culture featuring the tangible bottom lines of life—money, bodies, and brains—and the wordless deals with which one can be traded for another. A generation weaned on minimal expectations and gifted in the game of life is now avoiding meaning in a cumbersome society that, as they see it, offers them little" (p. 68).

As Baby Busters make the transition between school and work, moving from life with parents to life on their own, they can be reached through religious education approaches that allow for them to experiment with various views and ideology as well as through development of intense involvements with people. They are the least likely to attend church or synagogue regularly. They are most likely to be engaged in asking hard questions as well as participating in questionable, even illegal activities. Yet, they are the most open to change, have the lowest need for unchanging institutional structure, and most opposed to middle-class norms. They are the ones that change addresses most often according to the U.S. Census. According to recent research they are the coming wave that will test the church for their source of spiritual reality and hope. They are seeking for certainty, support, and a sense of belonging over against their loneliness and against Boomer rootlessness and self-seeking (Anderson, 1990).

Churched and Unchurched Young Adults

While unchurched young adults make up the majority of young adults between 18 and 35, there is by no means a commonality among them. They are different in terms of cultural backgrounds, are at different places in the life cycle, come in various shades of singleness and marital status, and have experienced a personally unique development.

In spite of so many differences, researchers report that there are few sharp distinctions in values between churched and unchurched young adults. In a

Gallup Poll 88 percent of the unchurched and 70 percent of churched young adults agreed a person can be a good Christian or Jew without attending church or the synagogue (Gribbon, 1990). When pushed further, nearly the same percent agreed that an individual should arrive at his/her religious beliefs independent of any church or synagogue assistance. A large majority of young adults appear to have a serious problem with the church and the religious education programs that are provided.

However, on any given weekend up to 40 percent of adults attend a house of worship and 60 percent claim to belong to a congregation. Barna (1991) found that 49 percent of 18 to 25 year olds and 62 percent of 26 to 44 year olds said that the word "religious" accurately describes them. Some 58 percent of Baby Busters and 67 percent of Back End Boomers strongly or somewhat agreed with the statement that "the Christian churches in your area are relevant to the way you live today" (Barna, 1991, p. 187). Gallup (1989) found that 34 percent of Boomers attend church and that 65 percent say they are church members. However, Patterson and Kim (1991) found that 58 percent of adults went to church regularly while growing up but less than 27 percent attend church now.

When religious education attendance was examined, 24 percent of churched Busters and 28 percent of churched Boomers said they regularly attend a Sunday School class (Barna, 1991, p. 264). Over 25 percent of churched Busters and 24 percent of churched Boomers say they regularly participate in a small group Bible study, fellowship group, or prayer group other than a Sunday School class (p. 266).

So, why do churched young adults attend? According to Barna (1991, pp. 259-60), when asked "What is the single, most important reason you attend church?", Baby Busters said, worship (35 percent), to study/learn about God (20 percent), and for personal growth/to become a better person (16 percent). Boomers answered in a similar fashion with 42 percent saying worship, 15 percent to study/learn about God, and 14 percent for personal growth. Gribbon (1990) reports that he found three major reasons why young adults attend church: a desire for spiritual refreshment, a need for fellowship or a sense of belonging, and a concern for their children or family. Because of the similar findings by these researchers, each of these ingredients should be part of the religious education programs for reaching unchurched young adults.

First, young adults who attend religious education activities may desire a sense of spiritual uplift, support, nourishment of faith, revitalization of their spirits, spiritual growth, and inspiration. Religious education programs for unchurched young adults will aim to meet these same spiritual needs but must initiate different forms that appeal to the unchurched and are held in neutral locations.

Second, young adults may attend religious education activities to experience quality relationships that affirm their uniqueness and support their spiritual belonging as a family, community, and fellowship. Some of these elements include unconditional acceptance, inclusiveness, leveling of status, mutual assistance, absence of competitiveness, bearing pain and crisis seriously, and loyalty to a transcendent God. Every church communicates its ethnic and social identity by its worship and music style, the language of its pastor, and the food that it shares. Young adults use these clues to select the church where they belong. While a sense of belonging may continue to attract a person long after the initial attraction to a program declines, religious education programs to reach unchurched young adults will focus on providing a sense of belonging that will be attractive to those who can identify with its participants.

Third, many young adults may attend church out of concern for their children and family (Hale, 1980). The young adult perceives the church as an institution supportive of the family by its preaching of moral values, worship of God, teaching of children, marital support programs, and activities for families. According to Gallup's poll having "a good family life" is very important to 80 percent of Americans while "being active in church or synagogue" is very important to only 40 percent (Gribbon, 1990). This suggests that the family situation will determine religious education participation. Because many couples come from different religious backgrounds or have disagreements about faith, this may be why a number of young adults do not attend.

While some young adults may attend religious education activities because of children, this initial motivation often loses influence unless they find something for themselves as well. While religious education programs may have focused on working with children and youth in hopes of drawing in the unchurched young adult parents, the children and youth are the ones that will most likely be the only ones affected. It was these early memories of church participation that assisted in drawing young adults back into the church (Gribbon, 1990).

Although the above research supports why young adults tend to participate in church, few unchurched young adults (12 percent) view church fellowship or worship as essential (Gallup, 1989). Most nonattendance seems to come from past negative church experiences, a lack of church experience or the lack of an internal motive to attend (Hoge, 1981). The next section examines why previously churched young adults are returning to the church.

Young Adults Who Are Returning to the Church

Gribbon (1990) found that unchurched young adults are returning to the church between 26 and 27 years of age over a three to four year period.

Many of those returning to the church have gone through a common cycle. Initially, many of them were involved in church as children. Often their parents brought them to church or sent them to religious education classes. A large number of those who were only sent and who had little to no home support of religious faith, returned years later to reexamine the church based on these memories. However, as many as 85 percent of the returning young adults had eventually dropped out of church between the ages of 13 and 23 with the most common age being 18. Eighteen was also the time of completing high school, leaving home, and entering the adult world.

These young adults report that they tended to drop out for three common reasons. First, many of the adult practices in church seemed boring. Church lacked any clear sense of meaning or importance in the things that were done. Second, many report that they seemed to outgrow their childhood beliefs. With their developing cognitive abilities, faith stories needed reinterpretation and application to their experience. Third, they left to explore life without any commitments to anything (see Hoge & Roozen, 1980; Hoge, 1981; and Hale, 1980 for past similarities).

Gribbon (1990) reports that many in his study of returning young adults were "developmental dropouts." By this he means parents stopped sending them to church, they moved away from home, or graduated from school, or started to focus on the opposite sex. On the average this period of noninvolvement lasted from two to eight years.

When young adults return around the age of 26 or 27, they return with a sense of tentativeness, exploring their options, and with a hint of wishfulness. Rather than returning out of a sense of commitment, they are checking out the option of church. Many of the returnees indicated that they had recently experienced a life transition or crisis event, but few of them connected either directly with why they returned. Involvement with the church came more as part of rethinking, restructuring or reorienting their lives. The most common events that preceded their return to church as young adults included moving to a new home, changing jobs, adding a volunteer activity to their schedules, experiencing a period of depression, birth of a child, moving to a new community, and new responsibilities at work. In a sense, these events have at least opened young adults to the possibility of reestablishing some link with the church.

While invitations to church activities had come in the past, many unchurched young adults report they turned them down until they found themselves in a time of readiness. During this time of readiness they report that at least one source encouraged them in their reentry. First, nonclergy witnesses to a vibrant faith attracted them to church. They were not so much attracted by their theological understanding but by their actions in repairing flat tires, helping with babysitting, and living a consistent life in the workplace or in the neighborhood. When they did discuss matters of faith they were attracted by their frankness, openness, and support in searching for personally owned faith commitments, not easy answers. The openness to accept an invitation to attend church often came from having a prior healthy friendship or respect for the person over a period of time (Hoge, 1981; Hale, 1980).

Second, ministers also served to facilitate the return of unchurched young adults to church. Often the young adult and minister would be similar in age, interests, and lifestyle. Thus, through visiting newcomers to town, or the area around a church, or meeting in community activities, the pastor became a gatekeeper until they attended church and built relationships with other churched young adults (Bast, n.d.). Gribbon (1990) reports that "liking the minister" is often given as a reason for joining with a congregation, even with groups that play down the role of the pastor.

Third, contact with a congregation drew unchurched young adults to become involved. Specifically, this includes five areas: the pastor, the church's atmosphere, relationships, invitations to help and programs. When they visit a church, the newcomer is looking at a number of factors. They are immediately attracted and affected by the words and style of the pastor. They judge the clergyperson on both personal and professional competence. Common characteristics include the ability to relate to people, level of education, confidence in self and others, ability to relate to everyday life, and friendliness of the spouse. In particular, the sermon was able to bridge easily between daily life and the spiritual realities of the bible (Hale, 1980).

Many of the unchurched young adults report making judgments about the atmosphere of the church starting from its external and internal conditions. This includes but is not limited to the attractiveness of signs and facility, maintenance conditions, style of worship, singing and preaching, and how people related to one another. Often they are looking for something familiar from their past experiences but with a new sense of spirituality, friendliness, and aliveness.

The friendliness of the people was not the primary reason for seeking a church for most unchurched young adults. However, friendliness often became the major attraction to stay with a congregation. They were drawn into church involvement through being greeted by name, knowing other people, feeling welcomed, and a sense of fitting into the group (Hoge, 1981).

Many of the unchurched young adults reported that the next step in being drawn into the church was an invitation to assist in the church's programs. By being asked personally to do something they felt welcomed, known, valued, and wanted by the church. Gribbon (1990) reports that young adults also appreciated being allowed to say no to tasks. It showed that people could be themselves, do what they wanted to, and not what someone expected them to do.

For some young adults specific programs were a strategic influence on their involvement with a church. Some of the entry programs included quality choirs for adults or children, the reputation of a church day school for their children, Sunday School, and preschool programs for their children. While parents tended to think of their children and attend religious education programs out of a sense of obligation, they became interested and committed as they learned from their studies. These programs gave them opportunity to rub shoulders and make friends with other persons of faith (Hershey, 1986).

While the above influences can be very positive, each of them may also serve as a barrier for reaching unchurched young adults. Table 2 presents some of the common barriers to reaching unchurched young adults. Some are put off by negative experiences such as the church being larger or smaller than their past experience, the different type of traditions that make up a service, poor maintenance conditions in the church, strange worship patterns, or the lack of friendliness of the people. Some have been put off by the large financial problems of a congregation, the focus on the church as a business or political organization, resentments of people toward them, lack of communication, difficulty in being accepted as a woman, older members unsupportive of their needs, changes to worship and infighting among church members, and/or staff (Miller, 1992).

Table 2	
Common Barriers to Reaching Unchurched Young Adults	
Anderson (1990)	Winfield (1989)
Focus on institution rather than purpose	Pastors not trained to run a
Socially self-perpetuating:	business
Exclusiveness of race, social status	Lack of capable trained
Minority rules not majority	lay leaders
Yesterday's innovator blocking change	Misplaced allocation of funds
Not inclined to take risks	Lack of lay accountability
Higher value on stability than innovation	Lack of targeting an audience
Protection of capital	Schisms between groups
Unwilling to suffer change	Cumbersome administrative
Unwilling to change personnel	procedures
Allowing tradition to rule	Scarcity of goals & benchmarks
Traditional worship	Ineffective communication

Some have been hindered by the pastor's boring sermon, lack of ability to administer the church, or inept pastoral care. More often they complain about the worship service being different from what they expected or that it has deteriorated and become uninspiring. At times they feel unwelcomed by the pastor, or don't fit into the congregation, or that the church is too family oriented or has inadequate children's programs (Miller, 1992).

Young adults have their own personal barriers to face as well. Those with young children and infants in particular are less likely to attend. Some couples have conflicting expectations and past experiences that keep them uninvolved. Some need space to handle their personal rebellion, doubts, fears, and frustrations. Some have conflicting work schedules. Some of these barriers can be overcome by a congregation's religious education program that provides excellent child care during services and programs and make it easy to attend. Other barriers require responses that will be more difficult and costly in time and reactions if they are to support a variety of lifestyles, be flexible in their scheduling, and affirming of those who are searching (Miller, 1992).

Insights from Research for Reaching Unchurched Young Adults

From Gribbon's (1990, p. 60) research we know several things about reaching unchurched young adults. First, "returnees and seekers affiliate with congregations in their twenties, in the course of building a first adult life structure." During this time period they are strongly influenced by their childhood images of what makes one an adult and by opinions about how life should be lived. His research shows that very few unchurched young adults have a conscious sense of guilt, duty, or the expectation that "I ought to go" as reasons for attending church.

However, Gribbon (1990, p. 60) found that many unchurched young adults "indicated that churchgoing was a normal, expected part of adult life, especially when they were ready." While this sounds encouraging it also raises a warning. Although they are committed to not making the same mistakes of earlier generations, they will most likely be more critical of churches when they fail to do things "right." This suggests that unchurched young adults between the ages of 26 to 30 will actively seek out religious education programs that will assist them in the rebuilding of their life structure which is now open to examining where spiritual values fit into life.

Second, from Gribbon's study (1990) we know that very few seekers turned to the church or a pastor when they were in a transition period or facing a personal crisis. In fact, it was not until several months later that they began attending church as part of rebuilding their life structure. However, when an unchurched young adult married a churchgoer, this was a major factor leading to church involvement. Unfortunately, the research shows that neither premarital counseling, child dedications or baptisms, nor specific religious educational programs related to life transition events have any significant influence on their church involvement.

While this finding may be discouraging, it reminds us of the difficulty of the task. There are so many types of transitions in young adult lives that no pastor or church or program could possibly be an expert in dealing with every issue. We are limited by church size, the number of lay leaders, and other resources. Positively, this suggests that a church seeking to reach unchurched young adults must selectively choose an area on which to focus its religious education energy. For example, "In one congregation a guild of young mothers visits parents when a child is born, provides a support group for mothers, and manages the church nursery. In another congregation lay persons conduct periodic spiritual journey retreats with groups of persons whose children are going to be baptized. One Roman Catholic diocese provides a training program for leaders of a citywide program for divorced Catholics, a program that has proved most important in the two-year adjustment period following divorce" (Gribbon, 1990, p. 61).

Third, short-term programs focused on young adult developmental issues such as parenting, child raising, etc., did not draw unchurched young adults into the church (Gribbon, 1990, p. 61). Rather, these programs were more successful in ministering to the young adults in the church when connected to some existing program. Thus, connecting a parenting seminar to an ongoing young adult Sunday School class provided for member needs and support for dealing with these life issues. However, this suggests that religious education strategies for reaching unchurched young adults must focus on moving outside of the church walls with programs geared to the unchurched for the unchurched. Unchurched young adults today are not reached so much through evening services, worship services, or Sunday School but rather through opportunities outside of the physical church building on different days of the week using different methods. Support programs focusing on Baby Boomer and Baby Buster needs may be effective if patterned after groups like Alcoholics Anonymous which reaches out to a whole community on a more focused needs basis.

Fourth, those seeking the church are focusing on the issue of intimacy rather than an intellectual search for truth and meaning (Gribbon, 1990 pp. 62-63). Most Far End Baby Boomers and Baby Busters are not talking about doctrine or intellectual struggles with the content of faith. Rather, they are seeking for friendship, looking for a community that shares their values, are seeking assistance in handling life tasks and developing a personal spiritual relationship.

Age Level Insights for Reaching Unchurched Young Adults

What can be done to reach unchurched young adult Baby Boomer or Baby Buster through religious education? Recognizing the great number of variables at play, the following suggestions should be received as a catalyst to developing any specific program.

Baby Busters between 18 and 22 are primarily single when they enter young adulthood but a majority will be married by the end of this period. Premarital counseling is the most likely link between the unchurched young adult and religious education. Pastors who specialize in this area should draw in married lay couples to discuss expectations for marriage. This approach exposes the unmarried couple to more than the pastor. Some pastors also ask the couple to attend the church for six weeks so they become aware of the church and what is taught. This is a strategic opportunity for witness to the young adult couple and those who attend the wedding.

In addition to premarital counseling, the other primary approach to this group is through personal contact. Lay people may desire to volunteer themselves to work with campus religious organizations, the church's young adult group, or introduce themselves to young adults who are part of their daily work or neighborhood experience. After initial personal contact has been made, the young adult may be open to any number of short-term activities such as a Bible study or participating in a service project or retreat.

Busters in their twenties are becoming more settled as they make decisions about their careers, marriage, and lifestyle. While they will delay and check out many alternatives, they are developing a greater sense of identity. Up to one-third of them will move in a given year, suggesting that they will be new to the community and be looking for a church for the first time. With many of them having negative views of organized religion, they will be tentative in exploring religious education programs. How they are greeted and introduced to the church could have a long-lasting effect. Religious education of those who greet visitors and strangers as well as a congregation emphasis on developing sensitivity to visitors are in order.

Community activities are a primary means for making contacts between the church and the young adult in transition. Some possibilities include sponsoring continuing education classes related to Baby Buster concerns (discerning vocational direction, ethical issues in the work place, how to do a job search for the unemployed, etc.); running a vacation Bible school for children with a focus on visiting in the homes of parents; sponsoring a barbecue or other such community activity; offering church facilities to community groups; sponsoring outreach ministries to various groups in the community such as teaching English as a second language for new immigrants, providing meals for the homeless, or organizing activities for the handicapped or apartment blocks.

Since many Baby Buster couples will have their first child later in their twenties, the church should have clearly developed religious education plans for infant dedications, quality nursery care, religious instruction for children, and parents participation in the life of the church. Programs focusing on prayer, study, and career tend to be successful in reaching unchurched young adults if they are well advertised, offered to the community at large, and occur at a time other than on Sunday mornings or evenings.

Back End Boomers are more likely to be settled down with responsibilities, well along in their careers, and have children at home than the earlier groups as you hit those in the thirties. They are usually very willing to assume responsibilities in the community because they tend to move less often. Their primary concern tends to be family life with children ranging from toddlers to teenagers. Single parents and blended families are more common. Divorce and its results drains a great deal of the energy of many of these Boomers. Unchurched Boomers may be particularly open to joining religious education support groups organized around parenting, handling difficult teens, working through all forms of past abuse, and recovering from divorce. A minority of them are very concerned about social issues related to the homeless and peace. Unchurched young adult Boomers may be attracted to service groups in these areas.

Insights from Practitioners for
Reaching Unchurched Young Adults

The following table identifies what various practitioners are saying is needed for the church to reach young adults at the close of the twentieth century.

Writing from the perspective that Boomers are broken, lonely, rootless, and

Table 3 Essentials For Reaching Unchurched Baby Boomers and Baby Busters Through Religious Education		
Schaller (1989)	Bast (No Date)	Anderson (1990)
Preaching	Strong worship focus	Worship & music
Vital worship	Meaningful educational	Spiritual gifts
Teaching ministry	program for all ages	Social responsibility
Changing priorities	Orientation toward	Entrepreneurial focus
Strong weekday program	experience and practical	Image
Strong music ministry	action; not theology	Consumer-responsive
Continuity of leadership	High degree of tolerance	priorities
Transformational leadership	and acceptance of diversity	Pre-evangelism
Challenge the people	Emphasis on inclusion of	relationships
Change-agent skills	women and newcomers	Large full-service
	in leadership	churches
	Informal relational style	Plurality of
		leadership

self-seeking, Miller (1992) identifies four things that will attract and reach young adults examining spirituality in the church. First, churches must provide opportunity for young adults to be actively involved in worship. He believes churches must scrap the choir and replace it with lively, upbeat singing led by a group of guitars, synthesizers, and drums playing and singing their own songs. He believes standing, clapping, and raising hands should become a standard practice if churches want to attract Boomers and Busters.

Second, young adults expect to be serviced. This includes a well-maintained, attractive and organized Sunday School and other children's programs to attract and keep the adults. The nursery should be state of the art with well trained caregivers. Miller (1992) also suggests that how people are greeted, visited, and followed-up will assist them in their seeking only if its done in a first-class way.

Third, young adults want contemporary teaching with helpful teaching aids such as using an overhead projector and making sermon outline handouts available. They desire a variety of classes and seminars as well as potential outlets for involvement where they feel capable of contributing. Faith must be encouraged to be active.

Fourth, young adults are attracted because they have multiple ways to be involved in leadership. This requires a pastoral team that is willing to delegate, train, and encourage spirituality in those they lead. In particular, Miller (1992) advocates the development of networking small groups where individuals are trained to provide care and encouragement to stimulate prayer and spiritual growth among one another (see George, 1991). These type of small groups tap the Boomer and Buster desire for interpersonal touch, caring, and independence.

The above points by Miller are echoed in the writings of Lyle Schaller (1985). He writes: "While precise numbers are not available, my observations suggest that a disproportionately large number of the persons born after the close of World War II can be found in a) "spirit-filled" or self-identified charismatic churches, b) new congregations organized since 1978, c) churches that offer a strong adult church education program (especially attractive to those born in the 1945-60 period), d) congregations with more than a thousand members and a specialized staff, e) the theologically very conservative congregations, f) churches that provide a Christian Day school for children of members, and g) congregations that offer the stability and relational advantages provided by a long pastorate" (p. 1).

Conclusion

To reach unchurched young adults like Bill, those in religious education must recognize the distinctive generational views of young adults toward life in general and the church in particular. We can no longer assume that Baby Boomer and Baby Buster young adults have the same experiences and values as older adults even though they face similar developmental issues. While these perspectives can provide some insight, each young adult must still be dealt with as a unique individual with their own history and story.

Unchurched young adults tend to have some to no prior experience in the church. Like Toni, some young adults are not ready to think about faith. Sometimes they enter because of marriage as in John and Mary's case, or they respond to a religious education program ministering to a felt need as in Linda's case. Since there are strong indications that young adults are beginning to return to the church, significant research findings on why young adults have returned is summarized. While specific suggestions are provided, the unique contexts of our location will continue to influence how unchurched young adults are reached through religious education.

References

Anderson, L. (1990). *Dying for change*. Minneapolis: Bethany House.

Barna, G. (1991). *What Americans believe*. Ventura, CA: Regal Books.

Bast, R. (N.D.). *Attracting new members*. No publisher, pp. 29-30.

Carson, T. (1986, November 10). Fast track kids. *Business Week*, 90-92.

Ehrenreich, B. (1986, September 7). Is the middle-class doomed? New York Times Magazine, 44, 50.

Gallup, G. (1989). *The people's religion*. New York: Macmillan.

George, C. F. (1991, January). Meta-Church, the church of the future. *The Pastor's Update, Charles E. Fuller Institute of Evangelism and Church Growth*, 3.

Gribbon, R. (1990). *Developing faith in young adults: Effective ministry with 18-35 year olds*. Washington, DC: Alban Institute.

Hale, J. R. (1980). *The unchurched: Who they are and why they stay away*. San Francisco: Harper & Row.

Hershey, T. (1986). *Young adult ministry*. Loveland, CO: Group Books.

Hofferth, S. L. (1985, February). Updating children's life course. *Journal of Marriage and the Family*, 99.

Hoge, D. (1981). *Converts, dropouts, and returnees*. New York: Pilgrim.

Hoge, D., & Roozen, D. (Eds.) (1980). *The unchurched American: A second look*. Hartford: Hartford Seminary Foundation.

Howe, N., & Strauss, W. (1992). The new generation gap. *The Atlantic Monthly*, 12, 67-89.

Klein, E. (1985, Winter). The gender gap: Different issues, different answers. *The Brookings Review*, 3, 35.

Lasch, C. (1979). *The culture of narcissism*. New York: Warner.

Light, P. (1988). *Baby boomers*. New York: Norton.

Littwin, S. (1986). *The postponed generation: Why American youth are growing up later*. New York: Morrow.

Miller, C. (1992). *Baby boomer spirituality: Ten essential values of a generation*. Nashville: Discipleship Resources.

Patterson, J., & Kim, P. (1991). *The day America told the truth*. New York: Prentice-Hall.
Roper Poll (1987, April). *American Demographics, 9*, (4), 56, 61.
Schaller, L. (1985). Whatever happened to the baby boomers? *MPL Journal, 6*, p. 1.
Schaller, L. (1989, March). *Net Results*, 64-68.
Wares, E., & Crandall, V. (1966). Social class and observed maternal behavior from 1940 to 1960. *Child Development*, 35, 1021-1032.
Winfield, T. (1990, September 15) Retailers needed to rescue hurting church. *Christian Retailing*.

CHAPTER TEN

The Religious Education of College Students

STEVE FORTOSIS

A special challenge inherent to this chapter is the fact that the age range of the American college student has been steadily expanding since about 1970 and is projected to continue to do so for the foreseeable future (Gribbon, 1981). Presently, the age of the typical college student is higher than in past decades, extending from about age 18 to the early 30s. This wide age range makes it difficult to place the student into a typical developmental paradigm and pinpoint religious programming for that specific group. Thus, in order to keep the chapter of manageable content and reasonable length, we will concentrate primarily upon those undergraduates from age 18 through the early 20s.

Today's College Student: A General Profile

Many of today's young men and women enter college unprepared. Nearly 40 percent of them are unable to draw inferences from written material, and only one in five can write a persuasive essay. The result is that 84 percent of all colleges and universities in our country must offer remedial programs (cited in McKinney, 1992).

Contemporary college students comprise a perplexingly paradoxical generation. A large percentage of those who actually graduate are among the best educated in U.S. history, but they do not seem sure how to give back to society what has been poured in. They are concerned about the problems the preceding generation will leave for them to fix but seem uncertain how to proceed.

They are the first generation of "latchkey" children. They virtually reared themselves, yet fully 75 percent of the males 18-24 are still living with their parents. They want successful marriages but hesitate for fear of failure (cited in Gross & Scott, 1990). A frighteningly large percentage of these students experienced physical, emotional, and/or sexual abuse as children (Elkind, 1984). Interestingly, one of the only commitments these young people seem dedicated to is providing loving care and a safe haven for their future children, a commitment their own parents were not willing to make.

An estimated 40 percent of early adults in their 20s are children of divorce. Perhaps they postpone marriage for fear that they will do no better than their parents (Gross & Scott, 1990). Some call them the "unromantic generation" because it is career, income, and rigorous, skeptical marital aspirations that seem to come first in their minds, not romantic love. Their moral standards may be slightly higher than their predecessors—the AIDS scare has placed new value upon virginity among young adults as a whole. A late 1980s syndicated article on virginity in sixty newspapers generated more supportive mail than any previous subject in that column (cited in Weber, 1987). However, many college students continue practicing high-risk sex and seem little concerned about the dangerous consequences. In a 1990 study, 79 percent of female students and 87 percent of male students reported at least one sexually active experience in the preceding year and 21 percent reported three or more sexual partners during that time (cited in McKinney, 1992).

The number one killer among college students is substance abuse, affecting more than ten thousand lives each year. Habit-forming drugs are not used as prevalently as in the 1970s, but at least 75 percent of the nation's college students drink alcoholic beverages (Ingalls, 1988).

Suicide is the second leading cause of death among college students; depression and disorders such as anorexia and bulimia are increasing at alarming rates (Blimling, 1989). Obviously, these young people are not strangers to deep emotional pain. Yet, as adults, they seem intent on avoiding risk, pain, and rapid change at almost any cost (Gross & Scott, 1990). They are not heartless or unimaginative—they are simply self-preoccupied. That seems a quality for which youthful generations have always been known. The difference is that this generation is fully aware of it and shows no widespread inclination to change (Weber, 1987). They want big money, but shun crass materialism. They want top jobs, but many want to travel first. They want role models, but see no one to emulate. They want a culture all their own, but settle for an aimless eclecticism.

What can the church-related college and the church do to help this generation of young people? These institutions can prepare them to say things well and do things efficiently as they enter the adult world. They can offer direction and give them a platform as they seek to speak out about needed reforms in society. They can give affirmation and also counseling to those who have experienced abuse or trauma in the past. They can suggest advice and model positive marriages and families, so that patterns of divorce and family dysfunction can be changed. Lastly, through spiritual example and teaching they can challenge students against sexual promiscuity and substance abuse and can offer spiritual hope to those vulnerable to depression and self-destruction.

Today's College Student: Social Tasks

Havighurst (1972) explains human development in terms of seven stages. Each stage is characterized by a set of achievements or tasks. According to Havighurst, the tasks of early young adulthood are: getting started in an occupation, selecting a mate, learning to live with a marriage partner, starting a family, rearing children, managing a home, taking on civic responsibility, and finding a congenial social group. Interestingly, five of the eight tasks relate to marriage and family issues. His apparent assumption that all young people will marry and rear a family may surprise some. Of course, when Havighurst formulated his task-based stages, there were not 70 million single adults in America (1990 census), and marriage was likely considered the norm for the large majority.

According to James Fowler (1981) the stage most characteristic of early young adulthood is the individuative-reflective stage. Coming out of a very peer-oriented synthetic-conventional stage, young adults must make critical choices in relation to their identity and faith. Identity must be based more upon inner convictions than outer relationships and roles. Concurrent with this critical, systematic selection of one's beliefs, values, and commitments, there must also be a fading dependence upon the borrowed beliefs and values of significant others.

Some young adults do not reach the individuative reflective stage. Sell (1991) states that there are several dangers inherent in a fixation at the synthetic-conventional level. First, this person is always subject to the despair that comes when one's faith sources betray or break down in some way. Second, sole identity with one's group can result in the stunting of ego development. In this case, one doesn't "own" himself or herself—in a sense the family or peer group does. Third, the expectations and evaluations of these significant others can be so compellingly internalized that it may be difficult to make autonomous decisions.

Fowler (1984) borrows Robert Lifton's "Protean" image of the evolving American young adult. Proteus was a minor Greek god who could easily change his shape, depending upon the situation. What he found difficult, however, was committing himself to a single form, unless he was actually seized and chained. It is easy to become overwhelmed by the relentless change, undigested media messages, and endless life alternatives open to the young adult. The days of one lifelong career, a peaceful family, stable friendships, a three-bedroom home, and secure settlement in a middle-class rural or suburban community are quickly becoming an ideal of the past. Fowler believes that in the face of this constant societal change, young adults have been forced to become "fluid, flexible, and frequently ready to modify fundamental convictions and outlooks as they face new environments and are constantly flooded with information" (1984, p.14). College students must be able to get away from the overwhelming pressures of life and the constant media overload. There must be significant periods of time that students are allowed to retreat to whatever place means safety and seclusion for them. In this way, the fragmented student can regroup and begin solidifying beliefs, convictions and life commitments.

Levinson's 1978 study of the social task orientation of 40 adult males is well known. In preliminary observations of his 1986 study of forty-five women, Levinson claimed that the initial hypothesis (1978) of both age-linked periods as well as their particular sequence also appears well-grounded in his intensive study of 45 women, as well as over one hundred adults from different countries and historical periods as sufficiently portrayed in (auto)biographies, novels, and plays.

Levinson hypothesized developmental stages of which, for our purposes, two are relevant. The first period, extending between age 22 to 28, Levinson terms "entering the adult world." The second, extending from age 28 to 33, he titles "changing the first life structure."

During the first period, the young adult makes and tests a variety of initial choices regarding occupation, love relationships, peer relationships, values, and lifestyle. The individual has two primary yet antithetical tasks: a) there is a need to explore the possibilities for adult living, keep one's options open, avoid strong commitments and maximize one's alternatives. The contrasting task b) is to create a stable life structure, become more responsible, and make something significant of one's life.

From his task orientation, Levinson appears to agree with Fowler that current societal pressures are proving very difficult for the early young adult in America. Levinson states that the participatory tasks associated with entering the adult world are intrinsically both trying and contradictory. The young adult senses pressure to establish a vocation, make an adequate salary, get married, rear children, fulfill religious obligations, maintain a network of friendships, and fulfill community responsibilities.

"One of the great paradoxes of human development," Levinson states, "is that we are required to make crucial choices before we have the knowledge, judgment, and self-understanding to choose wisely" (1978, pp. 82-83). Perhaps that is why Levinson found that 57 percent of his male, young adult sample experienced their lives as incomplete, oppressive, not going anywhere or heading in the wrong direction. Instead of communicating directly or indirectly that early young adults must make all the major life decisions immediately, adults in authority can take some of the pressure off. Religious educators can offer a relaxed haven for honest dialogue, letting college students know they are cared about and there is room for both successes and mistakes as they grow into full adulthood.

Levinson delineates the prevalence of vocational dreams among early young adults, as well as their seeking of mentors to bring the dreams to fruition. Emphasizing the importance of mentors for college students, Astin's (1977) research found that those students who interacted frequently with faculty tended to be highly satisfied with their college experience, whereas those who opted primarily for political involvement tended to be somewhat dissatisfied.

Perry (1970) observed that, while students do not uncritically accept the values of educators, they desire more "faculty-student contact." This represents a desire to know life meanings to which faculty have committed. Along with analyzing faculty meanings for possible adoption, students need a sense of hope that eventually they will be able to form valid life commitments for themselves. Interviews with college students indicate that they are not looking so much for "heroes" with whom they can fuse, as nurturers who can offer wisdom and support for their emerging selves. Parks (1986) states, however, that young adults are not so desperate for mentors that they will accept one who will betray the integrity of who they are or where they wish to go in life. Religious mentors should offer mature direction to students but not in an overbearing, superior manner. As difficult as it is, the successful mentor should wait until invited before assisting students in making life decisions.

Roger Gould's (1978) book *Transformations*, is based on examination of 5,000 males and females between the ages of 16 and 60. His findings seem to indicate that human development involves the replacement of false childish assumptions from the early years with more adult attitudes and presuppositions. According to Gould, ages 19 to 22 are characterized by the tasks of leaving the family and dealing with peer group orientations. Ages 23 to 28 are characterized by a developing independence and commitment to a vocation and possibly to children.

Four basic misconceptions that these early young adults must discard as they make the transition into settled adulthood are: a) rewards will come automatically if we do what we are supposed to do; b) there is only one right way to do things; c) my loved ones can do for me what I haven't been able to do for myself; and d) rationality, commitment, and effort will always prevail over all other forces. Perhaps more important than certain academic lessons, today's college student must learn that working hard does not unfailingly bring success, there is sometimes more than one right way, others cannot be expected to meet all their needs, and rational determination does not always prevail. In a firm yet gentle manner, these young people can be mentored through these sometimes jarring realizations about life—in a way that acquaints them with reality without destroying their robust sense of idealism.

Today's College Student: Psychosocial Development

Four of the primary psychological issues unique to early young adulthood are independence, identity, intimacy, and moral judgment. Erik Erikson's (1968, 1982) eight-stage theory assumes that the late-adolescent would typically have formed a solid and stable identity. However, though this may be ideal, many young males and females still struggle with aspects of their personal identity into young adulthood. Erikson refers to the chief psychosocial crisis of early adulthood as intimacy vs. isolation. He believes that if the young adult has developed a whole, healthy sense of identity in the previous stage, then he or she should be ready for intimacy. By intimacy he means "the ability to give oneself fully to another in shared experience of combined identity and mutual commitment" (1982, p. 101). These relationships can be with a marriage partner, class friends and mentors, or colleagues in the workplace. Closeness may evolve out of mutual battles or stresses, common religious beliefs, leisure activities, or living situations.

In a confusingly complex society such as ours, perhaps Erikson is being a bit idealistic to place the normal formation of the identity primarily in the adolescent period. Steele (1990) writes, "When I ask college students, both male and female, to identify which of the Eriksonian stages they think they are working through, invariably the response is both identity and intimacy."

Many college students have such a fragmented familial past that they are left with identity-confusion. Elkind (1984) explains that this may result in the "patchwork self"—an inability to decide what centers them. This is most obviously portrayed in individuals who change dramatically depending upon what person or group they are with. Young adults who are extremely insecure about their personhood may be unable to build healthy relationships. They may react by: 1) being easily threatened and withdrawing from interaction with others, 2) interacting only in necessary matters or in ways that are self-serving or, 3) seeking a negative form of intimacy often characterized by elitism and snobbery.

As early young adults struggle toward intimacy with others, they are also facing the decision of how to provide for the basic necessities. What is interesting in this paradigm is that issues of love and work often conflict. Most college students are struggling to develop intimacy, especially in relation to the opposite sex. In addition, many are not only juggling a job as they go through school but they are taking steps that will decide whether their future occupation is the type which allows ample time to pursue leisure and intimacy or one that allows little. One may question whether students realize the profound impact relatively flippant decisions made during college years will have upon the remainder of their lives.

Loevinger (1976) has constructed an interesting model of ego development. It is important that individuals entering young adulthood be moving from Loevinger's *Conformist* stage to the *Conscientious* stage and, in turn, to the *Individualistic* stage. Put simply, this means progressing from a focus upon external trappings such as social acceptance and material possessions to an awareness that the feelings and opinions of others must be taken into account when we are formulating our own. Moving, then, to the *Individualistic* level is reflected in an increased tolerance for self and others and an acceptance that some may be antagonistic to one's own striving for achievement or even one's moralistically conceived responsibility for the welfare of others (Loevinger, 1976).

It seems as if Loevinger would like to see in the early adult what Allport and Ross (1967) describe as "viewing oneself with complacency." This involves the ability to admit personal weaknesses and seek to deal with them. Religious educators can assist students in this area, first by admitting their own personal weaknesses and, second, by gently and, sometimes indirectly, leading students through experiences in which they will see their own weaknesses and be able to admit to them in a nonthreatening context. One such experience might be rock-climbing or stress camping. A survivalist setting like this greatly magnifies irritations and disagreeable characteristics of individuals, and it is in a setting like this that individuals must either face up to their weaknesses and learn to cooperate or else face dire consequences, the least of which would be a thoroughly miserable outing.

Today's College Student: Moral Development

In reference to moral development, Kohlberg (1978, 1982) does not equate a specific stage with young adulthood. Sell (1991) states that early young adults most typically operate on stages three or four, but others believe that he is being a bit too optimistic. These would hold that early young adults function at stages one to three. Respectively, stages one and two involve moral reasoning based on 1) consequences of actions or 2) on what will satisfy one's own needs. Stage three involves conforming to the expectations of others—being a good citizen, a nice person, a faithful religious devotee. Persons at this stage may easily engage in wrong actions, however, if the chance of being discovered is low. The stage four individual tries to make right moral decisions out of a duty to respect authority and conform to the social order. Human principles of justice, not particular expressions of law, guide the stage five behavior. These respect laws more out of commitment to the rights they protect than because society dictates them.

Of course, in 1982, Gilligan challenged Kohlberg's theory with the premise that female moral reasoning evolves from a different context than that of the male. According to Gilligan, the female context is essentially one of caring and interpersonal responsibility while, for the male, competition, individualism, duties, rights, and justice are primary.

Gilligan describes the moral imperative of women as an injunction to care and a responsibility to alleviate the troubles of the world. For men, the moral imperative appears rather as a standard to respect the rights of others and "get the job done." Admittedly, Walker's (1984) research casts some doubt upon Gilligan's assertions. He claims that "very few sex differences in moral development have been found" (p. 68). Walker concedes, however, Kohlberg's (1982) observation that the apparent lack of stage disparity between the sexes in moral reasoning does not preclude the possibility of sex differences in content within a stage or in the preferential use of varied orientations in the making of moral judgments.

In 1986, Baumrind wrote a rebuttal article to Walker's 1984 article. Baumrind differed importantly with Kohlberg and Walker in their assumption that when a control for education nullifies the gender difference in stage score level, it follows that the gender difference is spurious. According to Baumrind, education level legitimately effects gender differences in moral reasoning because education is the best single index of social niche and acculturated values of a large segment of Western society.

Even Ford and Lowery (1986), who are hardly sympathetic to Gilligan (1982), write: "This study provides some support for Gilligan's assertions that females are more attuned to issues of care in moral conflicts and males more attuned to issues of justice. However, it also supports the conclusion that the realm of care-giving is not an exclusively female realm" (p. 783).

William Perry (1970) begins from the premise that most students entering college are dualistic thinkers—that is, they see values, convictions, and moral issues as either black or white, right or wrong, with little or no legitimate gradation. With the ever-widening age span of individuals entering college, one may wonder if Perry's foundational premise is as true now as it was in the decade of the sixties.

In any case, based on a study of undergraduate students enrolled at Harvard and Radcliffe, Perry saw a nine-step line of development, beginning with a dualistic frame of reference and concluding with individual ideological commitment within relativism. Very briefly, the process begins with the student seeing the world in polar terms. There are absolute right or wrong answers for everything. Next, the student perceives diversity of opinion and uncertainty as unwarranted confusion caused by poorly qualified authorities. Third, the individual accepts diversity/uncertainty on issues as legitimate but still temporary. Fourth, the individual adopts two theoretical realms—a) authority still dictates only one right and wrong, but b) others have a right to their opinions. This often slides into an eventual perception that all knowledge and values are contextual and relative and "right/wrong" functions only in special cases. Sixth, the student realizes the necessity of orienting oneself in a relativistic world through personal commitments to beliefs and values. Beginning with an initial commitment in some area, the individual experiences the life implications of that commitment and others in an unfolding progression of personal lifestyle convictions. Perry acknowledges that these steps may be short-circuited if a student delays the process for a time, denies the need to progress to a further stage, or entrenches in a dualistic, absolutistic mindset.

Along with Perry, Kohlberg, Fowler, and Loevinger also identify a period of relativistic thinking for the typical early young adult. Loevinger (1976) defines the period more as a transition than a stage. She states that the "self aware" level is characterized in part by an awareness of 'multiple possibilities' in situations, rather than holding to a belief that there can only be one right answer.

Some religious educators would take at least partial exception to a sweeping relativism. Many of those from the Judeo-Christian tradition would support only a modified version of Perry's full schema. These would acknowledge that while some ethical issues are open to individual interpretation, those clearly delineated through divine revelation are to be considered absolute. In other words, "Thou shalt not murder" (Ex. 20:13) would be considered a moral absolute, but whether assisted suicide is murder would be an issue that each religious devotee would have to decide individually.

With or without the college experience, other religious individuals fixate in a dualistic mindset and may remain that way for life. For these people, there is no room for differences of opinion regarding values and moral issues. They not only have opinions concerning the rightness or wrongness of most issues but may seek to coerce those around them to share identical commitments.

Regarding moral nurture, religious educators must maintain a balance. On the one hand, religious educators and mentors should explain to students that, though they are free to establish their own personal moral convictions, the scriptures set certain moral parameters. On the other hand, students must also be assured that there are certain ethical issues which fall into a gray area, offering much room for diversity of opinion and conviction.

Today's College Student: Religious Effects of the College Experience

Astin's (1977) study of college students indicated that, generally speaking, students move toward a secularization of their religious beliefs—becoming more hedonistic and less religious. When they enter college, dormitory students appear to be no less religious than students living with their parents, but they are substantially less religious four years later.

In relation to parental influence upon early adult religiosity, Lindquist (1980) found that Protestant religiousness related positively with parental acceptance, and negatively with rejection and power control. The intrinsically oriented were associated with parental empathy, acceptance, and psychological control. Extrinsic religiousness was associated with an uncontrolled environment in which parents were perceived as distant. In a study by De Vaus (1983), parental support appeared to factor more importantly in the early adult religious *belief* than in religious *activity*. As adolescents moved into adulthood, while they still regarded religion as being of importance, they engaged in less overt religious activity, perceiving this as the adult model. A 1984 study showed 1) the degree to which freedom of thought was encouraged and 2) the degree that religion was emphasized in their homes in childhood as the two best predictors of their retention or rejection of religious involvement (Hunsberger & Brown, 1984).

Luft and Sorell (1987) found that students with less religious belief and devotion reported low previous parental control and nurturing, whereas those with greater religiousness reported high previous mother control and good communication or high control and high nurture. In most studies of this type, mothers showed greater religious effect on daughters, and fathers, on sons. However, generally speaking, mothers were considered more religious than fathers, and the mother's religious influence was considered more dominant (Wright, 1962; Acock & Bengston, 1978; Nelsen, 1980; Schmidt, 1981; Hunsberger & Brown, 1984; Dudley & Dudley, 1986). Parents should be made aware of their respective spheres of influence on sons and daughters. Student church attendance shows greater influence by fathers; practical application of religion, by mothers. However, it may not surprise some that mothers have a greater overall religious affect on both genders and are considered more traditionally religious. It seems that fathers should be encouraged to take greater initiative in the home, instead of leaving most of the religious training to the mothers.

By and large, university and college life does not undermine early parental influence if that influence is consistent and solid. There are occasional exceptions to this, such as Woodroof's (1986) study, which indicated that peer influence on the religious and sexual behavior of freshmen at Church of Christ colleges was so strong that despite their former influence, parents no longer constituted an effective reference group for these students. For other students who adopted varying religious beliefs from their parents during college years, higher educational achievement was most strongly associated with change of belief, followed by expectation of social mobility, and, among the women, an emotional disturbance, which either greatly strengthened religious belief or weakened it. Wadsworth and Freeman (1983) went on to hypothesize that the changing or dropping of religious practices among some college students may relate to their growing independence from home and family.

Based on a longitudinal study, DeVaus (1985) doubted whether the decline in religiousness of college students could be attributed to educational factors. However Astin (1977) found that students heavily involved in academics and athletics showed less likelihood to abandon their religious affiliations.

When college students in another study were asked which of eleven areas gave rise to personal problems, religious items were chosen by about a third. Religious problems were more frequent with women, and most were related to a loss of faith (Beit-Hallahmi, 1974). Hyde (1990) writes that in today's climate, beliefs are more likely to be discarded than allowed to trouble those who hold them. For these individuals, cognitive dissonance results in beliefs being rejected, rather than being rationalized.

Some studies, however, seem to indicate that persons with staunch religious beliefs, such as those belonging to campus religious organizations, tend to be more orthodox. Participants of these groups tend to become *more* religious during their student days, especially when personal friendships are also involved (Madsen & Vernon, 1983). In general support of this finding, Ozorak (1989) found that the college experience tends to polarize religious attitudes. The increase of religiousness among the more religious was matched by a decrease of religiousness among the moderately religious.

It is not certain why students heavily involved in academics or athletics appear less likely to abandon religious affiliations. Astin (1977) implies that this may be attributed to decreased interpersonal influence by diverse ideologies on campus. Somewhat disconcerting is the finding that religious beliefs are more likely to be discarded than allowed to trouble those who hold them. It seems as if religious educators and campus ministers could help bolster and nurture a college-age religious faith that is often is apparently not based upon a foundation that is solid enough to withstand the pressures and antireligious influences of university life.

In any case, it is well substantiated that the college experience tends to polarize religious beliefs—those who enter college with moderate to weak beliefs usually become less religious while those entering with staunch religious beliefs tend to become more religious. It may be that if better quality religious education is initiated in our churches and parochial elementary and secondary schools, greater percentages of early adults may develop the spiritual knowledge and stability to maintain a vibrant and growing faith throughout their college experience and beyond.

Spirituality and Today's College Student

There are troubling trends among college students, both in regard to their backgrounds and their present ethical values. Large percentages of these students come out of fragmented families in which moral standards were inconsistent and child abuse was not uncommon. Many suffer from mental health problems concerning which substance abuse only exacerbates the problem (McKinney, 1992).

The ethical values of students are reflected in the continued high percentage of promiscuous sexual activity, materialistic life priorities, and dishonest school behaviors. The high incidence of sexual contact, even with multiple partners has been mentioned earlier. As to life priorities, in 1967, eighty-three percent of American college freshmen cited "developing a meaningful philosophy of life" as a major reason for attending college. In 1988, the percentage dipped to 50 percent (cited in McKinney, 1992, p. 198). Perhaps materialism is now part of their "philosophy of life"—a 1988 freshman poll taken by Astin indicated 73 percent were attending college "to be well off financially," up about thirty percent from 1967 (cited in McKinney, 1992, p. 198). In the 1960s, many in early young adulthood decried materialism, but most did not embrace religious values in its place. If religious educators are to advise college students against materialism, biblical values such as generosity and devotion to spiritual treasures must also be taught or students will be left in a spiritual vacuum.

What can religious educators further do to nurture spirituality in college students? First, they must recognize, as was documented in the section on religious effects of the college experience, parental influence has a most profound effect on the spiritual decisions and growth of students during their college experience. That is one reason why religious educators must challenge the parents in their parishes to model and consistently train their children in the Judeo-Christian faith. If students enter college with strong religious convictions borne of consistent parental example and influence, they are likely to strengthen those convictions and continue to mature spiritually. However, the antithesis is also true.

Second, parents, religious professors, and pastors must take on a mentoring-nurturing role to encourage young adult spiritual maturation. We must help them move into Fowler's Individuative-reflective faith that takes seriously the responsibility for their own commitments, lifestyle, beliefs, and attitudes. It is not always easy for young adults to "transform their religious attitudes—indeed all their attitudes—from second-hand fittings to first-hand fittings of their personalities" (Allport, 1957, p. 36).

Some developmentalists believe that going through life crises of some kind are necessary for religious youth to attain adult faith. Indeed, the transition from a conformist faith to a mature, self-owned faith may be a rocky road, strewn with spiritual doubts and questions. Some never risk it. As Helminiac well states, "Too intent on becoming 'spiritual,' they follow the master, keep the rules, affirm the teachings, all without question or responsible criticism" (1987, p. 78). This results in a what Brueggemann (1979) terms a fake evangelicalism that speaks with shameless certitude and ignores the tough questions of life. Significant others must be willing to listen to student questions without intimidation or patronization, and assist students in finding answers that will satisfy them.

Third, in regard to moral reasoning, many of today's college students appear to functioning at stages one to three. It is no secret that religious individuals rarely test higher than stage four. There has been some constructive debate regarding whether this means that Kohlberg's model does not test religious thinking accurately, or whether evangelicals, among others, may be underdeveloped in the area or moral thinking oriented toward others. Students should be helped to realize that biblical law must be balanced with Christian freedom. Law orientation can exude calculating judgmentalism if lacking human warmth and compassion. Sell (1991) reminds us that our teaching of these lessons should not be in a sheltered, aseptic context far removed from the perplexities of life. Young adulthood is a time to face tough life issues and test one's developing system in the warp and woof of real life.

Fourth, college students should be assisted in the spiritual quest for both self-intimacy and intimacy with others. Self-intimacy has to do with a greater awareness of and comfort with oneself. In view of both one's past and present, to be able to value strengths and gifts realistically and admit mistakes and weaknesses with complacency, not hostility (Allport & Ross, 1967). As young adults achieve self-intimacy, they become more open to personal improvement and seeking help will be less threatening. Also, such persons can be more accepting of others with their peculiarities and flaws. One way to aid students in matters of self-knowledge and mature relationship is through mentoring/modeling. As an individual develops an intimate relationship with a mentor, he or she also learns by watching how the mentor develops bonded relationships. Another way is through "controlled disequilibration." Planned events such as relational retreats, stress camping, mission trips, and whitewater rafting can be a laboratory in which all the facades and emotional escape hatches are stripped away and individuals gain intimate knowledge about themselves and learn to form deep, lasting bonds with others.

Self-knowledge and acceptance results in the ability to be intimate with others. There are many situations that call young adults to risk some aspect of their self-definition. These situations include close friendship, group solidarity, social experiences of cooperation and competition, confrontive relationships, inspiring encounters with others, and/or sexual love and orgasm. An often-ignored aspect of adult intimacy is the ability to be isolated from others, to be selective in my love, to seek and savor periods of spiritual solitude— not out of fear or revulsion of others, but out of a need to commune with oneself and with God. Peter Berger (1961) observes, "He who would freely encounter truth must pay the price of being alone" (p. 120). Yet the structure of the typical academy offers little opportunity for pause or contemplation (Parks, 1986).

Of course, mature identity is drawn toward self-disclosure and empathy toward others yet wise caution and selectivity regarding appropriate exercise of such. A diffused identity cannot remain intact in close relationship, while an overly rigid identity allows too little flexibility in my sense of who I am, too little openness to learning something new about myself.

In friendship, early adults can reveal their true selves—their identity is tested, challenged with new information, modified and stimulated through interaction with another autonomous self (Whitehead & Whitehead, 1979). Thus, relationships should be encouraged both student-to-student and between students and significant older adults in their lives. Most important, early adults must be shown how to cultivate an intimate relationship with God— a unique friendship founded in mystical communion of the spirit—extremely challenging for sense-bound creatures.

In our culture, marriage is viewed as a social paradigm illustrating the achievement of spiritual and physical intimacy. Of course, there are many marriages in which little is shared and self-disclosure and empathy play little part. Both Levinson (1978) and Vaillant (1977) warn that marriages occurring during the first years of adulthood sometimes encounter great difficulty, partly because the parties are not secure enough in their identities to develop nonegocentric, mutual intimacy. It is not only important for mature adults to assist students in forming their identity but also to model for them what healthy, intimate marriages look like, even in the casual, mundane events of married life.

Campus Religious Education

Beginning with voluntary Christian associations in the late nineteenth and twentieth centuries, the church's ministry on college and university campuses was carried on in the 1920s, 1930s, and 1940s through various non-denominational groups, principally YMCA and YWCAs as well as through denominational student fellowships which began to organize on an inter-collegiate and national level as early as 1922. Between 1935 and 1955, a number of denominational national student work offices were initiated to take the lead in establishing other student centers of this type.

This work received more and more impetus as it became increasingly apparent that larger numbers of Christian students were finding their way to private and public colleges rather than to church colleges. Conservation of the faith of the faithful was the hope and the means was campus ministries designed to serve as centers of a religious social life and a spiritual and moral "haven" from the "godless campus."

During and after World War II, both the student movements and student church agencies became aware that theirs was a mission task and not merely a job of preserving faith in the faithful. The Christian community on campuses began to see its task not simply as holding the faithful or recovering the fallen, but as participatory evangelistic witness in the whole gamut of academic life. With this realization, parachurch campus organizations began forming and have expanded to hundreds of America's campuses during the past five decades. Four of the largest include InterVarsity, Navigators, Campus Crusade, and International Students Incorporated. InterVarsity employs 511 U.S. field staff affecting 48,000 students directly or indirectly; the Navigator organization has 281 staff on 136 U.S. college campuses. International Students Inc. employs 300 staff with access to 40,000 students, and Campus Crusade has 1,700 field staff on American campuses, working directly with about 18,000 students.

Sell (1991) writes that the need for religious campus groups "affirms the practice of having Christian groups on college campuses where religious youth can be discipled. If those groups allow for individual freedom, they will not hinder young adults' development but will be a necessary part of their progress" (p. 111).

The on-campus religious education minister must, first of all, exercise disciplined habits of study, meditation, and worship. Only from this spiritual overflow can effective ministry take place. In addition, there should be an ongoing habit of keeping in touch with the thought patterns and modes of expression common to students and to academic specializations within the university (Earnshaw, 1964).

Some student characteristics about which campus ministers should be familiar are partially borrowed from Gribbon (1981):
1) College students are more likely to act as responsible adults if they are treated as such. 2) The work and vocation of students *is* college life and deserves to be respected seriously—not treated as a carefree period before real life

begins. 3) College is often a time of stress, and depressed students should be helped and encouraged. 4) Students are typically busy people, so religious programs should be chosen and planned carefully, not added simply to make a campus ministry seem active. 5) Short-term programs, projects, and involvements draw more commitments from students than long-term ones; 6) Most students don't seek long-term counseling—they don't appear to want counselors as much as close and loyal friends in which to confide. 7) Students are experimenters—they experiment with life, limits, acquaintances, ideas, and roles. Also, their understandings and attitudes may change frequently. The caring constancy of campus religious leaders or mature saints can provide a countervailing security during this sometimes unstable experimental period. 8) Students bring with them energy and enthusiasm, a fresh perspective. They can be quick to question and eager to learn, idealistic and capable of deep devotion. Often, they have a reserve of skills and talents for leadership that needs to be tapped and trained. As we applaud their fresh insights, we should also help to unleash their contagious energy upon worthy causes, lest it be lost

In addition to these awarenesses, the campus religious education minister should provide a pastoral function for God's people in the academic community. In the gigantic complex of mass educational plants and commuter colleges, people get lost. There are the academic near-failures, the rejected lovers, the confused, the dazed, the insecure, and the homesick. There are the tremendous social and intellectual adjustments most entering freshmen must make—adjustments of dorm living, study routine, extracurriculars, dating, and many more (Earnshaw, 1964). Campus religious education involves giving encouragement to the discouraged, acceptance to the unacceptable, all in a language students can understand.

This brings up the need for staying abreast of ever-evolving societal thought forms and ideologies. Though the truth contained in the gospel is unchanging, the people of God must relate it in a relevant manner to each new generation within the academic community.

Not only must campus religious education ministers convey biblical truth in the language of today's students, they must also address felt needs of young adulthood: 1) Students must be assisted in developing independence, personal responsibility, and in redefining the relationship with parents. 2) As students encounter people with differing life priorities and values, they must be trained to examine them critically and clarify and select their own. 3) Some may seek spiritual guidance in the selection of a career, and campus ministers should be able to offer more than a prayer and a slap on the back. 4) Cultural diversities and competitiveness may make establishing college friendships difficult. In addition, students must be helped to learn how to relate to others adult-to-adult. 5) Campus religious education leaders can offer affirmation and feedback as students grapple with issues such as their personal identity, sexuality, dating and marriage.

Besides the spiritual influence of campus religious education ministers, we must not neglect that faculty can have immense positive impact on students. Citing a study by Philip Jacobs, Cantelon (1964) states personal contacts and relationships with faculty as the most valued aspect of the college experience according to students. Parks (1986) cites Perry's report of students asking for more "faculty-student contact," a request he felt represents a desire to know the meanings faculty have composed—not in order to accept those meanings blindly, but rather as a way of saying, "If you have been able to compose a valid place of commitment, it gives me hope that I will be able to also." In a section entitled "Professor as Spiritual Guide," Parks (1986) goes on to explain that young adults seek not heroes, but mentors—those who take into account the whole person—all the spiritual passion and potential waiting to be developed and unleashed.

Perhaps we can hear a little of that wistful desire for a mentor in a letter written by a university student to her grandfather. She speaks of slipping into the university chapel to sort out her spiritual questions and writes: "I'm fascinated by people who are able to open themselves to all the experiences life has to offer, accepting the harshness, pain, and tragedy without becoming callous or without withdrawing. Because of some elusive quality they call faith, they seem to retain their . . . humor, their humanity, and find strength to continue to fight for what they believe in. . . . I am intrigued, seduced, skeptical" (cited by Parks, 1986, p. 197). It is truly a privilege for professors who are farther along in their own spiritual pilgrimages, to serve as caring mentors to students such as this.

The College Student and the Church

The fact that a majority of church-going young people stop attending church when they reach college poses a significant challenge to the church (Sell, 1991). While young adults comprise more than 40 percent of the adult population in America, that same ratio is not found in churches.

These are the children of the former young adults who dropped out of churches in the 1960s, and they appear to be perpetuating the pattern of their parents (Stubblefield, 1986). Another factor affecting their low church attendance is that many move away from their home churches to attend college. Fifty percent of all American churchgoers attend the church they grew up in and those who have moved geographically are more likely to be unchurched. It is no less true for college students—very few transfer to a congregation at college (Gribbon, 1981).

Students boarding at resident colleges and universities have a special status—church members absent by reason of their vocation. The home congregation can remember them, keep in touch, minister when they are home, provide special opportunities for involvement, minister through their parents, and help others minister to them when they are away (Gribbon, 1981, p. 64). When students come home for holidays, it is important for home congregations to recognize them and plan meaningful events for them.

Churches can communicate care for their students over the miles. A box of cookies, a birthday card, or a personal note can be of great encouragement to those away from home. For students who indicate interest, cassettes of outstanding Sunday sermons from their home church can remind them that their spiritual well-being is important to those who care. Gribbon (1981) states that especially in cases where several students from one congregation attend the same college, some pastors would do well to plan a visit to the campus to renew relationships and communicate that students are not forgotten. Finally, the home church can minister to students by sending their name and address to the chaplain or local pastor near the college.

Even college students who attend church often move quickly from church to church. As long as they drift, they cannot truly identify with any one group. There is always the sense of being a visitor, and it is also difficult to establish any but the most superficial of relationships. If students are to be effectively channeled into a congregation near the college campus, church programs must be structured and organized to assist students with life issues they currently face and must include young adults as significant members of the congregation. The following points should be kept in mind as churches consider religious education and ministry with college students:

1) Church young adult programs should not be *to* students or *for* students, but *with* them. In other words, students strongly desire to not only participate but to partially control their own process (Lefeber, 1980).

2) In many cases, it is wise to offer program styles for both young and old. Some offer two worship service styles each week, one more contemporary than the other. In certain situations, whole churches have taken on an upbeat character, and appear to draw primarily young adult attendees (Sell, 1991).

3) Parks (1986) criticizes the Protestant church for rigidly dividing young adults into groups labeled married and single. In so doing, she states, the religious community has "defined participation in the religious community by forms of marital status rather than first by 'the work God calls us to do'" (1986, p. 201). While there seems to be some legitimacy to planning programs specifically for college students, Stubblefield (1986) reminds us that care should be taken to divide parishioners in congenial, compatible groups, not simply by decade or marital status. Some intergenerational parish activities should also be planned so that those of every

age group may benefit from the richness each group has to offer.

4) In addition, Parks' point is well taken in the sense that young adults should not be consigned to an obscure "singles" group, and thus excluded from church leadership roles. Sell (1991) rightly exhorts that students should be included in church ministry, social work, or even decision-making positions. The Apostle Paul warned against placing a neophyte into such a spot, but a neophyte is a new convert, not necessarily a young adult (1 Tim. 3:6). Thus, conscious attempt should be made to involve college students in all levels of church participation: worship, boards of deacons and trustees, religious education, special committees, and short-term mission opportunities.

5) The church can provide invaluable service to college students by offering a forum along with skilled, caring religious education ministers and other practitioners to help students sort through issues such as individualizing their religious faith, establishing their personal identity, improving relationships, dating and planning for successful marriage, and selecting a career that fits their aspirations and gifts. This input can be offered through weekly church education classes, student seminars, symposiums/forums, informal cell groups, as well as through personal mentorships.

6) Finally, it is important that college-age religious education ministries attract those who are alienated from organized religion. This attractiveness can be fostered in a number of ways. Meetings may be held in a hotel lobby or restaurant, instead of within church walls that seem threatening to some. A Sunday morning meeting may be casual in style and more redemptive or evangelistic in content. Indepth biblical teaching would then take place perhaps in weeknight home studies. Periodic social events in this milieu could allow the sort of modeling which would destroy myths some outsiders entertain regarding what religious young adults are like.

Conclusion

We must not forget that the deep hunger of the young adult world is for a dream that reveals the work to which we are called by God. Only if religion can demonstrate a robust capacity to 'make sense' in the reality of lived experience will young adults recognize religious institutions as contexts for the recomposing of a faith to live by (Parks, 1986).

References

Acock, A., & Bengston, V. (1978). On the relative influence of mothers and fathers: A covariance analysis of political and religious socialization. *Journal of Marriage and the Family, 40*, 519-530.

Allport, G. (1957). *The individual and his religion.* New York: Macmillan.

Allport, G., & Ross, J. (1967). Personal religious orientation and prejudice. *Journal of Personality and Social Psychology. 5*, 432-442.

Astin, A. (1977). *Four critical years.* San Francisco: Jossey-Bass.

Baumrind, D. (1986). Sex differences in moral reasoning: Response to Walker's (1984) conclusion that there are none. *Child Development, 57*, 511-521.

Beit-Hallahmi, B. (1974). Self-reported religious concerns of university underclassmen. *Adolescence, 9*, 333-338.

Berger, P. (1961). *The noise of solemn assemblies.* New York: Doubleday.

Blimling, G. (1989). *The experienced resident assistant.* Dubuque, IA: Kendall/Hunt.

Brueggemann, W. (1979). Covenanting as human vocation. *Interpretation, 33*, 115-129.

Cantelon, J. (1964). *A Protestant approach to campus ministry.* Philadelphia: Westminster.

De Vaus, D. (1983). The relative importance of parents and peers for adolescent religious orientation. *Adolescence, 18*, 145-154.

De Vaus, D. (1985). The impact of tertiary education on religious education. *Journal of Christian Education, 84*, 9-26.

Dudley, R., & Dudley, M. (1986). Transmission of religious values from parents to adolescents. *Review of Religious Research, 28*, 3-15.

Earnshaw, G. (1964). *The campus ministry.* Valley Forge, PA: Judson.

Elkind, D. (1984). *All grown up and no place to go.* Reading, MA: Addison-Wesley.

Erikson, E. (1968). *Identity: Youth and crisis.* New York: Norton.

Erikson, E. (1982). *Identity and religion.* New York: Seabury.

Ford, M., & Lowery, C. (1986). Gender differences in moral reasoning: A comparison of the use of justice and care orientations. *Journal of Personality and Social Psychology, 50*, 777-783.

Fowler, J. (1981). *Stages of faith.* San Francisco: Harper & Row.

Fowler, J. (1984). *Becoming adult, becoming Christian.* San Francisco: Harper & Row.

Gilligan, C. (1982). *In a different voice: Psychological theory and women's development.* Cambridge, MA: Harvard University Press.

Gould, R. (1978). *Transformations.* New York: Simon & Schuster.

Gribbon, R. (1981). *Students, churches and higher education.* Valley Forge, PA: Judson.

Gross, D., & Scott, S. (1990, July 16). Proceeding with caution. *Time*, 56-62.

Havighurst, R. (1972). *Developmental tasks and education.* New York: Mckay.

Helminiac, G. (1987). *Spiritual development: An interdisciplinary study.* Chicago: Loyola University Press.

Hunsberger, B., & Brown, L. (1984). Religious socialization, apostasy, and the impact of family background. *Journal for the Scientific Study of Religion, 23*, 239-251.

Hyde, K. (1990). *Religion in childhood and adolescence.* Birmingham, AL: Religious Education Press.

Ingalls, Z. (1989, September 6). Higher education drinking problem. *The Chronicle of Higher Education.*

Kohlberg, L. (1978). The cognitive-developmental approach to moral education. In Scharf (Ed.), *Readings in moral education* (pp. 38-51). Oak Grove, IL: Winston.

Kohlberg, L. (1982). *The psychology of moral development.* New York: Harper & Row.

Lefeber, L. (1980). *Building a young adult ministry.* Valley Forge, PA: Judson.

Levinson, D., Darrow, C., Klein, E., Levinson, M., & McKee, B. (1978). *Seasons of a man's life.* New York: Knopf.

Levinson, D. (1986). A conception of adult development. *American Psychologist, 41*, 3-13.

Lindquist, B. (1980). *Relationships among personal religion, dimensions of moral character, and parent-child interactions.* Unpublished doctoral dissertation, California

School of Professional Psychology.

Loevinger, J. (1976). *Ego development*. San Francisco: Jossey-Bass.

Luft, G., & Sorell, G. (1987). Parenting style and parent-adolescent religious value consensus. *Journal of Adolescent Research, 2*, 53-68.

Madsen, G., & Vernon, G. (1983). Maintaining the faith during college: A study of campus religious group participants. *Review of Religious Research, 25*, 127-141.

McKinney, L. (1992). Ministering to college students in the 1990s. *Christian Education Journal, 12*, 193-203.

Nelsen, H. (1980). Religious transmission versus religious formation: preadolescent-parent interaction. *Sociological Quarterly, 21*, 207-218.

Ozorak, E. (1989). *The development of religious beliefs and commitment in adolescence*. Unpublished doctoral dissertation, Harvard University.

Parks, S. (1986). *The critical years*. San Francisco: Harper & Row.

Perry, W. G. (1970). *Forms of intellectual and ethical development*. New York: Holt, Rinehart and Winston.

Schmidt, C. (1981). *The relationship of parents' belief systems to their parenting practices and to the belief systems of their children*. Unpublished doctoral dissertation, University of Colorado, Boulder.

Sell, C. (1991). *Transitions through adult life*. Grand Rapids, MI: Zondervan.

Steele, L. (1990). *On the way: A practical theology of Christian formation*. Grand Rapids, MI: Baker.

Stubblefield, J. (1986). *A church ministering to adults*. Nashville, TN: Broadman.

Vaillant, G. (1977). *Adaptation to life*. Boston: Little, Brown.

Wadsworth, M., & Freeman, S. (1983). Generation differences in beliefs: A cohort study of stability and change in religious beliefs. *British Journal of Sociology, 34*, 416-437.

Walker, L. (1984). Sex differences in the development of moral reasoning: A critical review. *Child Development, 55*, 677-691.

Walker, L. (1986). Sex differences in the development of moral reasoning: A rejoinder to Baumrind. *Child Development, 57*, 522-526.

Weber, B. (1987, April 5). Alone together. *New York Times Magazine*, 22-26, 58-62.

Woodroof, J. (1986). Reference groups, religiosity, and premarital sexual behavior. *Journal for the Scientific Study of Religion, 25*, 436-460.

Whitehead, E., & Whitehead, J. (1979). *Christian life patterns*. Garden City, NY: Doubleday.

Wright, D. (1962). A study of religious belief in sixth form boys. *Researches and studies, University of Leeds, 24*, 19-27.

CHAPTER ELEVEN

The Religious Education of Young Single Adults

MICHAEL ANTHONY

The religious education of young single adults is one of the most challenging horizons facing church leaders across North America today. One of the reasons for this challenge is the ever-growing number of single adults and the diversity of their needs. Nearly half of all adults living in America over the age of 18 are unmarried. These adults are active in civic, social, legal, and corporate settings. However, their role in the local church has been slow in coming. Part of the reason for this is the lack of knowledge that many pastors and church boards have regarding how they can reach out to single adults in a way that is appealing and consistent with their distinct needs.

This chapter will explore some of the more important issues which religious education leaders in the local church and central office must address in terms of effective religious education to young single adults. After a brief look at the historical development of single adults in America, a more detailed examination of current trends and considerations will ensue. The final section will deal with practical guidelines for designing and implementing a religious education ministry to young single adults in a local church.

The Historical Development of Single Adults

Recent demographic figures suggest that approximately 40 percent of the American population is not married (*U.S. Bureau of the Census*, 1992).

This represents a significant shift in population composition compared with the number of single adults who lived in America during its colonial heritage.

In colonial America the single adult population was approximately 3 to 4 percent. Very few adults were still single by the time they reached their 20s. The average age for a woman at first marriage was 13, and since there were more young women than young men in the population, there was rarely a problem finding a partner (Koons & Anthony, 1991, p. 47).

There were a number of social and economic reasons to explain the small number of single adults in the general population of America in the 1800s. It was considered a social disgrace for a woman to be unmarried once she passed her early twenties. Pejorative terms such as "ancient maid" or "thorn-back" were used to pressure young single adult women to marry at an early age. The feeling against bachelors was just as strong if not stronger than those toward single women. Unmarried men were treated somewhat after the manner in which we now handle criminals on parole. They were required to report to magistrates from time to time and give an account of their activities (Nimkoff, 1947). To discourage celibacy, the unmarried were taxed in some communities, while in others they were offered free land or given other inducements to marry. If, for some reason, an individual experienced the loss of a spouse, colonial society encouraged a speedy remarriage (Nimkoff, 1947; Seward, 1978). Society did not value or respect the adult who was not married—whether by choice or circumstance.

Beyond the social expectations for early marriage, there was also a practical reason related to economic necessity. America was primarily an agrarian culture; people lived on the farm in greater numbers than at any time in history. Farms require a great deal of labor and few farmers could afford to hire employees. Large families were the basis of economic survival. Family tradition required a young person to remain at home and help the parents with the work, so children were discouraged from leaving before they got married. In fact, even after marriage, more often than not, a section of land was given to the son with a small farm house on it so that he might remain with his family and continue helping his parents with the farm responsibilities (Seward, 1974).

As America moved into the twentieth century the Industrial Revolution exercised a profound impact upon the social fabric of our country. Urbanization brought the development of commercial establishments such as hotels and rooming houses, bakeries, restaurants, grocery stores, and laundries, making it possible for individuals to live apart from their families. This brought special significance for women, who no longer had to marry to have a place to live, and no longer had to stay married because there was no alternative; the divorce rate began to rise (Leslie, 1976). Men began to leave the farms in order to find better paying jobs in factories. Fewer hours of work and better benefits attracted many men from rural communities. Men began living away from home and the population of single adults began to slowly increase.

In 1917 the great World War required heavy machinery and weaponry. This need compelled many men to move from their farms into factories as an act of national pride and commitment. As young men went off to war the result was a continued increase in the number of single men and women in America. Almost immediately after the end of the war, however, the men returned home and those who had been forced to postpone marriage due to patriotic allegiance were now eager to get married and begin families.

The Great Depression had a profound effect on the demographics of America. Once again marriage had to be postponed while families stuck together to survive the economic hardships brought about by the loss of jobs and personal financial savings. Commitment to helping the family survive was seen as more important than fulfilling personal dreams of marriage and family.

As the effect of the Great Depression began to subside the world was once again thrust into turmoil with World War II. Young men and women were forced to postpone their dreams of marriage in order to build the great war machines that were needed. The protracted nature of this conflict resulted in large numbers of single adults throughout the nation. By the end of the war single adults represented over one third of America's population (Koons & Anthony, 1991, p. 51).

An interesting phenomenon took place shortly after the end of World War II. Once the men and women returned home, the subsequent marriage explosion resulted in the birth of what was to be known as the baby boom generation. The single adult population dropped to its lowest rates in the century, approximately 3 to 4 percent (Koons & Anthony, 1991, p. 51). America was happy to have its young men home and families began to live their dreams of marital success and happiness.

The dream was short-lived however, as families failed to live up to the expectations of their parents and the media. Television in the 1950s portrayed the family as having an endless supply of harmony and interpersonal cohesion. Television programs such as "Father Knows Best," "Ozzie and Harriet," and "Leave it to Beaver" depicted the perfect home where problems were solved in thirty minutes and family solidarity remained steadfast. Families could not meet these idealistic standards and the resulting disillusionment manifested itself in an increase in never-married singles and a rise in the divorce rate.

A dramatic increase in the population of single adults across North America between 1960 and 1990 can be attributed to several factors. Each factor played a significant role in changing not only the face of the family but also the character of the nation as a whole.

Factor one: The women's movement in America. By observing the methods of the civil rights movement in America during the 1960s women began to realize that if they were going to be given fair treatment and respect, they were going to have to join together and demand it. Eventually, women began to receive equal access to educational institutions and employment opportunities. As they gained these new opportunities they no longer felt the need for a mate to provide them with financial security. The age-old concept of having to be married to find security, protection, and provision was fast becoming a myth (May, 1983; Koons & Anthony, 1991; Jones, 1989).

Factor two: An increase in divorce. As was mentioned earlier, marriages which began in the 1950s began to disintegrate in the 1960s. Women had come to experience a degree of independence as a result of working in factories, schools, and hospitals during World War II and the Korean War. This independence gave them the confidence they needed to leave a dysfunctional marital relationship and still be able to survive as a single adult. This realization resulted in a dramatic increase in divorce among post-war couples. Today, nearly 16 million Americans are divorced—148 in 1,000. Thirty years ago 35 in 1,000 Americans were divorced (*Unmarried America*, p. 22).

Factor three: The hippie movement. This sociological phenomenon among young people was characterized by a questioning of American ideals and morality. Traditional values such as respect for authority and national allegiance were rejected for a lifestyle of rebellion and hedonism. Sexual activity outside of marriage was exploited for self-gratification and self-satisfaction. Reliable birth control devices gave these young adults freedom to explore the limits of their sexual fantasies. They remained single as marriage was no longer seen as a motive for sex. Free sex was common among young adults as moral standards became relative and ambiguous. A 1986 *Rolling Stone* survey found that 65 percent of those growing up in the 1960s had engaged in premarital sex, while 30 percent had lived with someone of the opposite sex before marriage (cited in Roof, 1993, p. 33).

Factor four: Postponement of marriage for self-gratification. The 1980s is commonly referred to as the "Me Decade" (Bell, 1993, p. 26). Young adults growing up in this decade heard their parents describe the sacrifices which they had to make while they were growing up. Baby boomers, by now in their thirties and forties, are often characterized by their "self-centeredness, greed, narcissism, and lack of commitment" (Roof, 1993, p. 255). Determined not to have to postpone gratification, these young adults desired, and even demanded the same lifestyle rewards that their parents had to work many years to attain. Marriage was postponed while they worked longer hours in order to indulge in frequent vacations, expensive clothes, new cars, and appropriate housing. Getting married was seen as a threat to accumulating the material possessions which they deemed as necessary. In 1989, the estimated median age at first marriage was 26.2 years for a man and 23.8 for women. The comparable figures in 1970 were 23.2 years and 20.8 years, respectively (Jones, 1991, p. 2; *Unmarried America*, p. 27).

The overall result of these four factors is a steady and consistent increase in the number of single adults living in America today. Marriages are delayed, divorces end nearly half of all marriages which are begun, and people are waiting longer to remarry. "Every year a smaller proportion of America is married. Every year the rate of people entering marriages drops, and the rate of people leaving them rises" (*Unmarried America*, 1993, p. 3). Current demographic statistics indicate that these trends show few signs of changing. It is little wonder that nearly half of the population of America today is single.

Types of Single Adults

Although people are coming to the realization that single adults represent a significant percentage of our population, most church and lay leaders make the mistake of grouping all single adults into one category. This is based upon the traditional way in which adults as a whole have been viewed. Adults were seen in the church as either married or unmarried. Few church leaders took the time to differentiate between the various types of unmarried adults which resided within their parish walls. In essence, there are four different types of single adults in America today: the never-married, divorced, separated, and the widowed. Figure 1 illustrates the percentage of single adults in each category by geographic region.

Figure 1 Single and Married Adults in the United States by Region					
	Total US	NE	MW	South	West
Total Singles & Separated	40.7	42.8	39.9	39.5	41.7
Never-Married	22.2	25.5	22.1	19.9	22.9
Divorced	8.3	6.3	8.3	8.6	9.9
Separated	2.6	2.7	1.9	3.0	2.6
Widowed	7.6	8.3	7.6	8.0	6.3
Married-Spouse present	58.5	56.5	59.7	59.8	57.2
Married-Spouse absent	3.4	3.5	2.4	3.7	3.8
Source: U. S. Bureau of Census, (1990) Marital Status and Living Arrangements, No. 450					

Each of the single adults in these four categories has distinct needs, interests, and concerns. Religious education programs which are designed for one category of young single adults may not work when directed at another category because the needs, interests, and concerns are different. Furthermore there are other important distinctions which affect single adult development. Once such distinction is gender. Men react and respond to their singleness differently than women for a variety of social, economic, emotional, and biological reasons. Those with children (single parents) will obviously view being single differently than those without children. Age is another issue, since people feel differently about being single depending on their particular stage of development. One way of looking at this multidimensional nature of classifying single adults is illustrated in Figure 2.

Figure 2 The Multidimensional Nature of Classifying Single Adult Development									
	Men	Women	With Children	Without Children	Age Differences				
					20	30	40	50	60+
Never-married									
Divorced									
Separated									
Widowed									

An effective program of religious education to young single adults must take into consideration the various types of single adults that are attending the church. For example, an aerobics program for single adults in your church may not be very well attended if the majority of your single adults are over the age of 60. Therefore, it is important for those who do religious education with single adults to understand, first of all, what type of single adults attend their church. Having determined this important consideration, they are better able to design a program which takes into consideration the felt needs associated with the single adult types in their church. George Barna (1991) writes concerning this needs base philosophy of ministry, "Several of the pastors had learned from prior experience that without a felt-needs approach, creating spiritual growth in the membership was often extremely slow, if not impossible. Instead, they saw a needs-based outreach as a way of plowing the fertile fields, and applying the truth of Scripture, guaranteed that they would have an attentive audience" (p. 107).

The Never-married Single Adult

These adults are single either by choice or by circumstance. In 1970, approximately 15 percent of the population of the United States had never been married. In 1980 that number had increased to approximately 20 percent (U.S. Bureau of Census, 1988, p. 72). According to the 1990 Census Bureau report, 22 percent of adults in America have never been married.

Although never-married single adults will be found in all of the major demographic categories, those between the ages of 21 and 35 make up the largest percentage of never-married singles. For example, "Since 1970, the proportion of persons age 25 - 29 who have never married has tripled for women and more than doubled for men" (Jones, 1991, p. 3).

Religious education programs that are most effective for meeting the needs of these young single adults include a large number of social activities and a strong focus on relationship building. Retreats, large group gatherings, recreational events, short-term elective seminars, and high energy events are welcomed and appreciated. Issues that might be especially pertinent to this group are dating, handling one's sexuality, loneliness, marriage, career, finding meaningfulness and purpose in life, and responsibility to the church. Small group discussions, panel discussions, and role plays are excellent techniques for addressing the aforementioned issues.

Never-married single adults should be encouraged to explore how they feel about singleness. Some of these single adults do not see themselves as making a conscious decision to be in a state of singleness, while others have consciously chosen this lifestyle (Sember, 1987). A simple technique the religious educator might use to help single adults explore their feelings about singleness is the *Circle Response*. In the Circle Response, questions are "posed to members of a group seated in a circle, each person in turn expressing a response" (Tighe & Szentkeresti, 1986, p. 94).

The Divorced Single Adult

Divorce in America has been on a steady rise over the past three decades, although the divorce rate has grown for at least a century. It picked up pace in the 1970s, but since 1980 the trend has been leveling off. Today, over 16 million American adults are currently divorced (*Unmarried America*, 1993, p. 63).

One of the primary reasons for this increase is that divorce is accepted by many as a reasonable alternative to an unhappy marriage. And while "the culturally based negative sanctions have diminished, so, too have the legal and economic constraints of obtaining a divorce" (Koons & Anthony, 1991, p. 104). For example, all but a few states have adopted some form of no-fault divorce, and reform of divorce laws "has generally resulted in a shortening of the required period of state residence and the required period of separation before a final decree is awarded by the court" (Koons & Anthony, 1991, pp. 104-105). "Although, of course, equal numbers of men and women divorce, the number of divorced women at any one time is greater than the number of divorced men because men are more likely to remarry, and do it

more quickly, than women. About five out of every six divorced men remarry, compared to three out of every four divorced women" (Stein, 1981, pp.
53-54).

A religious education program which seeks to meet the needs of a divorced
adult should include support groups, small group fellowships, divorce recovery seminars, and relational activities which foster an atmosphere of dialogue and interaction. Since some of these single adults will also have children, it would be helpful to include child care services for as many activities
as possible.

Religious education to divorced single adults should address issues such
as adjusting to divorce, remarriage, and handling transition and change. If children are involved, these individuals might need help in single parenting or handling custodial issues. Group seminars might be formed to enable single
parents to deal with child support payments, budget planning, and other
legal aspects of single parenting (Hunt, 1986). Some may be seeking forgiveness from God, from himself or herself, a former spouse, or children. They
may also be searching for biblical answers to questions related to marriage,
divorce, and remarriage (White, 1988).

The Separated Single Adult

Perhaps the most difficult classification of singleness to understand is
the separated single. Though legally married, this adult has removed him-
self/herself from his/her marital partner. In many cases, the couple has initiated the divorce proceedings and have begun the emotional process of
divorce. In some cases, the separated adults have chosen to remain legally married but are no longer living with their spouses. Generally, adults choose to
continue in this kind of arrangement for economic reasons such as allowing
both parties to receive health insurance benefits, residence status, or tax savings.

Religious education for the separated single adult should involve small
group workshops and seminars on special topics such as grief recovery and
surviving abusive relationships. Support groups and small group discussions
are also ideal in that they allow participants to self-disclose and share their
feelings in a supportive climate. Separated adults are individuals who are
in the midst of pain and stress, and any program which ignores the reality of
these pains will be ineffective and short-lived.

The Widowed Single Adult

Demographic figures indicate a continued increase in the number of adults
whose spouse has died. In 1987 there were 11 million widows and 2 million
widowers living in the United States. That figure represents approximately
5 percent of the. population of United States (Koons & Anthony, 1991, p. 60).

However, as one might assume, young adults make up a very small percentage of those who have lost a spouse through death (*Unmarried America*, 1993, p. 87).

Religious education for widowed young adults should be supportive (grief recovery seminars), as well as informative, and enabling (how to plan for future financial needs, navigating the job market for those who have been out for a while, health care issues while single). Many of these individuals need the reassurance of a small group of friends. However, they also need to be included in the larger activities of the church or they will begin to feel isolated and unwanted.

Myths and Misconceptions about Young Single Adults

Single adults have been and continue to comprise a growing percentage of the population. In 1970, there were a little over 37 million single adults living in the United States. In 1994 there are almost 70 million. This significant increase has brought about new societal attitudes, stereotypes, myths, and misconceptions, and in many cases, misunderstandings.

Young people experience a great deal of pressure to conform to commonly accepted social norms and standards of behavior. They live in a dichotomous world. It is no wonder that young single adults are bewildered as they seek to discover who they really are. Carolyn Koons (1988) says, "On one hand, we regard highly the values of individualism, being unique in thoughts and actions, and being competitive. On the other hand, we promote conformity, group consensus, and community" (p. 25). Duberman (1977) concludes, "The state of marriage is thought of as the natural order of things, and those who do not conform threaten this order; the result is that there is little room in the system for the unaccompanied person" (p. 115). Thus, the pressures and stereotypes begin and result in a host of misunderstandings, myths, and misconceptions. What follows are some commonly held myths about being a young single adult.

Myth #1: Young Single Adults Are Irresponsible
This misconception is based upon the belief that the apex of social stability comes when one is married, a home owner, and a parent (preferably with more than one child). Cargen and Melko (1982) comment on this common stereotype when they state, "The single is perceived to be less responsible, a swinger concerned with only having fun and looking after his or her own interests, a person lacking community ties and responsibilities; again, an immature and irresponsible person" (p. 21). One of the goals of those who are engaged in religious education ministry to young single adults should be to inform the members of the congregation about the pressing issues single

adults face. "When people begin to see singles as responsible adults it can significantly impact the way they respond to single adult needs and issues" (Fisher, 1992, p. 5).

Myth #2: All Young Single Adults Are Sexually Active

The media has traditionally portrayed the lifestyle of a young single adult as carefree and exploitive. The young adult experiences one sexual conquest after another with little regard for personal morals or standards of conduct. Although there may be a rare exception to this myth, the vast majority of single adults are not hopping from one bed to another. "According to several national studies of non-Christian singles, questions dealing with 'problem areas' and 'frustrations' indicate sexuality as fifth in concern. More important issues for singles were: (1) acceptable entertainment, (2) managing personal finances, (3) developing rewarding friendships, and (4) raising children as a single parent" (Koons & Anthony, 1991, p. 88).

Myth #3: The Young Single Adult Never Experiences Loneliness

This common misconception is based on the perception that young adults are always active and engaged in social interaction. For them, life is free of constricting responsibilities such as mortgage payments, health concerns, or caring for their parents. They are free to travel, pursue hobbies, and develop multiple relationships. In other words, "How could young singles ever get lonely?"

The reality is that young single adults are just as prone to bouts of loneliness as older single adults and their married peers. A recent survey of 27,000 people older than 18 found the highest rate of loneliness in those between 18 and 25 years of age (Meers, 1985, p. 32). "For some reason, college is the peak period when loneliness can invade the spirit as surreptitiously as a disease enters the bloodstream . . . . The fear of becoming a fringe person instead of one of the group. Above all, the fear that the real you does not matter to anyone" (Huggett, 1986, p. 1). Those young single adults who are not away at school also face their share of loneliness. It has been estimated that one-third of people in their late twenties who had never married still lived with their parents in 1990 (*Women delaying marriage*, 1991, p. 4). "These single adults may be extremely lonely, having few friends and few opportunities to make new friends. They may be hanging out at singles bars, seeking some kind of identity, seeking company" (Peak, 1990, p. 36).

Myth #4: Every Single Adult Wants To Get Married

This is a commonly held stereotype among churched adults. It is hard for many traditionally minded adults to believe that someone could actually enjoy being single and unattached. They assume that every young single adult wants to get married and that without a spouse they are facing frustration, anxiety, and pain. They want to help the young single "get fixed up with someone" as if they were somehow relationally broken. "Our society traditionally has said that singleness has too many disadvantages and a person is not complete until married" (Bell, 1992, p. 14). In a mild form of manifestation the single adult is the recipient of simple jesting and mild mannered prodding. The extreme form shows itself in a false theology which teaches that only a married man/woman could come to know and experience God's will for their life. Single adults become the brunt of jokes from the pulpit, and church leaders are often suspicious of the sexual orientation of single adults beyond the age of 30.

Many of these myths have been detrimental to the vitality of religious education ministry to single adults. Society's attitudes about single adults are often unfounded and based upon misleading media representation. Such commonly held stereotypes lead to misunderstanding. As with all myths, there may be an element of truth hiding in them somewhere, but a great deal of harm is done when such stereotypes form the basis of church policy toward the singles ministry.

The Sociological Phenomenon of Young Single Adults

Young single adults are distinct in their lifestyle from other demographic categories. Since over half (55 percemt) of the U.S. population of single adults are under 35 years of age (Hayner, 1987, p. 11) ministries which focus on this age group are usually well attended. In this category are two subgroups of young singles: those in a college/university and those active in a career.

Student Singles

Students attending college or university generally live away from home. Their lives reflect constant change as they begin to establish a lifestyle that is based upon personal values and standards as opposed to those of their parents. They are experiencing a new-found freedom and are experimenting with alternatives which are new and challenging. Education is a high priority to these single adults. In fact, many are consumed with the quest of academic discovery. Their lives are measured by units of time known as quarters or semesters. Their goals usually revolve around the completion of a degree or certification. They are flexible, generous, adventurous, transient, and open-minded about issues related to personal morality, social ethics, legal issues, etc. (Adams, 1992, p. 24).

Career Singles

Those who have left school, or who perhaps never attended college/university, comprise the second subcategory of young single adults. Within this subcategory are two classes. Some have chosen to enter a career and establish themselves in a stable lifestyle before settling down with a marriage partner. In essence, they have placed their personal careers before marriage, but they fully intend to marry at some future point. The other class of career singles are those who have made being single their career. They have no plans of getting married and have thrown themselves wholeheartedly into their careers. They have either chosen the single lifestyle or they feel that a single lifestyle has chosen them (Adams, 1992, p. 24).

The significant increase in the number of young single adults in the U.S. population has created a vast financial market. This sociological phenomenon has had far-reaching implications for corporations, educational institutions, health services, as well as the housing and travel industry.

Young single adults generally have more expendable income than their married peers. Wall Street marketing experts have acknowledged this economic power and have begun targeting the young single with advertisements and products suited for their unique lifestyle demands.

It is estimated that single adults spend up to 63 percent of their food budget on eating out. Restaurants are tailoring their decor, menu, and in-house entertainment to this segment of their customers. Young single adults also spend a good deal of their income on fashionable clothing. They are the biggest subscribers to fashion magazines, attend more movies and theaters than any other group, they join health clubs and fitness centers in larger proportions, travel more extensively, buy more expensive cars, and are more likely to go bowling than married adults (Jones, 1989, p. 51).

Stouffer's, one of United State's largest food companies, now makes over eighty-six different frozen foods designed to feed one person (Koons & Anthony, 1991, p. 55). However, just making food products for singles is no guarantee of success. Some companies have made the mistake of marketing their singles-oriented products with insensitive labels. Campbell Soup Company made that mistake with their Soup for One line. Robert Burnstock, a vice president for their soup division states, "Our consumers told us Soup for One is a lonely name. They are eating alone and don't need to be reminded. In 1990, after years of mediocre sales, the Soup for One label was removed. Single serving sizes now come without the offending label" (Jones, 1992, p. 5).

Since many of the single adults in this age category are beginning to move out and live away from home, they comprise a large percentage of the rental housing market. In addition, many of them are combining their incomes and purchasing single family homes and condominiums. The modern-day housing phenomenon known as the condominium community was designed specifically around the lifestyle of single adults. Today, hardly a community in the nation does not have a condominium complex within their city limits. Appliances such as refrigerators, microwave ovens, washers and dryers, coffee makers, and entertainment centers are all being built smaller to fit into these miniature homes.

Singles are demanding, and often getting, an increased voice in the policy decisions of many corporate institutions. Policies which have traditionally favored the married couple are being targeted by single adults for removal. Securing a home mortgage loan was once an opportunity primarily reserved for married couples since they represented an element of our society characterized by stability and secure risk. Purchasing a home is now a realistic option for even the single adult. Biased policies which adversely effect single adults in the health and automobile insurance industry are also being rewritten.

The power of young single adults is also being noticed in the voting booth. 1993 brought about the inauguration of the first United States president and vice president who were members of the Baby Boom generation. These individuals made campaign promises that were tailored to the interests and concerns of young single adults. Issues such as student tuition loans that could be repaid by national service, investment in job training, an end to employment discrimination, and broader rights for lesbians and homosexuals had a profound impact on the way these young and progressive individuals voted. Such power in the voting booth has far-reaching implications for the future shape of the nation.

Young single adults are flexing their economic and political muscles in ways never imagined by single adults who lived in the 1800s. No longer overlooked or viewed with disdain, this dimension of the American population is beginning to shape and influence the way America conducts business. They are indeed a new phenomenon in American society.

The Church's Response to the Singles Phenomenon

Though many industries and corporations across America have begun targeting young single adults because of their increased economic and political power, the church has been slow to recognize their available resources. These young adults have significant spiritual and emotional needs which only a relationship with Jesus Christ can meet. Many young single adults are experiencing pain and guilt from misplaced affections, poor financial decisions, broken interpersonal relationships, and feelings of isolations and shame. A personal relationship with Jesus can restore hope and bring healing to needy single adults. The Kingdom of God demands our response to those in such need.

Beyond the obvious biblical imperatives associated with ministry to the lost in our world, the church can also benefit from reaching out in a religious education ministry to young single adults. Once they are brought into a personal relationship with Jesus and their lives have begun to be transformed by the renewing influence of God's hand, they are able to make a contribution to the life of the church as well. With more time on their hands to fulfill leadership needs, more expendable income than married adults, increased mobility, and a host of other benefits, the church has much to gain from this untapped resource.

Dennis Chamberlain (1987) provides an excellent framework for the analysis of the church's religious education to young single adults. These "response levels" form a basis for determining the effectiveness of the local church as it seeks to reach out to young singles.

> *Response Level One*: This could be described as a "non-ministry" response. Churches that fall into this category may very well be healthy and active in their community, and they may also have a number of single adults within their general membership. However, this type of church sees no distinction between single adults and any other kind of adult . . . there exists no "directed" ministry toward the single person.
> *Response Level Two*: A church, particularly its leaders, is very much aware of the single adult's presence and there is a genuine concern; however, this church is unable to create any formal type of program for its single people. This church works to develop an atmosphere of acknowledgment and acceptance for the single person.
> *Response Level Three*: At this level there is specific organizational activity directed toward single adults. Church leaders participate in various ways to facilitate the development of a program.
> *Response Level Four*: This marks the beginning of the 'formal program' phase of development. On this level actual staff time is allocated for singles ministry as well as some means of financing the program.
> *Response Level Five*: This level continues the development with the hiring of a distinct staff person (at least half time) plus a formal budget allotment. By this point the single adult ministry is well-defined, well-supported, and easily recognized part of the overall church ministry. I would estimate that about 5 percent of the total number of churches today have developed a Level Five ministry (pp. 32-33).

These response levels help illustrate the stages of implementation which a church would undergo as they include a single adult ministry in their church goals. This ministry must be marked by purposeful planning, organization, and the allocation of appropriate resources.

Steps in Implementing a Religious Education Ministry to Young Single Adults

Beginning a religious education ministry to young single adults does not require extensive administrative finesse. It begins with a leader, either paid or volunteer, who has a call from God to reach young single adults. This divine motivation serves as a basis for the foundation of the group. This is the individual who is willing to invest the time and energy that is needed to lead such a group. Dyke (1989) suggests that this leader should be: "1) a person who is willing to accept responsibility for the ministry; 2) an individual of faith and vision; 3) an individual who can mobilize the gifts, talents, and resources of others; and 4) a person who can motivate people to active and effective involvement in singles ministry" (p. 23).

This individual should contact the leaders of the church (the Director of Religious Education, pastor and/or church board) and indicate a desire to begin a religious education ministry to young single adults. It is essential that the senior pastor, DRE, and/or church board be included in the initial stages of planning. Jim Smoke (1989) suggests that "the failure of the senior pastor and pastoral staff to understand and support the ministry will cause it to fail or at best, sputter and chug along" (p. 21).

Once the leadership of the church has agreed to begin such a ministry there needs to be a clearly developed philosophy of ministry. This philosophy should seek to answer questions such as, "What kind of young single adults does God want to reach at our church?" "Do we want to have an emphasis in outreach to nonbelievers, growth for believers, or a mixture of the two?" "Will the young single adult religious education ministry be integrated into the entire church membership or do we want it to be independent?" Questions such as these set the direction for the group and help insure that the desired outcome is met.

The next step in the process is to gather a team of young adult leaders who share in the vision and are willing to invest their time and resources in religious education to young single adults. The young single adult group should periodically elect a council of leaders who can work together as a team. These members should be representative of the types of young single adults that your church desires to target. This committee of leaders should be commissioned with the task of planning and organizing the ministry. A young single adult religious education ministry, like any other ministry in the local church, should have the involvement of its membership. Shared leadership was an important characteristic of the early church and should be reflected in our ministries as well. A group that does not have input into its goals and objectives will grow disheartened and decline.

The next step in the process is to establish some guidelines or standards of conduct. Each church will have different doctrinal or denominational distinctives regarding certain behaviors. For example, many churches do not allow dancing in their program activities. Most will restrict the use of alcohol at church sponsored functions. Another issue which is best tackled early is the church's position on single adults who are living together. Since the number of Americans living together outside of marriage has increased more than 400 percent since 1970 (Jones, 1992, p. 1) it is quite likely that you will encounter such an arrangement by a member of your group.

The DRE should have some input in the establishment of some of these standards. However, it is essential that the leadership council also have an opportunity to help establish these policies. Many of these issues will undoubtedly bring significant dialogue and discussion, but it is much easier to discuss these issues and come to a consensus regarding a policy decision before personalities get involved.

The final step is to advertise throughout the community. To attract young single adults, college and university newspapers are helpful publicity resources. Other possibilities are community newspapers, bulletin boards at local health clubs, radio spots, and public notices at apartment and condominium complexes. Young career-age single adults may be a bit more difficult to reach than other groups due to the diversity of their lifestyles.

These advertisements should highlight the positive dimensions such as contemporary music, small groups designed for support and encouragement, as well as quality teaching and instruction. Terminology should be inclusive and nonoffensive, and attempts to sensationalize the ministry should be avoided.

The initial stage of a single adult religious education ministry is critical. The church that invests in the lives of young single adults is investing in its future. The church congregation should be educated in the need and importance for the religious education of young single adults, and the leadership of the church should be united in their resolve and committed to the costs for such a venture.

Program Planning for a Religious Education Ministry to Young Single Adults

Getting a religious education ministry started is one thing, keeping it going and nurturing its development can be quite another challenge altogether. The following guidelines are provided to help the young single adult leader maintain a quality program of religious education.

Recognize Differences

Do not put all young single adults into one group. Those who work with young single adults must take into consideration the distinct differences between the college-aged single adults and the career single adults. Some churches have combined the two groups while the ministry gets started and then divide the group at a later date. That has proven to work well for many churches. The danger comes when the group begins to grow and the leadership wants to maintain a high profile by keeping the group together. Eventually, individuals will begin dropping out because of frustration.

The college-aged single adults will be frustrated by the lack of fun and impulsive behavior demonstrated by the more mature career-oriented single adults. Some of the career single adults will be divorced, and a few may even have young children. The college-aged single adults have difficulty relating to the issues often faced by these older single adults. Likewise, the career single adults will feel frustrated with what they perceive as irresponsible behavior on the part of the college-aged single. The career single adult watches the college-aged single adults spend several hundred dollars on a weekend ski trip, new trendy fashion outfit, or sound system for their car. Many of these career single adults are making payments on mortgages, alimony, or other long-term obligations. They are living in different worlds.

Due to these different sociological outlooks the two groups may be able to bond during the initial stages of development, but once the group gets established it will begin to show signs of strain and tension. One way to lower this tension is for the DRE to let the young single adults know at the beginning that the two groups will be together only for a predetermined period of time. If they know in advance that they will be together for only six months, or one year, they will not feel as threatened by the presence of the other single adults.

No Ministry Can Be All-Inclusive

Recognize that there are no perfect religious education ministries to young single adults. No one ministry can meet the needs of all of its members. Some single adult groups will attract, and therefore specialize in, divorce recovery. Other single adult groups may specialize in activities for never-married singles. It is a simple reality that few churches have enough resources to meet the needs of young single adults of all types. Some churches are limited by finances, while others are limited by the amount of available leadership. Few churches can do it all.

Expect Turnover

Do not be surprised if the young single adult religious education ministry experiences a great deal of turnover. Young single adults are transient people.

One of the primary reasons young adults choose to remain single is because they enjoy the freedom and mobility that a single lifestyle offers. Young single adult groups will experience a great number of visitors. The DRE and leadership council must address this reality and come up with a plan to enfold these visitors into the group. However, they will face disappointment if they expect the majority of these visitors to return. In most cases, visitors will come for only a week or two and then explore other opportunities. Relatively few of the young single adults will remain for a prolonged period of time.

Expect Misunderstandings

Do not be surprised when misunderstandings occur. Some degree of misunderstanding is likely to occur in a church where the married adults in leadership lack an understanding of single adult lifestyles. Sometimes these misunderstandings will come from the congregation that does not understand the complexity of needs which are faced by single adults in their church and community. Other times this misunderstanding may come from young single adults themselves, as they lack an understanding of how they fit into the larger sphere of the church community. The director of young single adult religious education will need to keep a lookout for these misunderstandings and make every effort to keep them distracting either the young single adults or the church membership as a whole.

The Use of Conferences

The use of large scale conferences for young single adults can be an excellent way to "kick off" a new single adult program. It can also be an effective means for starting a new theme or unit of discussion. These large group activities provide an opportunity for the singles in the group to bring their friends. Outside music and speakers can be brought in to allow variety from the normal routine. This approach is ideal when the religious education program for young single adults is combined with other churches in the area. Wood (1977) states, "One of the best examples of effective programming on a multi-church scale has been the single adult conferences, which, from beginning to completion, have reflected the needs and concerns of the singles in different churches. The themes of these conferences reflect a growth process on the part of the single adult and the single adult programs in the churches" (p. 155). These conferences can be held at a nearby retreat center, a cabin in the mountains which is owned by a member of the church, or perhaps at the local church itself.

Integration into the Church

It is important to integrate the religious education program of young single adults into the total church community. The religious education program should serve to bring young single adults into the full life of the church. There is a danger when a young single adult religious education ministry begins to grow and establish itself. If not kept in check, the temptation will be for the young single adults to view themselves as a small church within the larger body. One way to know if this has happened is by determining what percentage of the young single adults attend the regular Sunday morning worship service. Their involvement in the worship service is an indication of their involvement and commitment to the greater community of believers.

It is important that the religious education program of young single adults not be viewed as autonomous from the local church which serves to support it. Speaking of this danger, Terry Hershey (1986) writes, "The potential and temptation of any satellite ministry is that each satellite becomes a congregation unto itself. . . . Any program such as young adult ministry set up as a homogeneous support structure should serve as a funnel into the body, not as a funnel away from the body" (138).

Conclusion

As religious educators, we are compelled to reach out to those in need. Young single adults have long been overlooked in the church. Single adults have played an important role in the development of the plan of God for mankind. Many of God's leaders in the Old and New Testament including Ruth, Elijah, Daniel, Mary, and Martha, the apostle Paul, and of course our Lord, were single adults, at least during important phases of their ministry.

The church that begins and develops a program of religious education to young single adults is making a bold statement about the value of non-married adults. Whether never-married, divorced, separated, or widowed, the young single adult has needs which can best be met in the environment of a loving church. Scripture has much to contribute toward helping these individuals develop a biblically based self-concept, overcoming feelings of loneliness and isolation, establishing standards of conduct based upon moral absolutes, guidelines for the stewardship of personal resources, and a host of other related issues.

Single adults, especially those who are divorced, have felt left out and unwanted in many churches. The church has much to offer these individuals who are searching for answers to their hurts and pains. The destination of their search should be Christ himself. The door to finding that answer will be, in most cases, the local church. A church which provides varied religious education programming provides multiple avenues for coming into and strengthening a personal and communal relationship with God in Jesus.

References

Adams, M. (1992). Preaching with a single point of view. *Search, 21*, 23-27.

Barna, G. (1991). *User friendly churches*. Venture, CA: Regal.

Bell, H. R. (1992). Trends among American singles. *Search, 21*. 12-21.

Bell, J. (1993). *Bridge over troubled water*. Wheaton, IL: Victor Books.

Cargen, L., & Melko, M. (1982). *Singles: Myths and realities*. Beverly Hills, CA: Sage.

Chamberlain, D. (1987). Let's start at the beginning . . . Who are the single adults? In K. S. Welsh (Ed.), *Successful single adult ministry: It can happen in your church*. Cincinnati: Standard.

Duberman, L. (1977). *Marriage and other alternatives*. New York: Praeger.

Dyke, J. (1989). Signs of a successful single adult ministry. *National Single Adult Ministries Resource Directory*. Colorado Springs, CO: Single Adult Ministries.

Fisher, T. (1992). Will there be single adult supervision for your singles social? *Single Adult Ministries Journal, 9*, 5.

Hayner, J. (1987). *Growing together: Singles and churches*. Nashville, TN: Convention Press.

Hershey, T. (1986). *Young adult ministry*. Loveland, CO: Group.

Huggett, J. (1986). "The other side of loneliness." *His, 46,*1-4.

Hunt, R. (1986). Working with single parents. In N. Foltz (Ed.), *Handbook of adult religious education* (pp.151-180). Birmingham, AL: Religious Education Press.

Jones, J. (1989). Singles—The never-married. In D. Fagerstrom (Ed.), *Singles ministry handbook* (pp. 48-53). Wheaton, IL: Victor.

Jones, J. (1992). Unmarried couples living together. *Single Adult Ministries Journal. 9,*1.

Jones, J. (Ed.) (1991). U.S. single adult population nears 70 million. *Single Adult Ministries Journal, 8*, 3-6.

Koons, C., & Anthony, M. (1991). Single adult passages: *Uncharted territories*. Grand Rapids, MI: Baker.

Koons, C. (1988). Today's single adult phenomenon: The realities and myths. In D. Fagerstrom (Ed.), *Single ministries handbook* (pp. 25-30). Wheaton, IL: Victor.

Leslie, G. (1976). *The family in social context*. New York: Oxford University Press.

May, E. (1983). Great expectations: Marriage and divorce in post victorian America. Chicago: University of Chicago Press.

Meers, J. (1985, July). Loneliness. *Psychology Today, 19*, 28-33.

n.a. (1991, June). Women delaying marriage. *The Norman Transcript, 7*, 4.

Nimkoff, M. (1947). *Marriage and the family*. Boston: Houghton Mifflin.

Peak, G. (1990). Identify and enroll single adults. In R. A. Hill (Ed.), *Break through: Single adult Sunday school work*. Nashville, TN: Convention Press.

Roof, W. (1993). *A generation of seekers*. San Francisco: Harper.

Sember, T. (1987). Single young adults. In R. Bagley (Ed.), *Young adult ministry: A book of readings* (pp. 65-71). New Rochelle, NY: Don Bosco Multimedia.

Seward, R. (1978). *The American family: A demographic history*. Beverly Hills, CA: Sage.

Smoke, J. (1989). Thirteen reasons why a singles ministry can fail. *National Single Adult Ministries Resource Directory*. Colorado Springs, CO: Single Adult Ministries.

Stein, P. J. (Ed.) (1981). *Single life: Unmarried adults in social context*. New York: St. Martin's Press.

Tighe, J., & Szentkeresti, K. (1986). *Rethinking adult religious education*. New York: Paulist.

United States Bureau of the Census. (1990). *Marital status and living arrangements* (Current population reports. Series P-20, Population characteristics; no. 450). Washington, DC: U. S. Government Printing Office.

United States Bureau of the Census (1992). *Statistical abstract of the United States,* 112th ed. Washington, DC.

Unmarried America. (1993). Glenadale, CA: Barna Research Group.

White, W. (1988). Singles—The formerly married. In D. Fagerstrom (Ed.), *Singles ministry handbook* (pp. 57-60). Wheaton, IL.: Victor.

Wood, B. (1977). *Single adults want to be the church too.* Nashville, TN: Broadman.

CHAPTER TWELVE

Family Life Religious Education

NICK AND NANCY STINNETT

In Mark 12:28-31, an incident is recorded in which a Scribe, listening to Jesus talk with the Sadducees, Pharisees, and Herodians, asked which is the greatest commandment. Jesus answered, "The first of all the commandments is, Hear, O Israel; The Lord our God is one Lord: And thou shalt love the Lord thy God with all thy heart, and with all thy soul, and with all thy mind, and with all thy strength: this is the first commandment. And the second is like, namely this, Thou shalt love thy neighbor as thyself. There is none other commandment greater than these." Although only asked which is the first commandment, Jesus links the first which defines our relationship with God to the second which defines our relationships with other people. From this we may conclude that our healthy relationship with others is a central and obligatory part of a relationship with God.

Indeed, as young adults we are connected to many other people: our parents and relatives, friends, a spouse (for over 90 percent of adults) and in-laws, our children, co-workers, neighbors, and acquaintances (Stinnett, Walters, & Stinnett, 1991). Being able to establish close, significant relationships is vital all through life for the maintenance of identity and meaning, joy, and spirituality.

Why focus, then, on *family* relationships in young adult religious education? First, for most young adults, relationships within our families—with our parents, with a spouse, with our children—are the closest and most signifi-

271

cant relationships. Consequently most are aware of their need for improving family relationships.

Furthermore, Money (1987) states that the stability of the church is enhanced by the stability of families. He continues by observing that, "the family is the laboratory for Christian living. If it doesn't work at home, where does it work?" (p. 76). Sell (1981) notes that the dynamic aspects of family life such as cherishing, caring, encouraging, rebuking, repenting, forgiving, expressing kindness, and communicating honestly are also to be found within the church body.

The purpose of this chapter is to provide an overview of the area of family life religious education for young adults. Two major areas will be covered: concepts related to family life and methods for implementing a family life religious education program for young adults.

Concepts Related To Family Life

This section will address some significant concepts related to family life for young adults including family strengths, marital success, and effective parenting.

Family Strengths

In recent years some social scientists and the media have focused much attention on the problems and challenges of families. Indeed families are confronted with a variety of difficult situations: high rates of divorce, remarriage and stepparenting, teen pregnancies, AIDS and other sexually transmitted diseases, family violence, substance abuse, financial pressures, balancing work and family, fragmented family schedules, and suicide — to name a few. In spite of this, however, many families do *not* disintegrate or break apart. Instead they endure and many do well.

Understanding these families who do well, who are successful, provides a base of knowledge for programs of young adult religious education, counseling, and enrichment (Krysan, Moore, & Zill, 1990; Money, 1987). A family may be defined as successful by the characteristics of the individual members, by the characteristics of the family interaction, or by the extent to which it fulfills certain functions considered to be the responsibility of the family (Krysan et al., 1990). A strong family is one that creates a sense of positive family identity, promotes satisfying and fulfilling interaction among members, encourages the development of family group and individual members, and is able to deal effectively with stress and crises (Stinnett, Chesser, & DeFrain, 1979). Lewis and Looney (1983) propose that a family is successful to the extent that it provides an environment conducive to the development of child and parent alike.

For almost forty years, researchers have been generating sets of characteristics common to healthy, functional families. Although the researchers come from differing disciplines and perspectives, certain themes appear again and again. Some of these themes, which are often interrelated, are as follows:

- Commitment, connectedness (Curran, 1983; Hill, 1971; Lewis, 1979; Olson, 1986; Otto, 1963; Pollak, 1957; Schumm, 1986; Stinnett & DeFrain, 1985)
- Time together (Curran, 1983; Lewis, 1979; Schumm, 1986; Stinnett & DeFrain, 1985)
- Open communication (Curran, 1983; Lewis, 1979; Olson, 1986; Otto, 1963; Satir, 1972; Stinnett & DeFrain, 1985)
- Appreciation and encouragement (Curran, 1983; Epstein, Baldwin, & Bishop, 1983; Otto, 1963; Pollak, 1957; Schumm, 1986; Stinnett & DeFrain, 1985)
- Performance of roles (Beavers, 1977; Curran, 1983; Epstein et al., 1983; Hill, 1971; Olson, 1986; Otto, 1963; Pollak, 1957; Satir, 1972)
- Spiritual wellness (Curran, 1983; Epstein et al., 1983; Hill, 1971; Olson, 1986; Otto, 1963; Stinnett & DeFrain, 1985)
- Community involvement (Curran, 1983; Olson, McCubbin, Barnes, Larsen, Muxen, & Wilson, 1983; Otto, 1963; Pratt, 1976; Satir, 1972; Whitaker, 1980)
- Ability to Cope with Crises (Epstein et al., 1983; Olson, 1986; Otto, 1963; Pratt, 1976; Stinnett & DeFrain, 1985)

Commitment, connectedness. Although many people verbalize a commitment to family, members of strong families support their words with actions. They have made a conscious decision to value, sustain, and promote each family member (Stinnett & DeFrain, 1985). Family members demonstrate respect for each other (Curran, 1983; Otto, 1963) and report strong bonds of kinship (Hill, 1971).

At another level, commitment and connectedness are demonstrated by a valuing of the family unit and a sense of the family as a whole (Curran, 1983; Stinnett & DeFrain, 1985; Whitaker, 1980). Family members share a concern for family unity and have pride in belonging to the family (Olson et al., 1983; Otto, 1963). Rituals and traditions are important ways in which family identity is cultivated (Curran, 1983; Stinnett & DeFrain, 1985).

Time together. Another characteristic of strong families is that they spend time together. They enjoy being together in many areas of life — eating meals, doing house and yard chores, and sharing leisure activities (Curran, 1983; Olson et al., 1983; Stinnett & DeFrain, 1985). Members of healthy families achieve a balance between too much time together (enmeshed) and too little time together (disengaged) (Olson et al., 1983). It is recognized, too, that true *quality* time demands a certain quantity of time and that great quantities of poor quality time are not desirable.

Open communication. The presence of effective communication patterns is one of the most frequently reported characteristics of healthy families (Swihart, 1988). Communication in strong families is clear, open, frequent, and honest (Epstein et al., 1983; Lewis, 1979; Olson, 1986; Stinnett & DeFrain, 1985). Communication is both an effective skill for dealing with the challenges of daily life and a reflection of these family members' enjoyment of each other (Stinnett & DeFrain, 1989).

Members of healthy families are not exempt from conflicts and arguments. They are, however, skilled in resolving conflicts (Olson et al., 1983). For example, they attack the problem (rather than each other), discuss possible solutions and select one that is best for everyone (Stinnett et al., 1991). Humor is used to relieve tensions and to restore a positive outlook (Wuerffel, DeFrain, & Stinnett, 1990).

Appreciation and encouragement. Each of us likes to be with people who make us feel good about ourselves. Members of strong families express large measures of appreciation to each other; they build each other up psychologically (Stinnett & DeFrain, 1989). For example, we all do things each day that we're "supposed" to do—fix dinner, feed the cat, go to work. These tasks require time and effort; an expression of appreciation ("Good dinner!" "You work hard to provide for us.") boosts the self-esteem of the receiver and creates a bond of caring between recipient and giver (Stinnett & DeFrain, 1989).

On the other hand, a spirit of criticism can have far-reaching negative effects (Money, 1987). The recipient of criticism usually feels diminished and hurt. Very well-intentioned parents may assume that they must correct all of their children's short-comings and be liberal with "constructive criticism" in order to improve the children. Instead their efforts may backfire as children become discouraged and defeated; grades and behavior may deteriorate instead of improving (Hamner & Turner, 1990).

Performance of roles. Families that function successfully have clearly defined roles for family members (Beavers, 1977; Lewis, 1979; Otto, 1963; Satir, 1972). At the same time members of strong families often have an attitude of flexibility about the performance of roles; they share roles and are egalitarian in fulfilling roles (Beavers, 1977; Curran, 1983; Hill, 1971; Olson, 1986; Otto, 1963). With a clear, yet flexible structure in place, family members are aware of their responsibilities and the physical and emotional needs of family members are met on a daily basis. And in the face of a crisis, family members both know their roles and feel comfortable being flexible in meeting family needs. As a result the family's ability to adapt is enhanced (Krysan et al., 1990).

Issues of power—who decides what and how decisions are made—are also related to the concept of role definition. For example, within healthy families parents are clearly in charge. At the same time, parents remain open to their children's input and rarely are seen as authoritarian (Krysan et al., 1990; Lewis, 1979).

Spiritual wellness. Religious orientation has been identified as an important component of healthy family functioning (Curran, 1983; Stinnett & DeFrain, 1985). Many members of strong families express their spiritual nature by participation in organized religion—by membership in a church or synagogue and attendance at formal worship services and study groups. Others manifest their spirituality in concern for others, involvement in worthy causes, or adherence to a moral code (Stinnett & DeFrain, 1989). Members of healthy families have a set of values including a sense of right and wrong to guide their behavior (Curran, 1983; Epstein et al., 1983).

The religious quality in strong families could be described as the practice of spiritual health or wellness. Members of these families report that they have an awareness of God that gives them a sense of purpose and gives their family a sense of support. The awareness of God helps them to keep things in perspective, to be more patient, to be more positive, to get over anger, and to forgive more readily (Stinnett & DeFrain, 1989).

Community involvement. Successful families are not isolated from their communities and the wider society (Curran, 1983; Olson et al., 1983; Otto, 1963; Pratt, 1976; Satir, 1972; Whitaker, 1980). Instead they report a network of involvement in their communities in volunteer work, service to others, and fellowship with friends and neighbors. In return, strong families become aware of the resources within their community. They seek help when faced with problems, thus improving their ability to cope with life's difficulties (Curran, 1983; Krysan et al., 1990).

Ability to cope with crises. The family's ability to cope with stressful and potentially damaging events has been identified as a characteristic of strong families (Olson et al., 1983; Otto, 1963; Pratt, 1976; Stinnett & DeFrain, 1989). Members of healthy families utilize a combination of traits already mentioned to deal with crises: effective communication, encouragement of each other, humor, clear and flexible roles, spiritual wellness, commitment to each other , and community involvement. By calling on their resources (within the family and without) they are able to unite to face the crisis instead of being fragmented by it. And they are able, even in the most difficult situations, to see positives and to focus on them. It may be, for example, a renewed realization of how much they mean to each other (Stinnett & DeFrain, 1989).

Marriage Success

Marriage success is difficult to define. It is not necessarily how long a marriage relationship lasts, or the intensity which is experienced, or how little conflict occurs.

One definition of a successful marriage is that it is a relationship in which both partners feel they receive a high degree of personal satisfaction most of the time. The partners believe that their emotional, psychological, and physical needs are fulfilled by their involvement in the marriage relationship. They perceive that they have found the satisfaction they hoped for in the situation (Bowman & Spanier, 1978; Stinnett et al., 1991). Some of the most satisfying and least satisfying aspects of marriage, as reported in a survey of middle-class couples, are noted in Table 1.

Table 1
Most Satisfying and Least Satisfying Aspects of Marriage

Most Satisfying

For Men	For Women
Friendship	Friendship
Companionship	Personal growth
Shared interests and goals	Supportive partner
Building family together	Children
Children	Secure lifestyle

Most Unsatisfying

For Men	For Women
Not sexually satisfied	Sexual relationships
Money	Finances
Children too demanding	Husband's workload
Restrictions on personal freedom	Children

(Schlesinger, 1984)

Marriage success has remained an area of high interest for family therapists and social-science researchers. Much research has been conducted, identifying factors associated with marriage success over the past sixty years. Some of the major factors related to marriage success are now summarized briefly.

Personal happiness. Individuals who are happy are more likely to have successful, happy marriages (Leigh, Ladehoff, Howie, & Christians, 1985).

Parents' marriage. Children of parents who divorced are themselves more likely to divorce (Glenn & Kramer, 1987).

Parental approval. Approval of the marriage by the parents is important to marriage success.

Length of courtship. Longer courtships (one year or more) are associated with a greater likelihood of marital success (Whipple & Whittle, 1976).

Age of marriage. Couples who marry young (younger than age 20) have a higher rate of divorce and a greater degree of marital difficulties (Norton & Moorman, 1987; Price-Bonham & Balswick, 1980).

Premarital pregnancy. Marriages that are formed because of premarital pregnancy have a high rate of divorce, with approximately 40 percent to 50 percent ending within five years (Norton & Moorman, 1987; Price-Bonham & Balswick, 1980).

Reasons for marriage. That some individuals marry for negative reasons—to escape an unhappy home, to defy parents, or to reduce loneliness—does not necessarily mean the marriage will end in divorce, but it does add to the likelihood of dissatisfaction and to the greater probability of divorce (Stinnett et al., 1991).

Homogamy. While small differences can be stimulating in a marriage relationship, major differences in many areas are more often too challenging and stressful. For this reason, a couple similar in terms of race, ethnic group, socio-economic status, education, intelligence, sociability, mental health, general energy level, and values are more likely to experience marital success. (Knox, 1988; Price-Bonham & Balswick, 1980; Whipple & Whittle, 1976).

Personality characteristics. Unhappily married individuals are more likely to perceive their partners as being unkind, impatient, blunt, aggressive, complaining, gloomy, slow to forgive, skeptical, and distrustful. Many personality characteristics may contribute to marital unhappiness such as extreme aggressiveness, competitiveness, dominance, passivity, independence, self-centeredness, jealousy, and feelings of superiority (Luckey, 1964; Stinnett et al., 1991).

Individuals who possess personality traits that contribute to good interpersonal relationships in general are more likely to have happy marriage relationships. Certain personality characteristics consistently have been identified in research as being associated with marriage success (Bell, Daly, & Gonzalez, 1987; Fowers & Olson, 1986; Rao & Rao, 1986). They include the following:

Ability to express affection	Empathy
Self-control	Optimism
Emotional stability	Favorable self-concept
Stability	Honesty
Loyalty	Conventionality
Responsibility	Flexibility
Kindness	Generosity
Ability to handle anger and conflict constructively	Considerateness

Communication. Much research evidence indicates that the communication patterns of happily married couples differ from those of unhappily married couples (Alberts, 1988; Bell et al., 1987; DeFrain & Stinnett, 1992; Fowers & Olson, 1986; Rosenfeld & Bowen, 1991; Stinnett & DeFrain, 1989):

- They talk to each other more often.
- They demonstrate more sensitivity to each other's feelings.
- They more often convey the feeling that they understand what is being said to them.
- They make greater use of nonverbal methods of communication.
- They keep communication channels open more effectively.

Relationships with in-laws. Developing relationships with in-laws and extended family is one of the first critical adjustments that a newly married couple must make. Each partner must redefine the relationship with his or her own parents and must relinquish his or her primary relationship with the parents so that the new spouse may be primary. The new couple is more likely to experience marital satisfaction if they can develop a network of relationships with their in-laws that is positive and satisfying (Bader & Sinclair, 1983; Lingren, Van Zandt, Stinnett, & Rowe, 1982).

In a classic study of in-law relationships, Duvall (1954) found that the most frequent complaints against children-in-law were that they were indifferent, inconsiderate, and too busy to be interested in the parents' lives. The most common complaints against mothers- and fathers-in-law were that they were meddlesome, nagging, critical, and possessive.

Newly married individuals may develop positive relationships with in-laws by communicating with them, spending time with them and getting to know them as persons, respecting them and accepting differences, avoiding conflict over the trivial or what cannot be changed, and expanding the concept of family by regarding the in-laws as family (Stinnett et al., 1991). The development of good in-law relationships contributes to marriage success because in-laws are a potentially powerful network of support for the marriage relationship.

Religious participation. The positive relationship between religiosity and marriage success has been noted in numerous studies during the last forty years. Couples with a strong religious faith and who attend services frequently have fewer divorces and report greater marriage happiness than non religious couples (Brodbar-Nemzer, 1986; Fowers & Olson, 1986; Wilson & Filsinger, 1986).

Perhaps the major reason for the link between religious faith and marriage success is that the principal teachings of the major religions emphasize values that contribute to success in relationships in general. Values which most religions stress include love, commitment, respect, mutual support and aid, patience, forgiveness, service, and fidelity. Also, membership in a church or synagogue aids in integrating the family into the larger community. The family experiences social support, friends who value marriage and family, and assistance in times of crises. All of these help to provide stability for the marriage (DeFrain & Stinnett, 1992; Stinnett et al., 1991).

Relationship factors. Marital happiness is the result of the total interpersonal relationship between husband and wife in which positive psychological and emotional support is maximized (Stinnett et al., 1991). Relationship factors which are important contributors to marital happiness include mutual respect, expressions of appreciation and affection, commitment, and trust (Ammons & Stinnett, 1980; Stinnett & DeFrain, 1989; Stinnett et al., 1991). A good understanding of the types of behavior that promote a positive marriage relationship may be gained by considering the results of a study by Bell et al. (1987) who found that the wife's marital satisfaction was related to her husband's ability to be sincere and honest; to be physically affectionate; and to act in a caring, warm, and empathic manner.

Mate selection practices. One of most important influences on marriage success is wise mate selection. Specific mate selection practices which increase the probability of marriage success include: spending enough time together to really come to know each other well and to determine if the couple is compatible in terms of personalities, life goals, and interests; being oneself rather than pretending and playing a false role; participating in a variety of activities other than just entertainment, such as buying groceries and cooking dinner for some friends or volunteering in a program working with young children; and considering the probable effects of the relationship. For example, does the relationship bring out the best in both persons? Is each person happier and more optimistic as a result of being together? What will the relationship be like ten years from now?

Marital role expectations. Marriage success is positively affected by compatibility or similarity in marital role expectation. The more important the roles are to the individuals, the more important it is that those role expectations be compatible (Bokemeier & Maurer, 1987; Buunk & Van Yperen, 1991; Li & Caldwell, 1987).

Parenting

Although many couples do not think about it at the time of their marriage, most will eventually become parents. About 97 percent of persons able to have children do so (Hamner & Turner, 1990). Being a parent is a challenging and difficult role requiring knowledge and skills. Yet some persons assume that parenting "comes naturally" or that "loving a child is enough" to guarantee successful childrearing.

Being a parent is also a very rewarding role to fulfill and most parents gain a great deal of pleasure from their children. Having some information about the needs of children, the differences in parenting over the life cycle, and some specific skills for parenting makes the task of rearing children easier.

Needs of children. From research and observation in the field of child development, we understand that children have several important needs. Naturally, they need to have food, clothing, shelter, and health care. Children also need to be kept safe from a variety of hazards. In addition to physical needs, children have important emotional needs (Stinnett et al., 1991).

Bronfenbrenner (1985) states that the most critical need of a child is at least one person to be *irrationally* and *actively* involved in the child's life. By *irrational*, he means someone (usually parents or grandparents) who loves the child without any conditions attached, who thinks the best about the child, who accepts the child unconditionally. By *active*, he means someone who takes care of the child, talks and plays with the child. Bronfenbrenner says that the child benefits even more if there are two or more people irrationally and actively involved in her life and if there is peace between those people.

Another of the foundational needs of children is that of trust (Hamner & Turner, 1990; Stinnett et al., 1991). Parents begin meeting this need from the time the baby is born. When the baby is uncomfortable due to hunger and wet diapers or is lonely or is frightened, he cries. Parents who respond consistently and promptly to make baby comfortable teach that the world is good and reliable. The child learns a sense of trust. Children who consistently receive prompt, loving attention from their caregivers are more likely to be trusting and trustworthy in all their future relationships (Hamner & Turner, 1990; Stinnett et al., 1991).

Children have a need to explore, to become independent, to make decisions, and to learn. Parents are challenged to find the balance between too little freedom and too much freedom, because children also need the security of limits. Limits and boundaries help children to perceive the world as reliable and fair. They also demonstrate that someone cares enough to provide guidance. Limits and boundaries should be fair and reasonable or the child may become overly dependent, passive, or aggressive. Limits should always be stated with the reason behind the limit. For example, the parent says, "Pick up your toys from the floor when you're finished so no one will trip over them and be hurt." Such explanations help children develop the ability to reason (Hamner & Turner, 1990; Stinnett et al., 1991).

Clarke (1978) states, "Self-esteem is one of the greatest attributes a child can develop because learning, life, health, and even humanness itself are all functions of self-esteem" (p. 4). Persons need to feel whole, worthwhile, and valued to face life's experiences most effectively (Lee & Brage, 1989).

Most parents aspire to have their children develop positive self-esteem and the characteristics associated with high levels of positive regard for self such as: leadership, confidence, health, creativity, achievement, and optimism (Coopersmith, 1968). It has been suggested that self-esteem includes feelings of personal worth, competence (capability), and belonging. These are influenced by performance, appearance, abilities, and the judgments of significant others (Elder, 1968; Hamner & Turner, 1990; Lee & Brage, 1989). Parents who wish to bolster self-esteem in their children will express unconditional regard and acceptance of the child and will help the child to acquire skills and abilities. They also will recognize that self-esteem in childhood is largely dependent upon the recognition, attention, and encouragement received from others (Stinnett et al., 1991).

Parenting over the family life cycle. Family relationships can also be analyzed using a developmental approach. From a developmental perspective, each entity (person, family) passes through a series of stages. Each stage is characterized by tasks to accomplish and challenges to meet before the entity can move successfully to the next stage. This concept is called family life cycle or family career when applied to families (Aldous, 1978; McGoldrick & Carter, 1982; Stinnett et al., 1991).

The family life cycle begins when a couple go through courtship and marry. The birth of a child marks the transition to another stage of the family life cycle. The couple with young children face the adjustments of realigning the marital system to make space for the children, learning parental roles, and realigning relationships with extended family (who are now grandparents) (McGoldrick & Carter, 1982).

Children have differing developmental tasks as they grow, too. Infants are challenged to learn a basic sense of trust. Parents of infants may facilitate the development of trust by providing prompt, consistent care to the baby. Infants also need opportunities to form a close bond with their parents. This is encouraged when parents hold, cuddle, and stroke their infant. Even very young babies respond to verbal stimulation such as singing and talking; they are soothed by quiet music. The cognitive development of infants is stimulated by an environment rich with sights and sounds: brightly colored sheets, pictures on the walls, mobiles, and toys are all ways to enliven the surroundings (Hamner & Turner, 1990).

As children approach their second birthday, they need to make more decisions and to express their developing autonomy. Parents may help their toddler by allowing her to make many decisions appropriate to her age. The toddler can, for example, be allowed to choose milk or juice at lunch, which shirt (of two) to wear, or which bedtime book to read. Because toddlers are very active and mobile, safety is a major concern for parents. Cleaning materials, medicines, sharp objects, and other hazards should be put out of reach.

Additionally, children of this age require constant supervision (Hamner & Turner, 1990).

Preschool-aged children (3-5 years) are growing in a sense of initiative; they like to make things and to make things happen. Parents may nurture their developing abilities by providing opportunities and materials for playing and creating and making believe. A fenced yard with sandbox, swings, and tricycles is excellent for outdoor play. Crayons, paper, old magazines to cut, paste, brushes and paint encourage creativity. Old clothes, shoes, and hats spark hours of make-believe play. Parents should continue reading to their children and simple excursions to the zoo or park are fun family outings (Hamner & Turner, 1990).

As children enter school, they also enter the larger world around them. They become aware of their need to learn as much as possible and learn how to do things. Erikson (1963) termed this urgency to learn as a sense of industry. Children who perceive themselves as capable emerge from this stage with a sense of competence. Children, however, must learn a great many ideas and skills at this time. If they are not successful, they may feel as if they are failures and inferior. Parents assume the role of encouragers to their school-aged children to counteract the negative effects of failures (large or small). Parents may focus some efforts on building a cooperative relationship with the child's teachers, helping children with school work and projects. Parents should continue to remind children of their accomplishments, talents, and skills. Children of this age enjoy group activities such as Little League, Scouts, or church camps; and these provide opportunities to form friendships and to learn certain skills (Hamner & Turner, 1990).

As children approach adolescence—at about 12 years—they enter a time of upheaval and change. Rapid physiological changes are accompanied by many social and psychological changes. Adolescents want to know, "Who am I?" and set out to define themselves. They may experiment with various hairstyles, lifestyles, and attitudes in an attempt to discover their true identity. Teens are also moving toward a major transition for themselves and their parents—independence from parents. This transition is difficult for both parents and child. Both must find balance between too much independence too soon and holding on too tightly. In spite of a reliance on peers for advice and support, teens continue to need the solid environment of home and parents (Hamner & Turner, 1990).

The period of the family life cycle with adolescent children is a time of changes for parents, too. The nature of the parent-child relationship must shift to permit adolescents to exercise greater independence as they reach adulthood and eventually move out of the family home. Parents and children must then learn to interact with each other in an adult-to-adult fashion (McGoldrick & Carter, 1982).

Parenting skills. Many of the skills involved in parenting are the same as for other relationships or roles. Parenting requires skills of managing time and resources, for example. Some skills are particularly important to parents. Two have been selected for discussion in this chapter: communicating with children and providing guidance.

Communicating with children may well be the most difficult parenting skill to learn and to practice consistently (Hamner & Turner, 1990). Communication with children should start when they are newborns—with gazing, cooing, talking, touching. It should continue as children grow with conversations about topics of interest to the child as well as the parents. Some communication should be fun and pleasant—not only scolding, directing, or business.

Another helpful guideline for communicating with children is to treat them as persons. Recognize their feelings and needs. For example, some parents speak to their children in condescending tones so artificial that the children easily recognize it (Stinnett et al., 1991). Parents should be especially watchful to offer encouragement and praise in ways that are genuine (Faber & Mazlish, 1980; Popkin, 1983). A parent who feigns delight over a child's artwork, proclaiming it "the most beautiful picture ever" may be setting up unpleasant consequences. Children soon realize the artificiality and assume their work really isn't any good or that parents can't be trusted. Parents can strive to find real accomplishments and efforts to compliment as in, "You've worked hard on this picture. I like the sweeping red lines."

It is critical that parents learn to be active listeners. Active listening includes the process in which the parent attentively listens to both the content and the feelings of the child's communication. The goal of active listening is to understand the child. An integral part of active listening is the use of giving feedback (reflecting back what you think the child meant) to clarify the meaning of the message (Gordon, 1975; Stinnett et al., 1991).

Active listening is helpful when a child has a problem that may not be especially troublesome to the parent. For example, concerns about height (too tall, too short), freckles, all his friends going to beach, and small failures or difficulties may cause the child to feel awkward, inadequate, or lonely. From an adult perspective, parents may not be overly concerned. Active listening allows the parents to help the child identify feelings; and often the child will arrive at a resolution of the problem upon talking about it (Dinkmeyer & McKay, 1973; Gordon, 1975; Popkin, 1983).

At other times parents and children may be in conflict; both may be troubled by the situation. In these instances the use of conflict resolution techniques can be helpful. First parents and child sit down together and clarify the problem. Make it as clear and specific as possible. "We disagree about curfews" is better than "Mom and Dad never let me have any freedom," for example. Next make a list of possible solutions including all suggestions; do not evaluate them at this point. "No curfews," "child sets time of curfew," "parents set time," "don't go out," etc. Next evaluate the suggestions, eliminating the ones that are unacceptable and deciding on the one that is most suitable to everyone. Consider compromise. "Curfew at 9:30 on school nights; 12:00 midnight on weekends; special arrangements for special events such as prom." Implement the plan and evaluate from time to time to be sure it is working (Dinkmeyer & McKay, 1973).

The other area of parenting skills that will be discussed is guidance. Guidance differs from punishment in that the goal of guidance is to help children become self-controlling and self-directing. For example, the child stops hitting because she realizes that hitting hurts rather than because she will be spanked herself (Stinnett et al., 1991).

The age of the child involved and the nature of the misbehavior will both influence the type of guidance used. Many problems with very young children can be handled with redirection or diversion. For example, when the toddler is intent on taking a toy car from her cousin, mom may offer her another car (rather than scold or spank her). The preschooler who won't take turns on the tricycle may need redirected to an acceptable activity, "If you'll give him a turn on the trike, you can help me in the sandbox." Young children often lose control due to overstimulation or fatigue; they may hit or bite due to frustrations. In such instances, parents may use a time-out to allow feelings to calm. Some parents use a special chair in a dull location for time-out; use about one-minute-per-year-of-age as a guideline for timing. Do not lecture or scold the child while in time-out. A parent may say, "You were pulling the cat's tail and wouldn't stop. That hurts Kitty. Sit here until you get calmed down." Very young children may need an adult to sit with them—perhaps even to hold them.

Another guidance technique that many parents find helpful is the use of logical or natural consequences. Natural consequences are those negative results of a child's behavior. For example, a child who refuses to eat breakfast will be hungry before lunch. A parent who says, "You refused to eat breakfast. There will be no food until lunch," and then holds firm is using natural consequences. Logical consequences are similar inasmuch as they are related to the misbehavior. For example, the child who will not put his bicycle in the garage at night loses the use of it for a few days. Natural and logical consequences can be very effective in shaping a child's behavior. Because they are related to the natural order (Don't eat and you'll be hungry, for example.), they may be perceived as less punitive and arbitrary (Dinkmeyer & McKay, 1973; Faber & Mazlish, 1980; Popkin, 1983). Natural consequences should *not* be used in situations that might endanger the child.

In addition to using unpleasant consequences for misbehavior, many parents use rewards or motivators to encourage appropriate behaviors (Canter & Canter, 1985; Hamner & Turner, 1990). Rewards may be as simple as a hug or smile or "good job!" Young children like stickers or small treats such as raisins or gum. School-age children may cooperate with parents to collect points or tokens to be exchanged for a larger prize such as a movie ticket. Rewards or motivators may be used in conjunction with disciplinary consequences. For example the child may earn stickers for picking up her toys or lose the use of the toys left scattered about. Or an older child may earn a token each day he does his chores; ten tokens can be exchanged for a new book. If chores are not done, the child loses television time.

The information and suggestions in this section are not exhaustive. They do provide a foundation for parents and those who work with them.

Consequences for Religious Education

In most churches, religious education programs about family life are already underway in varying degrees—either formally or informally (Money, 1987). Hopefully this chapter will spark some ideas to improve the quantity and quality of existing efforts. In this final section some specific activities for family life religious education will be presented.

Prevention

A major part of the religious education effort in most churches will be aimed at the prevention of family problems. Serious family problems often start as small problems that could have been avoided or managed with a few easily learned skills (Money, 1987). Persons who are planning the young adult religious education program should keep the family life cycle in mind because transition periods, when one stage is left behind and another entered, are especially challenging (McGoldrick & Carter, 1982). Knowing about the family life cycle and the tasks at each stage can help families to cope more effectively with change. With prevention in mind, the topics for study are numerous: preparation for marriage, singleness, family financial management, stress management, balancing work and family, parenting, retirement, living with in-laws, drug/alcohol abuse, the empty nest, current issues of concern to families, grandparenting, sexuality, healthy family relationships, building a successful marriage, and dealing with conflict. This is not an exhaustive list, of course.

These topics could be presented in a variety of formats. One possibility is to have discussion groups (with a prepared leader) that meet to discuss material they have already read. Workshops or seminars can be planned for a short block of time such as a weekend (or a Saturday); these can include a variety of activities such as guest speakers, films, small-group discussions, and brainstorming sessions. Of course, formal classes scheduled to meet regularly for several months are a mainstay of any young adult religious education effort. In some instances it may be helpful to arrange classes of mixed age groups such as teens and parents meeting together to learn about "Surviving Adolescence."

People learn in different ways: Some learn best by seeing, some by hearing, some by doing. Although this is stated in simplistic terms it does emphasize the need to offer ideas in a variety of forms. Encourage teachers of classes and guest speakers to use audiovisuals, for example. Group discussions expose learners to the valuable resource of other peoples' experiences. And talking about ideas seems to help most people incorporate them into everyday life. Posters and bulletin boards, newsletters, bulletins, flyers and pamphlets are other media for sharing information. If resources permit, a library of books, materials, audio and video tapes is a bonus.

Counseling

Many churches provide counseling services for individuals and families under extreme stress or in a crisis situation (Larson, 1984; Money, 1987). Counseling is a natural part of the family life religious education program just as the services of a physician are part of a total health care effort.

A major thrust of counseling families is religious education for more effective living, communicating, and problem-solving. Many times support groups for persons with special needs serve the joint purposes of teaching, counseling, and comforting. Some possible support groups might include: widows, single parents, grieving persons, those with chronic illness, singles, divorced, those with addictive disorders, adoptive parents, or those caring for elderly parents.

Enrichment

Families also need encouragement in the areas of their lives that are going well. The first section of this chapter dealt with the idea of healthy, well, functional, strong families. This approach is positive and proactive. As a consequence, enriching family life is an important facet of religious education for young adults.

Young adult religious education programs may offer a range of activities that families can participate in as a "family"—thus encouraging time together, shared interests, and family fun. These activities may be oriented around recreation, service, learning, or worship and might include family camps or retreats, mother-daughter banquets, vacation Bible school, or allchurch picnics (Larson, 1984; Money, 1987). In other instances high school (or college) students and their parents are honored in a special ceremony at graduation, teens plan and execute a meal and entertainment to "appreciate" their parents, parent-child teams fill boxes with food for hungry persons, or volunteers help the infirm with household chores and shopping.

Outreach

Finally, many young adult religious education programs aim to serve the people of their community who may not be members of their church. In these religious education efforts an emphasis on areas of concern to families can be very beneficial. Most people are interested in improving family and interpersonal relationships and will respond favorably as they perceive that their needs are being met (Money, 1987). Many churches, through their religious education programs, open seminars, lectures or workshops on family topics to the public. These are advertised, are free or inexpensive, and many have child care or refreshments added as an incentive to attend. Other services that might be offered to the community include meals to shut-ins; tutoring; job placement counseling; food pantry; preschool, mom's day out, or daycare; daycare of adults; counseling services for divorce, addictive behaviors, or family violence (Money, 1987).

Conclusion

This chapter opened with the idea that human relationships are an integral aspect of a relationship with God. Certainly relationships with family members are our most important human relationships. In the pursuit of an improved relationship with God—and harmony within the church—young adult religious education leaders do well to improve the lives of families.

References

Alberts, J.K. (1988). An analysis of couples' conversational complaints. *Communication Monographs, 55*, 184-197.

Aldous, J. (1978). *Family careers*. New York: Wiley.

Ammons, P., & Stinnett, N. (1980). The vital marriage: A closer look. *Family Relations, 29*, 37-42.

Bader, E., & Sinclair, C. (1983). The critical first year of marriage. In D. Mace (Ed.), *Prevention in family services* (pp. 77-86). Beverly Hills, CA: Sage.

Beavers, W.R. (1977). *Psychotherapy and growth: A family systems perspective*. New York: Brunner/Mazel.

Bell, R.A., Daly, J.A., & Gonzalez, M.C. (1987). Affinity maintenance in marriage and its relationship to women's marital satisfaction. *Journal of Marriage and the Family, 49*, 445-454.

Bokemeier, J., & Maurer, R. (1987). Marital quality and conjugal labor involvement of rural couples. *Family Relations, 36*, 417-424.

Bowman, H.A., & Spanier, G.B. (1978). *Modern marriage*. New York: McGraw-Hill.

Brodbar-Nemzer, J.Y. (1986). Divorce and group commitment: The case of the Jews.

Journal of Marriage and the Family, 48, 329-340.

Bronfenbrenner, U. (1985). The parent/child relationship in our changing society. In L.E. Arnold (Ed.), *Parents, children, and change* (pp. 45-57). Lexington, MA: Lexington Books.

Buunk, B., & VanYperen, N. (1991). Referential comparisons, relational comparisons, and exchange orientation: Their relation to marital satisfaction. *Personality and Social Psychology Bulletin, 17*, 709-718.

Canter, L., & Canter, M. (1985). *Assertive discipline for parents* (rev. ed.). New York: Harper & Row.

Clarke, J. (1978). *Self-esteem: A family affair*. Minneapolis: Winston.

Coopersmith, S. (1968, February). Studies in self-esteem. *Scientific American*, pp. 96-106.

Curran, D. (1983). *Traits of a healthy family*. Minneapolis: Winston.

DeFrain, J., & Stinnett, N. (1992). Building on the inherent strengths of families: A positive approach for family psychologists and counselors. *Topics in Family Psychology and Counseling, 1*, 15-26.

Dinkmeyer, D., & McKay, G. (1973). *Raising a responsible child*. New York: Simon & Schuster.

Duvall, E. (1954). *In-laws: Pro and con*. New York: Association Press.

Elder, G.H. (1968). Adolescent socialization and development. In E.F. Borgatta & W. Lambert (Eds.), *Handbook of personality theory and research*. Chicago: Rand McNally.

Epstein, N., Baldwin, L., & Bishop, D. (1983). The McMaster family assessment device. *Journal of Marital and Family Therapy, 9*, 171-180.

Erikson, E. (1963). *Childhood and society*. New York: Norton.

Faber, A., & Mazlish, E. (1980). *How to talk so kids will listen & listen so kids will talk*. New York: Avon.

Fowers, B.J., & Olson, D. (1986). Predicting marital success with PREPARE: A predictive validity study. *Journal of Marital and Family Therapy, 12*, 403-413.

Glenn, N.D., & Kramer, K.B. (1987). The marriages and divorces of the children of divorce. *Journal of Marriage and the Family, 49*, 811-825.

Gordon, T. (1975). *Parent effectiveness training*. New York: New American Library.

Hamner, T.J., & Turner, P.H. (1990). *Parenting in contemporary society* (2nd ed.). Englewood Cliffs, NJ: Prentice-Hall.

Hill, R.B. (1971). *The strengths of black families*. New York: Emerson Hall.

Knox, D. (1988). *Choices in relationships*. St. Paul, MN: West.

Krysan, M., Moore, K., & Zill, N. (1990). *Identifying successful families: An overview of constructs and selected measures*. Washington, DC: Child Trends.

Larson, J. (1984). *A church guide for strengthening families*. New York: National Council of Churches of Christ.

Lee, P.A., & Brage, D.G. (1989). Family life education and research: Toward a more positive approach. In M.J. Fine (Ed.), *The second handbook on parent education* (pp. 347-378). New York: Academic Press.

Leigh, G., Ladehoff, G., Howie, A., & Christians, D. (1985). Correlates of marital satisfaction among men and women in intact first marriage and remarriage. *Family Perspective, 19*, 139-150.

Lewis, J. (1979). *How's your family? A guide to identifying your family's strengths and weaknesses*. New York: Brunner/Mazel.

Lewis, J., & Looney, J. (1983). *The long struggle: Well-functioning working class black families*. New York: Brunner/Mazel.

Li, J., & Caldwell, R. (1987). Magnitude and directional effects of marital sex-role incongruence on marital adjustment. *Journal of Family Issues, 8*, 97-100.

Lingren, H., Van Zandt, S., Stinnett, N., & Rowe, G. (1982). Enhancing marriage and family competencies throughout adult life development. In N. Stinnett, J. DeFrain, K. King, H. Lingren, G. Rowe, S. Van Zandt, & R. Williams (Eds.), *Family strengths 4: Positive support systems* (pp. 385-406). Lincoln, NE: University of Nebraska Press.

Luckey, E.B. (1964). Marital satisfaction and personality correlates of spouse. *Journal of Marriage and the Family, 26*, 217-220.

McGoldrick, M., & Carter, E. (1982). The stages of the family life cycle. In F. Walsh (Ed.), *Normal family processes*. New York: Guilford.

Money, R. (1987). *Ministering to families*. Abilene, TX: Abilene Christian University Press.

Norton, A.J., & Moorman, J.E. (1987). Current trends in marriage and divorce among American women. *Journal of Marriage and the Family, 49*, 3-14.

Olson, D., (1986). Prepared statement before the House Select Committee on Children, Youth, and Families. In *The diversity and strength of American families*. Washington, DC: U.S. Government Printing Office.

Olson, D., McCubbin, H., Barnes, H., Larsen, A., Muxen, M., & Wilson, M. (1983). *Families: What makes them work?* Beverly Hills, CA: Sage.

Otto, H.A. (1963). Criteria for assessing family strength. *Family Process, 2*, 329-337.

Pollak, O. (1957). Design of a model of healthy family relationships as a basis for evaluative research. *Social Service Review, 31*, 369-376.

Popkin, M. (1983). *Active parenting*. Atlanta: Active Parenting.

Pratt, L. (1976). *Family structure and effective health behavior: The energized family*. Boston: Houghton, Mifflin.

Price-Bonham, S., & Balswick, J. (1980). The noninstitutions: Divorce, desertion, and remarriage. *Journal of Marriage and the Family, 42*, 959-972.

Rao, V.P., & Rao, N. (1986). Correlates of marital happiness: A longitudinal analysis. *Free Inquiry in Creative Sociology, 14*, 3-8.

Rosenfeld, L.B., & Bowen, G.L. (1991). Marital disclosure and marital satisfaction: Direct-effect versus interaction-effect models. *Western Journal of Speech Communication, 55*, 69-82.

Satir, V. (1972). *Peoplemaking*. Palo Alto, CA: Science and Behavior Books.

Schlesinger, B. (1984). Lasting and functioning marriages in the 1980's. In G. Rowe, J. Defrain, H. Lingren, R. Macdonald, N. Stinnett, S. Van Zandt, & R. Williams (Eds.), *Family strengths 5: Continuity and diversity* (pp. 49-63). Newton, MA: Education Development Center.

Schumm, W.R. (1986). Prepared statement before the House Select Committee on Children, Youth, and Families. In *The diversity and strength of American families*. Washington, DC: U.S. Government Printing Office.

Sell, C. (1981). *Family ministry: The enrichment of family life through the church*. Grand Rapids, MI: Zondervan.

Stinnett, N., Chesser, B., & DeFrain, J. (Eds). (1979). *Building family strengths; Blueprints for action*. Lincoln, NE; University of Nebraska Press.

Stinnett, N., & DeFrain, J. (1985). *Secrets of strong families*. Boston: Little, Brown.

Stinnett, N., & DeFrain, J. (1989). The healthy family: Is it possible? In M. Fine (Ed.) *The second handbook on parent education* (pp. 53-74). New York: Academic Press.

Stinnett, N., Walters, J., & Stinnett, N. (1991). *Relationships in marriage and the family* (3rd ed.). New York: Macmillan.

Swihart, J. (1988). Characteristics of strong families. Unpublished paper, International Family Center, Logos Research Institute.

Whipple, C.M. & Whittle, D. (1976). *The compatibility* test. Englewood Cliffs, NJ: Prentice-Hall.

Whitaker, C. (1980, September 5). Characteristics of a self-actualizing family: A family that grows. Workshop presentation. Minneapolis.

Wilson, M.R. & Filsinger, E.E. (1986). Religiosity and marital adjustment: Multidimensional interrelationships. *Journal of Marriage and the Family, 48*, 147-151.

Wuerffel, J., DeFrain, J., & Stinnett, N. (1990). How strong families use humor. *Family Perspective, 24*, 129-141.

CHAPTER THIRTEEN

Religious Education and Marital Issues

EVERETT L. WORTHINGTON JR.

In the Judeo-Christian worldview, marriage and spirituality are intimately connected. Educating young adults about marriage provides an opportunity to educate them about spirituality (and vice versa). We are currently in a time of intense focus on both marriage and spirituality. The two topics will therefore not only be increasingly relevant, they might very well be the doorway to religious education and discipleship of young adults in the twenty-first century.

In this chapter, I first examine the connection between marriage and spirituality within the Judeo-Christian tradition. Second, I argue that marriage and theology need to be understood in light of a changing historical context and unchanging scriptural text. Third, I speculate about recent social, technological, and philosophical changes that have affected our lives and examine some potential effects on marriage. That leads to discussion about innovative methods and strategies for religious education of young adults.

Judeo-Christian Marriage-Spirituality Connection

In this section, a covenantal approach to life and thus to marriage is examined. This approach has grown from a covenantal world view put forth in both the Old and New Testaments.

The Covenant

Christianity is based on covenantal relationships—between God and Abraham set forth in the Old Testament, and between Jesus and his followers set forth in the New Testament. A covenant is a permanent blood oath in which participants pledge to value each other equally to or above their own welfare. Traditionally, at the making (or "cutting") of a covenant, animals were sacrificed and cut in half. Covenanting participants walked between the halves. Other forms of covenant involved (a) cutting participants and allowing their blood to intermingle in a cup of liquid, which was then drunk, or (b) cutting participants and holding their arms together, which allowed their blood to mingle.

Israel's animal sacrifices and Christian communion have symbolized the covenant between God and humans historically. Traditionally, loving self-sacrifice and faithfulness have been the two primary qualities that have characterized covenants.

The Old Covenant

The Old Covenant begins with the creation of a couple, Adam and Eve, because "it was not good for man to be alone" (Gen. 2:18). The covenant between God and Abraham (and later God and Israel) has been likened to a marriage covenant (Gen. 15: 9-11, 17-18). The husband-wife relationship was based on a covenant (Mal. 2:14) and was expected to be permanent (see Hosea). In the scriptures, God is referred to as husband and Israel as the wife (Jer. 31:32; Hos. 2:16; 3:1).

The New Covenant

Jesus' death is God's new covenant, based on Jesus' shed blood, with believers (Jn. 6: 53-4), and Paul likens marriage to the covenant between God (through Jesus) and believers. For example, Christ is referred to as the husband and the church as the wife in Ephesians (5:25-33), and Jesus is referred to as the husband and the believer as the wife (1 Cor. 6:16-17).

Christian marriage has been, therefore, symbolic of the covenant between God and believers. The families and friends of husband and wife sit on opposite sides of the church, and husband and wife walk between the divided body after they have taken their vows of covenantal commitment. The ceremony involves vows before God of partners' faithfulness and self-sacrificial love—for better or worse, for richer or poorer, in sickness and in health. The cleric closes by admonishing the couple, "What God has joined together, let no one break apart."

Clearly, then, in the Judeo-Christian tradition, there is a divinely mysterious similarity in the relationships between God and humans and between husband and wife. One logical conclusion is that educating people about marriage bears on the religious education and vice versa. Like a poem with two layers of meaning, like a metaphor, marital education informs about religious education.

One beauty of this connection is the ubiquitousness of marriage. Over 95 percent of adults in the United States will marry at least once (Cherlin, 1981). Even people who never marry—those celibate, homosexuals, and those who simply never find a mate—think about marriage from their earliest years. They hunger to find out about marriage, and even if they reject it as adolescents or young adults, they have pondered it and are still open to considering important principles of marriage even if they opt for a cohabitation or homosexual relationship. Thus, if in religious education we can communicate with young adults about marriage, we can often facilitate their simultaneous exploration of spirituality.

Marriage in a Societal-Historical Context

It is important for the young adult religious educator to understand the historical context of marriage. Most people's view of marriage—as a struggle between traditionalist and modern conceptions—is remarkably near-sighted. From that limited perspective, traditionalists want a strong nuclear family, headed by a husband who is family provider and nurtured and held together emotionally by a woman, who rears her children in the home and provides a haven for the husband. The modern conception of marriage is one of equality in duties and responsibilities, freedom of opportunity to work and earn money and power, and democratic child rearing. In Christian circles, traditionalists quote the Bible to prove their points, citing arguments about biblical authority and God's order in the family. Modernists cite feminist arguments and point to biblical passages concerning liberty and equality in Christ.

Paylor (1986) has outlined a historical perspective on marriage. He begins with Augustine's (early fifth century) conception of marriage, which emphasized three points: 1) marriage's purpose is procreation; 2) children are under the authority of their parents—including arrangement of children's marriages; and 3) marriage is a sacred bond, a symbol of the union between Jesus and his church.

The Augustinian view dominated theology until the twelfth century. In 1175, the archbishop of Canterbury held a council that proclaimed that if both partners do not consent to marriage, there is no marriage. This suggested that marriage depended on choice rather than parental prerogative. Also in the twelfth century, marriage became part of the Roman Catholic sacramental system, largely as a way for the church to control social power. Authority over marriage was moved from the family to the church.

With the Protestant Reformation, Calvin's view of humans' total depravity led to Wesley's theology of marriage, which emphasized absolute submission—of children to their parents, of wives to their husbands, of husbands to God. With Wesley, the goal of marriage was no longer to bear children; it was to *be* as children—submissive and obedient.

By the middle of the nineteenth century, society began to see children as individuals separate from adults, thus marriage was progressively emancipated from child rearing. The Industrial Revolution was underway in the United States, and the agrarian pattern of men working with and training their sons while women worked with and trained their daughters was abandoned as urban migration accelerated. Men went off to work, leaving child rearing to women. Women were custodians of both the children and the marriage, and marriage as an institution was separated from childbearing or rearing. Marriage was seen as an adult activity, based on choice, which usually involved children but which could be fulfilling even if there were no children.

From Paylor's (1986) summary of the history of marriage, the religious educator can draw several conclusions.

1. We are short-sighted about marriage and its historical interpretations. We believe we understand biblical Christianity when we are viewing that Christianity through the lens of relatively recent theological interpretations of scripture.

2. Emphases in many theologies of marriage were influenced by social and political changes. Theology is inevitably an interaction between biblical text and historical context.

3. What is thought of as "traditional" marriage today was once resisted as radically progressive. For example, during the Industrial Revolution, when a father went to work at the factory leaving his wife at home to be the primary child rearer, he was probably seen as abandoning traditional parenting, which was seen as biblical at that time.

In short, social and political changes can influence theologies of marriage. A caution is warranted concerning the inferences we might draw from Paylor's reasoning. The reasoning might suggest that perhaps theology *always* depends on social and political context. If that were true, we should be open to change, hesitant to retain any traditional views, because they are transitory. It also might suggest that social pressures will inevitably overcome tradition and that we should thus adapt to social changes.

The flaw in drawing such inferences is that Paylor recounted only the "successful" mutations in theology stimulated by social changes. Many cultural pressures did *not* change theology. Each generation must discern which contextual pressures might affect theology and whether they *should* affect theology. Some "successful" modifications in the theology of marriage might better have been resisted. For example, the principle that parents should be intimately involved in child rearing suffered when the industrial revolution essentially removed fathers from the home. Not all culturally induced theological changes are necessarily good—even "successful" ones. Rather, we must analyze cultural pressures against the enduring biblical text.

The Need for Analysis

Because culture is constantly changing, does that mean that the religious educator should continually reassess the meaning of marriage? No. Continual analysis would be mentally exhausting and would paralyze progress, which paradoxically requires stability against which to push.

Rather, let us use a developmental metaphor to explore this question. Individuals develop in stages. Generally, behavior for the individual is fairly constant and predictable within a stage of development. Behavior is matched to the environment well enough to allow minimal discomfort or dissonance. However, both the environment and the individual continually change. When discrepancies mount until the individual is troubled, the person is catapulted into a life transition during which the psychological and social anchors may be torn loose and the person may adjust his or her life to the new conditions.

Similarly, on the historical level, Augustinian theology of marriage served well for a "stage." However, environmental change—political and social changes—stimulated a transitional period in which the "rules" of marriage were rethought. That culminated in the twelfth century changes in theology of marriage. The Protestant Reformation and the industrial revolution stimulated other transitional periods.

At the end of the twentieth century, we are in another period of rapid and precipitous social, political, and ideological change. Reconsideration of the theology of marriage is to be expected.

Social, Technological, and Philosophical Changes

Further, the religious educator of young adults must consider the changes that are occurring and the likely impact that each will have on marriage. We will examine three: social, technological, and philosophical.

Social Changes

Two important social changes in this century are: 1) the increase in life expectancy due to advances in public health and medicine, and 2) the worldwide depression of the 1920s, which has led to baby boomers, busters, and boomlets.

Increased life expectancy. In 1900, the average life expectancy was about 45 years. People were born into families, grew up in families, married, and began almost immediately to rear their family. They may have reared ten or more closely spaced children. Most of life was spent growing up in or rearing a family.

Three major advances led to an increased life expectancy. First, changes in standards of public health eradicated diseases that caused earlier death. Second, biomedical research has increased our understanding of the human body and the mechanisms of disease and death. Third, technical developments in pharmacology, surgery, and preventive medicine have helped treat and avoid persistent diseases.

Today, the average life expectancy is closer to 78 years (United States Bureau of the Census, 1990; United States Senate Special Committee on Aging, 1986), and the life cycle has changed. People are reared in families for about eighteen years, but they enter young adulthood, where they live independently of the family for seven to ten years before marriage. First marriage is usually deferred until about 25 (on the average) and even after marriage many couples postpone having children until their mid-thirties. An increasing number of couples are childless voluntarily (Spanier, 1983; United States Bureau of the Census, 1990). An average couple has two children two years apart and thus spends twenty years at child rearing (United States Senate Special Committee on Aging, 1986). Once the last child leaves home, a couple can expect to live together or as a surviving spouse for the last thirty-plus years (United States Senate Special Committee on Aging, 1986). This pattern is complicated, of course, by a divorce rate of well over 50 percent, meaning that many people will likely spend even more time alone than the (atypical) couple that I have just described (Cherlin, 1981). The changing life cycle has a significant impact on young adults in that it increases emphasis on marital and individual concerns, and decreases emphasis on child-centered family concerns (Carter & McGoldrick, 1989).

The worldwide depression. In the 1920s, the global depression disrupted the family patterns that had arisen during industrial revolution (Cherlin, 1981). Many men lost their jobs and remained at home unemployed. Wives, though, were often able to obtain low-paying labor-intensive jobs, so they left the family to work. Much of the domestic care was assumed by the daughters. That generation of women matured in the mid-1940s, and after World War II, began to have children. In their early years, they had learned to value domesticity, so they had more children than had been the case in the previous few generations. Those attitudes, Cherlin (1981) identifies as the root of the baby boom generation—those born from 1946 through 1964 (Chandler, 1992; Collins & Clinton, 1992).

Environmental consciousness and disillusionment with "the establishment" resulted in the generation following the baby boom generation having fewer children than had the baby boomers. The years 1965 through 1985 are called the baby bust, because of the paucity of children in those cohorts. By the late 1980s, though, baby boomers were having children of their own, producing a baby boomlet, which is now in full swing (Collins & Clinton, 1992).

Technological Changes

The second great change of the twentieth century was stimulated by technological developments. Society has moved from an industrial nation in 1900 until, by about 1970, being a post-industrial, communication-based society (Naisbitt, 1984). Throughout most of the twentieth century, our mentality as a nation has been production-oriented. The result has been technical advances that have restructured society (Kipnis, 1991).

The electric light. First, electric lights were invented. The development of the electric light and widespread use of electric power created a society that could be fully urban. Lighting prolonged productive days in the factory and allowed cities to reorganize social life on a 24 hour cycle. By 1993, over half of the world's population resides within cities (Linden, 1993). The subsequent changes in time structuring, work, and urban life have profoundly influenced marriage and family life.

Individual transportation. Second, personal transportation developed markedly. The interstate road system has interconnected every concentration of population in the United States, making different regions of the country accessible to anyone. Consequently, society has developed a mobility that is not tied to mass transportation. This enhanced personal freedom, autonomy, and independence. In addition, air travel developed until intracontinental travel is easily possible within half a day and travel across the world can be accomplished within thirty-six hours by the average international business traveler. This has exposed more people to more regions of the country and to people from other countries and cultures within the world. Geographical mobility also disconnected married spouses from their families of origin.

Television. Third, almost every home in the country has at least one television. Most children and many adults spend at least two or three hours per week night (and more on weekends) in front of the television (Liebert, Sprafkin, & Davidson, 1982). The content of television programs has enormously affected our culture, many would say negatively, in terms of violence, perception of family interactions, and desire for continual change.

It is estimated that the average child will observe over 40,000 television murders by the time he or she is 18 years old (Liebert et al., 1982). Also viewable on television—more so on cable channels—are other violent acts including rape, abuse, and all manners of property crimes. Is it any wonder that most scholars conclude that watching television violence increases aggressiveness (Friedrich-Cofer & Huston, 1986; Singer & Singer, 1981; cf. Freedman, 1984), much of which occurs within families.

Television also has influenced the average television viewer's perception of family life. Based on the ubiquitous situation comedy, people expect the average family to be populated with smart-mouthed characters who say outrageous, hurtful things to each other weekly but end each episode with warm and tender feelings. The following week, they show no evidence of previous hurtfulness. This teaches viewers, especially children who are forming the vision of marriage they will carry toward adulthood, that one can say anything to another person without serious consequences. Television has also shown children that adults act abominably toward each other, show weaknesses, and make stupid mistakes (Gergen, 1991). Such things obviously happen in real life, but historically most children didn't know it. This has created a negative model of marriage that—to children who have seen thousands of bad and stupid adults on television—seems universal.

In addition, television continually stimulates people through change. People habituate quickly to continuous stimulation, so television frequently changes. Commercials change camera angles sometimes twenty times during a thirty-second spot. Programs change every thirty minutes. Trends change each year. One unintended consequence is that through television rapid societal change has been normalized. People expect to be constantly entertained with new stories, new images, new thoughts—to which they respond with increased passivity (Kubey & Csikszentmahalyi, 1990). That view generalizes to other aspects of their lives.

The VCR. In the last ten years, VCRs have become commonplace. People watch more movies than they ever have, and the nature of those movies has been transformed by the VCR. In the past, movies have been viewed by groups of strangers watching a bigger-than-life image, which produced bigger-than-life emotions. With the widespread use of the VCR, though, people now watch movies in family rooms, amid the distractions of home life, with one finger on the remote control pause button. To achieve a bigger-than-life emotional reaction from the modern viewer using smaller-than-life images, modern movies made with an eye to the VCR market often are more violent, more grotesque, more repulsive, more terrifying, more sexually explicit, and more shocking than ever before. Further, the natural tendency for people to adapt to their experience coupled with the tendency for people to watch two to five video movies per week, result in demands for movie producers to make ever more emotionally evocative movies.

Cultural metaphors help give life meaning by providing individuals with mental images of how people should and actually do behave. Traditionally, cultural metaphors have been provided by storytellers around the fire, later novelists, and now movie writers and producers. With the transformation of the nature of movies will inevitably come new cultural mental images of marriage. Of particular import is the microwave romance—hot and steamy in moments. Romances are conveyed as always fast-developing, usually sexually motivated, and almost always conflict-marred. In movies, male-female conflict is inevitable because it is necessary for drama that a story *changes* people and relationships. But in normal life, male-female conflict is not necessary nor do most people consider it desirable.

Computers and communications technology. Ten years ago, I had never heard of a personal computer or FAX. Today, scientists and business people communicate with people from other cultures almost instantaneously. Whatever information is needed is accessible from some computer, somewhere.

With the electronic linking of cultures has come the necessity to work with and understand other cultures. Multiculturalism has become a buzz word for the 1990s. While some may resist it, it is inevitable.

With advances in technology, especially communications and computer technology, our collective cultural mentality has changed. Information is everywhere and is, with new technology, not just accessible but too easily accessible. Individuals' major tasks have become, not discovering knowledge, but dealing with sensory and mental overload (Naisbitt, 1984). People have reacted with a societal sense of hopelessness and helplessness, which they have tried to cope with in two ways. Some specialize in minute areas of expertise, decreasingly small until the information is manageable. This is the general strategy preferred by most sciences. Others reject discernment and refuse to decide which things are important. If all the information cannot be accounted for, then, they think, it is better not to make *any* distinctions. This solution more often reflects the mentality of the politician and liberal artist.

Philosophical Changes

Four philosophical shifts have characterized the twentieth century. Generally, all philosophical changes have reflected a general drift from a communal approach to life toward an approach based on individualism.

Relativism. Social and technological changes have increased pressures toward individualism, abandonment of family ties, and hopelessness. They have paved the way for the widespread acceptance of a philosophy of relativism. Relativism is the belief that absolute truth does not exist (or is not discernible); thus, all truth is thought to be relative. Criteria for which truths are *useful* are varied (with the understanding that choice of criteria is not correct in an absolute sense). Francis Schaeffer (1968) traces the origins of the popularity of this philosophy to the writings of Friedrich Hegel.

Postmodernism. Postmodernism is a philosophical approach to life that has grown out of the idea that truth is relativistic. Postmodernism has permeated philosophy, art, and music for years, and is currently seeping more into general culture. Postmodernism is contrasted with premodernism and modernism. (For good summaries, see Doherty, 1991; Efran, 1991; Gergen, 1991; O'Hara & Anderson, 1991; Penn, 1991; cf. Minuchin, 1991).

Premodernism is a philosophical worldview in which cultural presuppositions are roughly uniform. Premodern times were roughly those prior to the industrial revolution. Modernism arose in the United States during the latter part of the nineteenth century as the industrial revolution brought large numbers of diverse peoples in close proximity. Religions and worldviews ceased being matters of presupposition and began to be debated and questioned. Despite the ensuing chaos, a thread unified culture: reason. The Enlightenment had lauded reason as the primary arbiter of truth. Even though people could not agree on exactly what *was* true, most people believed that truth was discoverable through reason, properly applied. Reality was thought to be undergirded by some sort of structure.

Modernist ideas were manifested in psychology by structuralists stage theories of Freud, Piaget, Kohlberg, Fowler, and others. In the modern world, while the structures were thought to be unseen, they were at least inferable.

Postmodernism arrived with the loss of a sense that there were absolute truths, but even more, a loss of the will to search for absolute truths. Individual choice is lauded. Religious and philosophical systems are thus seen as simply social constructions of reality, of which many compete in the marketplace of ideas. Truth is understood to be whatever is individually relevant. For example, a postmodern person might say, "Christianity may be true for you but not for me." Truth is seen as constructing a useful mental or psychological explanation for what happens to an individual. Truth is not expected to be consistent, which results in a fragmented identity.

The average person in the United States today—though he or she cannot articulate the philosophy undergirding the feelings—generally feels overwhelmed by choices, cut off from sure standards of decision making, unsure of what is true and what isn't, and sometimes even unable to judge what is real and what isn't. In short, the average person feels *postmodern.*

Of course, not every person is thoroughly postmodern. People vacillate between modern and postmodern thinking. They may advocate their adherence to the absolute truth of scripture at church on Sunday, but they shed that belief like a coat in a heat wave when they enter the workplace on Monday. They are bothered by their inconsistency, but quickly put the bother out of their mind because there are so many other choices to make. Mental life is more a collage than an painting.

Subjectivism. Plato described a metaphor of the relationship between human will and emotion. He pictured a chariot, pulled by a strong, fine horse—the passions. The charioteer, reason, guides the passions and channels their energy. This picture represents both the Greek and Christian view of the relationships between the passions and the virtues (Greek) or flesh and spirit (Christian).

Contrast that picture to another. The first time I rode a horse, the horse had been raised by three children. Its mouth was solid scar tissue. I was in the saddle, but the horse took me wherever it wanted. In this second picture of passions and virtues, the passions reign. Machiavelli popularized this second view, which contrasted with Plato's view, and since Machiavelli, this second picture of the passions and the virtues has gained prominence. Machiavelli reasoned that opposing the passions and the virtues, as Plato had done, was contrary to nature. He espoused natural rights, which argued that whatever the passions demand *is* virtue.

Today, we are experiencing the virtual full acceptance of Machiavelli's philosophy in common culture. Moral appeals are not generally couched in terms of absolutes. They are framed in terms of the contribution to a person's pleasure. For example, in reasoning about premarital sexual intercourse, most people openly favor premarital intercourse, feeling that it is "not wrong" if two people love each other. People should be able to make love if it *"feels right."* Even most of those who favor abstinence no longer argue that premarital sexual intercourse is morally wrong. They argue now that (1) a moment's pleasure from orgasm is not worth the guilt that one would feel or (2) one would risk catching a sexually transmitted disease or contracting the HIV-virus and the risk is not worth the benefit of sex. In short, the reasoning is not that the virtues should control the passions, but that the passions line up on the side of abstinence and a person should do what maximizes the passions.

Political free market consumerism. Fukuyama (1992) has argued that we are at the end of history, which he sees in neo-Hegelian light as the dialectical progress over time of great ideas in conflict. Fukuyama argues that liberal democratic capitalism has defeated all opposition, thus ending history as we know it. Democratic capitalism, then, is life's last great political idea. Free-market consumerism should logically be expected to pervade all of human intercourse—not insignificantly mating. In the Western hemisphere, we have always held to a modified form of free-market consumerism in selection of marriage partners; there is free-selection within social groups but selection across groups is discouraged. Given recent changes in the world economy in which trade barriers have been removed, we might expect similar lowering of barriers in mate selection, resulting in more marriages across different socio-economic class, educational range, race, and religion.

Some Impact of These Changes on Marriage
and Religious Education for Young Adults

The social, technological, and philosophical changes have affected culture's view of marriage. Notably, they have affected our understanding of commitment, models of marital communication and conflict, and expectations about marital intimacy. These in turn have consequences for religious education of young married adults.

Changing Understanding of Commitment

Two understandings of commitment permeate modern culture—one based on covenant, one on contract. Each view has different implications for marriage.

Covenantal or contractual commitment? Traditionally, the Christian concept of marital commitment has been built on covenant, as was explained at the beginning of the chapter. Covenantal commitment leads to a concern for the welfare of the other person. People care for and stay committed to a partner because they have staked their honor, word, and identity on fulfilling their covenantal obligations toward the other person regardless of what the other person does or doesn't do.

People living as if commitment were contractual may be highly stable in their careers, marriages, friends, or faith. Yet their commitment rests on reciprocity or exchange. Strong ties are forged in relationships when partners exchange things valued positively or when partners share resources needed by the spouse. Contractual commitment is built on mutual need fulfillment. The motivation for commitment is individualistic. Each person meets his or her obligations as long as the other person is thought to be reasonably likely eventually to meet his or her obligations. With contractual commitment, each person is mainly concerned with receiving the resources that the contract stipulates, which are his or her rights. Because humans are fallible, neither sense of commitment is perfectly stable.

The consequence for young adult religious education, is that for Christians who value covenantal commitment, religious education leaders will be increasingly talking at cross purposes to the cultural drift. To affect couples' view of the self-sacrifice needed in the Christian faith and in marriage, it won't be enough to give an occasional mention of covenantal commitment. We will have to bombard young adults in our religious education opportunities—classes, small groups, counseling—with a continual message of covenantal commitment. Less than a multipronged attention to covenant will be overwhelmed by the onslaught of common culture, which is heavily oriented toward contractual commitment.

A new model of marriage arising from a contractual view of commit-

ment. The model of marriage arising from contractual marital relations is one that may erupt in litigation at any juncture of the relationship at which a party feels aggrieved. Prenuptial agreements or contracts are natural to this way of thinking. Divorce is a natural outcome of failed contracts. People who divorce may approach scripture with the same (contract-oriented) frame of mind, searching for "loopholes" or clauses binding on the partner.

Knowledge of the adversarial position of many young adults reared on the contractual model of commitment will make the young adult religious educator tentative. Young adults evaluate the message of the religious educator, and at the slightest provocation may break the tacit contract between the educator and the young adult. The personal relationship between religious educator and young adult will likely take on added significance as young adults become increasingly likely to negatively evaluate a religious educator's message.

Marital Communication

The models of marriage conveyed to people through the visual media have affected views of marital communication (especially conflictual communication). The visual media have changed popular culture's vision of romance and marital life. A few detrimental effects of the visual media on marital life were mentioned earlier. However, there are also beneficial aspects of the visual media. For example, communication in television and movies is direct and economical. Because each line of dialogue should contribute to the plot, communication is generally more efficient than is most real-life communication. The visual media have also created a hunger for knowledge that was not previously experienced. People are thus inclined to search for information rather than assume that they know about the other person.

People are less inhibited about discussing taboo topics. While I am sometimes appalled that my ten year old probably knows more about sex than I did as a high school senior, the free examination of taboo topics on television and in movies has made them easier to discuss and has widened people's knowledge base.

On the other hand, conflict will probably increase as a consequence of television. Many controversial issues presented on television are framed as open questions, even when society doesn't frame them that way. For example, dramas on spouse abuse in which the wife murders the abusing spouse—such as *Sleeping with the Enemy*—may make a dramatic case for murder. In previous times, society possessed accepted answers for many of the tough social issues, freeing people from having to examine each issue anew. Now, people debate difficult issues. Such debate will probably increase domestic conflict. Marriages today must be robust enough to tolerate more conflict than in previous times.

The consequence for young adult religious education is that we must attend more to helping people develop adequate skills to reason and to resolve conflict rather than simply provide "answers" for them. Further, the religious educator must expect open discussion and conflict within the young adult congregation. Rather than shying away from conflict, we should provide groups that can allow discussion of difficult topics led by mature Christians who can model good communication and reasoning. Pastors, Directors of Religious Education, and young adult religious educators, rather than seeing themselves as the mature leader in every group, must diligently identify talented and skilled lay people, nurture their faith and leadership skills, and place them into positions where they can effectively educate couples about conflictual issues.

My wife and I currently lead a group for newly married couples. Unlike other groups years earlier that wanted to be told the "Christian position" on marriage, the current group is eager to discuss the options and investigate non-traditional alternatives to traditional marital roles and behaviors. Yet, despite their willingness to entertain new ideas, the couples are seeking God's will for their lives, and they want to arrive at a conviction that they are aligned with his will, so they do not rush willy-nilly into embracing avant-garde ideas.

Time Schedules and Intimacy in Marriage

In the twenty-first century, people are likely to be increasingly oriented to change. It is hard for us to imagine a more rapidly changing world than the early 1990s. The Berlin wall tumbled, the USSR crumbled, and George Bush fumbled record presidential popularity—within two years. Yet, in 1970, when Toffler published *Future Shock*, in which he warned of ever-increasing demands for change that would stress the next generation, few could conceive that life could become even more fast-paced than it was then. Twenty years after *Future Shock,* the 1960s look to us as if they were in slow motion.

One major pressure on young adults will be arranging their time schedules to accommodate to the change. High levels of activity can edge out marital intimacy. Too many demands on too few time slots will inevitably produce: 1) increased ego-centricism (when we are under pressure, we think of ourselves), 2) recognition of child problems at lower levels of child misbehavior (Brody & Forehand, 1986), 3) more stress-related illnesses (Weiten, Lloyd, & Lashley, 1991), and 4) increasing frustration at not being able to accomplish what we want. Marriages and marital intimacy could easily become casualties of increased time pressures if couples do not learn better time management, goal-setting, and efficiency-promoting skills.

Besides the obvious consequence for religious education that busy lives coupled with less cultural acceptance of religion may crowd out time for religious education, young adult religious educators must attend to helping couples learn better skills at time management, goal-setting, and efficiency-promoting. Couples want to know how to set priorities in marriage and balance the complex demands of their lives to follow through on those priorities. Religious educators of young adults are in a good position to teach this by working with married couples who want also to live as committed Christians.

Relativism and Marital Issues

As relativism and postmodernism have spread throughout this century, social mores have changed—even among Christians—until: 1) divorce is largely accepted within the United States, 2) remarriage after divorce is almost as widely accepted, 3) premarital sex has gained acceptance but is not yet normative within the church, 4) extramarital sex is increasingly practiced, though it is usually condemned, and 5) homosexuality is accepted by many as a valid sexual orientation and by some as a valid alternative to marriage. Social consensus, not scripture, is looked to for truth. With each passing year, fewer people consult scripture or even seek the opinion of the church on moral issues that affect their marriage.

From the theologically conservative, liberal, and moderate, the fingers of accusation point with equal condemnation. Conservatives accuse the church of abandoning scripture; liberals accuse conservatives of being unwilling to adapt to a changing world; moderates blame both sides for taking extreme positions that drive people away from the church. Regardless of who is at fault, religious education must address these moral social issues facing young adults—divorce, remarriage, nonmarital sex, and homosexuality—with straight-forward biblical teaching, and with a flexibility to speak the truth in love to a different world than existed in the 1950s. The church must practice love, while teaching doctrine as it is comprehended within its tradition. Often, the divorced, remarried person who has nonmarried sex or the homosexual are rejected by the church rather than lovingly accepted and taught as Jesus practiced with victims and sinners. Effective young adult religious education must be relevant. Furthermore it must strike a balance between love and acceptance, on one hand, and scriptural truth and discipline on the other.

Influence of Psychology on Spirituality

Psychology has increased individualistic subjectivism. By touting an epistemology that moves daily closer to postmodernism, psychology has helped eliminate moral categories, elevate the passions, eradicate objectivism, and exacerbate ego-centricism. Psychology has been effective because of its success at alleviating human suffering and at providing knowledge about human behavior. People disillusioned with traditional religion and seeking self-improvement or relief from distress have been open to the relativistic "truths" of psychology. With psychology's alleviation of suffering, though, have come individualistic emphases that have changed people's views about the nature of marriage.

Young adult religious education cannot ignore psychology. Psychology has become a part of the average person's worldview. Religious education, though, must filter psychology through the lens of biblical Christianity rather than filter Christianity through the lens of psychology. Religious education must reject the overemphasis on subjective individualism and must restore the biblical balance between communal and individual responsibility. In my opinion—and I'm a psychologist—religious education must teach love, altruism, self-sacrifice, and social involvement with greater emphasis than teaching individualistic recovery and self-esteem management (though we cannot ignore individual concerns). People receive so much emphasis on individualistic concerns from work, news and entertainment media, and popular culture that religious education must help achieve a balance by stressing the under-represented side of life in achieving a biblical balance.

Further Consequences for Religious Education

Most religious educators of young adults are familiar with the various theories of human development that reveal different aspects of the young adult (e.g., moral, intellectual, religious, psychological, and spiritual development). Steele, Clark, and Joy in the current volume review these aspects thoroughly.

Marital issues are good avenues for religious education of the young adult because the developmental tasks of young adulthood center on establishing an intimate relationship with another adult, a productive area of work, and a self-image that permits self-sacrifice during marriage and child rearing. Young adults struggle with balancing intimacy and productivity, self-advancement and self-sacrifice, and devotion to the partner, the family, and God. Young adults are primed to hear spiritual messages through dealing with the developmental concerns on which their lives are centered.

In promoting religious education for the young adult, we must superimpose a knowledge of young adult development, an understanding of how the forces of modern culture might show up in the young adult, and a grasp of the technology of delivering religious education in a way that young adults can receive it. Let us think about the technology of how to use marital issues to educate young adults about religion.

As we have seen, young adults currently bring many issues to the church. Religious education must respond to each.

1. People are spiritually hungry. Religious education must not just teach doctrine; it must also show people how they can be spiritually alive.

2. Numerous marital issues clamor for attention. Religious education must address the relevant issues, meeting young adults in the midst of serious moral and practical struggles.

3. Young adults are increasingly involved in cross-race, cross-religion, cross-ethnic, cross-cultural, cross-socio-economic status marriages. Religious education of young adults must emphasize the world church rather than a church within narrow regional or national boundaries. Young adults must be provided information about different cultures and allowed a forum to examine the difficulties associated with marrying someone who differs substantially from themselves.

4. Young adults increasingly embrace a contract (not covenantal) view of marriage. Young adult religious education must emphasize the covenantal nature of Christianity to a generation that lives in a world of legal contracts.

5. Young adults increasingly believe that the passions are more decisive than the intellect and that appeals to control the passions by rationality is against natural law. For religious education to be seen as useful, it must promote better feelings. Promotion of better feelings is the doorway to evangelism. After young adults become involved in Christianity, religious education must balance emphasis on the feelings with emphasis on social responsibility and self-denial.

6. Young adults have a sense of the normalcy of rapid, stressful change, but a feeling of burden that coping with change causes. Religious education must show young adults how to achieve the peace that surpasses understanding even within a stressful world.

7. Young adults believe that continual conflict and direct confrontation are inevitable in intimate relationships. Forums must be provided within the church where young adults can explore controversial issues within a format that allows questioning of authority. Religious educators must not take quick umbrage at having their authority challenged.

8. Young adults need to make many value choices but have a deficit in a) the moral foundation for making choices and b) an inability or unwillingness to discriminate among alternatives. Religious education must help young adults explore scripture's moral principles. Critical thinking must be taught within a framework that uses scripture to evaluate and choose among moral options.

9. Young adults are posing new questions about faith and marriage. Religious education must attend to the questions and not refuse to deal with them because they differ from tradition. Issues that were relevant in the 1970s are often irrelevant today, and many young adults are turned off by the lack of understanding they sometimes encounter within adult religious education.

10. Young adults often resist traditional modes of addressing their ques-

tions. New alternatives must be employed. Religious educators can learn much from modern technology of education in how to deliver effective religious education.

Modern Ways of Addressing
Religious Education Through Marriage

If churches embrace modern technology in young adult religious education, are they selling out to the world? Not necessarily. The fundamental message of evangelism is that each generation must speak the gospel so it can be understood. Jesus gave outdoor sermons with no audio-visual equipment. He talked to people in crowded market places. He chose twelve men and walked throughout the country teaching them intensely. Must all modern evangelism conform to the technology Jesus used to convey the gospel? How then can we religiously educate the modern Christian and how can we reach those who are not Christians with the good news of Jesus' love?

Congregational Formats

Congregational methods of delivering religious education are changing under the pressure of the changing society. The sermon or homily is being transformed, much as the lecture is being transformed within the university.

College lectures today usually involve high technology. For example, in my large class on Introductory Psychology I use music videotapes at the beginning of class to set the tone of the class. Rather than traditional thirty-minute educational movies, I use many short videotape clips. My notes are displayed on video screens and involve moving graphics. Charts and slides are shown on a large screen, as are cartoons and illustrations to break the flow of continuous lecture. I use at least one audience-participation exercise in each class, so that people feel involved. The room has the capability to beam in educational television, satellite conferences, and live, interactive interviews with famous people who are far from my classroom. As more college professors adopt similar methods and the methods spread to secondary and elementary education, religious education will be forced to keep pace or lose its audience.

Congregational religious education of young adults will integrate professionally produced video clips, dramas, audience participation, skits, and the like. Audience stimulation will drive the method of delivering religious information.

Telecommunications will play an increasing role in congregational religious education. Religious educators might show portions of talks and conferences by noted speakers on marriage, such as Gary Smalley, Norman Wright,

Larry Crabb, or James Dobson. Pastors might even show these as part of the homily or sermon. One could even imagine telecommunication-connected joint seminars centering on common themes, such as Christian marriage—not just across the city, but across the world. The technology is available today, but has yet to be exploited.

Helper Formats

People will always have problems which religious education must address, and during young adulthood many of those problems will center on premarital, postmarital, divorce, and remarital concerns. Young adult religious education programs must provide mechanisms that go beyond the pastor counseling of individuals and couples. Pastoral counseling, of course, continues, but it increasingly is supplemented by lay counseling, small groups, and psycho-educational groups. Lay counseling programs have sprung up across the country and many programs exist for training lay counselors. As churches become larger—especially in urban areas where the "mega-churches" of 3000 to 7000 members are not uncommon—people are hungry for fellowship with individuals. Religious education, especially in the form of small groups, is the backbone of the "mega-churches." Even in the smaller congregation, small groups provide more accountability and more opportunities for discipleship than do worship services and large congregational functions.

With marital problems being so prevalent, couples need to be trained as lay couple counselors. There are many programs in large churches that train lay counselors now (see Tan, 1991), but there are few programs that concentrate on lay counseling for marital concerns, yet those are the most frequent concerns presented to friends (Sell & Goldsmith, 1988) as well as to pastors for help (Benner, 1992).

Premarriage counseling is increasing throughout the country. In some states premarriage counseling is required by state law. In many churches, pastors refuse to marry couples who have not had premarriage counseling. Further, research is accumulating that shows that pre-marriage counseling can be effective. However, premarriage counseling is usually effective only if it involves specific training in communication skills, not merely the provision of information about marriage (Worthington, 1990).

Premarriage counseling—and by extension, marriage enrichment—continues to expand its methods to include multimedia approaches. Individual sessions with couples are supplemented by computerized personal and relationship assessment, group discussions and structured leveraged teaching within group sessions, and videotape-directed homework.

Marital counseling continues with little change in style. Most is conducted conjointly with a pastor, but churches are supplementing couples counseling by pastors with conjoint couples counseling by trained lay helpers and with psycho-educational group approaches.

Technological Formats

People are created for relationships, so technology will never replace congregational worship, helper ministries, or religious education. However, technological methods of transmitting information among Christians are only now beginning to be seriously explored. Some churches already have videotape and audiotape libraries of excellent speeches, conferences, workshops, and other resources. As technology continues to develop, parishioners, instead of checking out videotapes, which is highly inefficient, will access through home computers, modems, or more advanced telecommunication-computer work-stations, the church's on-line CD-ROM resource library at the touch of a finger. Further, as telecommunication workstations become widely available at lower cost, more young adults will work at home and be able to access information anywhere in the world.

Besides the obvious benefits to easily obtaining information about marriage and religious education, the growing use of home workstations may transform society. The trend toward urbanization may be reversed, causing migrations of people to rural areas because they no longer must commute to work. Further, husbands and wives may again be able to participate in child rearing. Day care will be unnecessary if both husband and wife are at home. If such a social transformation were indeed to occur, new societal standards would need to be developed to prescribe roles, boundaries, and norms within the family. The church, with its longstanding value on marriage and the family, would be well-positioned to help forge these standards.

Electronic college and postbaccalaureate education could abound. Correspondence adult education has already been transformed by innovative programs such as the Liberty University School of LifeLong Learning, which videotapes live courses that are viewed by correspondence students, who are examined in their home cities. Widespread telecommunications and computer work-stations could make interaction with faculty and examinations instantaneous within the adult student's own home.

Conclusion

Society and marriage have been and are being rapidly transformed, forcing us to rethink how we educate young adults in the faith. Religious education programs must respond to the challenges and can do so by using technology, understanding the young adult, and employing the relevant issue of marriage to teach young adults about spiritual truth.

References

Benner, D. G. (1992). *Strategic pastoral counseling: A short-term structure model.* Grand Rapids, MI: Baker.

Brody, G. H., & Forehand, R. (1986). Maternal perceptions of child maladjustment as a function of the combined influences of child behavior and maternal depression. *Journal of Consulting and Clinical Psychology, 54,* 237-240.

Carter, E., & McGoldrick, M. (1989). Overview: The changing family life cycle—A framework for family therapy. In B. Carter & M. McGoldrick (Eds.), *The changing family life cycle: A framework for family therapy* (2nd ed). (pp. 3-28). Boston: Allyn and Bacon.

Chandler, R. (1992). *Racing toward 2001: The forces shaping America's religious future.* Grand Rapids, MI: Zondervan.

Cherlin, A. J. (1981). *Marriage, divorce, remarriage.* Cambridge, MA: Harvard University Press.

Collins, G. R., & Clinton, T. E. (1992). *Baby boomer blues.* Dallas: Word.

Doherty, W. J. (1991). Family therapy goes postmodern. *Family Therapy Networker, 15* (5), 37-42.

Efran, J. S. (1991). Constructivism in the inner city. *Family Therapy Networker, 15* (5), 51-52.

Freedman, J. L. (1984). Effects of television violence on aggressiveness. *Psychological Bulletin, 96,* 227-246.

Friedrich-Coffer, L., & Huston, A. C. (1986). Television violence and aggression: The debate continues. *Psychological Bulletin, 100,* 364-371.

Fukuyama, F. (1992). *The end of history and the last man.* New York: Free Press.

Gergen, K. J. (1991). The saturated family. *Family Therapy Networker, 15* (5), 27-35.

Kipnis, D. (1991). The technological perspective. *Psychological Science, 2* (2), 62-69.

Kubey, R., & Csikszentmahalyi, M. (1990). *Television and the quality of life: How viewing shapes everyday experience.* Hillsdale, NJ: Erlbaum.

Liebert, R. M., Sprafkin, J. N., & Davidson, E. S. (1982). *The early window: Effects of television on children and youth.* New York: Pergamon.

Linden, E. (1993, January 11). Megacities. *Time, 141* (2), 28-38.

Minuchin, S. (1991). The seductions of constructivism. *Family Therapy Networker, 15* (5), 47-50.

Naisbitt, J. (1984). *Mega-trends: Ten new directions transforming our lives.* New York: Warner Books.

O'Hara, M., & Anderson, W. T. (1991). Welcome to the postmodern world. *Family Therapy Networker, 15* (5), 19-25.

Paylor, N. R. (1986). Working with adults in separation and divorce. In Nancy T. Foltz (Ed.), *Handbook of adult religious education* (pp. 181-206). Birmingham, AL: Religious Education Press.

Penn, P. (1991). *Letters to ourselves. Family Therapy Networker, 15* (5), 43-45.

Schaeffer, F. (1968). *Escape from reason.* Downers Grove, IL: InterVarsity Press.

Sell, K. L., & Goldsmith, W. M. (1988). Concerns about professional counseling: An exploration of five factors and the role of Christian orthodoxy. *Journal of Psychology and Christianity, 7* (3), 5-21.

Singer, J. L., & Singer, D. G. (1981). *Television, imagination and aggression: A study of preschoolers.* Hillsdale, NJ: Erlbaum.

Spanier, G. B. (1983). Married and unmarried cohabitation in the United States: 1980.

Journal of Marriage and the Family, 45, 277-288.

Tan, S.-Y. (1991). *Lay counseling: Equipping Christians for a helping ministry.* Grand Rapids, MI: Zondervan.

Toffler, A. (1970). *Future shock.* New York: Bantam.

United States Bureau of the Census (1990). *Current population reports.* Washington, DC: Government Printing Office, Series P-20, No. 445, June.

United States Senate Special Committee on Aging. (1986). *Aging America: Trends and projections (1984-85 ed.).* Washington, DC: United States Government Printing Office.

Weiten, W., Lloyd, M. A., & Lashley, R. L. (1991). *Psychology applied to modern life: Adjustment in the 90s* (3rd ed.). Pacific Grove, CA: Brooks/Cole.

Worthington, E. L., Jr. (1990). *Counseling before marriage.* Dallas: Word.

CHAPTER FOURTEEN

Young Adult Religious Education of Major Cultural Groups

HARLEY ATKINSON,
ELIZABETH CONDE-FRAZIER,
ANTHONY J. HEADLEY, DAVID WU

Introduction
(Harley Atkinson)

The ultimate goal in communicating the gospel is to present the supracultural message in culturally relevant ways. Missionaries have long grappled with the issue of presenting the message of the gospel to people of different customs, languages, values and belief systems. More recently careful efforts have been to *contextualize* the message to other cultures—that is to communicate the gospel in an understandable, culturally relevant form (Hesselgrave & Rommen, 1989, p. 2).

While we are sensitive to the principles of contextualization as we establish churches and do religious education in other countries, we often disregard cultural diversity when it comes to religious education in North America. For example, curriculum publishers tend to ignore specific cultures and pander to the dominant white, suburban, middle-class culture. Religious education textbooks and readings seldom focus on issues related to cultural differences. Yet education—including religious education—is very much culturally specific.

Furthermore, immigration to America is on the rise and plays an increas-

313

ing role in population growth—it is expected that it will account for nearly 40 percent of the growth we realize in the nineties (Barna, 1993). While at the turn of the century most immigrants came from Europe, the new wave is coming from southeastern Asian and Hispanic countries. Together these groups account for about two-thirds of all new residents (Barna, 1993)

This chapter will look at the young adult religious education of three major cultural groups that exist in North America—Hispanics, African Americans, and Asians. While generalizations may be helpful in understanding members of a minority group, two cautions must be identified. First it must be remembered that each member of a minority group does not necessarily share all or most of the traits identified with a particular group. "While generalizations may be helpful, we must be aware of the danger of over-generalizing and stereotyping minorities in contrast to the values of the dominant culture" (Pelaez, p. 50, 1987).

Second, we must recognize and understand the socio-historical differences within a major cultural group. For example, the Hispanic population, while sharing a common language, represents a variety of Latin American countries, the greatest percentage coming from Mexico, Puerto Rico, and Cuba. In addition to differences arising out of socio-historical backgrounds, "the Hispanic population also experiences intragroup differences. These differences are based on the length of residence in the United States, the degree of acculturation, and the extent of ethnic identity" (Birchett, Alvarado, & Lee, 1991, p, 378).

The terms African American or black American may include those who trace their ancestry to foreparents first brought here as slaves, as well as the more recent immigrants to America from African or Caribbean countries. Even within the native African American community intragroup differences exist. One attempt to identify such differences was that of Vontress (1971). From this earlier perspective, it was suggested that African Americans demonstrated differences in self-designation because of certain behavioral characteristics. For example, individuals who identified themselves as blacks tended to be better educated and were intolerant and hostile to racism. Persons who designated themselves as Negro were characterized by shifting values and were more willing to give whites a chance. Those who identified themselves as coloreds were more likely to gain their sense of identity from whites.

Perhaps the most diverse or pluralistic cultural group are made up by Asian Americans. The term Asian American encompasses many ethnic groups, each with distinct cultures and historical backgrounds, as well as different languages. The major groups include the Chinese, Filipinos, Guamanians, Japanese, Koreans, Samoans, and Vietnamese, with other Southeast Asian and Pacific people making up the rest (Birchett et al., 1991).

Hispanic Americans
(Elizabeth Conde-Frazier)

As with other cultural groups, Hispanic young adults are a largely diverse group. They may be single college students or professionals; they might be divorced and/or single parents, or young married couples; they may be first generation immigrants or fifth generation Hispanic Americans. Furthermore they represent up to twenty different Latino heritages, making the Hispanic population in the United States "a heterogeneous group, composed of people from many different countries, each with its own culture, ethnic values and history" (Birchett et al., 1991, p. 376).

In order to effectively do religious education with young adult Hispanics, it's important to recognize the unique issues that affect their lives. Perhaps the most critical is that of identity.

The Search for Identity

While for the first generation Hispanic issues include adaptation to the new environment, the establishment of new support systems, and new experiences coupled with the loss of others, for the second generation young adult, there arises the problem of identity. These individuals exist in two worlds. This means that they are interpreting everyday experiences, events, and values in the light of each cultural system, and choosing those needed to survive in each situation. The school and professional world represent one situation, while the family (that is, the nuclear family and very close friends who have become like family) and sometimes the church represent another. One may use a different language in each situation; one is an insider looking out and the other an outsider looking in. This creates the feeling of belonging to neither one of the two cultures, yet of being a mixture of both. Elizondo (1981) describes this as the *mestizaje*, and is characterized in many ways.

Language and code switching. One of the ways this ambiguity is evidenced is in what is called code switching. New generation Hispanics may switch back and forth from one language to the other, depending on the subject, and it is in this coding and decoding that we may observe aspects of biculturalism. English, for example, is used for professional purposes while Spanish is for more informal conversation, and for language used regarding church and God. During a worship service one may address God in code switching—"Thank you Jesus. *Gloria a ti, Jesus.*" Code switching may reflect the interior pilgrimage of the person in both cultures.

Religious educators must be sensitive as to how code switching signals the degree of comfort one has with a topic, the degree of intimacy expressed, and the relationship the person is forming with the group, the leader, and with Jesus. "When we touch the language structure of a person we touch the heart of his or her view of self and the world" (Villafane, 1991, p. 8).

Some second, third, and fourth generation Hispanics do not speak Spanish. Yet Justo Gonzalez (1988) states that "bilingualism is likely to continue being a feature of the Hispanic community in the forseeable future" (p. 33). He also gives this warning: "Let us not so idolize our culture that we oppress another Hispanic who does not speak as we do, or even one who has never learned how to speak Spanish because the pressures of society were too great" (p. 33).

Different family values. The mestizo Hispanic who has acquired the English language and has learned to adapt to the North American ethos enjoys a better socio-economic status. This may cause conflict with the first generation which has been poor, not as well-educated, and employed in low-wage service jobs or as laborers. They are Spanish dominant, and their value orientations are those of the country of origin. Family responsibilities and values are perceived differently by these two generations. The second generation naturally wants to spend more time with friends who are peers while parents feel that family should be a priority. Marriage may be postponed for career goals by the mestizo generation. Pressure may be placed especially on the female to give preference to forming a family.

Manuel Ortiz (1993) reflects on his life history by recounting, "my friends and I enjoyed both the Hispanic music we had grown up with at home and the contemporary music we heard in the community. But the adults made fun of this. Our parents felt we were betraying their culture and embracing another one instead. They viewed change as a denial of everything they believed, a rejection of everything they were. Conflicts flared up frequently between parents and children—sometimes subtle, other times quite confrontive" (p. 63). Such differences cause alienation between the generations.

One task of young adult religious educators is to provide ways for the two generations to come together to listen to the views they have on issues, to examine the origins of these views, and to explore the biblical and theological foundations guiding them. Group discussion is a technique which can be helpful in such situations.

For example, a question to explore in light of the scriptures is, "Can we shift or adapt the roles and responsibilities of the family and still be faithful to the gospel"? Answering this question calls for the formation of new biblical paradigms by the group, as they delineate the changes which migration brings to their lives and to their faith.

In teaching for affective and lifestyle change, the religious educator of Hispanic young adults will find experiential learning activities such as role play, simulation games, and case studies most helpful. For example the second generation Hispanic might take on the role of the first generation person, and vice versa. Group members can then discuss the feelings and attitudes they had as they took on the other's perspective.

A helpful technique for dealing with negative feelings is called "Dialogue Within Ourselves." The objective here is "to gain practice in listening to and making cultural interpretations based on an 'internal dialogue' about a cross-cultural issue or experience that has generated ambivalent thoughts and feelings" (Pusch, 1979, p. 124). The young adult students are asked to select a subject or experience that produces ambivalent feelings or thoughts within them. For example they might address the issue of being pressured into getting married and starting a family. They are then asked to listen to their ambivalent thoughts and feelings, and listen to the two sides of their internal dialogue. They can then do one of the following two exercises: a) describe in writing the two sides of the issues and the feelings accompanying them, or b) write down in a script of a play or conversation the dialogue between the two voices. Finally, the leader can ask for volunteers to read what they have written and discuss it with the rest of the class or group (pp.124-125).

Cultural identity and the church. Will Herberg (1960) argues that newcomers to America are overconscious of their identity, seeing themselves Italian, Polish, or German, for example, with greater intensity than they had in their home country. Members of the next generation tend to deemphasize their origins as they become Americanized. They seem to break away from the behavior patterns, religion, language, and the way of life of their parents. However in the third generation, they are drawn back to the country of origin as they search for a specific identity.

In a similar manner Daniel Sanchez (1991) describes second generation Mexican Americans as "Median Ethnics." They are English dominant, assimilated culturally, but not assimilated into the political structure. The third generation of Mexican Americans he places in the "Integrated Ethnic" category—81.8 percent of whom speak mostly English. There is more interracial marriage, they are more involved in the power structure of the dominant society and are very active in civil rights. Another group of Hispanics are called the "Revitalized Ethnic" or the "Renaissance Generation." These young adults examine their cultural heritage and are searching for a cultural identity which is different from that of the dominant society. They stress cultural revitalization.

We can observe in these different cultural adaptions the different strategies of survival, development, and revitalization. They have implications for the patterns of power relationships with the dominant society. These relationships range from powerlessness, to the establishing of political organizations, and a more forceful participation in civil rights efforts. These various dynamics influence the theology and spiritual pilgrimage of a group.

Manuel Ortiz (1993) says that for the most part Hispanics have long occupied communities of the United States without losing their identity. Unlike the Swedes, Irish, or Italians who have managed to join mainstream America, they have not followed the assimilation process (p. 32). Furthermore "more and more of them are joining together to attack the problems of poverty, unemployment, and underachievement in education. They are trying to do something about institutional racism and about their underrepresentation in community and state government" (p. 33).

However for those who come from families with stronger ties to evangelical Protestant churches it is sometimes more difficult. The church relates to the spiritual dimensions, but often these young adults are forced to move outside the church to give expression to their identity and heritage, or address issues related to their culture.

This is evidenced in interviews in the following ways. A 28-year-old woman from New York City says, "I really want to be used by the church. I have so much to offer. I'm really doing a ministry out there on my job and in the community. I wish my church would own these ministries in the areas of human and civil rights." A male, 33, from Boston expresses: "There is a lot of good that I do out there. I need the church to show me how the bible supports what I'm doing. It's never validated or informed by the church." A 31-year-old woman from New York says "I love my church but sometimes I get a lot more out of a conference I go to for my job, where we talk about current problems and find solutions for them. How does the Bible inform my work in the community and in the field of genetics where I'm trained? I hunger deeply for my faith to grow in those areas as well. I want that dimension added to my faith." A 23-year-old woman from Los Angeles adds, "As adults now we have so much love, so much energy and knowledge, and we need to be leaders of the church, but not just by collecting offerings and singing in the choir. The church won't listen to the vision God has given us."[1] Ortiz (1993) agrees. "The Hispanic evangelical church has always assumed that its commitment was more spiritual than social and that the social transformation was incidental, not primary" (p. 107).

Creating opportunity for sharing one's faith pilgrimage is a way of leading persons to recognize their common ground in the faith while getting to know the new dimensions, interpretations, and expressions which they give to their faith. The young adult religious education leader may arrange these expressions of faith chronologically and then add the church history pieces which reveal the communal expression of faith of each generation as it is revealed in the mission of the church. Needs and concerns of each generation will be listed next to each vision. Spaces will then be left open in the more contemporary era for the young adults to share their vision of mission. This celebrates the earlier visions and welcomes new vision. The discussion goes

---

1. The above remarks were made in an interview with Elizabeth Conde-Frazier.

on to look at the new gifts we also bring to the new vision as well as the gifts already present among all. Worship should be incorporated since it is common ground and becomes a community building element.

However it is the responsibility of religious education leaders to go beyond dialogue and reflection. They must provide and facilitate opportunities for young Hispanic adults to bridge the chasm between church and community; to equip them for addressing current problems in the community, and provide opportunities for them to integrate their faith, lifestyle, and mission. "They do not merely want to be pacified by a nice sermon; they want to know how they can bring about change in their situations. They want to be socially conscious in a responsible way and look toward the future, not just the present" (Ortiz, 1993, p. 72). In order to be successful with young adult Hispanics, the church must provide opportunities for them to give expression to their culture and heritage and equip them to bring an element of transformation and social change to their community. They must be included in the strategy for leadership, outreach and ministry (p. 83). The church, through young adult religious education, can offer classes or seminars that equip young adult Hispanics to bring social transformation to their community. Some issues to be addressed might include working with government agencies, fundraising, counseling, organization and administration, working with children and youth, and building relationships.

Identity, cultural heritage, and marginalization. A dimension of this identity issue is the struggle to attain one's socio-historical heritage, as the dominant society defines and marginalizes the group. Elizondo (1981) describes the process certain Mexican Americans go through, although the struggle is not unique to this group. "They began to dig into their past, to penetrate the development and meaning their historical process. . . . 'Who are we?' they asked themselves. And they began to search for their roots—not in order to go backward, but in order to go forward. The Mexican Americans realize that they have to rediscover their origin in order to appreciate and celebrate their historical process and their true existential identity" (p. 20).

There are so many names given to Hispanics, with much controversy surrounding the meanings, as well as discussion as to which ones should be used: Hispanic Americans, Mexican Americans, Cuban Americans, Newyoricans, Latinos, or La Raza. There is a need to belong to a cultural group which Hispanics define for ourselves and of which they can be proud. As Pelaez (1987) suggests, "Culture gives us a sense of belonging, a sense of identity" (p. 51).

Unfortunately, some individuals find themselves in a cultural limbo. "Heretofore, Mexican Americans have been a marginal people in sort of no man's land, caught between the polarizing forces of their cultural-linguistic, Indo-Hispanic heritage and their political-linguistic American context. They have become frustrated and alienated by the struggle between the system which seeks to refashion them in its own image and the knowledge of who and what they really are" (Ortega, 1971, p. 296).

Marginalization occurs when a person is unable or reluctant to give up some aspect of their cultural heritage. To live in the American context is to feel pressured and forced to incorporate social, political, and linguistic elements of the dominant society. One feels a confusion in the struggle between economic progress and cultural survival. Another dimension of marginality stems from the rejection some young adult Hispanics feel from the people of the country of origin. They are considered "ni de aqui, ni de alla" (neither from here nor from there).

At this point it becomes necessary for the religious educator to create a separate space for young adults to talk among each other about the daily inner conflicts and struggles as well as the advantages of being bilingual and bicultural individuals. Elizondo's *Galilean Journey* (1981) provides a theological perspective. The group may choose to read and discuss parts of it together as well as other short stories and poems written by others or themselves. These give voice to these struggles, as well as suggestions for new pathways to take, as young adults seek to maintain a creative tension.

Occasionally the religious education group may attend to these struggles by sitting in a circle. Everyone in the "ronda" is a pastor; there is absolute confidentiality in the "ronda." A question may be brought up by anyone, and those in the circle address the question. Questions should be addressed without attaching any form of judgment. If the group has not yet developed trust, then questions may be written down and placed in a box from where they will be drawn.[2]

The search for dignity. Closely related to the search for identity is the search for dignity—the overcoming of the negative self-image stereotypes. Manuel Ortiz (1993) says second and third generation Hispanics "must be given the dignity of their culture if they are to grow as balanced and progressive individuals in their present situation" (p. 81).

This can be pursued in at least two ways. First, young adult Hispanics must know their historical roots. Unfortunately most historical information given to young adult Hispanics ranges from nothing to inaccurate, misleading data (Ortiz, 1993). "History books downgrade the quality of the Spanish colonization; cartoons show a fat, mustachioed Mexican, sombrero pulled down over his eyes, sleeping in the middle of the day. Hispanics are perceived as inferior because they live outside the basic ethos of the North American republic. The tale has been so convincing that some Spanish-

---

2. The ronda was developed by Dr. Loida Martell-Otero, associate pastor of the Soundview Christian Church, Bronx, New York.

speaking have believed it themselves and have rejected their deepest traditions" (quoted in Ortiz, 1993, pp. 81-82). Providing young adult Hispanics with accurate historical data will help them understand who they are and give them a new sense of dignity or self worth.

Second, young adult Hispanics must be included in leadership and ministry opportunities. Often second generation Hispanics have been exluded by their churches and first generation leaders, fearing their inclusion will necessitate major changes in the way things are done (Ortiz, 1993). However the inclusion of young Hispanic adults in leadership is necessary not only for the success of the church in addressing the needs of the church and community, but in that it has a positive psychological effect on how they perceive themselves.

The religious educator needs to address the self-esteem issues that stem from this struggle with identity and marginalization. A new identity in Christ does not mean we become acultural beings. At the birth of the church in Acts 2, the Pentecost experience took into account the cultural diversity of those present, in order to evangelize them.

Relating Scriptures to Daily Living

Religious education for the mestizo generation does not begin or end with the classroom experience. It starts with the personal journey and the struggles of daily living, moves on to finding God's voice in the scriptures. The Bible plays an integral part in the development of one's faith. In interviews this writer conducted with young adults both in and outside the church, they expressed that "the Word of God is central to our lives." However, one of the main reasons for young Hispanic adults leaving the church is the church's inability to relate the scriptures to daily life. "We want to look at our lives in the light of the scriptures."

To do this the religious educator must first listen to the issues and experiences of the young adults and enable them to listen to each other. This may be done through one on one dialogue, or group discussions. The goal is to assist them to make sense of their lives through the lens of scripture. One 22 year old comments,

"I can sit with a bunch of friends to talk about similar experiences and we can relate to each other. I need that. It's important for putting things into perspective. However, as rich as they are, those conversations still have something missing. Sometimes it's meaning or purpose, sometimes it's a substantive answer or depth beyond where we are, but when we look at scriptures deeper questions arise. We can see more sides. An answer may not always come, but understanding and direction do. That direction may lead us into other issues and questions, but I know I'm growing."[3]

---

3. These remarks were made in an interview with the author.

Theological reflection is one way of doing this. The Whitehead and Whitehead model (1980) of theological reflection takes into account the elements of biblical tradition and culture, one's own culture, and personal experience. In these reflections one evaluates and critiques one's culture of origin alongside the culture of the dominant society. Then the question may be asked, "Which are the values that are congruent with scripture and which are not?" As young Hispanic adults wrestle with these questions, they may then begin to identify issues which emerge from these conflicting cultural values.

Furthermore, such theological reflection will help the young Hispanic to define a vision for mission, as oppressions and needs are identified. Politics, voting, ethical issues, education, health and other issues will come into full light of the gospel. At a point in their lives when they are learning the responsibilities of being citizens they face the responsibility of making ethical and moral decisions—in relationships, the workplace, political involvement, and sexuality. In accountability groups, young adults can not only discuss ethical, moral, and life-related issues in light of scripture but help and encourage each other in applying scripture to daily living. Young adult group members call each other into accountability by checking to see if and how they are applying scripture to various facets of living and issues.

Personal Faith Experiences

Personal faith experiences are also important. Like other young adults, Hispanics seek after and need a personal faith experience or testimony. Ruben Armendariz (1981) suggests that Hispanic spirituality is embodied in the notion that God will reveal himself through various means in the daily life. This revelation guides daily actions and decisions, as well as relationships. This approach not only leads to a strong commitment to responsible living but builds a very relational faith.

The religious educator might share his or her own faith journey and relationship with Jesus, then direct other young adults into their own search and relationship. Then they, in turn, can share their story with others. Another way faith can be shared is in the corporate worship experience. In worship we teach each other and embrace each other's faith journeys in a celebrative moment.

Non-Hispanic Churches

Marina Herrera (1979) identifies at least two challenges for the Anglo church in terms of religious education to Hispanics. First there needs to be an understanding of the history, language, and culture of Hispanic peoples. She suggests that all too often evangelization of Hispanics has been synonymous with Americanization. Pazmiño (1993) points out that in order to understand the world view and ethos of a particular ethnic group, non-

Hispanic religious educators must spend adequate time in the community with a variety of persons. Simply put, the religious educator must build relationships with Hispanics, take part in activities in the Hispanic community, get into their homes, and spend time dialoging with them. "The cultural differences among young adults need to be understood in context, not measured by the similarities or differences with the mainstream culture" (Palaez, 1987, p. 52).

The second challenge Herrera presents is the need for "a call of conversion to Christian values" (p. 462). For example, as some Hispanic young adults move up the economic ladder, they need to look at issues of Christian stewardship. Will they simply adopt the middle-class lifestyle of the dominant culture, or will they maintain the values of their cultural and religious heritage? The issues of resolving their marginality and desire to be a part of the American culture might push them toward an uncritical acceptance of a lifestyle which does not embody Christian values.

For those attending non-Hispanic churches the issue is intensified. A 29-year-old male from San Diego says this: "I now live in a different neighborhood. The Lord has been good to me. I walk into a church where the cars in the lot are mostly new and there are more Lexus, BMW's, and Jaguars than I am accustomed to seeing. Inside is a totally different world. The interests and concerns are very foreign to the ones I was brought up with. Do I accept this world and dive into it? The church I grew up in considered the poor before the personal acquisitions of riches. Here, accumulation of wealth is so natural and accepted. I want to know who is right."[4]

The non-Hispanic religious educator must provide the young adult Hispanic the opportunity to compare and contrast the worldview and ethos of the particular Hispanic group with the Christian faith and scriptures. Then, "In areas of confirmation and complementarity, the effort is to preserve and celebrate the culture. In areas of contradiction or conflict, the effort is by the grace of God to redeem and transform the culture wherever it is possible" (Pazmiño, 1993, p. 286).

Conclusion

The religious educator of young Hispanic adults must not see him or herself simply as a dispenser of biblical data, or an adherent to a set curriculum designed for a generic group of young adults. Rather, to teach is to center in a relationship and to guide others on a spiritual journey. Herrera (1984) describes the religious educator as one who will "share on the same level of humanness . . . as a fellow sojourner who has equal human needs for food, company and enlightenment. Without this ability to share in an equal fash-

---

4. These remarks were made in an interview with the author.

ion after an exchange of concerns and light, the relationship which evokes commitment will not exist. There will only be the relationship of a teacher and student which of its very nature places barriers to sharing the same table on an equal footing and deters people from personal involvement" (p. 44).

African Americans
(Anthony J. Headley)

The focus of this section is on the racial and cultural identity of young adult African Americans, and how identity impacts the religious education of this group. The dynamics of racial and cultural identity are critical to the task of religious education for young adults because they largely determine the openness of African Americans to religious education from persons of majority cultures. Furthermore, stages of racial identity have a great deal to do with learning styles, as well as critical needs and concerns of African Americans.

Religious Education of Young Adult African Americans

Leon McKenzie (1982, 1986) suggests that religious education must not simply be the telling of theological-scriptural truths. Rather, it is education that is derived from a religious framework but is addressed to the needs and interests of the learner. This does not mean that religious content is unimportant but that religious content is made relevant to the life situation of the learner.

This means that religious education must utilize the principle of inclusion whereby nothing human is alien to religious education. Any legitimate educational activity that takes place in a religious context (by that I understand that it also brings to bear the religious thought of that tradition) is religious education (McKenzie, 1986). Young adults have needs and tasks that are unique to their stage. For example, young adults are characterized by the psychological needs for independence, identity, and intimacy. In addition young adulthood includes the sociological tasks of searching for a meaningful occupation, establishing a family, and becoming a contributing member of one's community (Merriam & Ferro, 1986).

For young African Americans, religious education must address the major needs and tasks pertinent to young adults. However, given the reality of inequality that is yet evident in portions of society (including the church), religious education must do more. Religious educators must be concerned with prejudice and racism which may exist as barriers to the fulfillment of psychological and sociological tasks, as well as spiritual development. Religious education of young adult African Americans must be concerned with issues related to employment discrimination and fair and equal housing opportunities.

It must also make an effort to understand the black religious experience and how such perspectives may enrich ones faith.

Religious Education and Identity Seeking

McKenzie (1986) suggests that religious education is a process intended to enable the learner to acquire, explore, expand, and express meaning. He also argues that the acquisition of meaning is critical to the development of one's identity. Furthermore he suggests that the exploration and expansion of meaning can be facilitated by the exploration of the richness of one's religious tradition, by relating the religious tradition to one's life experiences, and by a critical examination of one's religious tradition. Finally, he says that the expression of meaning demands that religious education be action oriented.

These thoughts have several implications for the religious education of young adult black Americans. First, religious education must be concerned with identity formation as one of the outcomes of acquiring meaning. As indicated earlier, identity is a critical task of young adulthood, and this is intensified for young African American adults who may see their blackness devalued by society.

Second, religious education must allow for experiences that facilitate the exploration of the black religious experience and how that tradition relates to black life experiences, including oppression and suffering. This can best be done by introducing various elements of the black religious experience into religious education programs. This might include the study of black religious persons such as Sojourner Truth, Richard Allen, and Martin Luther King. In addition, religious expressions inherent in spirituals may be a fruitful area of study, since these provide keen insights, not only into the suffering, but also the faith African Americans have had in God and how this faith has supported them through countless sufferings. Such an approach can be found in the "Jesus as Liberator" unit in a project for religious education in black churches by Rogers and Rogers (1978).

Third, religious education must bring young African Americans to critically reflect on both their culture and their religious experience. Such critical examination will allow for one to appreciate what is best about his or her culture and religion, while allowing the scriptures to challenge both. Critical reflection can be facilitated through exposure to and discussion of the themes gleaned from the black religious experience.

Finally, religious education must be concerned with life and action—not mere theological reflection. The concern for action can be best met through encouraging individuals to become involved in activities that are designed to alleviate poverty, oppression, and injustice. This would be especially needful for middle- and upper-class African Americans who may have lost touch with the inner-city impoverished.

Developmental Models For Understanding Young African American Adults

As suggested earlier, an understanding of a developmental approach to racial identity will enhance the religious education process.

Cross model. One of the most helpful theories is the model of Cross (1972), a model which continues to receive much attention (Parham & Helms, 1981, 1985; Pomales, Clairborn, & LaFromboise, 1986; Ponterotto, Anderson, & Grieger, 1986; Pyant & Yanico, 1991). Cross's model suggests five stages through which African Americans pass in their identity seeking process. In the first, or *Preencounter Stage,* the individual is programmed to see the world as white, and to identify self with the dominant culture while distrusting blackness. The second stage is called the *Encounter Stage,* and is usually precipitated by some crisis that plunges the individual into a search for his/her blackness and an understanding of blackness. Stage three, the *Immersion-emersion Stage* is characterized by a renunciation of everything white, and a corresponding attachment to everything black. Stage four, the *Internalization Stage,* is where the African American develops a more secure sense of self and has a more flexible worldview that can appreciate elements of both whiteness and blackness. The final or *Internalization-commitment Stage* is closely related to stage four and involves a commitment to political action to bring about social change (Cross, 1972; Pyant & Yanico, 1991).

Minority identity development (MID) model. As the name suggests, this is a model (Morten & Atkinson, 1983) that extends to all minorities. The authors propose that minority attitudes are flexible and are a function of one's stage of identity development (Atkinson, Morten, & Sue, 1989). They further argue that although this model has distinct stages "the MID is more accurately conceptualized as a continuous process in which one stage blends with another and boundaries between stages are not clear" (p. 38).

The first stage is called the *Conformity* stage, and minority persons in this stage have a clear preference for dominant cultural values over their own. Stage two is called the *Dissonance* stage and as in Cross's (1972) Encounter stage, is usually precipitated by a critical event such as the assassination of Martin Luther King. Such an event throws the conforming person into a state of conflict regarding their racial identity. In stage three, the *Resistance and Immersion* stage, the black person moves to a complete endorsement of minority held views and rejects those of the dominant culture. Stage four, the *Introspection* stage, involves a greater degree of comfort with one's own sense of identity and greater personal autonomy. A person at this stage will also begin to realize that there may be some positive aspects to the dominant culture. The final stage of *Synergetic Articulation and*

Awareness involves "a sense of self-fulfillment with regard to cultural identity" (Atkinson et al., 1989, p. 43). In addition, "Cultural values of other minorities as well as those of the dominant group are objectively examined and accepted or rejected on the basis of experience gained in the earlier stages of identity development. Desire to eliminate all forms of oppression becomes an important motivation for the individual's behavior" (Atkinson et al., 1989, p. 43).

Not all minority persons experience all of these stages during their lifetime. Neither are the stages irreversible. In fact, individuals may be raised by parents functioning at level five, but in their own search for identity, may move from stage five back into lower levels. Each of these stages have their own characteristic attitudes in relation to self, members of the same minority group, members of other minority groups and toward the dominant culture. For instance, persons in the Conformity stage would have depreciating attitudes toward self and members of the same minority, a discriminatory attitude toward other minorities, while holding appreciating attitudes toward members of the dominant group (Atkinson et al., 1989).

The two theories (Cross, 1972; Atkinson et al., 1989) are presented in Table 1. The table demonstrates the overlap and similarity between the two theories. While both are concerned with social action in Stage 5, the MID model also captures notions of self-fulfillment and objectivity to other cultures.

Identity Development and Religious Education of Young African American Adults

Differences in racial identity may be much more fundamental in determining attitudes, values, and behavior than variables such as education and social class. One of the fundamental ways one's stage of racial identity will impact cross-cultural religious education is the degree of openness to persons of majority cultures (Cross, 1972; Atkinson et al., 1989).

Openess to cross cultural religious education. According to the Cross and MID models, one can infer that persons in stage 3 will be highly resistant to religious education from sources other than their own culture. Individuals at stages 1 and 5 would show openness to cross-cultural religious education but for drastically different reasons. Young adults in stage 1 would be interested in cross-cultural religious education because they hold that persons from majority cultures have a superior brand of religion. Certainly such a self and group depreciating attitude is not psychologically healthy (Parham & Helms, 1985; Pyant & Yanico, 1991). In addition, this stance is less likely to facilitate the mastery of the norms and beliefs of one's own religious tradition (McKenzie, 1983), since that tradition is laid aside for

Table 1
Stages of African American Identity Development

Cross (1971)		MID (Atkinson et al., 1989)
Stage	Attitude/Process	Stage
1. Preencounter	Preference for the dominant culture. Devaluation of blackness.	Conformity
2. Encounter	Conflict precipitated by some critical event. The search for new identity.	Dissonance
3. Immersion-emersion	Immersion in black experiences and culture. Rejection of dominant culture.	Resistance and Immersion
4. Internalization	Secure sense of self. Greater sense of autonomy. A more flexible worldview that neither automatically devalues whiteness or idealizes blackness.	Introspection
5. Internalization-commitment	Involvement in action to bring about social change. Sense of self-fulfillment of one's cultural identity. Desire to end all forms of oppression. Culture of others examined objectively and accepted or rejected on the basis of experience.	Synergetic Articulation and Awareness

the adoption of another. Finally, the wholehearted endorsement of majority values makes it less likely that the African American would engage in the critical reflection that is so crucial to the religious education process (McKenzie, 1983).

In contrast, young adults functioning at stage 5 are open to cross-cultural religious education because they recognize that traditions and values of both cultures can be beneficial to their spiritual development. Because of the appreciative stance toward their own traditions and culture, they are able to master the norms and beliefs of their own religious culture. At the same time, they are capable of objectively examining the traditions of other groups (Atkinson et al., 1989) to engage in critical reflection of culture and to value and appreciate traditions and norms other than their own.

Approach to religious education. Another way an understanding of identity stages can aid the religious educator of young adults is in the way religious education is approached. For example, when working with individuals at stage 3 (immersion in black culture; rejection of dominant culture) the religious educator should be especially careful to incorporate the symbols and heroes connected with the black religious experience as suggested by black theology (Eugene, 1987; Shockley, 1976, 1988; Stokes, 1982).

A different approach would be necessary for individuals at stage 5. Both the Cross and MID models suggest that individuals at stage 5 are concerned with the impact of oppression and social injustice on African Americans and other minorities (Cross, 1972; Morten et al., 1989). Consequently religious education with African American young adults at this stage must be concerned with issues of social justice, should provide opportunities for active involvement in social change, and should encourage compassion toward the oppressed.

Conclusion

This section has focused on racial and cultural identity of young adult African Americans and how identity impacts religious education of these people. Miller (1979) suggests that one purpose of religious education is "to nurture in individuals the formation of a unique and distinctive identity, one which faithfully represents the integrity and historical roots of the community of which one is a member" (p. 339). Similarly Tarasar (1988) argues that the task of the religious educator is to encourage the development of self-identity and the search for commonness.

The construction or shaping of one's identity is a unique concern of young adults (Merriam & Ferro, 1986), but given the minority status of young African American adults, this is an even greater need. Tarasar (1988) has rightly stated that "minority status, be it religious, political, racial, or economic seriously affects the attitudes of persons concerning their self-identity and their openness to others" (p. 203).

Asian Americans
(David Wu)

Much of what has been written about Asian American Christianity has not underscored the role of religious education. This section deals with the religious education of Asian American young adults in terms of some general characteristics of this group, their preferred instructional styles, and the development of content and curriculum. These topics are viewed against the backdrop of three factors that greatly impact Asian American life, namely immigration and assimilation, family ties, and education.

Immigration/Cultural Assimilation, and General Characteristics

A clarification of the terms "Asian" and "Asian American" is pertinent to this discussion. First, "Asians" are easily identifiable along ethnic and racial lines but are difficult to describe beyond generalities. Whereas formerly Asians in America were mainly Japanese, Chinese, and Korean, the United States Census Bureau currently enumerates seventeen Asian groups in United States,[5] each with its particular characteristics, ranging "from premodernized groups, such as the Hmong, to medical professionals from the Philippines and Ph.D.s from India" (Kitano & Daniels, 1988, p. viii).

Within the United States, most people have at best a superficial understanding that Chinese, Koreans, Filipinos, Vietnamese, and other Asian groups have different cultural backgrounds, languages, foods, and customs, and originated from different countries in the Asian continent. More likely, as Kitano (1981, p. 137) notes, two main stereotypes exist: that there is a presumed homogeneity and interchangeability among the different groups and their cultures, and that American-born Asians are expected to be familiar with the culture of their "home" country in Asia.

Second, "Asian American" is currently a politically correct term laden with sociological innuendos. Sociologists (e.g., Liu, 1980, pp. 282ff.) speak of a Pan Asian movement traceable to the late sixties and early seventies, and of a "new cultural synthesis" whereby, due to interethnic exchanges, the Asian American is less inclined to have a particular ethnic or racial orientation (e.g., as in being Chinese or Filipino). This cultural synthesis is noticeable among second-, third-, and fourth-generation Asians born in America who are highly assimilated and enculturated into mainstream American society.

Asian cultures undergo a gestalt transformation in America: the outcome is not simply part Asian and part American but a distinctive new cultural entity. Psychologists (e.g., Sue & Sue, 1973), in line with Park's (1928) theory, have used the term "marginal man" to describe the "distinct Asian American personality structure that is neither traditionally Asian nor American" (Hune, 1989, p. 35). The actual experience is one of racial liminality, an in-between state of identity where the Asian American asserts "I'm American," while others around say "You are Asian" (Matsuoka, 1990, p. 115).

Kitano and Daniels (1988, p.190 ff) suggest a model of adaptation showing four groups of Asian Americans according to the variables of assimilation

5. Asian Indian, Bangladeshi, Burmese, Cambodian, Sri Lankan, Chinese, Filipino, Hmong, Indonesian, Japanese, Korean, Laotian, Malayan, Okinawan, Pakistani, Thai, and Vietnamese.

and ethnic identity: a) a high assimilation and a low ethnic identity, persons who are more American than ethnic; b) a high assimilation and a high ethnic identity, bicultural persons who are comfortable in both the Asian and the American cultural settings; c) a low assimilation and a low ethnic identity, disillusioned and alienated individuals who are uncomfortable with both American culture and the ethnic ways; d) a low assimilation and a high ethnic identity, new immigrants and others who retain their lifestyles, languages, and values, and stay primarily within the confines of ethnic enclaves.

A clear profile of an Asian American young adult is difficult to construct. Studies on Asian American young adults have primarily focused on college samples. On the issue of assertiveness, for example, Asian Americans see themselves as being less assertive than non-Asians (Sue, Ino, & Sue, 1983; Okada, 1989). In situations where Asian students are the majority persons present, however, assertive behaviors are more easily demonstrated (Okada, 1989). But there is no empirical evidence from duplicated studies that Asian American young adults beyond the college ages of 18-22 have the same traits. Further, adaptation issues like assertiveness, the model minority image, equality issues in employment, and higher education admissions quota, are only small pieces in the puzzle of the heterogenous Asian American population. The concerns of college-educated persons are a far cry from the social-cultural experiences and spiritual passages of, e.g., young adult Asian women workers in clothing factories ("sweatshops") and restaurant workers in Los Angeles.

A demographic picture of Asian American young adults is within our grasp. Some general factors to consider include immigration, family ties, and education.

Immigration. The U.S. Immigration Act of 1990 currently favors family line immigration, and as long as there is no reversal to a policy favoring European immigrants, Asian Americans will continue to grow numerically and feel the impact of new Asians being transplanted and added into their communities. Two considerations should be noted. First, the population of Asians in America is a youthful one, averaging 30 years of age. Second, there is the phenomenon of the "reluctant" immigrants—persons who are transplanted from Taiwan or Hong Kong, because of perceived political insecurity in their homeland. These persons do not necessarily sever the financial ties back home but maintain business ties with affluent Pacific Rim countries.

Family ties. The Asian young adult's family is generally extended to include parents, siblings, aunts and uncles, grandparents, cousins, etc., who provide significant relationships, support, and demands; it is not a nuclear family. This family orientation is a boon from the financial standpoint. According to the 1990 Census Bureau reports, Asian Americans have higher house-hold incomes, the median household income being $36,102 in 1989 because of the greater number of wage-earners per household. Asian Americans are also the fastest growing and most affluent ethnic minority. They are highly urbanized, with 93 percent living in metropolitan areas like Los Angeles county and the Tri-State region of New York, New Jersey, and Connecticut.[6]

Education. As the perceived means to successful careers and financial upward mobility, education is highly valued. Two out of every five Asian American over the age of 25 years have at least four years of college, near-ly double the figure for non-Hispanic whites.[7]

Preferred learning and teaching styles. In teaching and learning styles, we see most clearly the fundamental problem of religious education for Asian American young adults: this is the conflict in basic philosophies of education, stemming from contrasting worldviews and ideologies, and a clash of different psychological conceptualization of human nature. This problem often con-fuses cross-cultural religious educators and Asian American young adults. Religious educators whose training and philosophical orientation are pri-marily drawn from Western theological institutions that do not have culture specific training curricula may find themselves contributing to teaching and learning processes that are ineffective and painful. Transplanted Asians, even after many years in America, may possibly continue to struggle with neg-ative learning experiences in a society that tends to view educational processes in a humanistic/existentialist light.

Selection of the right teaching methods and approaches for religious education, however, depends on the sensitivity of the educator toward the learner population. In an Asian church where there is a strong immigrant influence (i.e., low assimilation), chances are that the preferred approach is the Asian one adapted to American life. The instructional goals need to include the learning of life skills—problem identification and problem solv-ing from a Christian perspective that addresses the need of Asian young adults to deal with issues related to their development (e.g., Erikson's iden-tity, intimacy, and independence). The social context has to be Asian American, not an "old country" nor a white America orientation.

One teaching device that can be effectively used by the religious edu-cator of young adults is the contextualization of biblical parables for the purpose of developing moral reasoning. A sample session is given below, using Jesus' parable of the prodigal son in Luke 15. With the Sunday School class divided into three groups, each group is presented with a different ver-

6. See *The Wall Street Journal*, (1992, Sept. 28), B1; *American Demographics*, (1991, July), p. 16; *American Demographics*, (1990, Oct.), p. 26; *American Demographics*, (1990, May), pp. 48-50.
7. See the Wall Street Journal (1991, March 13), B1.

sion of the parable. In group 1, the prodigal son is a teenager who continues to live at home and exploits his parents financially in a lifestyle that rejects traditional Asian values as well as biblical teaching. There are episodes of violence, but the family is too ashamed to seek help from outside. In group 2, the prodigal son is a long-lost father who had chosen to live in Asia in debauchery, drunkenness, and irresponsibility; now terminally ill, he shows up at his children's doorsteps in Illinois with the hope that they will demonstrate filial piety to him. In group 3, the prodigal son is a young adult immigrant who has done well in America, but had "forgotten" about the parents back in Asia who had skimped and saved to send him to school in America.

The objectives for the above lesson would be to examine the application of biblical love toward the lost and solve each situation in a culturally appropriate manner. Using the discussion method, the problem-solving approach includes an integrational perspective: which of the three situations would merit a referral to a social work agency (the parents of the prodigal in group 1); which merits a referral to a Christian 12-step program that deals comprehensively with the issues of codependency and family dysfunction (group 2), and which would be best dealt with by a practical Bible study on adult child-elderly parents relationship (group 3). The problem-solving process therefore becomes an exercise in moral reasoning, a briefing on community resources for help, and a teaching on intervention and on the biblical meaning of love in action.

This learner-centered, cognitive skills learning approach also must focus on lifestyle application. There is little educational or sociological research for religious or other purposes to provide information on what is distinctly Asian American life and culture. On the issue of parenting, for example, while an Asian American young couple may desire to be effective parents, they may hesitate to accept a parent training approach which underscores either Asian or American values. As one young adult father remarked in church after a video-viewing of a lecture by a Christian psychologist: "Our parenting styles are in transition. We cannot bring up our children in the traditional (Asian) way; neither can we borrow wholesale the American way." In the absence of a clearly defined path shaped by adequate research findings, well-proven methodology, and well-thought curricula, learner participation in the educational process appears to an indispensable practice. This in essence means that religious education for the Asian American young adult must make the transition from a content-oriented, authoritative indoctrination to a pragmatic andragogy emphasizing life skills from a faith position.

Content and Curriculum

The modes of learning determine the content and curriculum for adults. Leon McKenzie suggests that there are two major modes. The *Notional* mode generally involves Bible study classes, discussion groups, and lectures, all focusing on explicit theological topics and concepts; the *Relational* mode of learning is "the often hidden learning that occurs from relation to others in a community of learners" (McKenzie, 1986, p. 14). There is, in other words, a distinction between teaching for a cognitive understanding of the systematic statements of one's faith traditions, and the nurture of concrete living and faithing experiences in relationship with other believers.

This separation of the two major modes of learning, becomes all the more crucial when one puts it in the Asian American experience: religious education in Asian American churches historically has adopted the goals and practices of American denominations because the church in Asia was greatly influenced by American churches since the turn of the century (Kim, 1990, p. 13). The interesting phenomenon here is that while the notional learning content of Asian American churches is derived from a Western theological paradigm, the relational content is not necessarily so. Asian American churches have had to fend for themselves by developing out of sheer necessity viable means of relational learning and communal life. This explains in part why most Chinese churches across the country have church luncheons each Sunday after the worship service. It is unclear how this tradition got started, but long before "community" was a fashionable word in the American church and in the days when Chinese churches were far fewer and served large geographical areas, Chinese Christians looked forward to Sunday as a time for extended social gatherings with friends and relatives from far and near. The after-service luncheon became an effective and much desired community-fostering activity.

Undoubtedly, there is tremendous potential for creative curriculum planning by using the two modes of learning effectively. For example, notional learning experiences of a biblical teaching on inward peace and joy may be complemented by another notional experience focusing on stress management, which culminates in a relational learning of Asian health food cooking.

While curriculum needs to be based on sound educational principles, substantive content has to "scratch where it itches," especially in helping Asian American young adults deal with their experience of assimilation. One example of curriculum that puts the assimilation experience in perspective is the *Sojourners in Asian American and Biblical History* project.[8] This curriculum attempts to validate Asian American identity and experience in relation to biblical perspectives. Curricula like this are too few. Christlikeness in character for Asian American young adults cannot be

---

8. Sojourners in Asian-American history. Asian-American Christian education curriculum project. Golden Gate Mission Area, Synod of the Pacific Presbyterian Church of the United States.

defined by a dominant culture that has yet to grasp the notion that Asia American Christian experience is a significant timely contribution, not a fringe existence. That contribution would certainly include the following dimensions: a) the unique experience of patience, hope, and faith by a minority ethnic group (which all Christians as a religious minority may learn from); b) the lesson in interracial integration among Asian groups, and how that translates to the multiracial Christian community at large; and c) the positive input of an ethnic church that has, to begin with, an understanding and nurturing of relationships and community that appears to be closer to the biblical culture.

Issues and Problems

Education is an activity by means of which the learner is led toward specific goals, outcomes, and experiences. The goal of Christian religious education is two-pronged—the spiritual formation of Christlikeness in character (Eph. 4:20-24) and the personification of that character individually and corporately in a needy world of multiple cultures. The Western church unfortunately has not always spent equal time dwelling on the interpretation of culture as it has on the exegesis of doctrine; its beliefs and practices along with the concomitant presuppositions and ideological bases are often presumed to be coextensive with all of Christian thought. One stark example is the psychological basis of theological anthropology: "the doctrine of humankind" traditionally viewed human beings as individuals and not as persons in community. Thus being Christians for many Asians meant accepting the individualistic self-perception prevalent in Western society. As Asians in America encounter on a daily basis the pressures to assimilate into mainstream culture, Christian religious education became for teachers and learners one more avenue for assimilation.

Asian American young adults face problems and issues which at first glance are not necessarily different from those of other American young adults. However, the social-cultural contexts, role expectations, priorities, and the possible intensity of difficulties are different. Religious education plays a crucial role in helping young adults grapple with issues related to their trajectories. The "sandwiched" generation in the Asian American church, being between children and middle to older adults, is the primary group to provide the educational leadership for the church's instructional programs. Like all other American young adults, they have to face many other demands for their time and resources, and they also have to deal with their particular social-cultural contexts. This includes the needs and demands of new marriages and young children within kinship systems which include the extended family to provide support and/or pressure; the Asian expectation of filial piety; and the stresses and grind of performance in new careers (or in graduate school) as minority persons. The management style of a religious education program for the Asian American church is a crucial issue in that it reflects the philosophy of ministry which the leadership espouses. Success or failure hinges upon the right management approach to programming. McKenzie (1982, pp.138-162) presents five different approaches to the development of adult religious education programs. He suggests that the approaches which satisfy the assumptions of adult education are the ones that have management styles that are consultative and adaptive. The consultative style seeks information and data from adult learners concerning their needs, while the adaptive style accommodates the decisions of teachers and learners who are viewed as capable of self-direction and wise choices. It remains to be determined by research which program development approaches are popular in Asian American churches and how Asian American young adult education can be directed toward the consultative and/or the adaptive approaches.

Most Asian American churches are fairly new and small. There are few openings for directors of religious education. For ministerial staff positions, Asian American churches tend to seek in order of priority, a senior pastor and an assistant pastor/youth worker before even creating the D.R.E. position. The result is that though the religious education program does somehow continue to operate, it is often managed by people trained in theological studies rather than in religious education. The Asian church in America is certainly one that needs D.R.E.'s who are astute in educational theory, capable of applying social-science research and theory to the development of programs that are culturally sensitive, and who can provide spiritual leadership.

Yet, while young adults are the age group looked upon to provide much of the leadership in education, they are likely to be excluded from the overall church administrative leadership. The presumed wisdom of older persons in Asian thinking accounts for this. Young adults must face squarely the issues of intergenerational roles and multiculturalism in church. Many Asian churches continue to be under a strong immigrant influence and maintain specific ethnic elements like language and management style; others believe that they are more effective in reaching out to persons who see themselves as Asians in a non-specific sense and who do not identify with any one Asian culture or race.[9]

Conclusion

Many positive and innovative steps need to be taken to improve the religious education program for Asian American young adults. A great poten-

9. See *Los Angeles Times* (1991, Aug. 11), Churches reach out to Asian Americans, B1-B3.

tial exists, requiring the effort and resources of Asian American researchers, theorists, and practitioners. Nevertheless, other Christians cannot stand by uninterested, as if to say "I have no need of you" (1 Cor. 12:21).

Summary
(Harley Atkinson)

Two major issues seem to emerge in the discussion of cross-cultural religious education of young adults. The first is the family, the second is identity formation. It is imperitive that religious educators recognize the need to be sensitive and responsive to these areas.

The Family

Each of the major cultural groups discussed in this chapter have distinct and unique perspectives, values, and traditions related to famliy and family life. There is often a struggle between generations as to whether traditions they bring from their country should be preserved, or whether they should adopt the values of the dominant culture.

Hispanics tend to maintain family values that are a part of their heritage. Barna (1993), based on research by the Barna Group, as well as other sources, says "Overall, Hispanics, more than any other ethnic group studied, feel a sense of loss over the deterioration of their traditional family structure. They are the least likely to expect America to return to the traditional family values of the fifties. . . . And they are more than twice as likely as white adults to describe marriage as an 'outdated idea . . . that does not fit American culture these days.' Although they are as likely as any other segment to believe that marriage should be conceived as a permanent arrangement between two people, they are also twice as likely as other adults to say that a person is better off these days remaining single and unmarried than getting married" (pp. 163-164). Barna goes on to suggest that the nineties might very well be a turning point for Hispanics, as they will probably reject the family values they brought from their countries of origin and adopt American ideals that see the family as a lower priority.

The situation for African Americans is significantly different. While many Asians and Hispanics are first and second generation Americans, African Americans (with some exceptions) possess generations of heritage in this country. They do not struggle with the same issues of assimilation and adoption of different cultural values and practises. Their battle is against poverty and economic inequality—three out of ten black families live below the poverty line and the median household income of blacks is about 70 percent lower than that of whites (Barna, 1993).

Consequently the black family has emerged significantly different from other racial and ethnic groups. For example, the divorce rate among African Americans is higher than any other ethnic group in America. Almost two-thirds of black women who give birth to children are not married at the time of the birth, and over three-quarters of black children born this year will live in a single or no-parent home before turning 18 (Barna, 1993).

Less data is available regarding the stability and makeup of Asian American families although, as Wu mentioned earlier, they constitute the most affluent and economically stable ethnic group. While Asians have displayed qualities of hard work, adaptability, and the pursuit of opportunity, there are problem areas in regard to the family. These include communication problems between generations, the breakdown of the traditional family structure, a desire for biculcuralism, parental role confusion, and domestic violence (Birchett et al., 1991).

It is imperitive that religious education of ethnic groups take serious the task of working with and stabilizing the family. Religious educators should encourage ethnic families to pass on their cultural heritage and positive family values to succeeding generations. We should encourage ethnic groups to celebrate their uniqueness rather than become more like white, middle-class Americans.

Special attention must be taken to offer strong biblical teachings in regard to familial issues such as marriage, divorce, parenting, and abortion. In addition young adults should be provided with classes and groups designed to strengthen and nurture strong families. Ethnic minorities that value family ties and extended families should be encouraged to maintain such relationships and structures.

Ethnic and Cultural Identity

While the issue of identity achievement is of special concern to the young adult, the task takes on additional relevance for members of a particular ethnic group. Ethnic or cultural identity refers to the extent that an individual chooses to identify with his or her ethnic group (its values, language, behavior, religion, and culture) or assimilate into the dominant culture (Birchett et al., 1991). Pazmiño (1993) suggests the challenge for young adults of ethnic groups is to balance these dual identities—of being North American and Hispanic, African and American, or Asian and American.

Perhaps the task of religious education should first be to help the young adult establish his or her true identity regardless of race, culture, or ethnicity. By this we mean establishing an identity that is founded first and foremost in one's relationship with God. We are all not only created by God but created in his image to worship and serve him—that should tell us more about who we are than the color of our skin or country of origin.

Nonetheless, culture is important. Culture does indeed give us a sense of belonging—a sense of identity (Pelaez, 1987). It becomes the task of religious education, then, to enable an individual to celebrate and affirm one's ethnic identity, yet explore and learn from the dominant culture. Furthermore religious education must facilitate the critical and biblical reflection of norms and values of both cultures.

References

Armendariz, R. (1981, November). Hispanic heritage and Christian education. *Alert,* 24-26.

Atkinson, D., Morten, G., & Sue, D. (1989). *Counseling American minorities.* Dubuque, IA: Brown.

Barna, G. (1993). *The future of the American family.* Chicago: Moody.

Birchett, C., Alvarado, M., & Ook Lee, J. (1991). Ministering to major cultural groups. In R. Clark, L. Johnson, & A. Sloat (Eds.), *Christian education: Foundations for the future* (pp. 367-391). Chicago: Moody.

Cross, W. (1972). The Negro-to-Black conversion experience. *Black World, 20,* 13-27.

Elizondo, V. (1981). *Galilean journey: The Mexican-American promise.* Maryknoll, NY: Orbis.

Eugene, T. (1987). Leadership for liberation: Catechetical ministry in the Black Catholic community. In (no editor) *Faith and culture: A multicultural catechetical resource.* Washington, DC: United States Catholic Conference.

Gonzalez, J. (1988). *The theological education of Hispanics.* New York: Fund for Theological Education.

Herberg, W. (1960). *Protestant, Catholic, Jew* (rev.ed.). Garden City, NY: Anchor Books.

Herrera, M. (1979). The Hispanic challenge. *Religious Education, 74,* 459-462.

Herrera, M. (1984). *Adult religious education for the Hispanic community.* Washington, DC: National Conference of Diocesan Directors of Religious Education.

Hesselgrave, D., & Rommen, E. (1989). *Contextualization: Meaning, methods, and models.* Grand Rapids, MI: Baker.

Hune, S. (1989). Introduction: Pacific migration defined by American historians and social theorists up to the 1960s. In H. Kim (Ed.), *Asian American studies: An annotated bibliography and research guide* (pp. 19-42). Westport, CT: Greenwood.

Kim, C. (1990). Asian Americans. In I. Cully & K. Cully (Eds.), *Harper's Encyclopedia of Religious Education* (pp. 43-44). New York: Harper & Row.

Kitano, H. (1981). Asian Americans: The Chinese, Japanese, Koreans, Philipinos, and southeast Asians. In M. Gordon (Ed.), *America as a multicultural society* (pp. 125-138). Philadelphia: The American Academy of Political and Social Sciences.

Kitano, H., & Daniels, R. (1988). *Asian Americans: Emerging minorities.* Englewood Cliffs, NJ: Prentice-Hall.

Liu, W. (1980). Asian American research: Views of a sociologist. In R. Endo, S. Sue, & N. Wagner (Eds.), *Asian-Americans: Social and psychological perspectives*, Vol.11 (pp. 276-287). Palo Alto, CA: Science & Behavior Books.

Matsuoka, F. (1990). The church in a racial-minority situation. In J. Seymour & D. Miller (Eds.), *Theological approaches to Christian education* (pp. 102-121). Nashville, TN: Abingdon.

McKenzie, L. (1982). *The religious education of adults.* Birmingham, AL: Religious Education Press.

McKenzie, L. (1983). Foundations: The scope, purposes and goals of adult Christian education. In Neil Parent (Ed.), *Christian adulthood.* Washington, DC: United States Catholic Conference.

McKenzie, L. (1986). The purposes and scope of adult religious education. In N. Foltz (Ed.), *Handbook of adult religious education* (pp. 7-23). Birmingham, AL: Religious Education Press.

Merriam, S., & Ferro, T. (1986). Working with young adults. In N. Foltz (Ed.), *Handbook of adult religious education* (pp. 59-82). Birmingham, AL: Religious Education Press.

Miller, D. (1979). Religious education and cultural pluralism. *Religious Education, 74,* 339-349.

Morten, G., & Atkinson, D. (1983). Minority identity development and preference for counselor race. *Journal of Negro Education,* 52, 156-161.

O'Hare, W. (1990). A new look at Asian Americans. *American Demographics, 12,* 26-31.

Okada, R. (1989). Dimensions of situational assertiveness and perceived amount of social support with respect to certain social settings. (Doctoral dissertation, California School of Professional Psychology, 1988). *Dissertation Abstracts International,* 49, 5028 B.

Ortega, P. (1971). The Chicano renaissance. *Social Casework, 52,* 294- 307.

Ortiz, M. (1993). *The Hispanic challenge.* Downers Grove, IL: InterVarsity Press.

Parham, T., & Helms, J. (1981). The influence of Black students' racial identity attitudes on preferences for counselor's race. *Journal of Counseling,* 28, 250-257.

Parham, T., & Helms, J. (1985). Attitudes of racial identity and self-esteem of Black students: An exploratory investigation. *Journal of College Student Personnel, 26,* 143-147.

Park, R. (1928). Human migration and the marginal man. *American Journal of Sociology, 33,* 881-893.

Pazmiño, R. (1993). Adult education with persons from ethnic minority communities. In J. Wilhoit & K. Gangel (Eds.), T*he Christian educator's handbook on adult education* (pp. 278-288). Wheaton, IL: Victor.

Pelaez, A. (1987). Multi-cultural dimensions of young adult ministry. In R. Bagley (Ed.), *Young adult ministry: A book of readings* (pp. 51-58). New Rochelle, NY: Don Bosco.

Pomales, J., Clairborn, C., & LaFromboise, T. (1986). Effect of Black student's racial identity on perceptions of White counselors varying in cultural sensitivity. *Journal of Counseling Psychology 33,* 57-61.

Ponterotto, J., Anderson, W., & Grieger, I. (1986). Black students' attitudes towards counseling as a function of racial identity. *Journal of Multicultural Counseling and Development, 14,* 50-59.

Pusch, M. (1979). *Multicultural education: A cross cultural training approach.* Chicago: Intercultural Press.

Pyant, C., & Yanico, B. (1991). The relationship of racial identity and gender-role attitudes to Black women's psychological well-being. *Journal of Counseling Psychology, 38,* 315-322.

Rogers, C., & Rogers, E. (1978). *Jesus as liberator.* Nashville, TN: Graded Press.

Sanchez, D. (1991). *An interdisciplinary approach to theological contextualization with special reference to Hispanic Americans.* Unpublished doctoral dissertation, Oxford Center for Mission Studies, Oxford, England.

Shockley, G. (1976). Liberation theology, black theology and religious education. In M. Taylor (Ed.), *Foundations for Christian education in an era of change* (pp. 80-95).

Nashville, TN: Abingdon.

Shockley, G. (1988). From emancipation to transformation to consummation. In M. Mayr (Ed.), *Does the church really want religious education?* (pp. 221-248). Birmingham, AL: Religious Education Press.

Stokes, O. (1982). Black theology: A challenge to religious education. In N. Thompson (Ed.), *Religious education and theology* (pp. 71-99). Birmingham, AL: Religious Education Press.

Sue, S., & Sue, D. (1973). Chinese-American personality and mental health. In S. Sue & N. Wagner (Eds.), *Asian-Americans: Psychological perspectives* (pp.111-124). Palo Alto, CA: Science & Behavior Books.

Sue, D., Ino, S., & Sue, D. (1983) Nonassertiveness of Asian-Americans: An inaccurate assumption? *Journal of Counseling Psychology, 30,* 581-588.

Tarasar, C. (1988). The minority problem: Educating for identity and openness. In N. Thompson (Ed.), *Religious pluralism and religious education* (pp.195-210). Birmingham, AL: Religious Education Press.

Villafane, E. (1991). *The socio-cultural matrix of intergenerational dynamics: An analysis of three basic elements and an agenda for the '90's.* Plenary address at the northeast conference on bilingual ministries of the Hispanic Association of Bilingual Bicultural Ministries, New York.

Vontress, C. (1971). Racial differences: Impediments to rapport. *Journal of Counseling Psychology,* 18, 7-13.

Whitehead, E., & Whitehead, J. (1980). *Method in ministry: Theological reflection and Christian ministry.* New York: Seabury.

Part Five: Programming Young Adult Religious Education

CHAPTER FIFTEEN

Setting Up a Young Adult Religious Education Program

TRENTON R. FERRO

Program planning is both a skill and an art (Easley, 1978; Knowles, 1980). While the planner or prospective planner can—and must—learn through reading and conversation from those who have a greater mastery over the process, there is no substitute for the experience gained from "hands-on" involvement. Skilled and competent religious education programmers become that way by planning programs and by paying attention to what they are doing, how they are doing it, and the results of what they have done.

Such learning-by-doing has been given careful attention in educational literature. According to Schön (1983, 1987), skills cannot be developed apart from the context in which those skills are applied. Furthermore, "the reflective practitioner" continues to develop competency and mastery not merely by repeating actions; the reflective practitioner both "reflects-in-action" and "reflects-on-action." Reflection-in-action is the developmental process and activity of paying attention to what one is doing while one is doing it and, as a result, making adjustments as one proceeds. Reflection-on-action describes the process of looking back over a completed project to consider what one has learned, how one has learned it, and what one might do better or differently the next time around.

Expertise comes, then, not merely through experience. Reflection is essential to making sense of, and extracting meaning from, one's experience

345

(Osterman, 1990). As the old saw has it, reflection is the difference between having twenty year's experience and having one year's experience twenty times. Reflection-in-action leads to "knowing-in-action" (Cervero, 1988, 1989; Schön, 1983, 1987). As the religious educator learns by doing, then he or she is able to deal intuitively with new settings, is able to work spontaneously, and even produces unexpected outcomes or surprises—and the cycle of reflection-in-action and reflection-on-action continues. Nor is this an esoteric or unreachable capability. It can be and indeed is learned (Dean, 1993; Imel, 1992; Peters, 1991).

Another way to describe this process is to borrow the concept of recursion from the lexicon of artificial intelligence (Hofstadter, 1979). The application here emphasizes the fact that the religious educator does not simply repeat an experience. Even though the topic or project may appear to be repetitive, it is a new experience each time it is revisited because the practitioner has changed—hopefully grown and developed—as a result of the previous experience (Ferro, 1993). Thus program planning is not simply cyclical in nature, with each endeavor being a duplicate repetition of a previous undertaking. Rather, the process is more like a spiral; it is additive and augmentative in nature. Not only the circumstances, the setting, the participants, and the content have changed, but the planner has also changed, grown, and developed. While there are elements in the planning process which overlap, there is also forward movement in the developing sophistication of the planner and an expansion of the planner's ability to use, apply, and manipulate the various steps and strategies connected with program planning.

The purposes of this introductory discussion are twofold. On the one hand, it is meant to encourage even the greenest of novices. Program planning, although it may first give that appearance, is not based on a reservoir of arcane knowledge stored away in sealed volumes to which only a small circle of initiates—modern day Merlins, so to speak—hold the key. It is not a possession, it is a process. Some practitioners have mastered a series of skills which have helped them become extremely competent in exercising that process. Yet they were once novices, too. Each fledgling programmer can take that first step toward becoming an expert. As detailed above, each effort leads to growth, development, and increased capability.

The introduction also serves as a caution or warning—there are no "cookbook" approaches to planning and setting up programs for the religious education of young adults. The prospective planner cannot find a formula or sequence of steps into which data can be plugged at one end and—*voila!*— a finished product spews out at the other. Rather, program planning is an interactive process (Dean, 1994; Murk & Galbraith, 1986; Pennington & Green, 1976; Simpson, 1982) which is mastered only by planning programs. While the printed page inherently forces a linear treatment of the subject, and the religious education planner can be successful in following the sequence of steps discussed here, the process of program planning as actually practiced is usually quite interactive. Working on one stage often involves working at another level at the same time, and change in one element or step will usually require alteration in another. In fact, Pennington and Green (1976) discovered that while most literature prescribes a linear, step-by-step approach to planning programs, these same planners used a variety of approaches and patterns in the actual development of programs.

Definition

What is a program? What is program planning? It is intriguing to note that the two books in the field of adult education (Houle, 1972; Knowles, 1980) which probably have had the greatest influence on the art and science of developing programs do not contain definitions of these terms, although both lay out detailed plans and sets of guidelines for planning programs. While there is no agreed upon definition of these terms, looking at several should provide a sense of what is meant by "program" and "program planning."

In an early effort to bring definitional order to the field of adult education, Verner (1964) defined a program as a "series of learning experiences designed to achieve, in a specified period of time, certain specific instructional objectives for an adult or a group of adults" (p. 34). He goes on to state that "program planning denotes the action of the agent in designing an educational activity such as preparing a meeting, structuring a class, or arranging a discussion group" (p. 35). For Verner, good practice in developing programs for adults requires "concentrating on learning objectives and developmental tasks related specifically to pertinent adult needs and interests" (p. 35).

Schroeder (1970) highlights the diverse uses of the term program by talking about "program areas" rather than actually defining the term program."Program, like most other components of the adult education structure, has an illusive character. The term has been variously used to refer to: (1) all the educative activities available to adults of a community . . . ; (2) the total adult education effort of a given agency . . . ; (3) activities designed for segments of the population . . . ; (4) social roles with which activities are related . . . ; and (5) the nature of a specific activity" (p. 38).

Kowalski (1988) arrives at a definition by limiting Schroeder's (1970) description of program areas. "Within the practice of adult education, the two most common uses of the term *program* relate to offerings within a given agency. The first is the concept of the *comprehensive program*. If one refers to all the adult education offered by an organization, one is talking about the comprehensive program. . . . The comprehensive program represents the macro view of planning. . . . Then there are the *individual programs*—the separate parts of the comprehensive program. . . . The individual program represents the micro aspect of planning. The distinction between comprehensive and individual programs is quite important. When planning is discussed, one should realize that the macro aspect is more entangled and requires a myriad of inputs. The micro aspect is much more specific, and the task of planning is simplified by the narrowness of the activity" (p. 88).

Kowalski defines planning simply as a "formalized procedure used to create programs. It is oriented toward the future and is the first step in creating programs" (p. 89). Sork and Caffarella (1989) provide this definition: "In its most general sense, planning refers to the process of determining the ends to be pursued and the means employed to achieve them. In adult education, planning is a decision-making process and a set of related activities that produce educational program design specifications for one or more adult learners" (p. 233).

For the purposes of this chapter, Kowalski's (1988) definitions will suffice. What follows is a developmental outline which discusses both the contexts or parameters within which program planning takes place and the processes involved in developing programs. Once again it should be emphasized that this is a descriptive, not a prescriptive, discussion. While what follows are necessary components of any successful religious education program for young adults, the process need not take place precisely in the manner or sequence presented. This outline is used for the sake of order and convenience. On the other hand, the novice may wish to follow quite closely the outline and procedures presented here until he or she feels sufficiently comfortable to strike out on his own. Ultimately, every religious education program planner develops his own model and sequence—one which works best for him.

The Contexts and Setting of Young Adult Religious Education Program Planning

Nothing happens in a social vacuum, especially highly human-intensive activities such as program planning. It is incumbent on professionals in religious, community, and human service organizations to recognize clearly the contexts, the settings, the parameters, and the restrictions within which they must operate or which they must consciously endeavor to alter. Any program is immediately under the influence of the roles, functions, and experiences of the participants or potential participants; the beliefs and attitudes of the program planner and religious educators; and the stated or implied mission, purposes, and goals of the sponsoring organization. The religious education program for young adults is also influenced indirectly by community expectations and standards, societal constraints, and world issues and events.

The Participants

Those who are participating, or may participate, in a young adult religious education program are the primary focus for any planning that takes place. Failure to focus constantly on the target audience is a sure invitation to program failure. Therefore, the program planner must understand her clientele, both generically and specifically (Apps, 1972; Dean, 1994; Dean & Ferro, 1991; DeBoy, 1979; Elias, 1982; McKenzie, 1982; Niemi & Nagle, 1979; Peters, 1989).

Generically, she must understand the psychological concerns and sociological circumstances of young adults (Merriam, 1984; Merriam & Ferro, 1986). Psychological concerns include the young adult's quest for independence, identity, and intimacy. Sociological circumstances describe the life tasks faced by young adults, such as seeking out, and receiving training for, an occupation; beginning and raising a family; and finding an independent and identifiable place and role in the community. In addition, the program planner working within a religious institution must be acquainted with the faith issues with which young adults struggle and the stages of faith development through which these participants are most likely to pass during their young adult years (Elias, 1982; Gribbon, 1990; Merriam & Ferro, 1986; Parks, 1991). These issues are discussed more fully in Chapters Four, Five, and Six.

In order to meet the actual requirements of young adults within a specific institutional setting, the planner must both get to know them directly as individuals and learn about them as a group. While personal acquaintance is highly desirable, it is not enough. Not only should the planner become acquainted with the demographic information available on these young adults (ages, marital status, family size and age of children, occupations, and the like), she must also understand their wants, needs, interests, and capabilities. How to collect information in these areas is discussed below in the section on determining needs.

The Planner

The ancient dictum, "Know thyself," is equally true for the program planner. He must have a clear understanding of his own orientation to, and attitudes about, adult learning and adult learners (Dean, 1994; Dean & Ferro, 1991; Houle, 1972; Knowles, 1980; McKenzie, 1982). What does he consider to be the overall purpose and ends of young adult programming in the religious organization? How does he view his relationship with these young adults? How does he understand his function as a planner and facilitator of learning and growth opportunities for young adults?

What planners do is shaped in part by their philosophical and theological orientation (Davenport & Davenport, 1985; Elias & Merriam, 1980; McKenzie, 1985; Podeschi, 1986; Zinn, 1990), by their own perception of the purpose and role of religious education programs for young adults. Knowing and owning their assumptions and beliefs openly will tend to make them better organizers and developers of such programs; they will less likely fall prey to irrational and inexplicable behavior and decision making. Aspects of this topic, the orientation of the planner/facilitator, are discussed in Chapter Seven.

The Sponsoring Organization

The religious organization or institution young adults belong to or identify with is the third key element in the planning context. Each organization exists for a purpose. That purpose is, or should be, stated clearly in a mission statement. Each institution also has a culture—the way things are done, who really makes the decisions, the values which are held—with which the planner must become aware. Every program developed and conducted within that organization or institution should help carry out its mission and conform to its values (Dean, 1994; Knowles, 1980; Kowalski, 1988; Merriam & Ferro, 1986; Offerman, 1989). A program's success or failure often hinges on this fit.

What, then, is the planner's role vis-a-vis the church or other religious organization? They might be several: 1) If the institution does not have a written mission statement she can take the lead in helping the institution develop such statements. 2) If there is a written mission statement, but the activities of the institution do not seem to agree with that statement, she can encourage a review of both the mission and the activities of the organization. The outcome should be a revision of either or both. 3) She might need to educate other members of the organization about the psychological and social needs of young adults if these members object to programming she has developed. If she is convinced that she is operating within the parameters of the religious organization's mission and purposes, she may need to take the lead in altering an institutional culture which is inimical to the very mission which the institution espouses. The role of the program planner within the institution, then, is to see that programs and institutional mission fit each other.

Larger Contexts

Every institution and, consequently, every program operates within, and is influenced by, the world around them and cannot function oblivious to these influences (Dean, 1994; Knowles, 1980; Kowalski, 1988; Smith &

Offerman, 1989). Therefore, the program planner must be aware of local, national, and world events and influences.

Community expectations and standards. Every institution or organization, and every program which it offers, both affects and is affected by the community in which the institution functions and the program operates. What a religious institution and its program planner offer, and how they offer their programs, must fit within the prevailing standards and expectations of the community if they are to be successful. This does not mean that the religious institution and the planner must compromise their own traditions and values. Nor does it mean that they should avoid programs which fit the institution's mission and are appropriate for meeting its goals but may not be of general interest to the community. And it does not mean that they should be reticent about offering programs which are new and different—on the "cutting edge." In fact, the success of an organization and its programming may well be their ability to be among the first to provide new opportunities and services.

Rather, the warning connected with the call for awareness of local standards is that any successful religious education program for young adults must start with the present situation and the current circumstances of prospective learners. The provider must build the bridge from current experience to new growth and learning; it cannot expect the participant to make a leap from the known to the unknown without any assistance. For example, while there is little question that a need exists to educate for awareness concerning AIDS and about methods to prevent catching and spreading the disease, there is considerable controversy in various parts of the country about how, where, and by what means such education should take place. Should the program planner see such education as a necessary and integral part of the religious organization's local offerings, he must develop a program which fits within, or at least starts with, local concerns and sensibilities. How such a program would be developed varies greatly from New York City to Alabama to Western Pennsylvania to Northern Illinois to San Francisco.

Program planners of young adult religious education also want to remain constantly aware of local conditions and sensitivities for several other reasons. Most religious organizations plan their education programs, not only for their own members, but also for others living in the surrounding community. In fact, their own members are also part of the local citizenry. Thus, while programming must fit within the mission of the organization, it also attempts to serve a larger clientele. In addition, planners may find that the success of their programs hinges on linkages with other local organizations, the need for resources which are available only from other sources, and marketing through other groups and local media. Knowing the community, then, is a requirement for good program planning.

Societal constraints. Local and community standards are embedded as well in regional and national values with which the planner must be acquainted. In fact, because both the organization and the planner live and operate within the region, they may already be conversant with the social milieu and societal values of that region. Because such values are often taken for granted, the planner may not even be aware of these constraints. If that be the case, the planner should become consciously aware of their existence lest she commit some grievous *faux pas*. On the other hand, and for the same reason, if the planner is relatively new to the sponsoring organization and to the region, she must spend some time learning the mores and folkways of the region, which vary considerably from region to region (Garreau, 1981). Such knowledge has an additional positive aspect—knowing the region and its idiosyncrasies also may provide a wealth of program ideas.

National and world issues and events. There is no question that we live today in a shrinking world and are affected by new technologies and by trends and events across the nation and around the world (Naisbitt, 1982; Naisbitt & Aburdene, 1990; Toffler, 1970, 1980). During a mere one hour of television viewing we can witness events that take place next door as well as those occurring on the other side of the world. No portion of the globe—and even much of the universe—seems impervious to the camera. By using the telephone and the computer we can communicate almost instantly with the next door neighbor, a colleague in another state, or an associate in another country and on another continent.

The planner of young adult religious education cannot ignore what is happening elsewhere. People are affected by these happenings—sometimes indirectly, sometimes directly. The demise of the Soviet Union, the tearing down of the Berlin Wall and the unification of Germany, Desert Storm, and civil war in former Yugoslavia have personally affected vast numbers of Americans. While political unrest in South Africa, famine in Ethiopia and Somalia, and the bloodshed of Tiananmen Square may not hit so close to home, these are still events which trouble us and about which we talk and express concern. World events and issues can often suggest ideas for programs or portions of programs for young adults.

While we may not be "of the world," we are certainly "in the world." The observant and competent program planner of young adult religious education must be aware of what is happening in the local community (the service area, so to speak), in the contiguous region, nationally, and internationally. Such awareness provides a yardstick against which the planner can measure his activities and offerings, keeps him current on what may be affecting program participants, and offers a wealth of new ideas and opportunities for program planning.

The Process of Program Planning for Young Adult Religious Education

The discussion to this point has highlighted the very important factors which influence, restrict, and direct any program which might be undertaken and implemented. Now attention turns to the various processes by which programs are developed (Knowles, 1980; Knox, 1986; Sork & Caffarella, 1989). Again the primary focus is on the young adults for whose benefit the religious education programs are being planned.

Targeting the Audience and Determining Needs

How does the sponsoring organization and the religious education program planner decide what programs to offer young adults? How do they know which programs will appeal to their young adults? How can they tell when a program has run its course? These are key questions—and there are no sure-fire answers. However, there are methods and techniques the planner can use which will improve the likelihood of success.

Generically, the process of collecting data for the purpose of making program planning decisions is called "needs assessment." There is considerable discussion in the adult education literature about what is actually meant by the term *need* (see, for example, the treatments by Cameron, 1988; Griffith, 1978; Knox, 1986; Mattimore-Knudson, 1983; Monette, 1977, 1979). Quite often *need* connotes the concept of deficiency or of a discrepancy between the present state and some desired state. Inherent to such a definition is the ability to compare the current situation with, or measure it against, some standard (Knowles, 1980; Kowalski, 1988). Such a concept usually does not apply to what would normally be developed as religious education programming for young adults—although some institutions may include among its offerings programs and courses designed to develop the skills and proficiencies of young adults in a variety of settings. More suitable terms might be *want* or *interest* (Knowles, 1980). If, then, the more traditional concept of needs assessment does not apply as well to the process of planning religious education programs for young adults, how does the program planner discover what young adults want or in what they might be interested? While a variety of methods and approaches are suggested in the literature (Cameron, 1988; Grabowski, 1982; Knowles, 1980; Kowalski, 1988; Niemi & Nagle, 1979; among others), the following outline should prove serviceable for the religious organization or institution.

Personal experience. As discussed in the introductory paragraphs of this chapter, the planner becomes increasingly skilled and artful as he plans programs. The planner who is intimately involved both with the young adults for whom he is organizing religious education programs and in the programs themselves is developing a growing sensitivity to the wants and interests of this group of participants (Dean & Ferro, 1991). This expanding reservoir of expertise becomes a source of information for the purpose of making program decisions and provides the basis for asking such questions as: What does my own experience tell me about possible program contexts and settings? About what the learners already know? About what interests they have? About what they will want and need to learn and/or to do?

The program planner should be wary, however, of depending solely on his own experience for determining want, need, or interest. No matter how capable the planner might be, his expertise is still bounded. His very expertise can cause a complacency that obscures his vision. He can slip into a rut; he can do things because they are comfortable and familiar; he may fail to see the signs warning that interest in some offerings or in certain types of programming is waning; he may miss the signals that changing events or new interests are beckoning him to new efforts and alternative programming. Therefore, he must also use other methods for collecting data.

Knowledgeable people. The astute planner of young adult religious education will want to develop and maintain a series of linkages and networks with those who are affected by what she does and with others who have similar concerns and responsibilities. The place to start is with participants and prospective participants themselves. The planner should work with a committee (Knowles, 1980), team (DeBoy, 1979), or advisory council (Kowalski, 1988; Kozoll, 1979) made up of selected young adults, as well as others who understand this group, who can represent the larger target audience of young adults and are able to generate ideas and state them clearly. Although one of the commonly accepted precepts of adult education is that adults are capable of making their own learning and developmental decisions (Knowles, 1980), many planners fail to follow through on that premise when actually developing programs (Thompson, 1992). Especially in settings where participation is completely voluntary, the wise planner certainly will want to develop a close relationship with those whom she is attempting to serve.

The successful planner of young adult religious education also seeks out colleagues with comparable roles in other organizations. An early task upon entering the position should be to approach others in the vicinity who have similar assignments and develop a network which meets on a regular basis (maybe over breakfast or lunch) to share experiences, problems, and attempted solutions. Not only will such a network help with the actual process of planning programs for young adults, it will also provide a support group. Often the planner will want or need to share frustrations or discuss ideas, but there may not be appropriate persons among his clientele or on the staff of his organization for this purpose. As the old Native American proverb intimates, those who walk in the same moccasins can best appreciate and understand both the difficulties and the exhilarations experienced by colleagues who share the task of working with young adults.

Another source of help is the regional or national staff of the organization to which the local institution belongs. An office, department, or division responsible for education, congregational or parish life, or similar functions often includes consultants whose professional portfolios include work with young adults. The planner of religious education programs for young adults will want to establish contact with such staff members, and with others around the country or the continent whose responsibilities include developing programs for young adults at the local level. The regional or national body may even hold regular meetings or retreats which provide special opportunities for educators and program planners to come together for learning, growth, sharing ideas and concerns, and relaxation.

Finally, organizational and denominational publishing houses may offer a variety of materials for young adults. These should be treated with some care, however, because programming for adults in general, and programming for specific segments of the adult population in particular, is a relatively new concept. Most of these publishers have a long tradition of producing materials for children and youth, but many have not given particular or special attention to adults until recently. Historically, materials for adults have been reworked from those published for children rather than starting with the adult population and building materials based on adult needs, interests, and learning principles. The planner should consult with her committee or advisory council members to get their reactions to such materials, both in terms of the topics selected as well as the way in which the material is handled. Nevertheless, there has been general improvement in recent years and this resource should not be overlooked.

Methods for gathering data. Now that the planner of young adult religious education has found a variety of information sources and developed contacts, committees, liaisons, and networks, how does he go about using them as resources for program planning? There are a number of useful methods available (Dean & Ferro, 1991; Grabowski, 1982; Kowalski, 1988; McKenzie, 1982; Smith, 1985). First, he can undertake actual interviews (Dean & Ferro, 1991). These can be conducted either in person or by phone. Beginning with questions similar to those listed above under "Personal Experience," the planner would prepare by making a list of things he wants or needs to know. After each item or question on his list, he can identify one or more human resources who may be able to provide insight and information. Then he would actually conduct interviews, record responses to his questions as well as other advice, ideas, and insights which come out of the discussions. He now has started a data pool to which he can add as he proceeds through other methods of collecting data.

If she is part of a group setting, such as her advisory council or the local network of program planners, she can initiate brainstorming sessions which might incorporate questions like the following: What are you doing that is working? Why is it working? What topics and activities do our young adults seem to be most interested in? Why? What special concerns are they expressing? What is going on in their lives that should be addressed? What is happening locally, nationally, and worldwide that might have an impact on these young adults? Responses to such questions can generate a large number of ideas and topics, as well as of ways to address those topics. All these can be added to her data pool. In addition, such interpersonal and interagency activity is invigorating in itself and might also lead to approaches and activities which a single organization would be unable to undertake.

A third way to identify the wants, needs, and interests of young adults is to collect information from them directly by using surveys and questionnaires (Dean & Ferro, 1991; Kowalski, 1988; McKenzie, 1982; Smith, 1985). Questions can be either open-ended or more structured. Open-ended questions allow for a greater variety of responses, while structured questions limit respondents' choices. Each has its usefulness and its limitations; therefore, careful attention must be given to the design of surveys and questionnaires. Often the planner will want to use a mixture of the two types of questions. Chapter Sixteen includes a section illustrating different types of open-ended and structured questions and how to write them.

The process of identifying the wants, needs, and interests of the target audience—the young adults whom the religious institution or organization is attempting to reach and serve—is two-fold (Dean & Ferro, 1991). The first calls for the planner to think through carefully what he needs to know from and about the prospective learners, what questions he can ask to find that information, how to phrase the questions, and what he plans to do with the information he gets. The second is to actually develop and distribute the survey or questionnaire and to collect the data he will use for program planning.

The planner of young adult religious education must be sure that she uses a sufficient number of sources of information (Dean & Ferro, 1991). Consulting too few young adults, or going back consistently to the same respondents, may not provide the wide spectrum of input necessary for developing a broadly diversified set of offerings. The planner should ensure that she is getting feedback from a random, representative sample of the total number of prospective young adult learners. If the number is small, the survey should be sent to everyone. If the group is larger, one way to obtain a representative sample is to place the names of all the young adults the planner is attempting to serve in a bowl and draw out 50 percent of the names. The planner then sends the questionnaire to this group with a cover letter introducing herself, telling why she is writing, and explaining the importance of responding to the survey. A follow-up reminder in about two weeks to nonrespondents usually increases the number of returns.

Identifying Potential Programs and Setting Goals

When the planner of young adult religious education has collected data by these various means from these different sources, he then is ready to begin the process of making program decisions: What will the religious program for young adults include? Why will it include these particular items? What does he expect to accomplish with this program, both totally and through its various segments? The process is one of identification, selection, and goal-setting.

Identifying and selecting potential programs and topics. This is the point in the program planning process that is most dependent on artistry and experience. However, if the religious education planner has executed well the various data gathering strategies and made use of a carefully selected variety of sources, she should have available to her an ample supply of ideas and suggestions (see also McKenzie, 1983). In addition, some of these should stand out from the rest because of the frequency of responses, the appropriateness of the topic to the time and setting, the requirements and expectations of the sponsoring religious organization, the recommendation of trusted experts, or other factors of sufficient import to cause the planner to give those recommendations special consideration.

As the planner begins to build the religious program for young adults, he will also want to select topics that will provide a diversity of options in both content and the time when and place where the program will be offered. A well-rounded program sponsored by a religious institution might provide the following opportunities:

1. Study of scripture (surveys of the entire scriptures as well as in-depth examinations of particular portions), including both historical and contextual elements and application to the life of young adults;

2. Study of the theology, history, and traditions of the sponsoring religious institution;

3. Topics of special interest, including current events, ethical and moral issues faced by young adults, keeping and living the faith throughout the week, and similar areas of concern;

4. Meeting the sociocultural needs and circumstances of young adults (Darkenwald & Knox, 1984)—job preparation skills, such as resume writing, interviewing skills, search strategies, and the like; career selection, advancement, and change; understanding oneself; interpersonal skills; mar-

riage preparation and marriage enrichment; parenting classes; and the like;

5. Preparation for assuming greater responsibility in the religious organization and society—including leadership training and development, teacher training, small group facilitation skills, organizational skills, how to run both informal (planning, working) and formal (business) meetings (including a healthy dose of Robert's Rules of Order for the latter);

6. Dealing with problems and special concerns—courses, self-help groups, support groups, group counseling, 12-step recovery groups, etc., as appropriate for such areas as job loss; death, divorce, and other grief situations; drug, alcohol, and other addictions; and other situations calling for help and support;

7. Opportunities, such as religious retreats, for spiritual renewal, recreation, and relaxation;

8. Opportunities for social, recreational, and physical activity;

9. Intergenerational programs and activities which include the family.

As suggested by the entire discussion up to this point, the actual selection process is guided by a number of factors: the expressed wants, desires, and interests of the participants themselves; the insight, expertise, and experience of the planner; the desires and needs of the sponsoring organization; and the influence and constraints of the various contexts within which the organization and its programs are situated and operate. Working within these parameters, the planner of young adult religious education makes topic selections and builds a program which is designed to appeal to the greatest number of the young adult population identified by the religious institution as its responsibility. The size of the program—the number of offerings—depends on how many young adults the religious organization is attempting to serve, the homogeneity or heterogeneity of that group, and the resources available to develop and support the program.

There is always—and there must be—an element of risk in all program planning, including planning for religious education of young adults. The planner must attempt to address the widest range of interests possible within the constraints just discussed. She must try new ideas and approach new topics. No young adult program should be an exact duplicate of the previous set of activities. Times change, people change, evaluations (to be discussed in the next chapter) reveal the need for change. Each new program should continue those offerings which have demonstrated staying power while providing new opportunities by which the young adults can continue their religious growth and development. Good programs include both successes and failures; in fact, failures can provide great opportunities for the professional development of the planner and even greater successes for the programs she plans in the future (Sork, 1991).

Setting goals and objectives. A purposeful, well-planned young adult religious education program is more than a mere collection of opportunities that are only incidentally related. In order to ensure that the wants, needs, and interests of the target audience are being met, the planner develops an overarching purpose or set of purposes for the entire program, as well as goals for each offering. In addition, objectives stating specific expected outcomes for each session are established, either by the program planner or by the facilitator of the course, activity, or workshop.

Goals and objectives are like road maps. They point out where the learners and religious educator intend to go. Not only do they help prospective learners chose the particular activity in which they wish to become involved, they also serve as guides or an outline around which the religious educator can design and develop each session and the sequence of sessions. In addition, goals and objectives provide a viable foundation for evaluating both the individual offerings and the entire program. Goals and objectives, including directions on how to write them, are discussed more fully in Chapter Seven.

Developing, Designing, and Organizing the Young Adult Religious Education Program

The steps and procedures described in this section are the "nuts and bolts" of the program planning process; they ensure that the goals and topics which the planner has identified, selected, and developed become reality in the form of activities which actually take place. These various aspects of the planning process call for careful attention to detail in order that the program proceed successfully and smoothly. If done well, few participants will notice what has been done. If done poorly—insufficient lead time, failure to give heed to particulars, lack of consideration for special needs and concerns, poor communication, to name a few—participation for all or portions of the program will decrease or be insufficient to maintain the program. Those who do participate will have an increasing number of complaints. The design phase incorporates the following items:

Master plan and schedule. Once the various topics and activities which will comprise the young adult religious education program have been identified, they must be built into a master schedule. The planner must determine a number of scheduling details:

1. The frequency of each module or portion of the program. Will it be weekly, bi-weekly, monthly, quarterly, or annually?

2. The length of each module. Will it be a one-time workshop or seminar; a short course of two to four weeks; a long course of three, four, six, or twelve months? Or will it be an on-going program based on establishing trust and relationships, such as self-help and support groups, or a series of unrelated topics for groups which come together on a regular basis because of common interests and concerns but not around a specific topic?

3. The time of the week or month each will meet. Will it be on Sunday mornings, evenings, weekday mornings, Saturday mornings, or over the lunch hour?

Laying all of this out on a master schedule offers the planner the opportunity to examine the adequacy of the variety of opportunities which have been developed. Furthermore, it guards against conflicts for the participants, the planner, others who will be involved in facilitating the various aspects of the program, and the sponsoring organization with its various programs. Plans can then be developed for each of the activities on a separate sheet with appropriate space for at least the items discussed in the following paragraphs. Some of these items, such as location and time, should also be noted on the master schedule.

Location. The identifying and securing of the proper location for each program portion is naturally dependent on the selection of the time of day and week for, and the duration of, each segment. Possibilities include the religious institution's own facilities, the homes or apartments of participants, restaurants, meeting facilities in community and business buildings, as well as retreat and conference centers. Naturally, the location should be appropriate for the activity, be able to accommodate the number of expected participants, and provide the proper ambiance and materiel to support the planned event.

These meeting sites should be reserved as the program is being developed so that the locations go on the master schedule. Such advanced preparation avoids the conflicts caused by scheduling more than one activity in the same place at the same time, as well as the confusion and decreased participation which naturally result when times, dates, and locations are changed after programs have been published and announced.

Educators and speakers. The success of programs and program segments often hinges on the competency and expertise of those who teach the various religious education activities. Care should be taken in the selection of these persons to ascertain whether they can relate well to the young adults for whom the program is being planned. Since the learners will be attending voluntarily, it is important that they feel comfortable, that their questions and concerns be addressed positively, and that they not feel threatened or belittled in any way. The attitude and demeanor of the religious educators is sometimes more important than the depth of their content knowledge. Even when content is of prime importance, a speaker with poor interpersonal skills can cause more harm than the good their expertise might engender.

Facilities. When the location for each program segment is being selected, the programmer must consider whether that site provides the appropriate facilities both to address the needs of participants and to meet the goals of the program. The setting should be clean, comfortable for young adults, and provide appropriate equipment (tables and chairs, podium, etc.) for, and food service capabilities suitable to, the intended activity. Unless the young adult religious education program emphasizes a presentation mode (such as a film or an important speaker who will be addressing a large audience with only a modicum of participant response or participation), there should be enough space for a seating arrangement which allows all the participants to easily see and hear all the other participants. Placing a person or group in charge of arranging furniture before the larger group arrives gives evidence that the planners and organizers of the event know what they are doing and have matters under control.

Child care, needs of persons with handicaps, and other special concerns. Because of its commitment to all persons, regardless of individual circumstance, the religious organization which sponsors education programming for young adults will want to be particularly sensitive to the special needs of any individual who may want to participate. Of prime importance to programming for young adults is the recognition that many will have small children and also be unable to find or afford suitable child care to participate fully in the various opportunities provided by the religious institution. Therefore, the provision of child care should be a regular component of every program. A nominal charge would be appropriate and manageable for most parents; however, the planner should be alert to situations where "grants" or "waivers" are appropriate. These should be handled with sensitivity and confidentiality so as not to embarrass and, consequently, lose participants. One method many groups have found workable is to hire members of either a youth or a senior citizen group to provide child care as one of their group's fund raising activities.

In a similar manner, appropriate arrangements must be made to accommodate learners with handicaps. Particular attention should be given to the needs of potential participants when choosing locations for the various activities which have been included on the program calendar. If such a project has not already been undertaken, the coordinator of young adult religious education programming can take the lead in developing a plan to study carefully the accessibility of the sponsoring institution's facilities and recommend alterations and additions that will provide persons with special needs access to all public areas. Such an effort will both serve the needs of all age groups and raise within the sponsoring organization the level of awareness of, and appreciation for, the young adults and their activities.

Other programmatic considerations include proper lighting (brighter lights are needed for activities requiring reading, use of maps, and the like), removal or reduction of distracting noises (hearing problems and difficulties are limited not only to older adults), and adequate ventilation and air circulation. Out of concern for the physical as well as the spiritual health of the young adults in attendance, smoking should be prohibited in all meeting and activity areas. A number of participants will have various respiratory problems which smoke will only exacerbate, and second-hand smoke is a serious health hazard for all. If the religious education planner and the advisory council so choose (and the sponsoring organization permits smoking on its premises), a smoking room apart from all public areas, including restrooms and restroom access, might be provided.

Materials and equipment. Appropriate advance preparation will ensure that all materials and equipment have been prepared and collected and are available in adequate quantities to meet the requirements of the expected number of participants. Duplicated readings should be clear and clean; words and diagrams must contrast sufficiently from the background to be read easily. Overhead transparencies should be prepared with large letters and avoid clutter (transparencies should never be used in place of copies of printed text). All pieces of equipment should be checked ahead of time to make certain they are in operating order. Replacement bulbs for projection equipment should be available in case any burn out while being used during the program; video and audio tapes should be forwarded beforehand to the proper starting position if the entire tape will not be used. By preparing and checking in advance everything that will be used for the program, the program planner will demonstrate his conscientiousness and proficiency.

Cost/fees. This topic broaches two separate but related issues. First, the actual expenses connected with sponsoring and producing a young adult religious education program need to be determined. Factors contributing to total cost include salaries which might be paid to religious educators and honoraria to speakers, the purchase of materials and supplies, rental of facilities, and the like. Some of the expenses connected with developing programs for young adults are usually included as line items in the sponsoring organization's budget, while others are not.

Determination of costs leads to the second aspect of this topic. Fees may need to be charged in order for certain activities to be conducted. The religious education program planner must scrutinize these program segments closely to make sure that such fees do not exclude those who would most benefit from participating. On the other hand, the sponsoring organization should not support financially those portions of the program which participants are able to pay for themselves. Careful attention to costs and who pays them will ensure the broadest possible array of program offerings.

Marketing. The best laid plans will go for naught if prospective participants do not know about them. Just as careful attention is given to the planning and development of the young adult religious education program itself, so should it be given to the marketing of the program (Shawchuck, Kotler, Wrenn, & Rath, 1992). The target market or audience has already been determined. What the marketing plan must do is provide a means of reaching that audience early and often. Many programs sponsored by religious organizations fail for no other reason than poor communication. Today's adults are active; they have full schedules and multiple interests and responsibilities. They need to know well in advance the details of planned events, and they need to be reminded regularly of the available opportunities. Saying something once is not sufficient.

The marketing plan might contain several elements. First, a quarterly calendar listing all planned events and activities could be sent to all young adults in the parish or local ecclesiastical jurisdiction. Of course, a mailing list for this purpose would need to be developed and maintained. Announcements then can be repeated in monthly or bi-weekly newsletters sent to the entire membership of the religious organization, in weekly bulletins, and at worship services and other public gatherings. In addition, regular announcements at young adult programs about future activities will reach directly prospective participants.

Finally, when a program has the potential of appealing to a larger audience, efforts should be made to announce such offerings through local media (newspapers, radio, and television—especially cable networks). Establishing contacts with the various media in advance eases access to these marketing resources when they are needed.

Conducting evaluations. People like to know how well they are doing. This is a natural human query. The same is true for the program planner, the teachers, and the participants involved in the religious program designed for young adults. Therefore, evaluation should be conducted at several levels throughout the process of program planning, development, and delivery. Since evaluation is as misunderstood and misused as it is important, it is treated as a separate topic in the next chapter.

Conclusion

As mentioned earlier, this discussion is not intended to be a prescription for a sequential process. The various aspects of program development often occur simultaneously and interactively as the religious education planner selects classes, workshops, retreats, projects, and activities which fit the needs and interests of the young adults with whom she is working, as she determines goals and sets objectives, and as she designs and implements the various program segments. Evaluative processes, to be discussed next, help her determine how well she has done and highlight areas requiring change.

As she gains expertise through experience, she will become free of such a sequential approach and develop her own unique model for the entire planning process.

References

Apps, J. W. (1972). *How to improve adult education in your church.* Minneapolis: Augsburg.

Cameron, C. (1988). Identifying learning needs: Six methods adult educators can use. *Lifelong Learning: An Omnibus of Practice and Research, 11*(4), 25-28.

Cervero, R. M. (1988). *Effective continuing education for professionals.* San Francisco: Jossey-Bass.

Cervero, R. M. (1989). Becoming more effective in everyday practice. In B. A. Quigley (Ed.), *Fulfilling the promise of adult and continuing education* (pp. 107-13). (New Directions for Continuing Education, No. 44). San Francisco: Jossey-Bass.

Darkenwald, G. G., & Knox, A. B. (1984). *Meeting educational needs of young adults.* (New Directions for Continuing Education, No. 21). San Francisco: Jossey-Bass.

Davenport, J., III, & Davenport, J. H. (1985). Andragogical-pedagogical orientations of adult learners: Research results and practice recommendations. *Lifelong Learning: An Omnibus of Practice and Research, 9*(1), 6-8.

Dean, G. J. (1993). Practice makes perfect—Or does it? The 3 R's of becoming a reflective practitioner. *PAACE Journal of Lifelong Learning, 2,* 71-73.

Dean, G. J. (1994). *Designing instruction for adult learners.* Malabar, FL: Krieger.

Dean, G. J., & Ferro, T. R. (1991). *AKC Judges Institute instructional design and teaching manual.* New York: American Kennel Club.

DeBoy, J. J., Jr. (1979). *Getting started in adult religious education: A practical guide.* New York: Paulist.

Easley, E. M. (1978). Program development. In C. Klevins (Ed.), *Materials and methods in continuing education.* Los Angeles: Klevens.

Elias, J. L. (1982). *The foundations and practice of adult religious education.* Malabar, FL: Krieger.

Elias, J. L., & Merriam, S. B. (1980). *Philosophical foundations of adult education.* Malabar, FL: Krieger.

Ferro, T. R. (1993). The authority of the word. In P. Jarvis & N. Walters (Eds.), *Adult education and theological interpretations* (pp. 35-52). Malabar, FL: Krieger.

Freire, P. (1970). *Pedagogy of the oppressed.* New York: Seabury.

Gadamer, H.-G. (1975). Truth and method (translation edited from 2nd German ed. of 1965 by G. Barden & J. Cumming). New York: Seabury.

Garreau, J. (1981). *The nine nations of North America.* New York: Avon.

Grabowski, S. M. (1982). Approaching needs assessments. In C. Klevins (Ed.), *Materials and methods in adult and continuing education* (pp. 60-65). Los Angeles: Klevens.

Gribbon, R. T. (1990). *Developing faith in young adults: Effective ministry with 18-35 year olds.* Washington, DC: Alban Institute.

Griffith, W. S. (1978). Educational needs: Definition, assessment, and utilization. *School Review, 86,* 382-394.

Groome, T. H. (1980). *Christian religious education: Sharing our story and vision.* San Francisco: Harper & Row.

Groome. T. H. (1990). Praxis. In I. V. Cully & K. B. Cully (Eds.), *Harper's encyclopedia of religious education* (pp. 493-494). San Francisco: Harper & Row.

Hofstadter, D. R. (1979). *Gödel, Escher, Bach: An eternal golden braid.* New York: Vintage Books.

Houle, C. O. (1972). *The design of education.* San Francisco: Jossey-Bass.

Imel, S. (1992). *Reflective practice in adult education.* (ERIC Digest No. 122). Columbus: ERIC Clearinghouse on Adult, Career, and Vocational Education.

Knowles, M. S. (1980). *The modern practice of adult education: From pedagogy to andragogy* (rev. and updated). New York: Cambridge.

Knox, A. B. (1986). *Helping adults learn.* San Francisco: Jossey- Bass.

Kowalski, T. J. (1988). *The organization and planning of adult education.* Albany, NY: State University of New York Press.

Kozoll, C. E. (1979). Communications and motivation of adult and continuing education staff. In P. D. Langerman & D. H. Smith (Eds.), *Managing adult and continuing education programs and staff* (pp. 323-349). Washington, DC: National Association for Public Continuing and Adult Education.

Mattimore-Knudson, R. (1983). The concept of need: Its hedonistic and logical nature. *Adult Education, 33,* 117-124.

McKenzie, L. (1982). *The religious education of adults.* Birmingham, AL: Religious Education Press.

McKenzie, L. (1983). Adult life goals and program planning: A research study. *Lifelong Learning: An Omnibus of Practice and Research, 7*(3), 20-23.

McKenzie, L. (1985). Philosophical orientations of adult educators. *Lifelong Learning: An Omnibus of Practice and Research, 9*(1), 18-20.

Merriam, S. B. (1984). Developmental issues and tasks of young adulthood. In G. G. Darkenwald & A. B. Knox (Eds.), *Meeting educational needs of young adults* (pp. 3-13). (New Directions for Continuing Education, No. 21). San Francisco: Jossey-Bass.

Merriam, S. B., & Ferro, T. R. (1986). Working with young adults. In N. T. Foltz (Ed.), *Handbook of adult religious education* (pp. 59-82). Birmingham, AL: Religious Education Press.

Monette, M. L. (1977). The concept of educational need: An analysis of selected literature. *Adult Education, 27,* 116-127.

Monette, M. L. (1979). Need assessment: A critique of philosophical assumptions. *Adult Education, 29,* 83-95.

Murk, P. J., & Galbraith, M. W. (1986). Planning successful continuing education programs: A systems approach model. *Lifelong Learning: An Omnibus of Practice and Research, 9*(5), 21-23.

Naisbitt, J. (1982). *Megatrends.* New York: Warner.

Naisbitt, J., & Aberdene, P. (1990). *Megatrends 2000: Ten new directions for the 1990s.* New York: Morrow.

Niemi, J. A., & Nagle, J. M. (1979). Learners, agencies, and program development in adult and continuing education. In P. D. Langerman & D. H. Smith (Eds.), *Managing adult and continuing education programs and staff* (pp. 135-171). Washington, DC: National Association for Public Continuing and Adult Education.

Offerman, M. J. (1989). Matching programmatic emphases to the parent organization's values. In R. G. Simerly & Associates (Eds.), *Strategic planning and leadership in continuing education: Enhancing organization vitality, responsiveness, and identity* (pp. 71-86). San Francisco: Jossey-Bass.

Osterman, K. F. (1990). Reflective practice: A new agenda for education. *Education and Urban Society, 22,* 133-152.

Parks, S. (1991). *The critical years: The young adult search for a faith to live by.* San Francisco: Harper & Row.

Pennington, F., & Green, J. (1976). Comparative analysis of program development processes in six professions. *Adult Education*, 27, 13-23.

Peters. J. M. (1989). Programming through the client's lifespan. In D. J. Blackburn (Ed.), *Foundations and changing practices in extension* (pp. 84-93). Toronto: Thompson.

Peters, J. M. (1991). Strategies for reflective practice. In R. G. Brockett (Ed.), *Professional development for educators of adults* (pp. 89-96). (New Directions for Adult and Continuing Education, No. 51). San Francisco: Jossey-Bass.

Podeschi, R. L. (1986). Philosophies, practices and American values. *Lifelong Learning: An Omnibus of Practice and Research,* 9(4), 4-6, 27.

Schön, D. A. (1983). *The reflective practitioner: How professionals think in action.* New York: Basic Books.

Schön, D. A. (1987). *Educating the reflective practitioner.* San Francisco: Jossey-Bass.

Schroeder, W. L. (1970). Adult education defined and described. In R. M. Smith, G. F. Aker, & J. R. Kidd (Eds.), *Handbook of adult education* (pp. 25-43). New York: Macmillan.

Shawchuck, N., Kotler, P., Wrenn, B., & Rath, G. (1992). *Marketing for congregations: Choosing to serve people more effectively.* Nashville, TN: Abingdon.

Simpson, E. L. (1982). Program development: A model. In C. Klevins (Ed.), *Materials and methods in adult and continuing education.* Los Angeles: Klevins.

Smith, D. H., & Offerman, M. J. (1989). The management of adult and continuing education. In S. B. Merriam & P. M. Cunningham (Eds.), *Handbook of adult and continuing education* (pp. 246-259). San Francisco: Jossey-Bass.

Smith, M. D. (1985). Fifty tips for using the needs/interest survey process. *Lifelong Learning: An Omnibus of Practice and Research,* 8(7), 29-31.

Sork, T. J. (Ed.). (1991). *Mistakes made and lessons learned: Overcoming obstacles to successful program planning.* (New Directions for Adult and Continuing Education, No. 49). San Francisco: Jossey-Bass.

Sork, T. J., & Caffarella, R. S. (1989). Planning programs for adults. In S. B. Merriam & P. M. Cunningham (Eds.), *Handbook of adult and continuing education* (pp. 233-245). San Francisco: Jossey-Bass.

Thompson, M. M. (1992). Learner participation in program planning. *PAACE Journal of Lifelong Learning,* 1, 27-39.

Toffler, A. (1970). *Future shock.* New York: Bantam.

Toffler, A. (1980). *The third wave.* New York: Bantam.

Verner, C. (1964). Definition of terms. In G. Jensen, A. A. Liveright, & W. Hallenbeck (Eds.), *Adult education: Outlines of an emerging field of university study* (pp. 27-39). Washington, DC: Adult Education Association of the U. S. A.

Zinn, L. A. (1990). Identifying your philosophical orientation. In M. W. Galbraith (Ed.), *Adult learning methods: A guide for effective instruction* (pp. 39-77). Malabar, FL: Krieger.

CHAPTER SIXTEEN

Evaluating Young Adult Religious Education

TRENTON R. FERRO

The mere mention of the word, "evaluation," elicits a reaction—usually a disfavorable or negative one (Dirks, 1990). Why might that be, especially in an age when fund granting agencies (governments, business and industry, communities, and—yes—religious organizations and denominations) are looking more closely at the way their monies are being used and at the results and outcomes of their investments? Such reactions stem from misunderstandings both about the purpose and function of evaluations, and also misapplications and improper uses of evaluative procedures. Many individuals have experienced evaluations which have been poorly planned, badly constructed, and unfairly administered. According to Knowles (1984), "Here is the area of greatest controversy and weakest technology in all of education, especially in adult education and training" (p. 134).

A perusal of some of the references cited in Chapter Fifteen of this volume underscores Knowles' observation. Works cited in that chapter which are devoted to the topic of planning and developing adult religious education programs vary in the extent of their treatment of evaluation, and none is very extensive. In some there is no, or only passing, reference to evaluation (Foltz, 1986; Girzaitis, 1977; McKenzie, 1982). Others contain brief discussions: Apps (1972) devotes 4 pages (out of 105) to the topic, while DeBoy's (1979) treatment covers 1 1/2 pages (out of 117). These observations

367

are not meant to impugn the motives and capabilities of these respected authors. Rather, these observations point out in vivid fashion the state of evaluation in both the general and the religious adult education literature.

However, by heeding the advice and processes outlined in this chapter, the planner of religious education activities for young adults will avoid inappropriate uses of, and allay misunderstandings about, evaluations. The desired outcome is that persons involved in the religious education of young adults recognize, accept, and use evaluation as a very serviceable tool for planning, assessing, altering, and/or maintaining program offerings. Properly conducted evaluations provide data which planners can use to determine whether they are accomplishing their participation and programmatic goals.

What Is Evaluation?

Attempting to find a definition of "evaluation" and "program evaluation" provides insight into the complexities and confusion surrounding evaluation. It is possible to peruse entire books—and very useful books at that—devoted to the subject and not locate a definition (for example, Anderson & Ball, 1978; Berk & Rossi, 1990; Grotelueschen, Gooler, Knox, Kemmis, Dowdy, & Brophy, 1974; Herman, 1987; Royse, 1992). While this chapter will provide descriptions of purposes, reasons, processes, methods, and models related to program evaluation, a serious effort will be made to define program evaluation.

Listed here are several definitions drawn from both the program planning and evaluation literature. Brookfield (1986) asserts, "Evaluation . . . is inescapably a value-judgmental concept. The word value is at the heart of the term, with all the normative associations this applies" (p. 264). According to Cranton (1989), "Evaluation of learning is not synonymous with testing or grading. Evaluation implies a judgment of quality or degree; it may or may not include testing (i.e., a structured instrument) or grading (the assignment of a number or letter to that judgment)" (p. 136).

Dirks (1990) provides a broader perspective: "Evaluation is determining what we are doing in comparison with what we ought to do. It involves three distinct activities: first, information is gathered; second, judgments are formed on the basis of factual data; and third, decisions are made to correct or improve" (p. 233).

Patton (1982), one of the leading theorists and practitioners in the field of evaluation, offers this comprehensive definition: "The practice of evaluation involves the systematic collection of information about the activities, characteristics, and outcomes of programs, personnel, and products for use by specific people to reduce uncertainties, improve effectiveness, and make decisions with regard to what those programs, personnel, or products are doing and affecting. This definition of evaluation emphasizes (1) the systematic collection of information about (2) a broad range of topics (3) for use by specific people (4) for a variety of purposes" (p. 15).

Rutman and Mowbray (1983) define program evaluation as the "use of scientific methods to measure the implementation and outcomes of programs, [sic] for decision-making purposes" (p. 12). Finally, Worthen and Sanders (1973) state: "Evaluation is the determination of the worth of a thing. It includes obtaining information for use in judging the worth of a program, product, procedure, or objective, or the potential utility of alternative approaches designed to attain specified objectives" (p. 19).

Several points stand out in these definitions. On the one hand, evaluation is a process, similar to needs assessment and research, both of which require the planned and organized collection of data and careful analysis and interpretation of that data. On the other hand, the purposes of evaluation differ from these other data collection modalities. Evaluation is conducted in order to place a value upon, or to make a judgment about, programs or program components. Therefore, a working definition of evaluation might be: To collect and analyze data in order to make an informed decision.

When Should Evaluation Be Conducted?

Evaluation is usually considered to be the final activity in any program. Consequently, it is usually the last programmatic element to receive attention during the planning process (oftentimes, of course, evaluation is conducted without any planning or forethought at all). Both assumptions are inadequate. First, if evaluation is to be anything more than *pro forma* ("Oh, yes, we have an evaluation form which we pass out after all our religious education programs!"), the planning of evaluation requires attention, along with the other elements of program development (see Chapter Fifteen), from the very beginning (Herman, 1987; Knox, 1986; Worthen & Sanders, 1973). Second, if evaluation purposes and processes are planned from the very beginning, religious education planners and facilitators will discover that evaluations can be conducted while classes, courses, and programs are being planned and delivered, as well as upon their completion.

The recognition that evaluation can be conducted both during and after the planning and delivery of programs is discussed extensively in the evaluation literature as formative and summative evaluation (Anderson & Ball, 1978; Beder, 1979; Brinkerhoff, Brethower, Hluchyj, & Nowakowski, 1983; Herman, 1987; Kowalski, 1988; Royse, 1992; Simpson, 1987; Worthen & Sanders, 1973). Usually carried out at the conclusion of the program, summative evaluation focuses on results. It seeks to answer the question, "How effective is the program?" Summative evaluation considers whether objectives have been met, activities completed, and participant competence improved (Anderson & Ball, 1978; Beder, 1979; Herman, 1987; Kowalski, 1988; Niemi & Nagle, 1979; Simpson, 1987). Some authors refer to this investigation of end results as evaluation or assessment of impacts (Courtenay & Holt, 1987; Knox, 1979; Rivera, 1984, 1987). "Evaluation of the impact of an educational program refers to the assessment of the degree the participant has reached the predetermined learning objectives and . . . performance criteria. Impact evaluation includes an assessment of participants prior to an educational experience; an assessment of participant's change in knowledge, skill, or attitude immediately after the educational experience; and a similar assessment after a predetermined time lapse following the program" (Courtenay & Holt, 1987, p. 169).

Formative evaluation, on the other hand, attempts to answer the question, "What can be done to improve the program?" Conducted periodically throughout program planning and implementation in order to improve the program in progress (Anderson & Ball, 1978; Beder, 1979; Deshler, 1984; Herman, 1987; Kowalski, 1988; Niemi & Nagle, 1979), "formative evaluation focuses on the interactive elements of the program, stressing process and indicators of progress" (Simpson, 1987, p. 159). Because they "are employed to adjust and enhance interventions," formative evaluations "are not as threatening and are often better received by agency staff than other forms of evaluation" (Royse, 1992, p. 38).

The timing of evaluation, then, depends on what the religious educator, the planner, and the sponsoring religious organization wish to accomplish. If the emphasis is on continuous improvement of the program and its setting, making appropriate accommodation for shifting participant interests, changing activities to increase participation, and the like, then evaluation needs to be ongoing (formative evaluation). If the concern is with outcomes, meeting objectives, changed attitudes and behaviors, and similar results, then evaluation needs to be conducted at one or more points following the completion of the program (summative evaluation). Very often, those with a vested interest in the programs offered for young adults by the religious organization will actually want to gather data for the purposes of both formative and summative evaluation. In order to accomplish either, however, the planning of the evaluation must be part of the program planning process. When to evaluate, then, is connected with the next two questions, "Why evaluate?" and "What should be evaluated?"

Why Evaluate?

This question and the one following, "What should be evaluated?" hold the keys to understanding the function and purpose of evaluation adequately and to conducting evaluations properly. Planners of religious education for young adults who carefully think through these two questions will not only carry out better evaluations, they will also conduct evaluations which have purpose and which make a difference in both the developoment of their programs and in the results which their programs produce. Simply put, "The primary purpose of [evaluation] is to improve teaching and learning" (Knowles, 1984, p. 134). Yet such a description raises as many questions as it answers. Other researchers provide greater insight into the purposes achieved by conducting evaluations.

One major reason evaluation is so problematic, misunderstood, and misused is that religious educators who conduct evaluations have not determined clearly what they want to evaluate and why. Two schemas or taxonomies display the diverse purposes of program evaluation. Anderson and Ball (1978) list six major purposes for evaluation:

1. To contribute to decisions about program installation.
2 To contribute to decisions about program continuation, expansion (or contraction), or certification (licensing, accreditation, and so forth).
3. To contribute to decisions about program modification.
4. To obtain evidence to rally support for a program.
5. To obtain evidence to rally opposition to a program.
6. To contribute to the understanding of basic psychological, social, and other processes (pp. 3-4, 15-35).

Cervero (1988) suggests seven categories of evaluation questions:

Program Design and Implementation. This category of questions assesses what was planned, what was actually implemented, and the congruence between these two dimensions. . . .
Learner Participation. This second category [and most common type] of evaluation questions has both quantitative and qualitative dimensions. . . . How many participants attended the program? . . . What proportion of the participants stayed for the entire program? . . . Qualitative types of questions . . . try to assess the degree to which the participants were involved or engaged in the flow of the program. . . .
Learner Satisfaction. The second most common way to judge the worth of a . . . program is to collect evidence about learners' satisfaction according to various elements, such as content, educational process, instructor, physical facilities, and cost. . . .
Learner Knowledge, Skills, and Attitudes. This category of evaluative questions focuses on changes in learners' cognitive, affective, or psychomotor competence. . . .

Application of Learning After the Program. This category of evaluative questions addresses the degree to which the knowledge, skills, and attitudes learned during the program are applied in the learners' natural envirnoment. . . .

Impact of Application of Learning. Evaluative questions in this category focus on . . . second-order effects of the educationial program. First-order effects are the accomplishments of those who participated in the program. . . . Second-order effects are once removed from the participants. . . .

Program Characteristics Associated with Outcomes. If evaluation results are to provide information that can be used for program improvement, data from implementation questions [the first set of three categories discussed above] should be linked with outcome data [collected under the second set of three categories] (pp. 135-146).

When discussing his categories, Cervero (1988) also issues a warning: "Evaluative information collected in one category is not inherently better or more useful than information collected in another category. The seven categories should be viewed as a hierarchy only in the sense that the evaluative information gathered at one level should not be used to infer success or failure at other levels. For example, if learners express satisfaction with a program, their satisfaction does not imply changes in knowledge, skills, or attitudes" (pp. 134-135).

Analysis of these two lists is enlightening. Concerns about formative and summative evalution are addressed in terms of two major dimensions, namely process and outcomes. For example, items 1, 3, and 4 in the list proposed by Anderson and Ball (1978) stress process or formative evaluation; items 2, 4, 5, and 6 emphasize outcomes or summative evaluation. The first and last of Cervero's (1988) categories deal with process or formative issues, while the remainder address primarily outcomes or summative concerns. Furthermore, of the six purposes listed by Anderson and Ball (1978), five deal with the program itself. Only the sixth seems to address what happens to the participant. On the other hand, five of Cervero's (1988) categories concentrate on the participant or learner; only the first and last, and to some extent the second, categories deal specifically with the program itself. Cranton (1989) observes this distinction by discussing the evaluation of learners and the evaluation of instruction in two separate chapters.

Sets of purposes presented by other authors both expand the terrain and emphasize the fact that the possible reasons for conducting evaluations are almost limitless. For example, Fellenz, Conti, and Seaman (1982) give the following reasons for conducting program evaluations:

1. To determine how well the program objectives are being achieved.
2. To make decisions related to program improvement and future operation.
3. To meet the requirements of the program sponsor.
4. To provide a feeling of worth or accomplishment to the program staff.
5. To describe what happened so that other educators can determine if they wish to duplicate the program.
6. To become or remain accountable.
7. To provide learning experiences for anyone interested in the program (pp. 342-343).

The list developed by Kinsey (1981) provides additional insight into the reasons for conducting evaluations:

1. An evaluation may be designed to provide a descriptive analysis—a description of inputs, activities, or purposes of the participants and their involvement.
2. An evaluation may be designed to solicit reactions and opinions—of individuals and groups on qualitative and quantitiative aspects.
3. An evaluation may be designed to identify and assess problems—the nature of problems, the importance of problems, and the causes of problems.
4. An evaluation may be designed to assess changes in knowledge, attitudes, and skills—the extent of changes and the relations of changes to goals and efforts.
5. An evaluation may be designed to assess behavioral changes—how clientele behave outside the program.
6. An evaluation may be designed to assess social impact—effects of the program upon the community or other collectives (In Kowalski, 1988, p. 153).

Careful scrutiny of these lists reveals again that evaluation is conducted both to improve process and to assess outcomes, to determine what happened with the participants as well as to decide the merits of the program itself.

Two discussions of religious education for adults also address the purposes of evaluation. Elias (1982) states, "The major purpose of evaluation is to improve the program by providing information to planners about all aspects of the program. Good evaluation leads to better decisions about continuing or discontinuing programs or teachers, improving practices and procedures, and adding specific strategies and techniques. A second legitimate function for evaluation is that it provides a measure of accountability to the parent organization, leaders, and participants" (p. 273).

Dirks (1990) is more singular and specific in his observation: "One of the primary purposes of evaluation is to assure that what we do helps achieve our objectives. This requires clearly established goals and criteria of effectiveness if evaluation is to be meaningful" (p. 233). The latter statement introduces how evaluations are conducted, a topic to which the discussion will turn shortly.

Purposes determine what is to be evaluated and the types of assessment and methods of data collection to be used in the evaluation process. Time spent on making such decisions early in the planning process will spare planners and facilitators the great disappointment that comes when they discover, too late, that the best opportunities for collecting useful and valuable data slipped by because evaluation was an afterthought rather than an intentional undertaking.

What Should Be Evaluated?

Not every person, thing, process, or outcome needs to be evaluated in every class, course, or program. As Knowles (1980) points out, evaluation has become a sacred cow: Just carry out an evaluation, and the program will be safe from scrutiny and intrusion from undesirable outside interference. That sort of attitude, of course, only leaves planner and participant open to the very risks they might be trying to avoid. Furthermore, facilitators and planners who are truly committed to helping the young adults grow religiously will definitely be interested in the results of what they are doing. They will want to improve, change, and adapt their religious education activities so as to be of optimum benefit to the young adult learners. Consequently, it is better by far to concentrate on a few aspects and elements which will actually receive attention than to conduct a massive, often time-consuming and expensive evaluation effort which will result in the production of a report that gathers dust on a shelf.

The question, then, of what to evaluate becomes vitally important. Both Dirks (1990) and this present chapter emphatically suggest that those who will use the evaluation results (called stakeholders in the evaluation literature) must first decide what they want to find out from the evaluation and what they will do with the data they collect. These persons may be most concerned about how the young adult learners view the religious education activities being evaluated. They may want to consider whether there are actual changes in cognitive, affective, and behavioral patterns in the young adult learners, as a result of their participation in the program. The concerns of those evaluated might be directed more to how well the program has been planned and conducted. They may want to discover which methods and activities were most effective; they may also want to determine the cost effectiveness of certain religious education programs for young adults, as compared to others. The planning and design of the evaluative process, are vitally important (Anderson & Ball, 1978; Beder, 1979; Brinkerhoff et al., 1983; Herman, 1987; Knox, 1986; Kowalski, 1988; Sork & Caffarella, 1989). The purpose of every legitimate religious education evaluation must be made clear to everyone involved. Then the stakeholders can go about the process of planning and conducting the evaluation components of the young adult religious education program.

How Is Evaluation Done?

Attention is now turned to the actual practice of evaluating young adult religious education programs. This section will look at evaluation modes, as well as various types of informal and formal evaluation.

Evaluation Models

A number of models for undertaking evaluation reside in the evaluation literature (see Brandt, 1981; Brinkerhoff et al., 1983, pp. 37-42; Brookfield, 1986, pp. 266-273; House, 1978; Kowalski, 1988, pp. 156-158; Steele, 1973, 1989; Worthen & Sanders, 1973, pp. 40-217). These models range from the simple to the complex, from the easily managed to the very sophisticated. Many models have been designed to assess the effectiveness of large, often multisite, programs with large budgets which have been funded by governments, foundations, and/or philanthropic organizations. Assuming the likelihood that most religious educators of young adults have little or no background in evaluative methods and procedures, only two approaches will be discussed here. As the religious educators of young adults gain competence and wish to explore more options, they can then consult the literature referenced at the beginning of this paragraph.

Informal Evaluation

While some evaluators consider informal evaluation to be repugnant (Anderson & Ball, 1978, pp. 62-63; Worthen & Sanders, 1973, pp. 107, 125), such a process has an important and useful place, especially for formative evaluation. As Knowles (1980) observes, "Informal evaluation is actually going on all the time. Some kinds of judgments are being made continuously about the worth of a program. Participants are constantly making complaints or paying compliments. Teachers and leaders are never without feelings about how well or how poorly things are going. The directors of programs are sensitive both to these judgments and to their own feelings. . . . But it does not serve the same purpose as periodic, systematically planned evaluation" (p. 203; see also Elias, 1982, p. 275).

Notwithstanding the statement made in the previous paragraph, informal evaluation need not be unplanned, unmanaged, and unaware of values and assumptions—those concerns which probably cause the reactions of detractors. Informal evaluation is undertaken to increase learners' awareness of their own developing and changing cognitive, affective, and behavioral attainment; to increase participants' self-confidence and commitment to learning or their involvement in the planned activity or process; to improve communication between facilitator and participants; to determine what should be undertaken next; and to establish or alter the pace of the learning activity. The religious educator seeks regular feedback concerning the materials, methods and strategies, pacing, and setting of the activity. Feedback allows for prompt adjustments which will benefit both religious educator and the young adult learners. Prompt response to learner input (either at the present session or the next one if immediate remedy is impossible) sends positive messages to the learner that both their presence and their involvement are desired and prized.

Informal observation is carried out through personal assessment by the religious educator after each session and by asking relevant questions of the learners. Some of the questions the religious educator might address through observation and reflection or ask outright of the young adult learners include: Do they appear to understand me? Are they following the materials? Are they participating in the activities? Is there any apparent confusion regarding the directions or explanations I have given? Do the learners appear to be comfortable? Is the heating (or air conditioning) and lighting adequate? Asking these types of questions, and responding promptly in an appropriate manner, keeps the religious educator in touch with the learners and demonstrates to the young adults the active interest and concern of the facilitator.

Formal Evaluation [1]

Formal evaluation, whether formative or summative, is a planned process which follows a definite sequence of steps (Anderson & Ball, 1978; Beder, 1979; Brinkerhoff et al., 1983; Herman, 1987; Knowles, 1980; Kowalski, 1988). As indicated above, a number of functional and useful models exist; however, the one presented here should be easily grasped by, and prove quite serviceable to, the religious educators of young adults. The

1. I wish to express a deep sense of gratitude to James H. McElhinney and George S. Wood Jr., colleagues of mine at Ball State University during the 1989-1990 school year, during which time I taught a course *Evaluation of Educational Programs*, using a great deal of material developed by these two scholars and educators. Much of the content in this section was gleaned from this material.

reader is referred to the works cited in this paragraph and in the list of references for more extensive treatment of both the entire process and the individual steps.

Focusing and Designing the Evaluation

The first key step in the evaluative process—and one that is frequently overlooked, especially when standard evaluation forms are used only at the end of programs—is to focus the evaluation (Beder, 1979; Brinkerhoff et al., 1983). Focus involves asking such questions as: Who needs to know? What do they need to know? Why do they need to know? What questions must the evaluation address in order to achieve its purpose? Knowles (1980) calls this step "formulating evaluative questions" (p. 205), with the questions falling into two categories: those having to do with operational objectives and those dealing with educational objectives. Operational objectives are concerned with organizational climate and structure, assessment of needs and interests, definition of purposes and objectives, program design, program operation, and program evaluation (Knowles, 1980, pp. 205-208); "educational objectives always define behavioral changes an educational experience is designed to help participants achieve" (p. 208).

Cranton (1989) also emphasizes course components: "The instructor who has conscientiously applied the planning principles . . . will have at this point: a list of objectives, a planned sequence, a selected set of methods and materials, and techniques for the evaluation of participants' learning. Depending on the situation, the instructor may wish to obtain feedback on the effectiveness of some or all of the following components:

- Objectives (clarity, relevance)
- Sequence
- Readings, books
- Audio or visual media
- Outside resources (guest speakers, clinical facilities, library services, etc.)
- Internal resources (labs, computer facilities, physical environment)
- Special methods (modules, computer assisted instruction, ield trips)
- Assignments, projects
- Techniques for providing feedback, evaluation
- Grading procedures, where relevant" (p. 183).

Thus, evaluation can look at the process and/or at the outcomes (DeLoayza, Grosser, & Bulkin, 1988). It should also be patently obvious why planning the evaluation must be part of the whole program development phase. If any of the questions in the evaluation focus on aspects of the process, data collection instruments and procedures must be in place and ready for use when that part of the process takes place. Such opportunities will be missed if planners and facilitators wait until the program is over before designing and attempting an evaluation.

Identifying objectives. As Knowles (1980) intimates, a good place to start the evaluation procedure is with the objectives which have been developed during the program planning and development process (see Chapter Fifteen). As discussed more fully in Chapter Seven, objectives are written with the learner as the subject; use precise, active verbs; and are as direct as possible in stating desired outcomes (Dean & Ferro, 1991; DeLoayza et al., 1988). Basically, learning objectives take the form: "Who will do what by when." When writing objectives, religious educators must strive to develop statements which can actually be tested in some way.

One way to test the utility of an objective for evaluation purposes is to ask, "Why?" If the question can be answered, "Because that is how the participants will behave" (or some variation on that theme), then the objective states an outcome—acquired knowledge, attitudes, or action patterns—which can be assessed by gathering data during the evaluation. If the "Why?" question cannot be answered, the objective probably states an activity—what participants will do in order to gain the desired knowledge, attitudes, or action patterns—rather than an outcome. Should this be the case, the objective will require rewriting in order to prove serviceable for evaluation.

The purpose of objectives-based evaluation is to collect and analyze data on the inherent and/or acquired knowledge (cognitive domain); attitudes, feelings, and behaviors (affective domain); and skills and action patterns (psychomotor domain) of all groups involved in the young adult religious education program: participants, planners, facilitators, staff, boards and committees, Director of Religious Education, etc. The objectives are stated as outcomes of the program: If the program works, what is present (stated in terms of objectives and all groups involved)? What happens/will happen/will have happened if/when the program is successful? Who needs to know what information? Why?

What questions should the evaluation provide in order to answer these previous questions?

Determining indicators and criteria. Clear, precise, and well-written process and outcome objectives (written in the form: Who does/shows/demonstrates/knows/feels what?) allow for the development of criteria, or indicators, for collecting and analyzing data. Criteria or indicators, which should have the same subject as the objective they measure, provide the basis for answering the question, "How can stakeholders (all groups involved in the program) tell when a learner has accomplished a specific learning outcome?" Elias (1982) calls these the "values" which indicate the "expected reactions and attitudes of participants, learning outcomes, behavioral outcomes and tangible results" (p. 276). They are statements of concrete evidence which will be used to test how well the objectives have been met by the organization, planner, religious educator, and participants. If the program has identified desired outcomes, these outcomes should be clearly stated in terms of knowledge gained, attitudes and behaviors exhibited, and skills developed, and should also be observable.

Collecting Information

This step is composed of two interrelated parts: 1) developing and/or selecting appropriate data collection instruments and 2) using those instruments in the actual data collection process. This is another place where many evaluations often break down. Because of lack of planning, the right questions are not asked, and the right methods of data collection are not used.

The development and selection of data collection instruments hinges directly on the objectives and indicators which have been identified for the evaluation. At least one data collection item should be included in the collection instruments for each criterion. Ideally, since several types of data collection should be undertaken, several data collection items of different types should be developed for each criterion. This use of multiple and varied data collection items for each criterion is called triangulation (Patton, 1987; Royse, 1992). Steele (1989) describes the strength of this procedure: "Information about the same program secured through two or more independent means often provides better understanding and sounder conclusions than one large study. In the same fashion, viewing a program or its results from several perspectives . . . gives a better understanding of the value of the program" (p. 270).

Figure 1, which illustrates the relationships among objectives, indicators (criteria), data collection instruments, and data collection items, also demonstrates how to plan for triangulation.

Data Collection Instruments

There are three primary data collection procedures: talking with people, having people write, and observing people. Hence, there are three major types of data collection instruments: interviews, surveys and questionnaires, and observation. Each of these procedures will be discussed in turn, and advice will be given on planning and constructing each type of data collection instrument.

Interviews. The strength of the interview is that it allows respondents the opportunity to construct their own responses. Interviews also allow the evaluator to pick up on verbal and visual cues and pursue these as additional avenues of information. In addition, a symbiotic relationship can develop; the interviewer and respondent are "in this thing together." Consequently, the

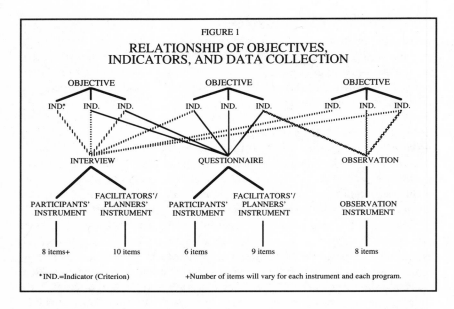

FIGURE 1
RELATIONSHIP OF OBJECTIVES,
INDICATORS, AND DATA COLLECTION

source of the data has a freedom in responding which is not available through the use of questionnaires and observations.

On the other hand, interviews require a great deal of time. An entire group of participants can respond to a questionnaire in less time than it takes to conduct one interview. Furthermore, data collected from interviews cannot be reported easily and quickly. Considerable "massaging" of raw interview data (demanding greater skill on the part of the researcher or evaluator) is required in order combine responses from several sources and "reduce" them to reportable form. Nevertheless, religious education evaluators who wish to be thorough and comprehensive (to "triangulate" their findings) will select indicators or criteria for which they will collect data by interview.

Before actually conducting interviews, evaluators need to develop an interview protocol, namely the list of questions to be asked of each respondent. The protocol is developed as follows:. First, the evaluators select those criteria or indicators for which they wish to collect interview data.

Second, the evaluators develop clear, specific, and precise questions which will elicit the type of data which can be used to evaluate each indicator and the objective under which each indicator falls. These questions should be phrased in such a way that respondents are encouraged—and must—respond with their own thoughts, feelings, and reactions. Since questions can be intimate and personal, great care needs to be taken both in deciding what questions to ask (they should seek only information that is pertinent to the established criteria and objectives) and how to ask them. Evaluators avoid questions which can be answered simply by "Yes" or "No." They usually do not use interviews to ask for demographic or factual information which can be gained as easily through the use of a questionnaire.

Third, the evaluators sequence the questions in such a way that allows for a comfortable, yet informative interview. Questions to which respondents are expected to respond quickly and readily are placed first; those calling for greater thoughtfulness—or which may be more sensitive—come later. In this way a certain rapport or trust is established before respondents are asked to "bare their souls." Evaluators also sequence the questions so that each one flows as naturally as possible from the previous question and response.

Fourth, the evaluators conduct the interview. If interviewer and respondent know each other, establishing a comfortable climate is usually not difficult. If they do not know each other, some time and effort must be devoted to establishing such a climate. The interview should be conducted in a place where the respondent feels at ease—at the respondent's home, in a restaurant, at the program site, or some other place of the respondent's choosing. Some casual conversation which allows the two be get acquainted should precede the actual use of the protocol. The task of the evaluator is to get the respondent talking; the purpose of the protocol is to provide "prods" when the discussion lags. The evaluator should not interrupt the respondent in order to follow the sequence of the protocol; the evaluator should only be concerned that all the questions have been covered, even if out of order. While the respondent is talking, the evaluator takes notes or, if the respondent agrees, records the conversation.

Fifth, as soon as possible after the interview, evaluators need to attend to several particulars. They should transcribe the interview (if it was electronically recorded), review their notes and add any observations or materials which they did not have time to record during the interview, and prepare a summary which highlights specific responses to each of the questions asked. The more time that passes between the interview and these activities, the greater the likelihood that important information will be lost.

Surveys and questionnaires. In many ways the strengths and weaknesses of surveys and questionnaires are the opposite of interviews. These prepared forms on which respondents record their responses allow for the collection of data from a much larger group of people. These forms are also useful for the collection of factual and demographic data. On the other hand, except when open-ended questions are used, responses usually are limited to the specific questions which are asked. Furthermore, evaluators do not have the opportunity to follow up on enticing comments or to ask for clarification of responses. Consequently, great care must be taken in the construction of question items so that they are perfectly clear to the respondents and they elicit the types of responses desired by the evaluators.

The preparation process for developing surveys and questionnaires begins in a fashion similar to planning interviews.

1) The evaluators select those criteria or indicators for which they wish to collect data by questionnaire. 2) They develop clear, specific, and precise questions which will elicit the type of data which can be used to evaluate each indicator and the objective under which each indicator falls. At this point evaluators must also decide what types of questions they wish to ask. Dean and Ferro (1991) describe and illustrate five types of questions: fill-in-the-blank, scales, multiple choice, check list, and open-ended. Other authors provide different schemas and examples (Courtenay & Holt, 1987; Cranton, 1989; Knowles, 1980; Patton, 1982; Royse, 1992).

Fill-in-the-blank items are used primarily to gather descriptive information about participants. This information can be collected beforehand to help religious educators better plan and prepare a prospective program, or it can be collected after a program to determine the level of a participant's involvement. Examples of questions asked before a class, workshop, or program begins might be:

How long a member of this religious group? _____.
No. of previous programs/classes attended: _____.
Favorite books/portions of scripture (here several blanks might be provided): _____.
What types of programs interest you the most (again, several spaces might be provided)? _____.

Examples of questions following a program might be:

No. of sessions attended: _____.
No. of suggested activities tried at home: _____.
Names of activities tried at home (several spaces might be provided):
_____.

Rating scale items allow participants to express their personal reactions to a particular statement or their feelings about a specific position; they are especially useful for eliciting attitudes and values. There are several ways to structure such items. One is to use a *Likert scale*, a line or continuum which offers a sequence of choices, from one pole to another, in response to a particular statement. Respondents circle the number which best corresponds to their position or feelings. A Likert scale looks like this:

I feel that every engaged couple should participate in at least six hours of formal marriage preparation sessions before their wedding day.

```
1               2               3               4               5
├ - - - - - - - - - ┤- - - - - - - - - -├ - - - - - - - - - ┤- - - - - - - - - ┤
Strongly      Disagree          Not            Agree         Strongly
Disagree                        Sure                          Agree
```

Of course, the poles and other positions in between would need to reflect the type of statements being made. Other sets of contrasts might be low—high, weak—strong, like—dislike, approve—disapprove, and so forth. In a *modified Likert scale* the responses are placed in a list rather than on a scale, and respondents place an "X" or a check-mark before their desired choice:

I feel that every engaged couple should participate in at least six hours of formal marriage preparation sessions before their wedding day.
____ Strongly Disagree
____ Disagree
____ Not Sure
____ Agree
____ Strongly Agree

Rank order provides a list which allows participants to indicate the importance they place upon, or their preference for, each of the items on the list by ranking them in a sequence. Here is an example:

In the following list rank all of the items in order from 5 to 1. Place a 5 in front of the topic you most prefer to discuss and a 1 in front of the topic you least prefer.
____ Body language.
____ Dealing with difficult people.
____ How to remain religious and keep my job.
____ Job search and interviewing skills.
____ Social etiquette for young professionals.

Multiple choice items can be used 1) to check learners' knowledge or understanding of a topic or 2) to have them select from among options.

Example 1: Which of the following is not a book in the Hebrew scriptures? (Circle the appropriate letter.)
a. Ezekiel
b. Hezekiah
c. Isaiah

d. Jeremiah
e. Obadiah

Example 2: Which of the following do you consider to be the most important trait for a married couple? (Circle the appropriate letter.)
a. Faithfulness
b. Honesty
c. Open communication
d. Reliability

Check lists allow participants to identify those items which are important to them, which they know, or which they prefer. The usefulness of this
type of item is that the respondents can make as many checks as they want.
For example:

Place an "X" by the skills and services you would be willing to provide to
community volunteer and nonprofit organizations and agencies:

____Cook   ____Babysit
____Companion   ____Counselor
____Office help   ____Yard work
____Phone hot line   ____Fund raising

Open-ended questions allow respondents to write out an answer to a question. They are not limited to selecting only those responses which have been
provided or anticipated by the planner, religious educator, or evaluator. The
difficulty with using these types of questions is that they take longer to complete, and many people do not want to take the time to write out their responses. Two examples are provided:

Example 1: How can this religious organization best help you grow and
develop spiritually, mentally, emotionally, socially, and physically?

Example 2: What do you believe are the most important traits for new
parents to acquire?

In order to be most effective and to elicit the type of information desired
by evaluators, open-ended questions must be written in such a way that participants cannot respond "Yes" or "No." Rather, questions are written which
allow respondents to state their beliefs, attitudes, ideas, or knowledge about
a particular topic. When developing the actual questionnaire, evaluators
need to leave sufficient space for participants to provide a developed response.

3) After evaluators have developed the questionnaire, which will usually contain several types of questions as described above, they determine the best time for its administration. If they are looking for information to assist in program planning, they will look for a time and place when the target group will be gathered or can be gathered well in advance of the scheduled program. If the questionnaire seeks participants' reactions to an actual program, then a time near the conclusion of the program itself will be used.

The evaluation, however, should not be the very last activity. Possibly it can be administered when the group reassembles following the last break in the program, or it can be the first activity of the final morning or evening if the program is spread over several days or weeks. By allowing sufficient time for completing the evaluation, planners and religious educators communicate nonverbally the importance placed both on the process and on the information respondents are asked to provide. Asking participants to complete the instrument as they are gathering their belongings and putting on their coats elicits hurried responses at best or, more often than not, no responses at all.

4) Again, as with interviews, the data gathered by means of the questionnaires should be tallied as soon after administration as possible. By examining the results promptly, evaluators can also use their fresh memories of the program or activity to help them better understand, interpret, and use the responses provided by participants.

Observation. As the name suggests, this mode of data collection allows evaluators to actually view a group in action. Observation data are not dependent on reports of others which, of course, can be tainted, distorted, or skewed if those reporting are not skilled in this technique, or if they have their own agendas. On the other hand, observations can require considerable time in order to gather sufficient data, and they do call for some skill on the part of observers. For additional information on observation see Henerson, Morris, and Fitz-Gibbon (1987); Herman (1987), Jorgenson (1989); and Spradley (1980).

Before actually conducting an observation, evaluators need to develop an observation guide or instrument. This instrument includes definitive statements itemizing specific behaviors which are to observed and noted. Observation is not a process of simply watching everything that is going on. Rather, it is a disciplined activity requiring evaluators to look for certain actions or modes of conduct and to disregard extraneous activity.

The guide is developed as follows: First, the evaluators select those criteria or indicators for which they wish to collect data by observation. Second, evaluators develop a clear set of definitive statements describing as precisely as possible the action or condition to be observed together with the overall context in which that condition or behavior is to occur. The item should also indicate if the frequency of the condition or behavior is to be recorded. Most observed behaviors are not dichotomous. Rather, they occur to a degree or with relative frequency. When constructing items to be observed, a good practice is to utilize a recording continuum not unlike the Likert scale discussed earlier. The ends of the continuum should be marked with the absolute presence or absence (i.e., always—never) of the behavior or with terms or quantification symbols which are as universally understood as possible. When a continuum is used, it is often desirable that points along the continuum be marked and that the observer record only at the marked points so that data from more than one observer or observation can be combined. Here is an example of an observation item using a continuum:

All activities are
purposeful and   No activity has
task oriented.   () () () () ()   purpose or goal.

Third, evaluators conduct the observation. Proper arrangements are made in advance with facilitators so that they are at ease during the observation. Providing the religious educator with a copy of the observation guide in advance helps with this process because they know what the evaluators intend to observe. Further, coaching the religious educators to conduct business as normal establishes an observation setting which actually produces usable data. In addition, religious educators make themselves as unobtrusive as possible so that their presence does not distract from or alter the normal sequence and scope of activities, behaviors, and conditions. If the evaluators are already participants in, or known to, the group, their presence will not be problematic.

Items on the observation instrument should be marked when the evaluators feel they have enough exposure to make an accurate observation. They do not depend on memory. If at any time they observe a behavior that would contribute to the content of an item, but which is not built into the guide, they write a note on the guide explaining the contributing behavior.

Fourth, as with interviews and questionnaires, the data should be tallied as soon after the observation has taken place as possible. By looking at the results promptly, evaluators can also use their fresh memories of the program or activity better to help them understand, interpret, and use the observations which have been recorded.

Analyzing Data and Drawing Evaluative Conclusions

Once the data has been gathered according to these guidelines, evaluators prepare a report which presents the collect data and analysis of those data. Analysis is, first of all, a process of answering the question, "What do the data say?" "What do the data tell us?" A second step asks the question, "What do the data mean?" "How do we interpret the data?"

This report is shared with all stakeholders who are then brought together with the evaluators for an oral report. Evaluators and stakeholders then go back to the evaluative questions which were asked during the process of focusing the evaluation process. With data in hand, this group then agrees on answers to those questions and determines the course, or various courses, of action they now wish to pursue—what to change or alter, what to augment, what to stop, what to begin. In the process, new questions may arise which will serve as the basis for a new evaluation cycle or sequence.

Conclusion

Conducting valid and reliable religious education evaluations requires much planning and thoughtfulness in order to solicit, gather, and interpret information (data) which form the basis for making decisions about program components, procedures, and results. Although the prospect of undertaking an evaluation may appear daunting to the novice, it can be done—and done well—even by the most inexperienced planners if they proceed with care. As with the learning of any skill, planners must take their first plunge. With each repetition they will learn, both from their mistakes and from what goes well, and become increasingly proficient at the process.

References

Anderson, S. B., & Ball, S. (1978). *The profession and practice of program evaluation.* San Francisco: Jossey-Bass.

Apps, J. W. (1972). *How to improve adult education in your church.* Minneapolis: Augsburg.

Beder, H. (1979). Program evaluation and follow up. In P. D. Langerman & D. H. Smith (Eds.), *Managing adult and continuing education programs and staff* (pp. 263-283). Washington, DC: National Association for Public Continuing and Adult Education.

Berk, R. A., & Rossi, P. H. (1990). *Thinking about program evaluation.* Newbury Park, CA: Sage.

Brandt, R. S. (Ed.). (1981). *Applied strategies for curriculum evaluation.* Alexandria, VA: Association for Supervision and Curriculum Development.

Brinkerhoff, R. O., Brethower, D. M., Hluchyj, T., & Nowakowski, J. R. (1983). *Program evaluation: A practitioner's guide for trainers and educators.* Boston: Kluwer-Nijhoff.

Brookfield, S. D. (1986). *Understanding and facilitating adult learning.* San Francisco: Jossey-Bass.

Cervero, R. M. (1988). *Effective continuing education for professionals.* San Francisco: Jossey-Bass.

Courtenay, B. C., & Holt, M. E. (1987). Evaluating program impact. *Materials and methods in adult and continuing education: International—Illiteracy* (pp. 168-174). Los Angeles: Klevens.

Cranton, P. (1989). *Planning instruction for adult learners.* Toronto: Wall and Thompson.

Dean, G. J., & Ferro, T. R. (1991). *AKC Judges Institute instructional design and teaching manual.* New York: American Kennel Club.

DeBoy, J. J., Jr. (1979). *Getting started in adult religious education: A practical guide.* New York: Paulist.

DeLoayza, W., Grosser, R., & Bulkin, E. (1988). *A source book for evaluating special projects.* Altamont, NY: Interorganizational Relations.

Deshler, D. (Ed.). (1984). *Evaluation for program improvement.* (New Directions for Continuing Education, No. 24). San Francisco: Jossey-Bass.

Dirks, D. H. (1990). Evaluation. In I. V. Cully & K. B. Cully (Eds.), *Harper's encyclopedia of religious education* (pp. 233-234). San Francisco: Harper & Row.

Elias, J. L. (1982). *The foundations and practice of adult religious education.* Malabar, FL: Krieger.

Fellenz, R. A., Conti, G. J., & Seaman, D. F. (1982). Evaluate: Student, staff, program. *Materials and methods in adult and continuing education* (pp. 335-345). Los Angeles: Klevens.

Foltz, N. T. (Ed.). (1986). *Handbook of adult religious education.* Birmingham, AL: Religious Education Press.

Girzaitis, L. (1977). *The church as reflecting community: Models of adult religious learning.* West Mystic, CT: Twenty-Third Publications.

Grotelueschen, A. D., Gooler, D. D., Knox, A. B., Kemmis, S., Dowdy, I., & Brophy, K. (1974). *An evaluation planner.* Urbana, IL: Office for the Study of Continuing Professional Education, University of Illinois at Urbana-Champaign.

Henerson, M. E., Morris, L. L., & Fitz-Gibbon, C. T. (1987). *How to measure attitudes.* Newbury Park, CA: Sage.

Herman, J. L. (1987). *Program evaluation kit* (2nd ed.). Newbury Park, CA: Sage.

House, E. R. (1978, March). Assumptions underlying evaluation models. *Educational Researcher,* 4-12.

Jorgensen, D. L. (1989). *Participant observation: A methodology for human studies.* (Applied Social Research Methods Series, Vol. 15.) Newbury Park, CA: Sage.

Kinsey, D. C. (1981). Participatory education in adult and nonformal education. *Adult Education,* 30, 155-168.

Knowles, M. S. (1980). *The modern practice of adult education: From pedagogy to andragogy* (rev. and updated). New York: Cambridge.

Knowles, M. S. (1984). *The adult learner: A neglected species* (3rd ed.). Houston: Gulf.

Knox, A. B. (Ed.). (1979). *Assessing the impact of continuing education.* (New Directions for Continuing Education, No. 3). San Francisco: Jossey-Bass.

Knox, A. B. (1986). *Helping adults learn.* San Francisco: Jossey- Bass.

Kowalski, T. J. (1988). *The organization and planning of adult education.* Albany, NY: State University of New York Press.

McKenzie, L. (1982). *The religious education of adults.* Birmingham, AL: Religious Education Press.

Niemi, J. A., & Nagle, J. M. (1979). Learners, agencies, and program development in adult and continuing education. In P. D. Langerman & D. H. Smith (Eds.), *Managing adult and continuing education programs and staff* (pp. 135-171). Washington, DC: National Association for Public Continuing and Adult Education.

Patton, M. Q. (1982). *Practical evaluation.* Beverly Hills, CA: Sage.

Patton, M. Q. (1987). *How to use qualitative methods in evaluation.* Newbury Park, CA: Sage.

Rivera, W. M. (1984). What's a program for?—The question of impacts. *Lifelong Learning: An Omnibus of Practice and Research*, 7(5), 10-12.

Rivera, W. M. (1987). Making impacts: The educational end result and its measurement. *Materials and methods in adult and continuing education: International—Illiteracy* (pp. 161-167). Los Angeles: Klevens.

Royse, D. (1992). *Program evaluation: An introduction*. Chicago: Nelson-Hall.

Rutman, L., & Mowbray, G. (1983). *Understanding program evaluation*. Newbury Park, CA: Sage.

Simpson, E. L. (1987). Program development: A model. In C. Klevins (Ed.), *Materials and methods in adult and continuing education: International—Illiteracy* (pp. 154-160). Los Angeles: Klevens.

Sork, T. J., & Caffarella, R. S. (1989). Planning programs for adults. In S. B. Merriam & P. M. Cummingham (Eds.), *Handbook of adult and continuing education* (pp. 233-245). San Francisco: Jossey-Bass.

Spradley, J. P. (1980). *Participant observation*. Fort Worth: Holt, Rinehart and Winston.

Steele, S. M. (1973). *Contemporary approaches to program evaluation: Implications for evaluation programs for disadvantaged adults*. Syracuse, NY: ERIC Clearinghouse on Adult Education.

Steele, S. M. (1989). The evaluation of adult and continuing education. In S. B. Merriam & P. M. Cummingham (Eds.), *Handbook of adult and continuing education* (pp. 260-272). San Francisco: Jossey-Bass.

Worthen, B. R., & Sanders, J. R. (1973). *Educational evaluation: Theory and practice*. Belmont, CA: Wadsworth.

CONTRIBUTORS

MICHAEL ANTHONY is chairman of the Department of Christian Education and Associate Professor of Christian Education at Biola University/Talbot School of Theology at LaMirada, California. He is also the pastor to young families at Mariners Church, Newport Beach. He holds a Ph.D. in Life Span Development from Claremont Graduate School, and an Ed.D. in Educational Administration from Southwestern Baptist Theological Seminary. Dr. Anthony is the editor of *Foundations of Ministry: An Introduction to Christian Education for a New Generation* and co-author of *Single Adult Passages: Uncharted Territories.*

HARLEY ATKINSON is Assistant Professor of Christian Education at Toccoa Falls College. He holds doctoral and master's degrees in Christian Education from Biola University/Talbot School of Theology. He has served as youth pastor and pastor in Christian and Missionary Alliance churches, and has worked with young adults in a variety of capacities including young singles ministry, home Bible studies, and Sunday School classes. Dr. Atkinson has contributed several articles to the Christian Education Journal.

M. CAROLYN CLARK is assistant professor of adult education in the Department of Educational Human Resource Development at Texas A&M University. She received her M.A. from Creighton University in Christian spirituality, and her Ed.D. from the University of Georgia in adult education. She is the co-author of the book *Lifelines: Patterns of Work, Love, and Learning.* Dr. Clark has extensive experience in ministry, working in the area of spiritual formation of adults and adolescents in retreat and parish settings, as well as leadership development of laity.

ELIZABETH CONDE-FRAZIER is the director of Orlando E. Costas Hispanic and Latin American Ministries Program, Andover Newton Theological School. She holds a M.Div. from Eastern Baptist Theological Seminary. For the past fifteen years she has conducted workshops and seminars on ministry with Hispanic young adults in the northeastern part of the United States. Rev. Conde-Frazier has also served as pastor for churches in New York City and Connecticut.

GARY DEAN is Associate Professor and Department Chairperson in the Department of Counseling, Adult Education, and Student Affairs, at Indiana University of Pennsylvania. He received the degrees of M.A. and Ph.D. in Adult Education from The Ohio State University. He is the author of *Designing Instruction for Adult Learners*, co-author of *Adult Career Counseling: Resources for Program Planning and Development*, and a contributor to a number of journals. Dr. Dean is co-editor with Trenton Ferro of the *PAACE Journal of Lifelong Learning*.

JOHN ELIAS is Professor of Religious Education at Fordham University. He holds an Ed.D. from Temple University and an M.Div. from St. Charles Seminary. His books include *Paulo Freire: Pedagogue of Liberation; Moral Education: Secular and Religious*; and *Foundations and Practice of Adult Religious Education*. Dr. Elias is also the author of numerous journal articles and has served as a consultant to churches.

TRENTON FERRO holds the positions of Assistant Professor and Coordinator in the Master of Arts Program in Adult and Community Education at Indiana University of Pennsylvania. He received an Ed.D. from Northern Illinois University, as well as master's degrees from University of California (Berkeley) and Concordia Theological Seminary. His publications appear in *Handbook of Adult Religious Education Learning Opportunities Sourcebook; Education Through Community Organizations; Adult Education and Theological Interpretations*. Dr. Ferro served as parish pastor for a number of years, with primary responsibilities in youth ministries and adult programming.

STEVE FORTOSIS holds master's and doctoral degrees from Biola University/Talbot School of Theology. His publications include numerous journal articles which concentrate on Religious Education. He has served as a youth pastor for six years, as volunteer staff person for a singles ministry, and more recently as a worker in adult Christian education.

ANTHONY J. HEADLEY is Assistant Professor of Counseling at Asbury Theological Seminary. He studied at Asbury where he received his M.Div., and University of Kentucky where he earned master's degrees in Counseling Psychology and Family Studies and a Ph.D. in Counseling Psychology. His ministry experience includes nine years of pastoring in the United States and Antigua, as well as directing and teaching young adult extension studies.

DONALD JOY is Professor of Human Development and Christian Education at Asbury Theological Seminary. He holds an M.A. from Southern Methodist University and a Ph.D. from Indiana University. His numerous books include *Moral Development Foundations: Alternatives to Piaget-Kohlberg; Bonding: Relationships in the Image of God; Re-bonding: Preventing and Restoring*

Damaged Relationships; and *Becoming a Man: A Celebration of Sexuality, Responsibility, and the Christian Young Man*. Dr. Joy has conducted over 500 seminars and lectures relevant to young adulthood.

LES STEELE is Professor of Religion at Seattle Pacific University. Dr. Steele's degrees include an M.A. in religion from Azusa Pacific University, an M.A. and Ph.D. in Education from Claremont Graduate School. He is the author of *On The Way: A Practical Theology of Christian Formation*, as well as a number of journal articles. He has served as Minister of Christian Education, with the tasks of coordinating and teaching adult Christian education. He currently serves as a teacher and adult education committee member in a local church and frequently speaks to adult groups.

NICK STINNETT teaches and conducts research in the Department of Human Development and Family Studies at the University of Alabama, Tuscaloosa. He has been involved for about twenty years in a national ongoing study of successful families, the results of which have been published in a book *Secrets of Strong Families*. Nick and his wife NANCY are the authors of *Relationships in Marriage and Family*. Nancy is the head of the Infant/Toddler Laboratory in the Department of Human Development and Family Studies.

R.E.Y. WICKETT teaches in the College of Education at the University of Saskatchewan in Saskatoon, Saskatchewan, Canada. Dr. Wickett, who holds an Ed.D. in adult education from the University of Toronto, is a member of the National Advisory Committee on Adult Religious Education for the Canadian Conference of Catholic Bishops and serves on the Advisory Committee for the Anglican Church of Canada. His numerous published works include *Models of Adult Religious Education Practice*.

FRED R. WILSON teaches in the Christian Education Department at Wheaton College. He has a Ph.D. in Adult Education from Kansas State University and a Th.M. from Dallas Theological Seminary. His articles have appeared in *The Christian Educator's Handbook of Adult Education* and in a variety of journals. Dr. Wilson has also worked with Inter Varsity Christian Fellowship and served as the President of the North American Professors of Christian Education *(NAPCE)*.

EVERETT L. WORTHINGTON is Professor of Psychology at Virginia Commonwealth University. He holds a Ph.D. in psychology from the University of Missouri (Columbia) and studied nuclear engineering at MIT and the University of Tennessee (Knoxville). He is the author of *Hope for Troubled Marriages: Overcoming Common Problems and Major Difficulties*, and *Marriage Counseling: A Christian Approach for Counseling Couples*. He is the editor of Psychotherapy and Religious Values, and has made a number of contributions to journals. Dr. Worthington, along with his wife, leads pre-marital counseling groups and groups for newly married couples at his church and has taught adult Sunday School classes for twenty years.

DAVID WU is currently Program Director with the Community Assistance Program for Seniors, Fuller Theological Seminary. He studied at Biola University/Talbot School of Theology, where he acquired the M.A. and Ed.D. degrees in Christian Education. Dr. Wu served as Director of Young Adult Ministries and Christian Education at the Jachin Chinese Alliance Church in Costa Mesa, California and is currently a Bible study teacher at a men's group home for recovering addicts. His professional articles have appeared in the *Christian Education Journal.*

Index of Authors

395

Index of Subjects